SEVEN SAGES
The Story of American Philosophy

SEVEN SAGES
The Story of American Philosophy

FRANKLIN	DEWEY
EMERSON	SANTAYANA
JAMES	PEIRCE

WHITEHEAD

by

H. B. VAN WESEP

1724

LONGMANS, GREEN AND CO.

NEW YORK   LONDON   TORONTO

1960

LONGMANS, GREEN AND CO., INC.
119 WEST 40TH STREET, NEW YORK 18

LONGMANS, GREEN AND CO., LTD.
6 & 7 CLIFFORD STREET, LONDON W 1

LONGMANS, GREEN AND CO.
20 CRANFIELD ROAD, TORONTO 16

SEVEN SAGES

PUBLISHED SIMULTANEOUSLY IN THE DOMINION OF CANADA BY
LONGMANS, GREEN AND CO., TORONTO

FIRST EDITION

LIBRARY OF CONGRESS CATALOG CARD NUMBER 60–15278

Printed in the United States of America

Contents

Prefatory Note

THE FIRST PURPOSE of this book is to make it clear that America does have a philosophy of its own. Two devices are used to help the reader see this. First of all, only the seven truly outstanding leaders of American thought are considered, so that the bold outline of their philosophy is never, not even for a moment, allowed to get lost in a tangle of lesser men. Secondly, by presenting the biography and the historical setting of each leading thinker, as well as his philosophy, the reader is led to discover that all these men were working at different times and in different ways on one and the same philosophy. Perhaps the unanimity came from having back of them always a free and unified people to whose views they gave a voice. Thus an attempt is made to bring home to the reader the fact that among the countries with a clear and distinctive philosophy of their own America can take an honored place.

The second and main purpose of this book is to dig into the contents of this American philosophy, show what its main tenets are, why its central significance has never changed, and how this philosophy has managed to keep on strengthening itself and growing. The reader is shown this, first, by letting each man speak out briefly but to the point on each important facet of his own philosophy exactly as he saw it. Secondly, the reader is aided by having each leader in turn, and in the right succession, shown exactly how and by what steps a simple but enlightened pioneer philosophy of colonial days could, by incorporating the steady advances of science, grow into the mature, consistently democratic, but still daring and dynamic outlook of today. The Seven Sages of American philosophy thus come to stand also for the seven stages through which this philosophy passed on its way from Franklin to Whitehead.

The reason the fundamental unity of American thought has sometimes not been apparent is that either the thought is watered down with too much small-fry and unoriginal thinking or an attempt is made to pin the whole system on to one man. In either case the result is an inadequate view of something that with all the main contributions clearly in place gets to be a highly original, well-rounded, and naturally developing philosophy of audacious impact. Around it still linger overtones of bold experimentation.

This book aims to present no more than an introduction to this philosophy and to present this introduction worded untechnically, and in such a way as to hold the interest and remain within the understanding of the general reader. In recent years the public has been given a number of readable books through which the nonspecialist in science could get a good idea of what the new sciences, from archaeology to nuclear physics, are all about. This book aims to do something similar for philosophy. The specialist in a field other than philosophy, the scientifically trained student, or the literary-minded reader who may wish to get some notion of how philosophy brings together the viewpoints of art, literature, religion, science, and practical life will find himself in sympathy with what is here put down. It is intended to induce the nonspecialist in philosophy to take a greater interest in this broadly human subject and if possible to lead him to read the philosophers themselves.

Although this story deals only with the founders of American philosophy, the history of the United States is so new that the general message of these Seven Sages sounds surprisingly up to date. These founders carry the story well through Einstein. They represent a new beginning. In fact American philosophy is chiefly the story of the recent revolution which all human thinking has had to undergo, since in the past one hundred fifty years the mechanical forces of a Newtonian world have reshaped themselves into the dynamic and organic world of today with its frightening symptoms of world wars, atomic explosions, and space flights. The interest is in finding the contours and directions of these new currents of thought in the hope they may continue to prove a guide for further action.

Selecting the seven leading thinkers is in itself an exploratory orientation. It is also a challenge. In writing about American philosophy no one wants to consider men who merely copy ancient European or other Old World points of view; but do we have in these Seven Sages all the important originals? Do Franklin, Emerson, James, Dewey, Santayana, Peirce, and Whitehead represent the properly spaced peaks in this New World landscape? The answer is to try to think of seven other men, or even of a single entirely suitable substitution. There is no doubt that these are the outstanding thinkers and that Franklin, Emerson, James and Dewey are dyed-in-the-wool native products, and that Peirce, if anything, is even more so. The same quality, only slightly less homespun, comes out in the adopted American Santayana, and in Whitehead, the latecoming but almost violent convert to America. These men are called Sages, not only because they laid the foundations but also because their contributions are now all finished, so that they can be weighed together to show how really significant they are. Whitehead died in 1947, Dewey and Santayana in 1952, and Volumes VII and VIII of the *Collected Works* of Peirce, never before published, appeared only in 1958, although Peirce died in 1914. What these men achieved can now be considered as a whole. In that sense this book represents a timely summing up of a New World movement in philosophy just now reaching its maturity.

In this story the stress is put on how seven separate views dovetail into each other. All seven are needed to complete the picture. The seven men back of them waste no time on fighting each other. They do not cancel each other out. On minor points they do sometimes correct each other, and certainly in a large way each supplements the other, but always they remain in essential agreement in setting forth the same outlook on life. United they stand for the best thought of a united people, as its separate states represent the United States. All agree in being realists, pluralists, evolutionists, freedom lovers, and antiabsolutists, the last-named in the sense that they leave the system open at the end for still further growth. All stand for a broadening of intellection to include elements formerly considered too everyday, too practical, too emotional, or even too irrational to be a part of the intellect. All are secularly minded in the sense that they seek for man a better life right here in the New World. From the start these men have been united in trying to make varied human beings live together and feel more at home on earth. Thus we get a philosophy with a nonescapist outlook, rooted in the entire man, and dedicated to a coolheaded control over the constantly increasing facts, scientific and otherwise, of present-day living. American philosophy is presented as the distillation, through a handful of its own geniuses, of the point of view arrived at, perhaps inarticulately, by a conglomerate but essentially single-minded, freedom-loving people, who in the New World sought to set up and are still clinging to a new way of life.

The Seven Sages, fulfilling each other but never steering other than a common course, thus constitute a thought movement that parallels what has at the same time being going on in Western Europe. In this book it is shown how American philosophy differs from European existentialism, and also how it resembles and, in a sense, goes beyond it. It is also made clear why our views are less bleak and pessimistic. However, in calling this philosophy American there is no attempt to see it as other than a development, with a sea change, of something started in, and rooted in, the original mother country of Great Britain. American philosophy is built on English and French philosophy, but by now is so different that it has a stature and a flavor of its own. Like the British empiricism from which it stems, and which has in its designation the same Greek root that is found in the words "experience" and "experimental," American thought leans strongly on scientific experimentation and its findings. Each of the Seven Sages draws for his inspiration on a different science. Each takes the new facts from some particular science of his day for his own province and weaves them into his thought. Franklin absorbed the expanding Newtonian astronomy; Emerson got an uncanny feeling for the implications of the rising geology of his day; James appropriated biology; Dewey, cultural heredity; Santayana, aesthetics; Peirce the new logics; and Whitehead, relativity and mathematics—all with the, perhaps partly instinctive, purpose of completing and rounding out the same basically explorative philosophy. The cumulative effect is startlingly forward-looking. This universal interest in the new facts of science also gives the philosophy its emotional drive, for it is through the increase of knowledge that man has always attempted to conquer the world.

Since in America, as is the custom of free men who stand for free thought, the road to further discoveries is always left wide open, the job of philosophy gets to be to help mankind in its constant adaptation to a changing world. Thus in the short space of American thinking deism and transcendentalism bob up only to give way to a broadly pragmatic meliorism. James sometimes calls his views meliorism. Nor is this the end, because, concomitantly, determinism of the fatalistic variety gets more and more discredited in favor of spontaneity, creativity, and the clear recognition of powerful organic forces compelling people and things into new self-controlled combinations and into new behavior. Thus any short-term or prematurely stabilized form of optimism is soon outdated, making room for something quite different, a deeper preparedness, provisionally dubbed excelsiorism. It is so called because of its open mind to the acceptance of unlimited new discoveries, possibly radical in scope. The result is a wary but hardheaded approach to life, treasuring fiercely what has already been achieved, but ready also to face whatever new advantage or danger may turn up, always with a weather eye out for the one thing that really counts—the survival of the human race on this planet of which America is a cooperative segment.

Benjamin Franklin:
Statesman-Philosopher

1. An American Socrates

EARLY IN LIFE Franklin patterned himself for a time on the Greek Socrates. As part of a strenuous course in self-education through reading, Franklin shortly after the age of sixteen thoroughly digested an English version of Xenophon's *Memorabilia*. In this book Xenophon tells how the shrewd and brilliant Socrates used to buttonhole talkative Athenian youths and propound to them a series of apparently innocent questions.

To start things going as smoothly as possible the cagey Socrates first of all pretended that he himself knew nothing about the subject under discussion. Disarmed by this confession and flattered at being consulted at all, the rash youths unloaded their opinions. Presently the debate that started so soothingly took an unexpected turn. Interlocutors who thought they had all the answers found themselves enmeshed in a tangle of contradictions. This technique with its deceptively simple beginnings delighted the young Franklin, who confesses that as a lad he loved to rush headlong into arguments.

In the hands of Plato, that other biographer of Socrates, the Socratic dialogue was soon developed into a highly finished art form. The same game of Socratic questions and answers, especially with a few additional rules, such as: Answer, Yes or No, is still in full operation in the courtrooms of today. The youthful Franklin discovered in it a splendid whetstone for his already keen young mind.

Socrates himself, if we are to put the best construction on the procedure he invented, was interested not so much in besting his opponent as in teaching him something. Plato hints that Socrates by this means hoped to dig out the truth regarding certain questions on which Socrates himself was still genuinely puzzled.

3

Franklin, to begin with, had no such high aims. Franklin enjoyed putting on the humble inquirer because, as he himself says, he found this way of arguing more effective than his former abrupt contradictions and positive statements.

"I took delight in it and grew very artful and expert in drawing people, even of superior knowledge into concessions, the consequences of which they did not foresee." However, the astute Franklin soon discovered that this was not a good way of making and keeping valuable friends. "I continued this method for some few years, but gradually left it, retaining only the habit of expressing myself in terms of modest diffidence."

What Franklin learned from this youthful encounter with Socratic irony was that making yourself less important than you really are may enable you à la Tom Sawyer to get things done by community effort. Not that Franklin himself was either lazy or averse to effort. Far from it. His name has come to be a synonym for industry, frugality, and thrift, all of which virtues he cultivated with zeal both in his youth and long after; but you get better results, even with thrift, if you do not too crassly put yourself in the foreground—and results are what count.

A little later in life, when he had become a solid citizen, Franklin used the Socratic method with good effect in getting subscriptions for a public library in Philadelphia. Establishing the first public library in this country was entirely Franklin's idea, but, said Franklin, "I put myself as much as I could out of sight, and stated it as a scheme of a *number of friends* who had requested me to go about and propose it to such as they thought lovers of reading. In this way my affair went on more smoothly, and I ever after practiced it on such occasions, and from my frequent successes, can heartily recommend it."

That Franklin set afoot in this way a typically American public relations practice by inculcating the Art-of-How-to-Make-Friends-and-Influence-People is at this juncture not the point. Rather the aim is to display at the start the pragmatic bent in this pioneer philosopher. Even in doing good, do good by stealth, if need be, but do it. Get it done. Show results. That what you get done should preferably also be something of benefit to the public hails from a second something that Franklin also took over from Socrates, namely, a firm conviction that virtue can be taught—and a far greater thing this was than mock modesty could ever be.

The belief that virtue could be imparted to others was not to Franklin just a broad faith in the powers of education, but a much more profound and possibly naïve creed that men not only can be taught about virtue but by the teaching of virtue be transformed into more virtuous beings. Only a very young republic, such as the Greece of 399 B.C. (the year when Socrates in a show of heroic respect for democratic law drank the hemlock) or the America of 1776 (with its ringingly youthful pronouncements put forth in a new Declaration of Independence), could with confidence uphold so bold a doctrine. That human nature can be changed through education has, however, remained a cornerstone of American philosophy.

"Men should be taught as if you taught them not," said Franklin, ostensibly quoting Pope. Teach by the example of your own life. Franklin was no saint. Perhaps neither was Socrates. But Franklin did freely and openly put down the details of his own life, faults and all, as illustrations of what worked and what did not work in the pursuit of virtue. Franklin was deeply persuaded that the teaching of virtue "is the subject of an art." "It is," said he, "as properly an art as painting, navigation, or architecture. If a man would become a painter, navigator, or architect, it is not enough that he be *advised* to be one, that he is *convinced* by the arguments of his adviser that it would be for his advantage to be one, and that he resolves to be one; but he must also be taught the principles of his art, be shown all the methods of working, and how to acquire the habit of using properly all the instruments . . . My *Art of Virtue* has also its instruments, and teaches the manner of using them."

All his life Franklin wanted to write that book on the *Art of Virtue*. He was born in 1706. In 1761 he wrote: "You will not doubt my being serious in the intention of finishing my *Art of Virtue*. It is not a mere ideal work. I planned it first in 1732. . . . The materials have been growing ever since. The form only is now to be given." Even earlier than 1732, on February 18, 1728, the twenty-two-year-old Franklin, in some newspaper pieces which he wrote under the name of Busy-Body, was telling his readers that the Persians, "in their ancient constitution, had public schools in which virtue was taught as a liberal art, or science." Throughout his life Franklin could not praise this idea too highly.

The gist of his doctrine about virtue was that "vicious notions are not hurtful because they are forbidden, but forbidden because they are hurtful, the nature of men alone considered; that it was therefore everyone's interest to be virtuous who wished to be happy even in this world." He thought it important "to convince young persons that no qualities were so likely to make a poor man's fortune as those of probity and integrity."

In his busy life he never did get around to finishing that treatise on the *Art of Virtue*, but he did do something just as good; he wrote, and managed to finish after a fashion, an *Autobiography* of his early years that had the identical purpose of teaching the young how to succeed in life. Socrates tried to make his young men think. He compared himself to a midwife, because he said it was his business in life to help the Greeks give birth to new ideas. Sometimes he compared himself to a gadfly stinging people into thinking. Modeling himself on the Athenian gadfly, Benjamin Franklin made a slight change in the Greek approach by adding hard work to hard thinking.

To take full advantage of life in the day and age of the new America, it was not enough just to think. Franklin's life included hard thinking, but it did not stop at thinking. The peculiar twist that Franklin gave to the teaching of virtue was to change the "Know thyself!" of Socrates into his own, strictly American, "Make something of yourself!"

To the early Greek and democratic way of encouraging free thought by free men, Franklin attached the all-important item of self-help. Unlike the Greeks, Franklin did not condone slavery. There are some strong direct antislavery statements by Franklin, but as convincing as any words could possibly be was his own personal and Gargantuan toil. Sloth, either intellectual or physical sloth, was to him one of the Seven Deadly Sins. For a man who loves to do things for himself it is not necessary to get things done by slaves. The American idea cuts deeper than the Greek.

In the pioneering days of America, slavery had not yet become the festering problem of a later day; but a minor form of it, indenture as an apprentice, Franklin tasted as a personal experience, and later on circumvented when as a youth he ran away from Boston to Philadelphia. Indentured to his brother, who owned and ran a newspaper, Franklin left for the record a description of how his own brother treated him. "Though a brother, he considered himself as my master, and me as his apprentice. My brother was passionate, and had often beat me, which I took extremely amiss; and thinking my apprenticeship very tedious, I was continually wishing for some opportunity of shortening it, which at length offered in a manner unexpected." Before telling how he managed to run away to Philadelphia, Franklin adds in a footnote: "I fancy his harsh and tyrannical treatment of me might be a means of impressing me with that aversion to arbitrary power that has stuck to me through my whole life."

This is the brother who began by never suspecting that his young brother-apprentice might know how to write. To get around this the young scamp of sixteen at night slipped some of his own well-written compositions under the door. When these, after being found each morning, were promptly printed as good pieces by a new anonymous contributor, Franklin figuratively rubbed his hands with glee. The pseudonym used by Franklin for these contributions was Mrs. Silence Dogood, supposedly the name of a virtuous and highly respected widow. Does this prefigure the future philosopher's preoccupation with doing good and not blabbing too much about it, or does it simply mean that colonial Americans had no patience with pretentious behavior?

2. From Rags to Independence

It is not surprising that early American philosophy should take on, in form at least, the shape of a boy's book. By that I do not mean a child's book, but a book, say, for a boy of twelve at least. A boy of that age is in many ways a remarkably clear-eyed individual. He no longer believes in Santa Claus. He knows a good deal about mechanical things. He is not yet sentimental about girls. He has a complete blueprint of all the foibles of his elders. With other boys, and possibly girls also, he gets along just fine. If he is any sort of normal boy he has already worked out some compromise between ambition and the love of play. He has all the rudiments of that same down-to-earth horse sense that Franklin so unmistakably exhibits in all of his writings.

Franklin pitched his *Autobiography* on the highly intelligent but still unsophisticated and unromantic level occupied by those preparing to lay aside childish things. Moreover, like *Gulliver's Travels* the *Autobiography* has in it more than meets the eye. To be sure, it is a treatise on how to practice virtue, but it is a treatise with meat on its bones. A living personality, with living companions, stalks through this book and, like the Bible, it is a plain-spoken book good for young and old alike. In addition to inculcating in the minds of the young habits of thrift, independence, and civic virtue, Franklin's masterpiece contains a well-anchored creed for adults. As Franklin saw it, the three tasks confronting incipient manhood are:

(1) Keep alive. Learn how to make money. Learn how to provide well for yourself and for your family. Taking care of yourself and of your own is important, and it is something that all by itself can keep you busy and out of mischief for life.

(2) Get along with other people, and make a business of it.

Learn how to handle yourself, and also how to handle other men, so that you and they can get things done together. We have here in full preformation an embryonic public relations cult.

(3) In addition to being a self-supporting, civic-minded citizen, do something over and above all that for the welfare of mankind in general. This Franklin himself interpreted as a call to promote science. When with his kite he drew the lightning from the skies he was doing the kind of scientific research from which men keep harvesting new crops of useful knowledge, and for which foreign universities gave him, who had never had more than two years of elementary schooling, a doctor's degree.

To his injunction to go out and make money, Franklin added one important proviso: Be sure to stop in time. As soon as you have a comfortable living, retire and get busy on civic and philanthropic affairs. Franklin, the future statesman, himself retired from business in his early forties, thus setting an exalted but thoroughly American example of how a public and a private life can supplement each other. In this the Franklin saga of a rise to fame was well ahead of the vulgar "rags to enormous riches" of a later day. Yet the robustness and the gusto of an undiluted individualism was there. This was the age in which Adam Smith published his famous book showing that when a man seeks his own welfare he promotes the welfare of his nation, and in which Bernard de Mandeville (Franklin met him in London) wrote his celebrated *Fable of the Bees*. Once upon a time in a hive each bee was very busy looking out for himself, fighting, killing, stinging others, but storing up the honey. The hive thrived. Then along came a reformer who said: Be less selfish! The bees obeyed, but in doing so they cut the nerve of enterprise. The hive drooped and died. Take the freebooters off the seas and down goes England. Stop robbing the colonies, and England starts robbing itself. But Franklin was an American, and that made a difference.

Better than most men Franklin could lay his finger on the weakness of a lusty age, and also on its strength. That strength lay not in riches, not even in tolerance, nor in religion, but in ethics. Never, never let ethics (virtue), doing good, get lost in the shuffle. You do not have to be rich to be virtuous, but riches are not wrong and can be a help. In developing that theme Franklin was plowing furrows around the well-tilled field of Protestantism. Nor do you have to be a sniveling Puritan, although Franklin did come from a long line of dyed-in-the-wool Dissenters. "This obscure family of ours . . . early in the Reformation . . . had got an English Bible, and to conceal and secure it, it was fastened open with tapes under and within the cover of a joint-stool. When my great-great-great grandfather read it to his family, he turned up the joint-stool upon his knees, turning over the leaves then under the tapes. One of the children stood at the door to give notice if he saw the apparitor coming, who was the officer of the spiritual court. In that case the stool was turned down again upon its feet, when the Bible remained concealed under it as before. This anecdote I had from my uncle Benjamin."

That Franklin even in his early days was not just a money-grubber does not come as a surprise to later generations, but in his own day many misunderstood him, and the English gravely misjudged him. Because he was, in age, a generation ahead of men like Washington and Jefferson, most of Franklin's life was spent as a loyal citizen of England. He helped the English to subdue frontier Indians, staking his whole personal fortune, at one time, on getting help to General Braddock in time. Nevertheless, the British regulars did not do so well against the Indians, and Franklin got the idea that Americans, knowing frontier ways, could better themselves undertake their own protection. With his genius for organization it was easy for him to get up a colonial army which he himself led against the Indians.

Englishmen began to fear this American with an army of his own, but when one colony after another appointed him their agent in England to redress grievances and get privileges, for a time their respect for him and his abilities outweighed their fear of him. Franklin's qualities made him our first foreign ambassador even before we were an independent country.

The eighteenth century was a corrupt age, with widely prevalent spying and bribery, but no one could corrupt our pioneer foreign ambassador, who practically invented honesty as the best policy. The shrewd but honest Franklin somehow generally got the best of every bargain. Then by chance there occurred an incident which led his English detractors to think that for once

Homer had nodded. The great man had finally tripped himself up by (as they thought) giving out for publication certain private and privileged letters—a thing no gentleman or man of honor could ever do. So they decided to show up the American boor.

The story of the Hutchinson letters is well known. It is mentioned here only to show that the practical Franklin could on occasion display a noble and extremely farsighted attitude. It seems that some of the highly placed men in colonial America, in cahoots with England, were telling the king just how he could impose taxes and otherwise discipline and bring to terms the colonies. Somehow Franklin got hold of some letters containing information of this sort and sent them back to America, not for publication but by private messenger and to be read privately by a few men whom he wished to acquaint with this type of fifth-column work going on in high places. Someone bungled, and the letters, through no doing of Franklin's, were published. Accusations, flying back and forth, landed on innocent heads. There was even a famous duel. To protect others, Franklin came out into the open, saying only that it was he who had sent back to America the letters, most of which were written by Governor Hutchinson of Massachusetts.

Thereupon the king, the prime minister, and the other high notables of England forced Franklin to appear in open court. The most able, but also the most unscrupulous, of the prominent lawyers of the day was hired to pour it on. By making a public spectacle of this American upstart it was hoped once and for all to dispose of him. While the lawyer excoriated him at length, and all the lords and personages present guffawed and slapped their thighs outrageously, Franklin stood for several hours next to the fireplace without moving a muscle. No one came to his aid, and when the turn came for him to reply, what did he do? He could so easily have defended himself by saying he had never ordered and had never intended the letters to be published, but something led him to do the one thing that in his opinion the occasion called for. Something caused him to keep on standing there silent before his judges, without uttering so much as a mumbled word. He just let them have their fun. Imagine the effect! What, no answer? Did we do something wrong? At one stroke Franklin emerged with dignity and as master of the situation. Nor did he afterwards reply. He merely shrugged his shoulders and said the English were like that. They liked from time to time to bait their public men and they certainly had a fine time goading him. That was all there was to it.

His usefulness in England was at an end, and the colonies with great acclaim called him back. This matter of the letters showed once and for all that in spite of his ten-year stay in England he had not become a Tory. Since war was about to be declared in any case, can it be that Franklin, sensing the situation, applied just the right touch to make him change colors under the spotlight, and emerge, presto, a one hundred per cent loyal colonial? If so, he was still a great and shrewd diplomat, who knew when to act philosophically and could be trusted to handle ticklish situations well.

Money-making, since it was never to Franklin an end in itself, did not lead him to neglect the building of character. He knew that into the making of character goes a great deal of habit formation and steady work. A job or a trade was to Franklin better than a fortune because it built character and promised independence. He proved the worth of early conquering a trade when, as a penniless youth still under twenty, he made his first two-year trip away from America. Good journeymen printers, especially those who not only printed but also read good books, were still rare even in London. He had no trouble getting and keeping a job in England.

Franklin's *Autobiography* starts out as a declaration of independence for the common man, then coming in large numbers from Europe to America to start their lives all over again. For hundreds of years, says Franklin in effect, people in Europe have been taking off their hats to kings and bluebloods who inherited wealth, but in this country there is a new doctrine. Every man can make his own fortune. He takes off his hat to nobody, not even to a king. No wonder the French later affectionately dubbed him "the Quaker."

In Franklin's day such economic individualism was a new and heady wine. In previous ages the common man had little chance to indulge in opinions of his own, but now that very printing press of which Franklin is almost a symbol was helping to change all that. Magic wings to written words was the something new that was added to the life of the lowly in the age of Franklin, who immediately saw what new power this gave to publicity. A reading public clamorous enough to support its own authors came into the world between 1720 and 1750. Before that literature had needed patrons, but now came literature read and paid for by the people. Englishmen, perhaps not fully realizing what they were doing, wrote novels which made the lives of ordinary people interesting enough to read about. In America, and elsewhere, discussions burst forth into printed pamphlets. Franklin published and promoted his own newspaper and almanacs.

When in a London coffeehouse Franklin met that poor but gifted weaver, Thomas Paine, he promptly sent the man to America with letters of introduction. Paine arrived in 1774. By 1775 he was the most articulate patriot. "Others can rule, many can fight, but only Paine can write for us the English tongue," said Franklin—which from a man himself a master stylist was high praise indeed. Franklin did much to establish in the colonies these new highly readable and rapid-fire types of literature. He also got a postal system established, which, in turn, helped him to circulate his newspapers, and incidentally built up good roads.

If in all this Franklin was outspoken on the advantages of capital, consider what ready money meant in a world just emerging from an age in which there was almost no hope of rising above the station in which you were born. Generations no longer within hailing distance of feudal conditions can hardly grasp how deeply in Europe that canker of heredity had sunk in. Your birth determines your fate. A king is a king because his father before him was a king. Ever since the Roman Empire, if your father was a slave you were a slave. All through the Middle Ages the shoemaker was told to stick to his last. Do not step out of your class!

This was the kind of talk that Franklin with his newspapers and his almanacs was fast throwing overboard. By using his mind, or even his hands, the common man could better himself. Now, two hundred years later, we fail to see what rank heresy it was in Franklin's day to smash heredity. The new incendiary talk, which was getting into type and spreading everywhere, almost went so far as to wipe out the distinction between rich and poor right then and there. Paine in his book *Common Sense* harped on a single theme: Down with the king! To ignore a king is not treason but common sense.

In England well before 1776 inherited privileges could be purchased. The Renaissance had given the rich man of lowly origin his chance, since with money he could bribe or wangle his way to preferment. England had rotten boroughs by means of which votes could be manipulated. So could titles and honors. Deplorable as this corruption might be, it helped to break the implacable chain of heredity. At least a poor man, if he could lay his hands on money, could buy his way in.

Concerning money, and the making of money, the Americans of New England learned every trick in the English book. But from the beginning Americans went England one better in trying to make a clean sweep of political advantages based on either birth or wealth—no titles, no hereditary nobility, and no special status just because you are well-to-do. Every liberalizing step after the American Revolution has been in the direction of letting people, without regard to wealth, both exercise their vote and get an education for their children. A good head and a pair of willing hands were all the capital needed to gain independence—that was the main idea back of Franklin's thrift and statesmanship. Breaking down heredity has its philosophical and even theological implications in that it puts Franklin at the head of the newly ambitious, free-will iconoclasts. In rubbing out heredity Franklin was rubbing out the taint of original sin as something age after age had passed on from father to son. This stampede toward liberty is not going to stop until it storms the Bastille of determinism, and a leading figure in stirring all this into motion was Franklin.

3. Was Franklin a Philosopher?

THERE IS MUCH more to Franklin than is set forth in the simple biography of his early life, but one reason for considering him a philosopher is that he did write a book on how to live. Most men, even those who lead very full lives, do not bother to write things down. Socrates fortunately got Plato and Xenophon to do it for him. Franklin did it for himself. He left not only maxims and rules and much besides but, in addition to all that, he went over his own life in homely detail and underlined his mistakes. No other great statesman of the day—and there were many—did just that. For this reason, and for other reasons which will presently come crowding upon us, I call Franklin a philosopher, and I am not the only one to call him that.

"America has sent us many good things, gold, silver, sugar, tobacco, indigo, etc.; but you are the first philosopher, and indeed the first great man of letters, for whom we are beholden to her," said David Hume, an English contemporary of Franklin and a first-rate philosopher in his own right. James Truslow Adams, in his *Epic of America*, hits off Franklin as follows: "If American culture was as yet a little thin, it was genuine, though European. In many ways, perhaps, Franklin typified it best. Making Philadelphia his home, though born in Boston, he occupied in more ways than geographically a middle position in colonial life. Shrewd, practical, always alive to the main chance, anxious to make money and rise in the world, yet keenly alive to a life above money grubbing, he had on the one hand, none of the genuine depth or the religious fervor of the New England intellectual (nor his conscience), and, on the other hand, none of the humane quality or natural gentility of the Southern gentleman. Always something of an actor, with genuine ability, a self-made man in every way, he was ever ready to make the best of every situation and *if* there were two, of both worlds. Complete intellectual disinterestedness was as foreign to his nature as religious exaltation. He could draft a plan for the union of the colonies or invent a stove or a lightning rod, yet there was also that in him which brought the French to pay homage to him as a philosopher. If we were as yet unable to say what an American is, we might name him as the first."

Being a philosopher means more than just having a philosophy. In a sense every man on earth has a philosophy of his own. The beliefs he acts on are his philosophy, and such beliefs, though they be no more than an inherited patchwork, are proudly worn. Without a point of view from which to get his bearings, whether inherited or not, a man is lost. To get around in his own town a man needs in his head a map of some sort. He may not consciously have seen or have studied such a map. He may just have learned about his town step by step through practice, but the map is there just the same, and when he gets beyond the local confines the same man again needs a wider map or he is once more lost. In a sense a philosophy is a guide or map of what to do in life; and whether Franklin had a good guide in his head on what to do in growing America depends on how well he knew his way around.

Old John Adams, who knew Franklin, was not a man given to overstatement, but he seems to have considered Franklin as a man who knew and was known by the whole world. "Franklin's reputation was more universal than that of Leibnitz or Newton, Frederick or Voltaire; and his character was more beloved and esteemed than any or all of them. His name was familiar to government and people, to kings, courtiers, nobility, clergy, and philosophers, as well as plebeians, to such a degree that there was scarcely peasant or citizen, a valet de chambre, coachman or footman, a lady's chambermaid or a scullion in a kitchen who was not familiar with it and who did not consider him a friend to human kind. When they spoke of him they seemed to think he was to restore the golden age. His plans and his example were to abolish monarchy, aristocracy, and hierarchy throughout the world."

Ralph Waldo Emerson in a letter to his aunt, Mary Moody

Emerson, wrote in 1824: "Was Dr. Franklin (one of the most sensible men that ever lived) as likely to be born elsewhere as at Boston in 17 . . . ? Don't you admire (I am not sure you do) the serene and powerful understanding which was so eminently practical and useful, which grasped the policy of the globe and the form of a fly with like facility and ease; which seemed to be a transmigration of the genius of Socrates—yet more useful, more moral, and more pure. . . . Franklin was no verbal gladiator, clad in complete mail of syllogisms, but a sage who used his pen with an effect which was new and had been supposed to belong to the sword. He was a man of that singular force of mind (with which in the course of providence so few men are gifted) which seems designed to affect by individual influence what is ordinarily accomplished by the slow and secret work of institutions and national growth. . . . Many millions have already lived and millions are now alive who have felt through their whole lives the powerful good effect of Franklin's actions and writings. His subtle observation, his seasonable wit, his proved reason, and his mild and majestic virtues made him idolized in France, feared in England, and obeyed in America."

Asking whether Franklin and Emerson were philosophers is a little like asking whether Socrates and Plato were philosophers. Socrates was a stonecutter, Franklin was a printer. Plato was an aristocratic gentleman who instead of writing philosophical treatises wrote brilliant essays in the form of dialogues. Emerson was an ex-preacher who wrote poetic essays and lectured in scintillating fashion on heterogeneous subjects, as Plato did. In and underneath the conversations and dialogues of Socrates and Plato there is revealed the structure, or theory, of the Greek and democratic way of life. In the same way Franklin and Emerson, spaced a generation apart, give us immortal crosscuts of American life, with perspectives that let us grasp clearly the principles around which in those days American life was built.

There is a further analogy between the first democracy of Europe and the first democracy of the New World in that the pre-Socratic Greeks made no distinction between philosophy and science. Nor did Franklin; nor did Emerson, whose exalted prose is a kind of scientific poetry. When Franklin uses the word "philosopher" he is designating the kind of man we today would call a scientist. Before science found a bailiwick of its own it was called natural philosophy. The American Philosophical Society, which Franklin founded, was interested in science and scientific experimentation. Emerson too is forever studying—at least he does his best to study—nature and nature's laws.

Science, history, art, logic, and life must be blended into one to make a philosophy, or at least the material for a philosophy, and into it too must go the rules of conduct that shape the life we have in the world we live in. Early American and early Greek thought agree in respecting this universality of the scope of a philosophy. Just look at what Franklin did, and you cannot miss the breadth of the man. He is vitally interested in every phase of human endeavor. So were Socrates and the pre-Socratics. Later came specialization, but it is refreshing to see Franklin jump from lightning rods and stoves to gulf streams and thoughts on slavery. There is something salutary in the way he ties up all his thinking, even his religion, directly with Newtonian astronomy and with what we today call the sciences. I am not sure but what this gives his thoughts their central force. Perhaps science and philosophy should never have been divorced. They were not in the early days of Greek and American thought.

Philosophy has to be man's most comprehensive view of life. It cannot afford to be less. It suffers when it leaves any field untouched. Every broad contribution of knowledge is needed to round out a proper view of man and his relations to himself, to his fellow men, and to the universe. Thus philosophy covers the range from common sense to scientific theory and metaphysics. It includes, and must seek to weave into a single presentation, the contents of the storehouse of knowledge.

On the other hand, although comprehensive, it cannot be just an omnium-gatherum. To throw all we know or think we know into a grabbag might make some sort of encyclopedia but never a good philosophy. The whole mass of information must be put together in a way that gives sense to the total. There must be insights as to how part relates to part. A philosophy not only leaves nothing out but fits everything in. Its success, like that of a scientific theory, is measured by what it accounts for and how well it does so. This success is always relative. Each philosophy should be more adequate than the one that preceded it, but none so far has or perhaps ever will speak the final word, because the world and our knowledge of it keeps growing. Experience keeps piling up and will continue to do so as long as the universe spins and the brains in it remain receptive.

On this basis, was Franklin a philosopher? He did cover the ground. He was not averse to discussing any subject on earth. He did try over and over again, and with considerable success, to put all he knew into a revealing and readable form. He even gives us in full his views on religion. In science he was an original contributor, in mechanics an inventor, in speculation a bold spirit, in the field of common sense an uncommonly successful businessman, and in statesmanship almost without a peer. He might have been and done all that and still not have been a philosopher, if he had not formulated his own views and put them down on paper. But he did, and in doing so he gave us our point of departure for an American philosophy.

Not only did he mold in his own head all he learned, but he gave this hoard of information a slant of his own, thus pushing American philosophy definitely in a certain direction from which —at least in the six men here considered as following him—it has not departed. He gave the original impetus to a respectable and highly original school of thought, pragmatic, hardheaded, and optimistic, worthy of a hearing because it claims much. It claims to be a voice of free democracy. This huge and sprawling new democracy growing up in the New World of Franklin's day claims to be a continuation of that earlier and more compact one that worked and spoke and thought in Greece. Franklin's voice is therefore setting the tone for a modern free democracy.

But I am getting ahead of my story in the sense of formulating conclusions long before completing the narrative. Hear me out on Franklin at least because this chapter has a reverse twist at the end. Not only for his general views is Franklin rated among the philosophers. It is not too generally known, and it is never at all stressed, that very early in life the precocious Franklin did write a strictly philosophic dissertation and that, of all things, he gathered up all the copies of it that he could find and burned them! Nevertheless, the treatise survived, and today we read it and think it a cogent piece of work. What we have to explain is why he wanted it destroyed. Was he right in thinking, and deciding for himself, that that particular piece at least was away ahead of his time and had better be suppressed?

4. The Good Neighbor Policy

DEEPLY EMBEDDED IN Franklin's autobiographical homily is a secularized version of the old commandment: Love thy neighbor! In making yourself independent and, if possible, important, never neglect or outposture your neighbor. Above all things, be tolerant. Remain ready to learn. Be humble. Be cooperative. Franklin was an early expert on the basic everyday principles of human cooperation. In defending your own right you can at the same time defend the rights of others. It is not necessary to ride roughshod over your fellow men in order to develop your own personality. The entire Declaration of Independence, the spirit of it, can be put into four words: Live and let live!

To solve the problem of how not only big and little people but also big and little states could work together, Franklin introduced his famous compromise of proportional representation in the House and equal representation in the Senate. As he put it: "When a broad table is to be made and the edges of the planks do not fit, the artist takes a little from both and makes a good joint." Every individualist needs a little planing in the direction of good will. If you are not naturally friendly, appear to be friendly. The appearance may become real. Such politeness and such a restraint put on your own orneriness is not insincerity; it is a necessary step in establishing your better and more cooperative self.

The first move toward being a good neighbor is to be a good fellow and at least listen to the other side. Franklin's method was to throw out a hint and see if he could get other people to believe that the new idea was not his but their own. Ideas are not something you force down other people's throats. Franklin was the one founding father who had an outstanding sense of

21

humor. It took Balzac to say that Franklin had invented three things: the lightning rod, the republic, and the hoax. Franklin was famous for his hoaxes.

One day, as friends were having a heated argument on tolerance, Franklin picked up a Bible and read from it a solemn page about how Abraham had pressed a wayfarer, biding under a tree, to come into his house and eat with him. When the stranger, on eating, blessed not God, Abraham's wrath was kindled. After a violent quarrel with the stranger Abraham "arose and fell upon him, and drove him forth with blows into the wilderness." Then in the sudden way of the Old Testament the Lord appeared and reproved Abraham: "Have I not borne with this man these hundred and ninety and eight years, and nourished him, and clothed him, notwithstanding his rebellion against me; and couldst not thou, who art thyself a sinner, bear with him one night?" Abraham repented, ran after the aged stranger, treated him kindly, and on the morrow sent him on his way with gifts. All this Franklin read to his visitors, and what he read was clothed in such good biblical style that he had people hunting for weeks thereafter in their Bibles for this nonexistent passage.

Franklin was a printer, and what he had done was to have a special copy of the Bible bound up with this extra page in it. Where he got the original story of Abraham and the Stranger has kept scholars busy ever since. They traced it to Jeremy Taylor's *Liberty of Prophecy* (1657), and then to a rabbinical work, *The Rod of Juda,* in which the Stranger is a fire worshiper, and that version back again to the Persian poet Saadi, who says the tale was "something he read once upon a time." All this only goes to show how far Franklin roved to find gems for his many hoaxes and collections of old tales, sayings, proverbs, and anecdotes. The whole lore of stored wisdom was grist to his mill, much of it reappearing in the pages of his yearly almanacs.

For eliminating personal bias Franklin in a playful way advocated moral algebra. Sometimes when your feelings get to be too personal, substitute for your own highly colored opinion the letter x. Then calm down and see if you can write an equation with the pros and cons, whittled down to their bare bones, on opposite sides of a sheet of paper, cancel out the equals on both sides, and look for the weight of evidence. When you are so angry that you have neither the time nor the patience to get out the paper and practice moral algebra, at least stop and count to ten. This gives the still, small voice of reason a chance to remind you that if you have the right to get mad enough to murder somebody else they have the right to do the same and exterminate you. Thus the very first principles of self-preservation lead straight to a decent regard for the basic rights of others. By the same token it pays to be patient in engaging the help of others. One man avails naught against an army. It is by cooperation in which many heads and hands contribute something that all the great and important things of life get done; so do not always hold out for the seeming perfection of your own point of view.

Franklin started his public career by putting in many years as the clerk of a legislative assembly. He had the advantage of a long unhurried study of how men in practice work together. Then he spent a major part of his life among the wrangling absentee landlords and profit-seekers in England, advocating patiently the rights of the colonials. When patience failed, he left England to continue his invaluable efforts to aid the colonies first at home and then in France. At the time of the temporary crisis with England, Franklin, as our ambasador to France, did more for the colonies in getting supplies, establishing credit, and gaining good will in Europe than whole armies together. He turned out to be a good hater, but even there, in tune with eighteenth-century usage, he still deployed diplomacy, as when he ended a very polite letter to a former English crony with the "You are now my Enemy and I am Yours."

Earlier in the game he had wanted America and England to form a federation instead of a one-sided combination in which the mother country exploited the daughter. He even envisioned America as one day becoming the more important part of England. After the war he applied to the conduct of nations the same principles that worked in private life. If a mistake had been committed, recognize it as such, write it down in your diary as an *erratum*, forget it, and start all over again as soon as possible on a path which avoids repeating that particular error.

Crowning a lifetime of conciliation he put his signature on the American Constitution. Before doing so he made a speech or, rather, had a speech read for him as he sat by, at the age of eighty-one, infirm in body but with a mind as strong as ever. The words of that speech are well known, but his phrases bear repeating for their excellent restatement in modern language of the Second Great Commandment. "Mr. President, I conceive that there are several parts of this Constitution which I do not approve, but I am not sure that I shall never approve them. . . . For having lived long, I have experienced many instances of being obliged by better information, or fuller consideration, to change opinions even on important subjects, which I once thought right. . . . I doubt too whether any other convention we can obtain may be able to make a better constitution. For when you assemble a number of men to have the advantage of their joint wisdom, you inevitably assemble with these men all their prejudices, their passions, their errors of opinion, their local interests and their selfish views. From such an assembly can a perfect production be expected? It astonishes me, Sir, to find this system approaching so near to perfection as it does; and I think it will astonish our enemies, who are waiting with confidence to hear . . . that our States are on the point of separating only to meet hereafter for the purpose of cutting one another's throats. Thus, I consent, Sir, to this Constitution because I expect no better, and because I am not sure it is not the best. The opinions I have had of its errors are sacrifices to the public good."

Almost sooner than anybody else Franklin saw that slavery was a blot on democracy. His very last public act was a memorial addressed to Congress and signed by him as president of the Abolition Society. He asked the members of Congress to "devise means for removing this inconsistency from the character of the American people" and "to step to the very verge of the power vested in you for discouraging every species of traffic in the persons of our fellowmen."

And that was not all. He died, eighty-four years old, on April 17, 1790; but on March 23, 1790, he had sent to the papers the last but not the least of his many hoaxlike parodies. This was a piece on the slave trade. "Reading last night in your excellent paper," Franklin began, "the speech of Mr. Jackson [a Southern senator] in Congress against their meddling with the affair of slavery, or attempting to mend the condition of the slaves, it put me in mind of a similar one made about a hundred years since by Sidi Mahomet Ibrahim, a member of the Divan of Algiers, which may be seen in Martin's account of his consulship, *anno* 1687 . . . " And so on and on. Every point made by Jackson in his speech was paralleled by an argument from the Mohammedan pirate in favor of capturing, buying, and selling Christian slaves. There was not an American alive who did not detest and abhor the way Algerian pirates had practiced slavery on what to them were Christian unbelievers. But the Divan, as a public body, came to the conclusion that it was clearly in the interest of the state to go on plundering and enslaving as many unenlightened but able-bodied Christians as possible.

Individualism is not incompatible with a strong feeling for the solidarity and brotherhood of all mankind. Franklin, a former slaveowner but not averse to letting slaves slip quietly away from him in England and to changing his mind on the subject altogether, had this feeling to a remarkable degree. It became in a sense almost a religion.

5. The Scientist

ALL THIS ABOUT enlightened self-interest, good neighbor policy, good public relations through working together, and even the passionate pleading late in life against slavery, lays bare a good part but by no means all of the underlying sinews of Franklin's philosophy. Beyond America, beyond England and France, beyond patriotism, stands the international figure of Franklin the scientist. The reason for spreading out before the reader some brief account of what and how much Franklin did in science is that, perhaps imperfectly aware of the full purport of what he was doing, Franklin here took a giant step toward making thoughts for the welfare of all humanity a part of the daily thinking of even ordinary men. All his efforts in science flowed from his desire to do something for all mankind.

When Millikan, the physicist, as Bernard Jaffe points out in his *Men of Science*, was asked to select the influential scientists of the eighteenth and nineteenth centuries, he named just thirteen men: three Englishmen—Faraday, Maxwell, and Darwin; two Germans—Karl Gauss and Helmholtz; two Frenchmen—Pasteur and Fresnel; one Italian—Volta; and two Americans—J. Willard Gibbs and Benjamin Franklin. Prominent among the world scientists chosen by the National Academy of Sciences for bas-relief portraits on their Washington Building is the portrait of Franklin. Of course Franklin was among the first to be elected to the Hall of Fame, but he enters that Hall as a statesman and not as a scientist.

In Franklin's day there were no Nobel Prize winners, but Franklin did get the Copley Medal from the London Royal Society, the highest scientific honor then available. The small but famous Junto that Franklin organized early in life was in essence a scientific society. To get in you not only had to have a strong interest in scientific knowledge but also no prejudices. You had to declare that you loved your fellow men regardless of their religion or profession; promise to see that no one was harmed in body, name, or goods for holding speculative opinions; love truth for truth's sake; and search for the truth as well as communicate it to others. No more than twelve members were permitted, but each member could start a new Junto of his own. The Junto idea he put into practice in 1727. Much later, in 1743, he founded the American Philosophical Society, which might be considered an expanded Junto on a scale definitely international. What he was launching here was world-wide, cooperative, scientific research.

Much of Franklin's own scientific work had a practical, but never a personal or selfish, aim. In the popular estimation Franklin the inventor overshadows the original investigator; it is forgotten that he did important original research work. It is also overlooked that he turned none of his inventions to private profit. On patents Franklin held that as we enjoy great advantages from the inventions of others we should be glad of an opportunity to contribute inventions of our own. The governor of Pennsylvania offered Franklin a patent on his stove but he declined. The lightning rod too was a free gift to the world.

At the time when Franklin became interested in electricity is was thought that electricity was of two kinds: one produced by rubbing glass with silk and the other by rubbing sealing wax with fur. The glass attracted a pith ball, the wax rod repelled it. People spoke of electricity as being either vitreous or resinous. Franklin said there was only one kind, and "it is not created by friction but collected, being really an element diffused among matter. The electrical matter consists of particles extremely subtle. . . . Hence have arisen some new terms among us: we say B is electrized positively; A negatively. Or rather B is electrized plus; A minus." He was the first to speak of plus and minus in connection with electricity. A few more of the now well-known electrical terms introduced by Franklin were: armature, conductor, battery, and electrician. Generalizing far beyond glass or wax, Franklin concluded that if a body or substance possessed too much electricity it was charged plus; if it had not enough it was charged minus; if it had just the right amount it was neutral.

Franklin's contribution to electric theory is thus summed up by Jaffe: "So deep and clear was Franklin's creative imagination that he came very close to arriving at the modern conception of the electrical nature of matter, with its electrons (negative particles of electricity) and protons (positive charges of electricity)." Jaffe also quotes J. J. Thomson, Nobel laureate in physics and discoverer of the electron: "A collection of electrons would resemble in many respects Franklin's electric fluid, the idea of which was conceived in the infancy of the science of electricity." All of Franklin's researches in electricity took place in the six years 1746–1752, when he was between the ages of forty and forty-six. The genesis of his book on electricity which achieved fame long before the *Autobiography* did, is well set forth in Verner W. Crane's book on Franklin:

"Already the Philadelphia experiments had begun to arouse interest among the Europeans. . . . Franklin reported them all in lucid detail in letters to scientific friends, in the first instance to Peter Collinson. As Franklin had expected, Collinson shared the letters with other members of the Royal Society, who cited them with approval in papers printed in the *Philosophical Transactions*. . . . Meanwhile, Collinson's friend, Dr. John Fothergill, another Quaker and a famous London physician, was preparing them for the press, and they were printed by Cave in April, 1751, as *Experiments and Observations on Electricity, made at Philadelphia in America, by Mr. Benjamin Franklin, and Communicated in several Letters to Mr. P. Collinson of London, F.R.S.* This was the first slender edition of the most famous and influential book to come out of America in the eighteenth century. It is still, historically, one of the major works in science. Five English editions, besides supplements, were published in Franklin's century, three French editions, one Italian, one German. When the fourth English edition appeared in 1769, William Bewley declared in the *Monthly Review, London,* that these papers constituted 'the *principia* of electricity.' "

Crane also tells us how Franklin described an experiment whereby from a high steeple, in a rather dangerous manner, it could be proved that lightning was electricity, and how Jean François Dalibard on May 10, 1752, first performed Franklin's experiment. Meanwhile Franklin had thought of a simpler method by using a kite armed with an iron point, and in June, 1752, before he heard of the success of the French, he went out into the fields with his son William, then 19, and proved the point himself. He waited till October to flash the news in an advertisement in the *Pennsylvania Gazette,* referring to the forthcoming 1753 edition of his Almanac. In this Almanac tucked away near the end was an eighteen-line paragraph on *How to Secure Houses, etc. from Lightning.* "The lightning rod," says Crane, "along with the kite, at once became the popular symbol of Franklin's fame as an electrician."

Other things Franklin did or invented were: a flexible catheter, the first in American medicine; bifocal glasses; watertight bulkheads for ship construction; explanation of why boats pull harder in shallow water; magical numerical squares made for amusement; a harmonica or arrangement of glass hemispheres revolving on an iron spindle which he learned to play with skill (Beethoven and Mozart wrote music for such an instrument). He studied storms and the Gulf Stream constantly, having an inveterate interest in meteorology possibly because of his travels and his post roads; he studied the effects of oil in soothing the surface of the water, carrying oil in the hollow of his walking stick for these experiments; studied heat conductivity by placing black and white pieces of cloth on bright snow, concluding that people should wear black in winter and light clothes in summer. The list of his scientific interests could be extended.

"I leave them," said Franklin of his scientific opinions, "to take their chances in the world. If they are right, truth and experience will support them, if wrong, they ought to be refuted and rejected. Disputes are apt to sour one's temper and disturb one's mind. I have no private interest in the reception of my inventions by the world, having never made, nor proposed to make, the least profit by any of them."

Franklin, in writing about heat as early as 1757, said: "As by a constant supply of fuel in a chimney you keep a room warm, so by a constant supply of food in the stomach, you keep a body warm." Lavoisier in 1774 discovered that burning was the rapid union of the substance with oxygen, and for the first time asserted that in the process of assimilation in the body food was oxydized, providing a slow burning. Benjamin Thompson, toward the end of the eighteenth century, established that heat was a form of energy due to vibration of particles of matter. Sometimes in his *aperçus* Franklin was right, and then again he was good and wrong. In 1791 John Fitch took out his steamboat patent. Three years earlier Franklin had taken a look at Fitch's invention. Franklin was then eighty-two and refused to give any aid to the unfortunate Fitch. He could see no future in this newfangled contraption.

Joseph Priestley drew a parallel between Franklin and Newton, maintaining that Franklin had passed on to posterity the true principles of electrical science, just as Newton had given the world the true principles of natural science in general. Men were beginning to look upon science as a revelation of true principles.

Newton believed that opposing forces were so regulated in the physical world that this world became a self-regulating mechanism in which each part controlled, held in check, and worked harmoniously with every other part. God could afford to be a spectator, standing off to admire the variety, ingenuity, and utility of his handiwork. In America it was thought that similar principles could be applied to government. Franklin went along with the Constitution in its setting up of separate, self-balancing branches of government which served as checks one on the other. The idea of opposing forces holding each other off and working together appears also in Franklin's negative and positive electricity, and later this same idea was developed more fully in Emerson's ideas on the Laws of Compensation.

For two hundred years preceding Franklin's day the natural sciences had gone from one triumph to another. Bacon sounded the trumpet call of the new learning. Galileo, Harvey, Gilbert and others worked away quietly, and then came the incomparable Newton. All this took place in England and in Europe, but

Franklin knew his Europe and his England as well as anyone born over there. By building ahead on the solid achievements of English thought, America was making itself a newer and more youthful England. Certainly the two giants of English thought, Locke and Newton, were towering figures also in America. Both of them Franklin read in his impressionable years, and in them the roots of his own thinking burrowed down.

The English Enlightenment with its new learning flowered in the heads of all our founding fathers. From them we get English thought with a sea change. No one read more widely, had a deeper sense of humor, or gave his heart more fully to the problems of mankind than Franklin; and some of the serenity surrounding this early sage and much of his tolerance came, I am sure, straight from his deep contemplation of the Newtonian heavens. I cannot help thinking that Paine, Franklin's emissary, when he wrote his famous book *Common Sense* was going back to the same source of inspiration. The central idea in Paine's book is that in this country we substitute for monarchy a reign of law. The majesty of law, as set forth in our Constitution, is our king, and that idea of the supremacy of natural law came straight from Newton.

Then, as now, men were stirred by the grandeur of the Newtonian astronomy. Newton gave the world an entirely new conception of things physical. After Newton a reign of law extending from the remotest star to the tides of the sea united the whole universe of matter. The majesty of it was overwhelming. In 1728, when he was twenty-two years old, Franklin wrote: "When I stretch my imagination through and beyond our system of planets, beyond the visible fixed stars themselves, into the space that is every way infinite, and conceive it filled with suns like ours, each with a chorus of worlds forever moving round him, then this little ball on which we move, seems, even in my narrow imagination, to be almost nothing, and myself less than nothing, and of no sort of consequence. I cannot conceive otherwise than that He, the Infinite Father, expects or requires no worship or praise from us, but that He is infinitely above it."

In the light of the new grandeur given to things material some men were asking, But what about the human mind? John Locke addressed himself to this question. The reputation of Newton as a student of celestial mechanics was matched by that of Locke as a student of the human mind. Locke's psychology was a companion piece to Newton's physics. John Locke and Isaac Newton were contemporaries and firm friends for life. There was nothing in the writings of Newton or Locke which could arouse official opposition from the powerful ecclesiastical organizations of their day. These men wrote books both orthodox and bold, both subtly subversive and openly liberal. It was on these books that American Romuluses and Remuses were suckled.

In his study of the human mind Locke recognized and re-emphasized some old conclusions. It had been the fashion for centuries, and it had recently been newly clarified by Descartes, that everything in the world could be reduced to two basic substances, mind and matter. This Locke accepted. But if mind is a substance, it is obviously quite a different kind of substance from that of which the material world is made, argued Locke. The effect of matter on matter, as Newton made plain, is to retard or accelerate motion. The effect of matter on mind is something quite different, in that instead of causing acceleration it causes sensations of sound, sight, odor, pain, or pleasure. The scientific way, therefore, of defining mind is to say that it is the kind of substance which is affected by matter in such a way as to produce in it colors, sounds, tastes, smells, and a variety of feelings. So far so good, but this rather abstract and highly ingenious bit of reasoning was not what made Americans excited about the doctrines of Locke.

Further conclusions drawn by him were that each person represents a fresh and independent piece of mind substance. Moreover, the mind at birth is a blank. It starts from zero. Its business is to translate matter into sensations. Every mind makes matter its own property. It feeds on matter and builds up from it all its own rich content of sensation and feeling. The furniture of the mind comes into existence from the lowly material stimuli encountered in nature. And here Locke was laying the foundation for a new doctrine of human equality. The mind is not subject to matter. Man is born free to utilize matter. All men can begin from scratch the pursuit of the good things of life.

This was a doctrine to attract the keen minds in the malleable youths of the Age of Enlightenment. Americans liked the naturalistic setting which Locke gave to human dignity. They liked the way in which he stressed the political rather than the exclusively religious angle.

There is nothing in the mind that it did not get through the senses. Thus Locke reaffirmed another ancient view, but a view that gives a new centrality to experience, the experience we get in life through the senses. Experience and experimentation become the King and Queen of Progress. The colonists, born experimenters, were avid for a new land full of new experiences. Most of the men who came here were not averse to trying something novel. They wished to live in a different country, in a different way, free independently to explore new ways of life and new political setups in a new country.

It is possible that the American Revolution was fought with greater determination because the colonists, a motley crew, could unite on some, perhaps vaguely felt but general and nonsectarian, ground in the conviction that all men are born with an equal chance. Instead of merely holding that men were equal in the sight of God hereafter, as had been the custom for ages, they found, following Locke, some reason for saying that one man is as good as another in his fundamental rights here on earth. With incomparable popularizers like Paine and Franklin to present these views in words and parables that all could understand, Locke's thought found in the New World a new birth. Right here the question is not whether Locke's view of mind-substance, as different from matter, was a true guess or merely a halfway house to a more adequate psychology—the latter is certainly the case—but the point here is that for their day and age the views of Locke, as developed and promulgated in this country became a bright new center surmounted by a high banner around which men of all faiths, many of them of small learning but bold in spirit, could unite.

6. The Religion of a Deist

DEISM MAKES SENSE only against the excesses of religious practices and the fierce religious wars of the two hundred years preceding it. The inhumanities publicly practiced in the years 1500–1700 are often with a good deal of justice ascribed simply to the crudeness of the times. In a two-volume account of the *Christian Saga* by E. T. Boggs there is a description of the punishment inflicted on the murderer of William the Silent. Five times they beat him with sticks most cruelly. Then they smeared his body with honey and let a goat with a very rough tongue lick him all over in such a manner that skin and flesh were stripped off at the same time. Next they extended his body on a bench and tore apart one after another the muscles and the bones. During all this time the man being punished never once cried out or seemed to feel the least pain. Modern psychologists might explain this as the total anesthesia typical of certain psychoneurotics. The Hollanders believed that the man was possessed of the devil; the Spaniards believed that God was helping him. The fact remains that even in a liberal country like Holland cruel and unusual punishments were not only tolerated but demanded by government and populace alike.

Burning at the stake was at one time prescribed in England for an attempt on the life of a noble. An early French law demanded that the wife of a thief be buried alive. Impaling, flaying, burying alive, and boiling in oil were recognized forms of execution. Tens of thousands of malefactors died by crucifixion, which was for centuries a standard method of execution. Torture by brigands, pirates, and outlaws for obtaining money and by constituted authorities for obtaining confessions was common practice. For heretics a brief burning here on earth, when God was going

34

to burn them in hell forever anyway, seemed, it is shocking to say, almost a fit entrance into that greater fiery furnace. It is only against these backgrounds of almost universally tolerated violence and cruelty, condoned even in the name of religion, that the reaction into the comparative mildness of deism gets to have real meaning.

Brinton in his sane and balanced account of the sixteenth century says that three things are necessary before persecutions can flourish: men must believe that they are right, that the point in question is highly important, and that coercion is effective. An inquisitor in the Low Countries at the time of the Tyndale trials is quoted as saying: "It is no great matter, whether they that die on account of religion be guilty, or innocent, provided we terrify the people by such examples; which generally succeeds best when persons eminent for learning, riches, nobility or high station are thus sacrificed."

Things had to get worse before they got better. Dealing out death to infidels, sorcerers, devil worshipers, and heretics brought things to such confusion that at one time in England, where an intermediate church had been established, the same cart carried both papists and dissenters to the same horrible and untimely end. The autos-da-fé spread to South America, the witch hunts to North America, and then mercifully, both in the Old World and in the New, fury burned itself out and slowly a new sanity dawned. No wonder the eighteenth century is called the Age of Enlightenment.

It had been abundantly proved that men of every stamp knew how to die for their ideals, and that the ideals they died for could be of the most varied sorts. Now came the different and equally hard lesson of learning how to retain ideals when one did not have to die for them. This difficult phase of passing to a less theatrical but more sanely balanced plane of living was getting under way in America, where a real effort was made not only to have different sects live side by side in peace but also to kindle their interest in new ideals. Between New England and the South, with its Cavalier traditions, lay that large middle area in colonial America where Dutch traders along the Hudson practiced tolerance for good commercial reasons; Rhode Island,

where Roger Williams, driven out of Massachusetts for personal
reasons, practiced and preached the gospel of toleration; Mary-
land, where Lord Baltimore, himself a Catholic, had broad views
on toleration as political expediency; and finally Pennsylvania,
with its chief city Philadelphia, home of the Quakers, themselves
persecuted for a time in America and now on principle cultivating brotherly love and protesting against war even with the
Indians. In this conglomerate central portion of the colonies
the tough business of living side by side, ambitiously yet without
coming to blows, was hammered out by Franklin and others.
Franklin was above all a conciliator. The greatest domestic
differences in the colonies were not nationalistic, or even economic, but religious.

"I had been religiously educated as a Presbyterian," says
Franklin, "and though some of the dogmas of that persuasion,
such as the eternal decrees of God, election, reprobation, etc.,
appeared to me unintelligible, others doubtful, and I early
absented myself from the public assemblies of the sect, Sunday
being my studying day, I never was without some religious
principles. I never doubted, for instance, the existence of the
Deity; that he made the world, and governed it by his providence; that the most suitable service of God was the doing good
to man; that our souls are immortal; and that all crime will be
punished, and virtue rewarded, either here or hereafter. These
I esteemed the essentials of every religion."

In his *Articles of Belief and Acts of Religion,* written when he
was twenty, Franklin's religion reflects Newton's cosmology with
a slightly pagan and polytheistic tinge. "I conceive then, that
the Infinite has created many Beings or Gods, vastly superior to
man, who can better conceive his perfection than we, and return
him a more rational and glorious praise. . . . I believe there
is one supreme most perfect being, author and father of the
gods themselves. . . . It may be that these created gods are immortal, or it may be that after many ages they are changed,
and others supply their place. Howbeit, I conceive that each
of these is exceeding wise, and good, and very powerful; and
that each has made for himself, one glorious sun, attended with a

beautiful and admirable system, that I propose for the object of my praise and adoration."

Concerning the ritual Christianity of churchgoing and prayers, he wrote: "The faith you mention has doubtless its use in the world; I do not desire it to be diminished, but I wish it were more productive of good works than I have generally seen it; I mean really good works, works of kindness, charity, mercy, and public spirit; not holiday-keeping, sermon reading or hearing, performing church ceremonies, or making long prayers, filled with flatteries and compliments, despised even by wise men, and much less capable of pleasing the Deity. The worship of God is a duty, the hearing and reading of sermons may be useful; but if men rest in hearing and praying as too many do, it is as if a tree should value itself in being watered and putting forth leaves, though it never produced any fruit."

Toward the very end of his life, March 9, 1790, he wrote: "As to Jesus of Nazareth . . . I have . . . some doubt as to his divinity. . . . I see no harm, however, in its being believed, if that belief has the good consequences, as perhaps it does, of making his doctrine more respected and more observed." How he arrived at these astonishingly direct and frankly utilitarian points of view, he explains in his *Autobiography:* "I was scarce fifteen, when, after doubting by turns of several points, as I found them disputed in the different books I read, I began to doubt of Revelation itself. Some books against Deism fell into my hands; they were said to be the substance of sermons preached at Boyle's Lectures. It happened that they wrought an effect on me quite contrary to what was intended by them; for the arguments of the Deists, which were quoted to be refuted, appeared to me much stronger than the refutation; in short, I soon became a thorough Deist."

The incorrigibly practical Franklin saw clearly that in this world it makes little difference what you believe concerning the next. For your fellow men it is what you do here that counts. An unbeliever can be a good neighbor. Actions speak much louder than words. Above all, having your words say one thing and your deeds another, is something no man of common decency can stomach. As Franklin put it in one of his doggerel quotations:

> A man of words and not of deeds,
> Is like a garden full of weeds.

Outspoken, but not censorious, Franklin was likely to find some good in almost any religion, even in the old-fashioned Calvinistic preaching of the Cotton Mather variety. Late in life he wrote to Samuel Mather, son of Cotton: "When I was a boy, I met with a book, entitled *Essays to Do Good,* which I think was written by your father. It had been so regarded by a former possessor, that several leaves of it were torn out; but the remainder gave me such a turn of thinking, as to have an influence on my conduct through life; for I have always set a greater value on the character of a *doer of good,* than on any other kind of reputation; and if I have been, as you seem to think, a useful citizen, the public owes the advantage of it to that book."

He explained to his sister Jennie how he never tried to get rid of or to sidestep religion: "You express yourself as if you thought I was against the worshipping of God, and doubt that good works would merit heaven; which are fancies of your own, I think, without foundation. I am so far from thinking that God is not to be worshipped, that I have composed and wrote a whole book of devotions for my own use; and I imagine there are few if any in the world so weak as to imagine that the little good we can do here can merit so vast a reward hereafter." Further to his father: "I think opinions should be judged by their influence and effects; and if a man holds none that tend to make him less virtuous or more vicious, it may be concluded he holds none that are dangerous; which I hope is the case with me."

It is hard to find a more clearly formulated platform for pragmatism. Later William James is going to take exactly these points of view and weave them into a characteristically American philosophy more fully worked out than that of Franklin. The main tenets of early pragmatism are all here, with the stress in Franklin, as in James, on tolerance and sympathetic understanding of varying points of view. Cultivate agreements, not differences, is the practical application. Franklin often went to church but always he looked for preachers who came out for general virtues such as might be fostered among any group of decent men. He avoided disputes. As he put it in a letter to his father: "My mother grieves that one of her sons is an Arian, another an Arminian. What an Arminian or Arian is, I cannot say that I very well know. The truth is, I make such distinctions very little my study. I think vital religion has always suffered when orthodoxy is more regarded than virtue; and the Scriptures assure me that at the last day we shall be examined not on what we thought but what we did; and our recommendation will not be that we said 'Lord! Lord!' but that we did good to our fellow creatures."

In frontier America it was good form to ask, What can you do to be useful? and not What do you believe? Putting into the background the differences that led to bloody feuds in Europe was one of those sensible steps forward shown by all subsequent testings to have been sound practice. At the same time the soft-pedaling of weighty questions leading to sharp differences did not necessarily betoken indifference to either religion or metaphysics. These were the days of a return to a simpler humanistic religion, coupled with a strong belief that scientific attention to nature would greatly benefit mankind. Franklin, in addition to his civic activities, was forever on the alert to find new ways of putting nature to use for the benefit of all.

I. Woodbridge Riley has pointed out that Franklin's summary of the main points of his religion coincides exactly with a much earlier five-point summary made by the picturesque Herbert of Cherbury (1583-1648), who died a hundred and fifty years before Franklin was born. Herbert of Cherbury goes down in the history of philosophy as the "Father of Deism." It is of course obvious that deists and theists alike believe in God, *deus* and *theos* being just the Latin and Greek names for God, and therefore of no help at all in distinguishing between the two terms. Undoubtedly theism is the more general term. A theist is practically the same as a monotheist, a believer in one God as opposed to the polytheist, who believes in many; and then if you are a theist, and moreover believe that God created the world, there comes the further question: Did he thereafter leave it alone or is a continual process of creation and maintenance still going on?

A deist is a special kind of theist who does not identify God with nature (pantheism) nor necessarily conceive of him in human terms, such as walking in a garden and thinking and feeling much as we do (anthropomorphism), but who believes in a transcendent God who made a self-sustaining universe, organized under its own laws, so that he seldom need interfere with it. The deist, following Herbert of Cherbury, stresses the main points that all the great religions have in common. These points, practically identical with those Franklin emphasized, were:

1. There is a God;
2. God should be worshiped;
3. Virtue and piety are the important parts of religious practice;
4. Vices and crimes (sin) must be expiated by repentance;
5. Rewards and punishments come during and after this life.

Lord Herbert of Cherbury in 1624 published a famous book of which *De Veritate* is the shortened title and which contained in the end of it a short but clear account of deism. The author of this book was first of all an accomplished courtier, who came from a distinguished family. When only 15 he married his cousin Mary Herbert, but it is not clear whether this early entry into domesticity had anything to do with his seeking an adventurous career outside the home. At any rate he was a gifted man. His brother was George Herbert, the poet, and some consider Edward Herbert, who later became a lord, a better poet than the well-known George. Twice for excitement Edward joined the army of the Prince of Orange in Holland. As a spirited soldier, who loved dueling, Edward once challenged anyone from the opposing side to a duel. When the Spanish commander refused to sanction any such shenanigans, Herbert persisted, dashing over into the enemy's camp. He was complimented on his bravery by the Spanish commander, who gallantly invited him to dinner. Presumably he was allowed to return to his own camp unharmed.

All this and more the founder of deism tells us in an *Autobiography*, which Horace Walpole, the first editor of Herbert's self-written life, calls "perhaps the most extraordinary account that ever was given seriously by a wise man of himself." Herbert wrote it after he was sixty: "My age being now past three-score, it is fit that I should examine what I have done well or ill." The volume is still to be had in cheap editions. It is a most readable book, vain and boastful, but not offensively so. In it occurs an account of the circumstances surrounding the writing of his earlier book, *De Veritate*. "My book *De Veritate* . . . was about this time finished, and I communicated it to Hugo Grotius, that great scholar, and others who exhorted me earnestly to publish it. But though encouraged, being still doubtful, one fair windless day in summer, kneeling by the open casement with my book in my hand, I did devoutly ask God for some sign. Immediately a loud though yet gentle noise came from the heavens (for it was like nothing on earth), which did so comfort me that I took my petition as granted and resolved to print my book, which was done in Paris. At first I divulged it only to worthy readers, but afterwards reprinting it in England, I not only dispersed it among the prime scholars of Europe, but was sent to from the furthest parts of Christendom to desire the sight of it."

In a quite different vein in that same autobiography he tells the reader: "That summer I spent in the Low Country with the Prince of Orange, who, as there was no fighting forward, played chess with me or took me as his companion when he went lovemaking." Herbert of Cherbury's contacts with the religious wars of his day and his creditable but difficult negotiations at the French court, where he later served with distinction as the English ambassador, made him look at religion as a statesman does. His brilliant inspiration was: why not stress what religions have in common instead of the points of difference? In coming out boldly and unreservedly against sectarian dogmatism, he remained a lone figure for at least fifty years, when another writer, Charles Blount, published *Anima Mundi*, essentially a rehash of

Herbert's ideas. Another fifty years were to pass before we get the standard authors on deism: John Toland (1670–1722); Anthony Collins (1676–1729); Thomas Woolston (1670–1733); and Matthew Tindal (1653–1733), the fullest and most complete of them all. Herbert of Cherbury's seed, so prayerfully planted, fell on late-blooming but fertile soil. All these men expanded but did not radically change the basic ideas set forth by Herbert, but they did make sure that these sensible ideas finally received the kind of wide publicity that assured their spread to America.

At that Herbert of Cherbury, in making common agreement the test of truth, was merely continuing a very old idea, clearly stated by Cicero with his *Omnium consensus est naturae vox.* Unfortunately Herbert considered that men had an innate knowledge of these general ideas which all men held in common. By instinct, Herbert thought, they knew and could listen to the voice of nature telling them about God, who invites worship and inculcates virtue; but shortly after Herbert's time the great Locke made a special point of demolishing the notion of inborn or innate ideas. To him the mind of an infant was a blank tablet with nothing inscribed upon it. This weakened Herbert's position somewhat, but some of the later deists repaired this damage, among them William Wollaston, the second edition of whose book, *The Religion of Nature Delineated,* we find the young Benjamin Franklin setting up in type during the first year of his first stay in London. Wollaston's book was published in London in 1722, almost a hundred years after Herbert of Cherbury had planted the basic ideas.

The men whom Herbert consulted about the advisability of publishing his book also helped his central idea along, especially Grotius, the great jurist, who in his own *Rights of War and Peace* also equated natural law and right reason. Nature's law flowers in human reason. Emerson will take up anew that same idea. According to Grotius, reason forbids what nature forbids, and since God is the Author of Nature, the voice of reason gets to be the voice of God. In war Roman lawyers permitted fraud of any kind, but Grotius holds that a promise is a promise, even if made to an enemy. The white flag, ambassadors, women and children, even scholars and merchants, should be respected. The trend toward a greater humanitarianism is evident. It was men like Grotius, Herbert, and the still-earlier Montaigne who really started the big task of making the world a less harsh place to live in. Montaigne settled for reason in all things except the doctrines of the Catholic Church. These he accepted on faith. That was in that early day the safest and easiest way of keeping out of serious trouble, but it was the deists who made the first determined and large-scale attempt to turn religion itself into something simpler and more humane and that, moreover, did not need prodigies of faith to find acceptance. The fact that they made it something simple enough to be understood and embraced by all was what appealed to Franklin. Franklin, Washington, Jefferson, most of the leading men of the day were all deists of some sort.

7. The Dissertation

THE *Dissertation*, written by the young Franklin and purposely destroyed by him, was occasioned directly by the setting up in type of the Wollaston book while Franklin was working at the printing house of Palmer's during the first year of his first stay in London. Later he worked at an even larger printing establishment called Watts's. Both were prominent London printing firms.

Franklin had come to London in the first place merely to buy type to set up a printing shop of his own in Philadelphia. Governor Keith of Pennsylvania, with whom the precocious and gifted Franklin was on friendly terms, egged him on in this enterprise, promising him valuable letters of introduction and perhaps even the loan of money. Letters from the governor with their precious contents were to reach Franklin on the boat. They never came, and Keith went down in Franklin's books as a conspicuous example of one of the men in high places who cannot be trusted. In London he had quickly to find work or starve.

He made good at both printing places where he worked, and at Watts's, during the second year of his stay in London, we find him getting into the kind of situation that perfectly displays the way the mind of the young Franklin was operating. His conduct exemplifies a thesis that was also set forth in the *Dissertation*. In this larger house he undertook presswork which meant carrying heavy type forms up and down stairs. Most of the men in the place took two hands to a form, and wondered where the new youth from America got his strength to carry one in each hand the way he did, especially since he drank nothing but water.

The other men were great guzzlers of beer, even during working hours, the beer being supplied by a boy they hired to bring it from an alehouse across the way. Strong beer made strong men, and they jeered at the "Water-American," making the young show-off contribute to the kitty required to keep the beer and the beer boy going. This Franklin considered unfair. He protested that, as he himself drank only water, he did not need to chip in on the beer, and he even got the foreman to agree with him and announce that he need not pay. But soon queer things began to happen. "I stood out two or three weeks, was accordingly considered as an excommunicate, and had so many little pieces of private mischief done me, by mixing my sorts, transposing my pages, breaking my matters, etc., etc., if I were ever so little out of the room, and all ascribed to the chappel ghost, which they said ever haunted those not regularly admitten, that, notwithstanding the master's protection, I found myself obliged to comply and pay the money, convinced of the folly of being on ill terms with those one is to live with continually."

You cannot always be logical, Franklin decided. It is the way people behave that counts, and that should shape your own conduct. Do the thing that works rather than the thing that is strictly just or logical. This bias for the kind of conduct that works and brings results comes out also in Franklin's refusal to accept his own very logical *Dissertation*. In fact, the very question posed by the *Dissertation* was: Shall I accept a belief that is logical or a belief that works? In cases of this sort the incipient pragmatist ran true to his principles; he chose what works.

The *Dissertation* deals with a considerably more important matter than whether or not you should pay for the beer you did not drink. It has to do with the deism propounded by Wollaston in his very learned book replete with footnotes containing hard to set Latin, Greek, and even Hebrew quotations. Franklin not only breezed through the typesetting task, but he also read the book for its meaning and, what is more, disagreed with minor but crucial points. These disagreements he put in a pamphlet. The pamphlet was the *Dissertation*.

According to Franklin, the pamphlet "occasioned my being more considered by Mr. Palmer as a young man of some ingenuity, though he expostulated with me upon the principles of the pamphlet, which to him appeared abominable." Wollaston's book reads very well, and at first glance it is hard to see what Franklin might have against it. Carl Van Doren, in his extensive and valuable biography of Franklin, says: "Wollaston, in answer to the deists, had attempted to prove with geometrical rigour that even if there had never been a divine revelation there could still be support and reason in nature itself for all the essential beliefs of orthodox religion. Some acts of men, he claimed to prove, are naturally good, some naturally bad, and some naturally indifferent. Franklin, who at fifteen in Boston had been turned to a logical deism by reading the arguments against it, now was turned to an indulgent pantheism." It is still not clear just how Franklin differed from Wollaston, nor does it appear that Franklin was ever any sort of pantheist. For that matter Wollaston was not answering the deists; he was one himself.

In his book written over a hundred years after Herbert of Cherbury's *De Veritate*, Wollaston tries to answer two questions: Is there any such thing as a natural religion? If there is, what is it? He starts with a good deal of straightforward exposition, following Herbert and the deists, but not making Herbert's mistake of accepting innate ideas. All knowledge comes through the senses, but by a rational synthesis our reason organizes our sense experiences and thus arrives at clear notions of what our duty is. No wonder the Germans make much of Wollaston, whom they consider as plainly a forerunner of the great Kant, who likewise has reason organize sense experiences.

Through reason man discovers the law of nature which is also the law of God. Wollaston gives more convincing detail than Grotius does. Just as conformity of thought to reality gives us truth, so conformity of actions to reality gives us goodness. Wollaston was looking for an objective way of finding out what was right. He found one which has a close analogy with the criterion for truth. To see and to report things as they are leads to truth. To act in a manner that treats things as they are leads to goodness. Truth and goodness are not identical but they are analogous. For example, you might treat an animal as if it had no feelings. An animal does have feelings. Treat it as such. Do not be cruel.

In the same way it is wrong to enslave a man because then, even if you treat him kindly, you are treating him not as a responsible human being but as an animal. Wollaston keeps on saying: "Men by their actions deny truth." He handles morality in terms of truth. Logic says that A is A, and morality says that A should be treated as A. Men should act in conformity to the truth of the case.

Wollaston has three general rules: piety to God, benevolence to men, and sobriety to self. What contradiction is to theory iniquity is to conduct. The rational life is guided by self-knowledge, self-revelation, and self-control. We should so behave as to treat everything as being just what it is.

To none of this could Franklin possibly object. Franklin is not against treating things as they are. What he hits in the *Dissertation* is the one great weakness of the Wollaston book, namely, its uncritical assumption throughout that these views are compatible with belief in an All-Wise and All-Powerful Deity or, in other words, that natural and revealed religion coincide. This really unnecessary article in the deist creed Wollaston gratuitously accepts, and it is here that the astute Franklin crosses swords with Wollaston.

In his brash *Dissertation* the nineteen-year-old Franklin starts by propounding the great question of all time: Whence comes evil into the world and who is responsible for it? In the words of his treatise, the full title of which is *A Dissertation on Liberty and Necessity, Pleasure and Pain* (London, 1725): "*Unde Malum?* has long been a question. That there are both things and actions to which we give the name of *evil* is not here denied, as *pain, sickness, want, theft, murder, etc.* . . . All the heavenly bodies, the stars and the planets, are regulated with the utmost wisdom! And can we suppose less care to be taken in the order of the *moral* than in the *natural* system? It is as if an ingenious artificer, having framed a curious machine or clock, and put its many intricate wheels and powers in such a dependence on one another, that the whole might move in the most exact order and regularity, had nevertheless placed in it several other wheels endowed with an independent *Self-Motion*, but ignorant of the general interest of the clock; and these would every now and then be moving wrong, disordering the true movement, and making continual work for the mender; which might better be prevented by depriving them of that power of self-motion, and placing them in a dependence on the regular part of the clock."

Who can disagree? An expert artificer would certainly not make a clock in which certain wheels, not connected with the mainspring, ran wild. In a good clock every wheel is geared in with every other, including the one motivated by the mainspring. But if the world is constructed on this plan, what becomes of free will and moral responsibility? It would be hard to put the riddle of "Whence evil?" into a plainer image than this. Franklin draws the inevitable conclusion: "If a creature is made by God, it must depend on God, and receive all its power from Him; with which power the creature can do nothing contrary to the will of God, because God is almighty; what is not contrary to his will, must be agreeable to it; which is agreeable to it, must be good, because He is Good, therefore a creature can do nothing but what is good."

Franklin had no objection to the details of Wollaston's intellectualist theory of morals, but Wollaston was a clergyman and assumed that man still lived under a Deity who is All-Wise and All-Powerful. Here is where Franklin inserts the crowbar of his logic. The *Dissertation* poses a dilemma: Either God is almighty, and then there is no difference between good and evil, or there is a difference, and in that case one must detract from God's power to the extent that he is not almighty.

Now, if Franklin had known about Spinoza, he could have discovered an interesting way in which one of the world's great minds worked on that selfsame problem and arrived at a solution, satisfactory to himself, by the simple expedient of identifying God with nature. This leads Spinoza to advocate for mankind a not unhappy sort of stoical submission in which a human being slowly learns to see all things under the timeless aspect of eternity. But Spinoza, who already had been dead almost sixty years when Franklin wrote his *Dissertation*, had to be dead another forty years before some of the world's great literary men, including Goethe, began to read him again and to make his views known to the world. Anyway, Spinoza's magnificent effort would not have been considered a success by Franklin. Spinoza's passively contemplative view of life would never have suited the extremely extroverted and public-minded Franklin. If Spinoza chose one horn of the dilemma, Franklin would be bound to choose the other.

But Franklin did not exactly choose the other. He temporized. It is not so much at the denial of omniscience or omnipotence to the Deity that he boggled. He took a much more direct approach. If an omnipotent Deity wipes out the distinction between good and evil, then the conclusion would have to be that God is not good, and this is something that Franklin with his inveterate belief in virtue and a virtuous God would never accept. Even at nineteen, the efficacy of virtue was rooted in his bones. The *Dissertation*, which in its unbreakable logic equates vice and virtue, therefore gets to be a reduction to absurdity. Most people might fail to see that. So he burned the *Dissertation!*

He destroyed his own smooth-sounding and irrefutable arguments. He might so easily have explained that the old doctrines about the omnipotence and omniscience of the Deity might need a little revision, and that God could help us even if he is not almighty. Not even the most rabid theologian believes that there is nothing God cannot do. He cannot do evil. He cannot be untrue to his own nature. He cannot make A be both A and not–A, or commit other essentially illogical acts. To that extent he is not omnipotent. Franklin could easily, as many thinkers and theologians do today, have turned God into just a powerful, but not omnipotent Coworker. But Franklin disliked theological thinking and theological disputations, and he did not want to get in any deeper. So he obliterated his whole perfectly good *reductio ad absurdum* argument and threw it into the fire. Like Montaigne, but in a milder manner, he settled for the conventional but uncritical idea of a God who can be worshiped, who hates vice, and who is himself in no way responsible for evil. With such a God of common sense to help him, man could build up a good character. This to Franklin was important. He condemned everything that does not make for character. Hence he condemned his own *Dissertation*.

In his *Autobiography* Franklin gives a mellowed-down and totally undramatic account of all this. "My printing this pamphlet was another *erratum*." Nevertheless, the pamphlet made friends. "My pamphlet by some means falling into the hands of one Lyons, a surgeon, author of a book entitled *The Infallibility of Human Judgment*, it occasioned an acquaintance between us. He took great notice of me, called on me often to converse on those subjects, carried me to the Horne, a pale-alehouse in ―――― Lane, Cheapside, and introduced me to Dr. Mandeville, author of the *Fable of the Bees* who had a club there, of which he was the soul, being a most facetious, entertaining companion. Lyons, too, introduced me to Dr. Pemberton, at Batson's Coffee-house, who promised to give me an opportunity, some time or other, of seeing Sir Isaac Newton, of which I was extremely desirous; but this never happened."

He ties the contentions of the *Dissertation* up with his early wayward notions, and sums it all up by saying: "I began to suspect that this doctrine, though it might be true, was not very useful. My London pamphlet, which had for its motto these lines of Dryden:

> Whatever is is right. Though purblind man
> See but a part o' the chain, the nearest link;
> His eyes not carrying to the equal beam,
> That poises all above . . .

and from the attributes of God, his infinite wisdom, goodness and power, concluded that nothing could possibly be wrong in the world, and that vice and virtue were empty distinctions, no such things existing, appeared now not so clever a performance as I once thought it; and I doubted whether some error had not insinuated itself unperceived into my arguments, so as to infect all that followed, as is common in metaphysical reasonings. I grew convinced that *truth, sincerity* and *integrity* in dealings between man and man were of the utmost importance to the felicity of life; and I formed written resolutions, which still remain in my journal book, to practice them ever while I lived."

Franklin printed a hundred copies of the *Dissertation*, gave a few to friends, and burned the remainder. His burning all but a few copies was an empty gesture so far as really destroying the work was concerned. As a printer Franklin should have known that *scripta manent*. Without the knowledge or sanction of Franklin someone reprinted the pamphlet a few years later. It is not at all hard to obtain copies of it even now. It was reprinted with loving care in New York in 1930 by the Facsimile Text Society from the original London (1725) edition of which at least one copy had evidently survived through all these years. You cannot get rid of books by burning them. The *Dissertation* is included in such specialized texts as I. Woodbridge Riley's *American Philosophy, the Early Schools,* and the book by Anderson and Fisch, *Philosophy in America,* but not in Franklin's *Collected Works.*

The *Collected Works* of Benjamin Franklin have been issued by different editors no fewer than four times: first in 1818, in three volumes; then successively in 1840, 1887–1889, and 1905–1907, each time in ten volumes, and each time presumably more complete, but none of these contain the *Dissertation.* Albert Henry Smyth, the 1907 editor, refused to print the *Dissertation,* remarking: "The work has no value and it would be an injury and an offense to the memory of Franklin to republish it." The comprehensive new edition of the Franklin papers now projected by Yale University and the American Philosophical Society will doubtless contain it.

Franklin prejudged his own *Dissertation* because there were arguments in it that seemed to wipe out the distinction between virtue and vice, but there is more to this treatise than just a clever disputation that from some points of view there is no evil. There is *Section II: Of Pleasure and Pain,* which has in it the gist of a doctrine of compensation for good and evil right here on earth. This doctrine is developed much more fully by our next philosopher, Ralph Waldo Emerson, but Franklin gets off to a good start on it.

Pain and pleasure, Franklin points out, play a universal role in life. Pain he identifies with uneasiness. "This uneasiness, whenever felt, produces desire to be freed from it, great in exact proportion to the uneasiness. Thus is uneasiness the first spring and cause of all action. . . . I might also observe, how necessary a

thing in the order and design of the universe this pain and uneasiness is, and how beautiful in its place. . . . To exemplify this, let
us make a supposition; a person is confined in a house which appears to be in imminent danger of falling, this, as soon as perceived, creates a violent uneasiness, and that instantly produces an
equally strong desire, the end of which is freedom from the uneasiness, and the manner or way proposed to gain this end, is to
get out of the house. Now if he is convinced by any means, that
he is mistaken, and the house is not likely to fall, he is immediately
freed from his uneasiness, and the end of his desire is attained
as well as if it had been in the manner desired, viz. leaving the
house.

"All our different desires and passions proceed from and are
reducible to this one point, uneasiness, though the means we
propose to ourselves for expelling of it are infinite. One proposes
fame, another wealth, a third power, etc., as the means to gain
this end; but though these are never attained, if the uneasiness be
removed by some other means, the desire is satisfied. Now during
the course of life we are ourselves continually removing successive uneasinesses as they arise, and the last we suffer is removed by the sweet sleep of death.

"It is owing to their ignorance of the nature of pleasure and
pain that the ancient heathens believed the idle fable of their
Elizium, that state of uninterrupted ease and happiness. The
thing is entirely impossible in nature! . . . No state of life can
be happier than the present, because pleasure and pain are inseparable. . . . I am sensible that the doctrine here advanced,
if it were to be published, would meet with but an indifferent
reception. Mankind naturally and generally love to be flattered.
Whatever soothes our pride, and tends to exalt our species above
the rest of creation, we are pleased with and easily believe, when
ungrateful truths shall be with the ultmost indignation rejected.
What! bring ourselves down to an equality with the beasts of
the field! with the meanest part of the creation! 'Tis insufferable!
But (to use a piece of common sense) our geese are but geese
though we may think 'em swans; and truth will be truth though
it sometimes prove mortifying and distasteful."

Here in an intermezzo in the body of his *Dissertation* Franklin is building up an argument against immortality—which may be another reason why he did not want the *Dissertation* to stand. Yet the language is unmistakably pithy and Franklinese: "One of the most common arguments for the future existence of the soul, is taken from the generally supposed inequality of pain and pleasure in the present; and this, notwithstanding the difficulty by outward appearance to make a judgment of another's happiness, has been looked upon as almost unanswerable: but since pain naturally and infallibly produces a pleasure in proportion to it, every individual creature must, in any state of life, have an equal quantity of each, so that there is not, on that account, any occasion for a future adjustment."

Not that Franklin did not acknowledge the terrific inequalities in the distribution of pleasure and pain that sometimes occur within a single life, but "one single moment of pleasure may outweigh and compensate an age of pain." He also has an entirely independent argument aimed at hitting those who stress the immateriality of the soul. When the body is gone all activity of the soul ceases, "and to cease to think is but little different from ceasing to be." Nevertheless, the soul might be given a new body and start up thinking again "but in that case it is no longer the same self but a new being."

All this doubting of Providence and doubting of immortality Franklin consigned to the flames. Like Montaigne, he settled for the conventional religion of his day which in Franklin's case meant deism. When it came down to making a final decision, Franklin chose the course that is most efficient and produces the best results. A world without a belief in virtue does not work. A machine that does not work is thrown out. Better to use an old model than a new one that does not work. Use the old one at least until the new model can by removing its imperfections be made to work. He chose the best model of religion available at the time, for, in his opinion, men must join hands in doing good or they cannot live at all. A philosophy that does not work is not a philosophy at all.

Deism transferred some of the immensity of God himself to God's own handiwork, the universe. The new blowup of the universe, its vast increase in scope through a multiplication of planets, suns, and stars, following Copernicus, had the effect too of placing God further off in the distance somewhere, with little more to do, so far as we are concerned, than to watch this huge mechanism perform; and secondly, it had the effect of inclining a number of thinkers, including Franklin, toward the acceptance of a lesser and more intimate, perhaps an additional subordinate, Deity, not so powerful but more closely related to our own planetary system. Such a Deity would be interested more directly in human affairs and in our human efforts here on earth to be good rather than vicious.

The belief in a universe infinite in extent also had the indirect effect of removing the spotlight from the individual and letting it play instead upon the whole human race, now shrunk in size to a spot in a galaxy no bigger in size than one man among a billion. Concern for the race replaces concern for any single member of it. Only a slight readjustment changes it to a blueprint of the future of humanity here on earth rather than to the saving of a handful of souls for some indefinite world to come. The "choir invisible" of heroic strivers for mankind replaces the "heavenly host" of elected souls saved from the burning. Helping science to achieve permanent improvements in the future lot of man begins to have an almost religious significance.

Franklin had a deep concern for making the world a better place to live in. First find something that works—this is pragmatism; then use it to make the world a better place to live in—this is meliorism; third, place no limits on how far this improvement may go—this is, let us call it, excelsiorism. Just as the Peking man may have had only a dim idea of the achievements of today, so we of today should put no hasty limits on what the men of future ages may achieve. It is a homely business to put in street lights, public libraries, post roads, and lightning rods. In the same way to perfect instruments of government by setting up a representative double house with no king or nobility, with separate executive and judiciary, are only first steps. The main thing is that this whole setup, both of government and of scientific achievements, be self-correcting. This leaves the road open to endless improvement. The switch from total depravity to infinite perfectibility is not the affair of a generation or two.

It is essentially a change in direction rather than a goal already achieved.

Hence the insistence by Franklin everywhere on character. He fully recognized the downright cussedness of many specimens of the human animal, but refused a wholesale condemnation. By keeping everlastingly at it, much can be done in the building of character. Errors are not fatal so long as the path of error is not made permanent by accepting views that do not work. Franklin did no more than lay a foundation for this pragmatic view. It is the contention of this book that all the thinkers herein described and discussed worked together on a single philosophy. There are not seven different philosophies and seven different men, so much as one philosophy at which seven men were working, each advancing and strengthening the emerging structure.

8. Preliminary Preview

FRANKLIN DEFINITELY turns away from dogmatism but not from rationalism. He extends rationalism by a new reliance on practicality. Practicality, or paying attention to the thing that works, is beginning to be with Franklin, for the first time, a recognized extension of the logic of the head. The hands join the head. Later will come also the heart and the whole nervous system. The work of our hands and good old horse sense in getting along one man with another receive initial recognition as new and essential ingredients in building up a broader philosophy. As the body grows, clothes must be enlarged. As the facts going into the mind grow in volume and complexity, the mind must expand. As the mind expands, the garment of the mind, or its philosophy, also must have its seams let out.

The narrowly intellectual attempt of the mind to arrive at a solution, using Aristotle's logic and a limited body of facts, may have been a failure, but the human system has other resources, not yet tried. There is no call to despair. The brain has its roots in the rest of the nervous system and the entire nervous system is in turn rooted in the body molecules. First, join theory to practice. This is the starting point insisted upon by Franklin. Next, keep on experimenting, and let the experiments be undertaken jointly as well as singly. Men working together with heads and hands, making over that portion of the earth included in the New World, is enough for a start. In America men had to work with their hands, clearing the land and laying out arteries of future transportation routes.

Because there was more scope in this country there was less of a feeling of limitation. America is not dying and has never been defeated. Large parts of the land have not thus far been bombed out, nor have portions of the population been forced to live under alien domination. Frantic groans are out of place. It is somewhat silly to compare Franklin and Kierkegaard, but Kierkegaard too came out strongly against the official churches of his day. He had his own type of practical piety, as did Franklin. But he lived in a narrower world, and his sense of guilt and entrapment was correspondingly stronger. He clung with overwhelming desperateness to Revelation. He made anguished choices. Kierkegaard turned down his Regina, refused to live an ordinary married life, and preached a method of living in which outré choices were central. A man selects his own hairshirt and wears it. Franklin, after some wild oats, settled down to a prosaic but happy marriage with a woman who never left this country and who was in no sense his intellectual equal. He lived in Europe twice for ten years at a time, but was always mindful of his family, remembering how in the early days, his Debby had kept store for him and helped him build a competence. Always intensely practical, Franklin used common sense, as Kierkegaard used moral sense, in building a strong central core of character. Franklin chose a resolute way of life that broke with theological creeds and enlisted, as in the case of Kierkegaard, certain parts of the human organism other than the brain centers dealing with abstractions. Kierkegaard loathed Hegel, who stood for a kind of cerebral web-spinning, and Franklin loathed, or at least scorned, theological hairsplitting that divided men on such (to him silly) subjects as Arianism and Athanasianism.

Franklin saw more clearly that the whole movement is one of secularization. Pulling our roots out of the sky may cause acute pain and deep misgivings. These were felt here as in Europe, but not to the same extent. Here, not only symbolically but literally, there were directly at hand new worlds to conquer. It may be expected therefore that the great secularization should proceed here with fewer jolts and fewer backward turnings to new revelations. Franklin rejected revelation. He set his hand to practical things and to a social rebuilding of this continent. A United States of Europe is still in the making.

The American movement in philosophy, with its back against a wall of wide democracy and strong initial inclinations toward pragmatism, has greater scope. The pragmatism is only a first phase. It has from the start been closely interlaced with the second phase of ameliorating human conditions; and this in turn may lead to succeeding phases, having to do with world unity and further secularization. Who knows—and future philosophers are going to stress this—what may happen if humanity survives and if the road to self-correcting research is left open? Hence the American movement has thus far remained much more romantic than the European one. There is hope that in an expanding universe an expanding humanity, or congeries of spirits perhaps from different planets, may play a constantly more controlling role in a universe of which we are essentially a part. Something is brooding even on this little planet. Franklin felt a modicum of this ferment. His successors also felt it. And each succeeding sage will have something to add to what Franklin had to say. The story does not begin to be told until all have spoken.

Ralph Waldo Emerson:
Gentle Iconoclast

1. Out of the Burning Bush

BETWEEN THE TWO peaks of high endeavor, 1776 and 1864, when a Union of States in America was first set up and then preserved, lay a period of moral stagnation when America tried for a time to ignore or to circumvent the question of slavery. John Jay Chapman put his finger on the sore spot when he quoted from a diary of that period by an Englishwoman, Harriet Martineau, who, overcoming the handicap of deafness from childhood, discoursed brilliantly on current topics. Concerning a visit to Boston she wrote: "It was not till months afterwards that I was told there were two reasons why I was not invited there as elsewhere. One reason was that I had avowed, in reply to urgent questions, that I was disappointed in an oration by Mr. Everett; and another was that I had publicly condemned the institution of slavery. I hope the Boston people have outgrown the childishness of sulking at opinions not in either case volunteered, but obtained by pressure. But really, the subservience to opinion at that time seemed a sort of mania."

A part of this period opening up the nineteenth century is called "the Era of Good Feeling." Perhaps, for a change, it did feel good to bend every bone and muscle to the building of a bigger America. This was one way of sidetracking the bothersome promptings of conscience. Every nation at times seems to drift into a moral holiday, when, likely as not, there are underneath hidden forces getting ready to explode. In the United States there did remain a corporal's guard sufficiently alert to keep on hearing the knocks of fate about the coming trouble with slavery and to counsel a more mature attitude, not only toward slavery but also toward all the main issues of life and death.

One such was a boy, to be briefly noted here before going on to the main subject of this chapter. This particular boy, who was

growing up in New England in the very first years of the nineteenth century, had a perceptive brain in a very large head. His
head was so large that his father, a Massachusetts country doctor,
had him soak it every morning in a cold spring to see if that
would shrink it. Born in 1794, this boy at the age of seventeen
wrote a poem. His father, finding the poem in the family desk,
sent it on to Richard Henry Dana of the *North American Review.*
The editor rubbed his eyes. He could not believe that anyone this
side of the Atlantic could write a piece as good as that. He printed
the poem to which the boy had given the high-sounding title of
Thanatopsis. The poem treated with mature dignity and at length
a tragic theme which a much earlier poet, Ecclesiastes, had disposed of in a single line: "Man goeth to his long home"—and, said
the boy, face it like a man—this natural fact of death. "So live, that
when thy summons comes . . . Thou go not, like the quarry-slave
at night, Scourged to his dungeon." But the run of mankind in
America was not then, and perhaps is not even now, prepared to
meet death, or any great vital issue, on that mature, calm level
envisioned by the seventeen-year-old William Cullen Bryant. It
so happens that Bryant in that poem struck the note that could
serve as a motto for this whole chapter on Emerson. Emerson
says: Look nature and look human nature in the face. Have the
courage to be what you are and live what you are, meeting the
problems of today and solving them not in the vague hereafter
but today.

The French historian, Alexis de Tocqueville, in his well-known
Democracy in America (1835–1839), tells us from firsthand observation that philosophy in America during the years covered by
his book was at low ebb. "I know of no country in which there is
so little independence of mind and freedom of discussion as in
America." On the general absence of good literature he remarks:
"If great writers have not at present existed in America, the reason
is very simply given in the fact that there can be no literary genius
without freedom of opinion, and freedom of opinion does not exist
in America."

The slavery scandal that America had on the brain was causing
a momentary paralysis of thought. The whole upper crust of
America suffered from cerebral doldrums. Chapman called it a

martyrdom. "The white-lipped generation of Edward Everett . . . suffered the most terrible martyrdom that can fall to man, a martyrdom which injured their immortal volition and dried up the springs of life." According to Chapman, "the years between 1820 and 1830 were the most pitiable through which this country ever passed." It was a "time of humiliation, when there was no free speech, no literature, little manliness, no reality, no simplicity, no accomplishment . . . the era of American brag. We flattered the foreigner and boasted of ourselves. We were oversensitive, insolent, and cringing. . . . So long as there is any subject which men may not freely discuss, they are timid on all subjects. They wear an iron mask and talk in whispers. Such social conditions crush and maim the individual, and throughout New England, as throughout the whole North, the individual was crushed and maimed."

Stalling on the slavery question put leaden shoes on every forward step. "Compromise neither slumbered nor slept. . . . The conservatism of politics reinforced the conservatism of religion; and as if these two inquisitions were not enough to stifle the soul of man, the conservatism of business self-interest was superimposed." Chapman drew a stark picture of a New England judge, almost up to the verge of the Civil War, enforcing the Fugitive Slave Law. As early as 1830 the social fruits of these heavy conditions could be seen in the life of the people.

However, as always there were exceptions. One exception was the lad who wrote the poem briefly stippled out above, and now emerges a second figure. He is slight of build and youthful. Through the fog we see him, at first dimly, then more clearly, a stooped and scholarly form. His shoulders are curved slightly forward. He wears a thin black coat. He mounts a speaker's platform. His name is Ralph Waldo Emerson. By 1836 he has struck his stride, but he is not at all like that other famous early American, Benjamin Franklin. This man will never grow a paunch. The floor does not creak under his hearty step, but he does have that same enigmatic Mona Lisa smile that Franklin had, only a little more melancholy, and he too has something to say. In his hand he carries written notes, for, like Franklin, he is a scribbler and from these notes he reads his lectures. And such lectures! Who could have expected that from this mouselike figure with the wiry frame would issue such a voice. Nathaniel P. Willis who heard it says:

"It is a voice with shoulders in it, which he has not; with lungs in it far larger than his; with a walk which the public never see; with a fist in it which his own hand never gave the model for; and with a gentleman in it which his parochial and 'bare-neces-sities-of-life' sort of exterior give no other betrayal of. We can imagine nothing in nature (which seems to have a type for every-thing) like the want of correspondence between the Emerson that goes in at the eye and the Emerson that goes in at the ear. A heavy vaselike blossom of magnolia, with fragrance enough to perfume a whole wilderness, which should be lifted by a whirl-wind and dropped into a branch of aspen, would not seem more as if it could never have grown there than Emerson's voice seems inspired and foreign to his visible and natural body."

James Russell Lowell, after hearing one of these orations of Emerson's, gives us a picture. The oration "began nowhere, and ended nowhere, and yet, as always with that divine man, it left you feeling that something beautiful had passed that way. Every possible criticism might be made of it but one—that it was not noble. There was a tone in it that awakened all elevating associa-tions. He boggled, he lost his place, he had to put on his glasses; but it was as if a creature from some fairer world had lost his way in our fogs, and it was *our* fault, not his." At another place Lowell said of Emerson that his words were "like gold nails in temples to hang trophies on."

There was an occasional nobility in Franklin, as when he said nothing on being torn to pieces over the Hutchinson letters, but it was a noble side rarely displayed; in Emerson you have it morn-ing, noon, and night, lighting up one of the drabber periods in our history, the period of backing and filling which preceded the abolition of slavery.

Chapman thought that much of what Emerson had to say, for example on love and marriage, lacked virility. He thinks Emerson was bred to the priesthood. But Emerson was not really a priest. He had a family, and his heart could bleed when a young son died. Even so, priests can talk, and when Emerson talked men all over the country were willing to come miles to hear him. They listened with rapture and were heartened. There is not a pusillanimous word in the whole Emersonian output. As Franklin stood for thrift and industry, so Emerson stood for self-reliance and moral courage.

These were the two commodities in low supply in the United States that greeted the early life of Emerson. It may be doubted whether Chapman gave the whole reason for the stagnation of the early decades of the nineteenth century. Perhaps its origin in part at least went back to another, more remote catastrophe that had just taken place in Europe. Ever since Lafayette, the United States had had a warm feeling for France, but the catastrophe that numbed the world, and had a deadening effect also in America, was the terrifying French Revolution symbolized by the dreadful guillotine.

Deism died in the French Revolution. That gentle quasi-universal religion never survived the excesses that took place in France just before Napoleon took over. Just as Puritanism blew up in the Salem witch trials, so deism blanched in the face of the French Revolution. It was not a pretty picture to see the finely dressed and finely mannered French aristocracy beheaded. To the cross and the stake the religion of reason now added the guillotine. There was nothing at all wrong with the mild doctrines of deism, nor with the humanitarian religion of a man like Franklin. It required a monstrous distortion of the golden rule and of humanitarianism to produce the stake and the guillotine. But that monstrous distortion did come about in the French Revolution when a pent-up fourth estate wreaked vengeance on a wastrel and a criminally stupid aristocracy.

Carlyle published in 1837 a history of the French Revolution written "flamingly from the heart." At the beginning all was held in check by Mirabeau. "When I am gone," said Mirabeau, "the miseries I have held back will burst from all sides upon France." Mirabeau at least died a natural death, but what he said was true, and now Paris explodes. "Terror is in her streets, with defiance and frenzy. From a Sunday night to Thursday are a hundred hours, to be reckoned with the Bartholomew butchery; prisoners dragged out by sudden courts of wild justice to be massacred.

These are the September massacres, the victims one thousand and eighty-nine." And this was only a beginning. Regicide and reginacide were still to come. "The guillotine goes always, yet not fast enough. . . . Besides which, behold destruction of the Catholic religion; indeed, for the time being, of religion itself; a new religion promulgated by the Goddess of Reason."

When the king was brought to the guillotine "beside him, brave Abbé Edgeworth stands, saying, 'Son of St. Louis, ascend to heaven'; the axe clanks down; a King's life is shorn away. At home, this killing of a king has divided all friends; abroad it has united all enemies. England declares war; Spain declares war; all declare war. 'The coalized kings threaten us; we hurl at their feet, as gage of battle, the head of a king.'"

The whole world turned on France, in which the new religion, so bravely begun in deism, was discredited. It was not stamped out forever, but it arose under a new form, known to history, in America at least, as transcendentalism. Somewhere in this account of Emerson an attempt must be made to give a clear picture of that transcendentalism which like a penumbra surrounds the figure of Emerson. Calvinism, deism, transcendentalism—the religious history of America proceeds. It is folly to try to write about philosophy without weaving into it the outstanding religious motivations of the day. What a man does, what he believes, do not his religious convictions enter into that also? In the story of the long climb to brotherhood it is impossible to leave out those aberrations which sometimes from the highest of motives make us kill our brothers as unpleasantly as possible, instead of cherishing them as pleasantly as possible.

The world-wide revulsion of feeling following the excesses of the French Revolution caused everywhere a retrogression from the horrid present into the remoter and more romantic fastnesses of history, a return also to older and partly discredited institutions, including a formalized church and a re-embracing of reactionary conservatisms. The French Revolution also had something to do with the sudden reversal of cultural progress, the halting of reforms, and the general miasma that settled down on the America of that day. Fortunately this story deals not with the prevailing numbness but with the man who helped to overcome it.

2. The Impact of Geology

THERE IS plenty of evidence that for Emerson's philosophy the impact of natural science, and more particularly the impact of geology, was decisive. Just as a new realization of the tremendous extent outward in space of the universe enabled Franklin in his own mind to push a sectarian God into the background and ethics into the foreground, so the tremendous extent of the earth backward in time, giving elbow room for self-creating forces to do their work from day to day through geological epochs, enabled Emerson to see these same creative forces doing their work on earth right here and now, thus enabling him to quit stressing the single great creation of the past in favor of a continually active creative process going on in the present moment of the "deep today." This gave Emerson, in an age of stagnation, a new and a dynamic beginning.

Emerson was born in 1803. The vigor of his life preceded the Civil War. Although he lived much longer, the pre-Civil War period is the one to which he belongs. The golden age of Emerson coincided with the intellectual depression continuing on through the 1830's. His message came early, but at one time late in life there still sputtered forth from the Sage of Concord some of the old flickerings. In 1880 he gave a lecture in the Concord Lyceum, his hundredth before that body. "His mind," says Perry Miller, "was then dissolving into benign vagueness, but the address was pieced together, with the help of a secretary and his daughter, out of older jottings (mostly from the year 1867); hence it still exudes that sense of freshness and excitement, combined with a cool, ironic appreciation . . . which from the beginning was Emerson's peculiar qualification."

In this final summing up Emerson recalls when he too was one of the young men "born with knives in their brains" ready for sharp criticism of old views. He speaks of the severe shocks which the religion of the fathers received, first from the Arminian backsliders of Calvinism, then from the English theologians following Locke, then above all from the new learning in Germany, brought over by Edward Everett, who spent five years studying there and and who then poured it all out in lectures at Harvard attended by Emerson. "In the lecture-room," Emerson says, Everett "abstained from all ornament, and pleased himself with the play of detailing erudition in a style of perfect simplicity." Emerson gives pages to the American reception, chiefly through teachings at Harvard, of European critical scholarship, and then in a final word brushes all this aside:

"But I think the paramount source of the religious revolution was Modern Science: beginning with Copernicus, who destroyed the pagan fictions of the Church, by showing mankind that the earth on which we live was not the centre of the Universe, around which the sun and stars revolved every day, and thus fitted to be the platform on which the Drama of the Divine judgment was played before the assembled Angels of Heaven— 'the scaffold of the divine vengeance' Saurin called it—but a little scrap of a planet, rushing around the sun in our system, which in turn was too minute to be seen at the distance of many stars which we behold. Astronomy taught us our insignificance in nature; showed that our sacred as our profane history had been written in gross ignorance of the laws, which were far grander than we knew; and compelled a certain extension and uplifting of our views of the Deity and his Providence. This correction of our superstitions was confirmed by the new science of Geology."

The word "geology" should have been written by Emerson in capital letters, for it was geology with its way of turning the earth's crust into an ever-continuing and presently operating, creative agency, that gave Emerson his central view of human life. It made Emerson, the ex-preacher, see God himself still operating in nature, and through nature in the hearts of men. Geology and paleontology were the two new sciences added to the store of human knowledge in the period between Franklin and Emerson, and in any up-to-date pre-Darwinian view of the world the new information given by these two sciences had to be assimilated. This Emerson did.

Philosophy is like Wall Street. It discounts quickly, almost before it is going on, whatever is happening in the world of human information. The perceptive Emerson, as he had his antennae out during the Everett lectures, as he visited the Jardin des Plantes in Paris (age thirty), as he read his beloved Buffon, sized up and instantly absorbed the effect of geology on antiquated doctrines long before others even sensed what was going on. His philosophy is one long paean to creative nature, of which we are a part, in action around and within us in the past as in the present day. Hence no need of a far-off creation, the first and only of its kind, which thereafter left the world untouched. The creation never stopped. It is still going on, as is the creative ferment in our own breasts.

Morris R. Cohen in his *American Thought* stresses that evolution did not come to America through Darwin but much earlier, through Coleridge, through translations of Schelling, Goethe, and other German as well as French authors, steeped in the broad ideas of pre-Darwinian evolution and avidly read at least by certain select souls among the intelligentsia of America. Georges Louis Leclerc, Comte de Buffon, was a man of the world, a prolific writer, and a ladies' man. Everyone remembers his *mot* that "Style is the man," but what he was really famous for was his numerous books on nature and natural history, especially animals. He is suspected of having written secretly some of the articles on zoology for the French Encyclopedia, the Bible of the French Revolution, but Buffon (1707–1788), lived and died before the fury of that revolution burst upon the world.

In a work on geology Buffon swept aside the Mosaic account of creation and pictured the earth as a dislodged fragment of the sun, still cooling off. "Ages ago the Earth was a dislodged fragment of the sun, which gradually congealed in the chill of outer space. It was not until this splinter of the sun had cooled to a certain extent that life began upon it. For life is not the salamander of the legends, which lives on fire. It exists at an intermediate stage between the heat of the sun and cold of ice. Its pre-eminence on our planet will not last long."

Herbert Wendt, who gives us the above quotation, goes on to describe an experiment which Buffon made. "He heated two metal spheres and then allowed them to cool. In so doing he took note of two moments: that at which he could touch the spheres again without burning himself, and that at which the temperature of the spheres coincided with the average temperature prevailing in Paris. He converted the figures thus obtained to apply to a sphere of the size of the earth. The first moment represented that at which life began, and the second the contemporary period. . . . It would take 168,123 years, Buffon calculated, for a white-hot sphere of the size of the earth to turn to ice. The earth was 74,832 years old, and life could have existed upon it, theoretically, for the last 40,062 years. It had another 93,291 years before it froze over."

These figures are of no significance except that they began to get people used to the idea that the earth was old, much older than had been thought. Buffon was a writer of popular science, but Frank Dawson Adams in his present-day account of *The Birth and Development of the Geological Sciences* gives his frontispiece to a portrait of the great James Hutton (1726–1797), whose strictly scientific *Theory of the Earth* was published in 1795, eleven years before Emerson was born. Hutton was the first to explain the changes in the earth's crust by natural agents still operative at the present time. Whether the chief agency in the past was water or fire gave rise to the early schools of Neptunists and Plutonists. Buffon and Hutton held with the Plutonists, who won the day. Adams explains the early bitterness of this fight:

"This celebrated controversy between the Neptunists and Plutonists was one of the greatest and most bitter controversies in the history of geology, one which was prosecuted with a vigor and even a virulence which at first seems quite surprising and difficult to understand, for it passed beyond the field to which such scientific discussions are usually confined, and made itself widely felt in the literature of the time. This was due chiefly to the fact that by some persons the controversy was thought to have a religious aspect. The Neptunian theory was believed to conform to the teaching of the book of Genesis. It presented a finished world whose development might—with the exercise of some considerable imaginative effort—be compressed into the creative week; while the Plutonic theory, on the other hand, displaying an unfinished world, which showed so Hutton said, 'No trace of a beginning and no prospect of an end,' a world, furthermore, which must in any event have required untold millions of years for its present development. . . . Perhaps the most striking emergence in the literature of the time is its appearance in Goethe's Faust." In Act II of the Second Part of *Faust* there is a dialogue between Seismos and the Sphinxes, representing the two sides of the controversy. Goethe sided with the milder Neptunists represented by the Sphinxes.

Sir Charles Lyell, the first edition of whose *Principles of Geology* appeared in 1830–1833, differed with Hutton on the part played by subterranean heat, but agreed with his forerunner in ascribing all geological transformations to the slow agency of existing causes. The main purpose of Lyell's work was to show that all past changes in the earth's crust were referable to causes now in operation. Darwin considered himself a disciple of Lyell, and had a copy of Lyell's book constantly with him. Long before Darwin's own book came out there was a widespread interest, also in the United States, in books on geology. One text, not an original work but a school textbook, *Elements of Geology* by an Amherst professor ran through thirty-one editions from 1840 to 1860. The subject was very much under discussion and study.

Emerson visited Buffon's stamping ground, the Jardin des Plantes in Paris, in 1833. He was tremendously impressed by the fifteen rooms full of carefully arranged and classified exhibits. "Except to naturalists I might hesitate to speak of the feeling it excited in me," said Emerson. "The universe is a more amazing puzzle than ever, as you look along this bewildering series of animated forms, the hazy butterflies, the carved shells, the birds, beasts, insects, snakes, fish, and the upheaving principle of life everywhere incipient, in the very rock aping organized forms. Whilst I stand there I am impressed with a singular conviction that not a form so grotesque, so savage, or so beautiful, but is an expression of something in the observer. We feel that there is an occult relation between the very worm, the sprawling scorpions and man. I am moved by strange sympathies. I say I will listen to his invitation. I will be a naturalist."

Three years later Emerson told an audience of the "system of Lamarck" which "aims to find a monad of organic life which shall be common to every animal, and which becomes an animalcule, a poplar-worm, a . . . mastiff or a man, according to circumstances. It says to the caterpillar 'How dost thou, Brother! Please God, you shall yet be a philosopher.'" Thus almost gaily Emerson adumbrates the coming upheavals in biology. Presently he wrote in the same vein his *Nature,* a little volume of 96 pages, his first book, which reads more like a poem in prose than a treatise on nature, but which started him off on a brilliant literary career.

The reason so much of Emerson's early work sounded for his day and age so strangely dynamic and full of new touches was that he was preparing the way for the acceptance of evolution. The idea was in the air a hundred years before the patient further researches of Darwin finally clinched the whole matter and before William James began even more resolutely and definitely than Emerson to reshape philosophy along evolutionary lines.

3. The Law of Compensation

NEARLY EVERY ESSAY that Emerson wrote has in it something, or touches at some point, on either self-reliance or compensation. Compensation, or the law of compensation, is Emerson's designation for the general way in which nature operates. The first big surprise in Emerson, the one that catches you midships as you read him, is his insistence on compensatory justice as a process going on all around us and in human life here and now. Into the word "compensation" Emerson compresses his own deepest insights of how beneath our eyes each day the mills of God are slowly grinding out rough retribution, not just of the human variety but somewhat in the way of establishing a broad equilibrium between gigantic as well as minor forces in nature.

At first sight it seems incredible that this type of natural justice should apply also to us. For ages it has been drummed into us that it would take an eternity to right our wrongs. We postulate elaborate metaphysical structures stretching out into an endless future after death just to make things come out even. Not necessary, says Emerson. Sweep all that away! Open your eyes to the things happening around you today! Learn to live deeply in the present. Don't dream, live! This second philosopher, very much like Franklin in this respect, is also an activist. He advocates a type of practicality that in its own way cuts even deeper than the workaday views of the widely active Benjamin Franklin. Emerson is more ruthless about tradition. Often what we need, both as individuals and as a nation, is a clean break.

Emerson himself made several such breaks. He broke with the church. He left his pastorate and stopped preaching. His young wife died. Presently he married again, starting life anew.

Then his young son Waldo, age five, lay dead upstairs from scarlatina, and the gentle Emerson, meeting friends who inquired about the boy, led the way upstairs and opened the door. These adjustments, personal and professional, all came the hard way.

His father, a hard-working bright-enough preacher, died when Emerson was eight. There were four children. The mother struggled along, kept boarders, and saw to it that the boys somehow, mostly through self-help, got educated. As soon as he could, the older brother started teaching, to help the family, so that others in turn could go to school. Franklin used to push a wheelbarrow through the streets to show his creditors how hard he worked; Emerson waited table to pay his way through Harvard. Later the older brother went to Germany to study theology. He urged Ralph to go there too and learn all about the higher criticism, but Ralph, except for comparatively short visits to England and main points on the Continent, stuck to America.

Here was his mission, a man trained in divinity, dealing out lay sermons to his fellow Americans. "Every day is doomsday. . . . The present hour is the decisive hour. . . . Each person is a new creature. . . . All power is of one kind, the sharing of the nature of the world." Emerson, the ex-preacher, went to church one day and heard another preacher, "a man esteemed for his orthodoxy, unfold in the ordinary manner the doctrine of the last Judgment. He assumed that judgment is not executed in this world; that the wicked are successful; that the good are miserable; and then urged from reason and from Scripture a compensation to be made to both parties in the next life."

It astounded Emerson that no one took offense at this far-fetched suggestion. What this really means, says Emerson, is: "You sin now, we shall sin by and by; we would sin now, if we could; not being successful we expect our revenge tomorrow. . . . The fallacy lay in the immense concession that the bad are successful; that justice is not done now. . . . When I talked to an ardent missionary, and pointed out to him that his creed found no support in experience, he replied, 'It is not so in your experience, but it is so in the other world.' I answer: 'Other world; there is no other world. God is one and omnipresent; here or nowhere is the whole fact.' The one miracle which God works evermore is in Nature, and imparting himself to the mind. When we ask simply, What is true in thought? What is just in action? It is yielding of the private heart to the Divine mind; and all personal preferences, and all requiring of wonders are profane."

Paragraph after paragraph Emerson marshals his arguments that heaven and hell are within you. These paragraphs occur in essay after essay. It is not just the old adage about virtue being its own reward. It is that a certain Presence or inspiration that children and poets sometimes feel, "the heaven that lies about us in our infancy," need not depart when childhood goes and childhood doctrines fail. One keeps or one acquires a deeper faith in a Presence that like blindfolded Justice, and possibly in a more intimate and personal way, deals out compensations. To Emerson the Presence was not a remote Lawgiver far above the minutiae of the world but a pulsation from within of a not too awesome Power, operating also all around us, a part of ourselves and a part of the world, pushing in the direction of justice.

There are accidents and there are cases of justice unachieved and of justice overflowing, sometimes all within the single life, but the life span of an individual is not the only measuring unit in the universe. The Power operating, sometimes vaguely but always gently and steadily in the direction of justice, works through us as well as through nature. If all does not get done, the fault may in part be ours. The very circumstance that things cannot be left entirely to nature, and certainly not to a hereafter, means that something should be done to right the wrongs about us now. There are examples to be set. There are changes to be made. There are challenges, especially for youth, to meet and to answer.

Between "Early to bed and early to rise, Makes a man healthy, wealthy, and wise" (Franklin, 1735) and "If a man can make a better mouse-trap, than his neighbor, though he builds his house in the woods, the world will make a beaten path to his door" (Emerson, 1871) lay more than a century of sturdy human development. Daily good habits, and increasing ingenuity, are not the whole story. There were crises: our own Revolution, the French Revolution, a terrible Civil War—in depth as well as in

breadth the human spirit is put to the test. The kingdoms of
heaven here on earth do not just glide into being without throes
and upheavals. Can it be that nature pushes forward, often stum-
blingly, making use of such faulty instruments as happen to be on
hand?

Long before the protest against slavery came to a head, America's treatment of the Indians, the needless extension of slavery
and the acts of aggression preceding the Mexican War, had so
angered Thoreau, one-time handy man around the Emerson place
and coprophet with Emerson, that he wrote his *Essay on Civil
Disobedience,* a little classic that later served as a model to
Gandhi. "Go put your creed into a deed," Emerson had said.
Thoreau did just that. He refused to pay taxes to such a government. The story goes that "when Thoreau was in jail, Emerson
came to visit him, and standing outside his cell, called to him in
shocked tone, 'Henry, what are you doing in there?' and Thoreau
replied, 'Waldo, what are you doing out there?'"

Others found it necessary to do much more than go to jail
before the injustices of slavery were finally in a measure redeemed. Now, first frightened by the guillotine and then chas-
tened by the greater carnage at home, America was no longer a
land of untried pioneers. A Great Emancipator had lived and
died, imparting a new solemnity to human solidarity from coast
to coast. While all this was happening, Emerson was facing in
a deeper dimension the same three subjects confronting Franklin:
individualism, neighborliness, and philanthropy, the last in the
etymological sense of trying to do something for mankind in
general.

There is more to individualism than just earning a living and
being a good citizen. Emerson kept pointing out that you need
confidence in your stature as a man. In addition to being independent you must learn to draw on hidden powers of growth and
self-reliance. It was not enough to be just a yes man, or even an
agreeable, hard-working average citizen; be ready to be different,
to start new things. Of course, Franklin had stressed that too, but
Emerson did it all over again, and in his own way so that he in
turn, as Franklin did, became an inspiration for young men. John
Dewey stresses Emerson's appeal to the intellect: "Emerson has

taken away the barriers that shut out the sun and has secured the unimpeded, cheerful circulation of the light of heaven, and the wholesome air of day. . . . There are times, indeed, when one is inclined to regard Emerson's whole work as a hymn to intelligence, a paean to the all-creating, all-disturbing power of thought."

And in that second ingredient of getting along with other people, did Franklin really disclose the whole secret of his leadership? Was it just hard work and honesty? Mechanical perseverance, plus good habits, may not be enough to release the extra courage needed to go at times beyond the call of duty. Who can tell us how to find the way to deeper sources of inspiration and insight? This is the problem Emerson was working at. Franklin spoke to boys, Emerson to youths. To the youth of seventeen, with new hormones coursing through his veins, a steadying influence in the way of a deeper hold on himself may be a godsend. To him Emerson had much to say. The world has great need of its exceptional men, and Emerson knows how to brew within his adolescents the stirrings of ambition to leadership.

Nor does Emerson let you down on that third item of doing something for the world, as so many supercharged boys and girls would like to do. No need to give up those larger ideals when turmoils from within and new responsibilities from without confront you. The answer is to keep your mind alive. It is not just a case of contributions to science or invention; leadership is needed also in artistic and cultural fields. Here again Emerson, who is more of a poet than Franklin was, casts a wider net. He agrees with Franklin that as the youth grows into a man no previous ideal need be impaired. Emerson builds right on to Franklin, just as the age of Jackson builds right ahead on top of and all around colonial America.

Emerson had to grope deeper than Franklin did for his moral supports. A faraway God who just looked on and somehow kept smiling was no longer enough. Emerson substituted a closer and more constant dependence on some divine element in nature to which the poetic inner core of him seemed intimately attuned; and yet in some strange and fundamental way both men cultivated all the homely virtues and continued to be practical. The prag-

matic element in Emerson will presently be stressed; it is allied
to his optimism. Franklin was greatly concerned about the way
a large part of humanity kept going to the dogs. He had intimate
experience with rascals of all kinds. To Emerson with his inde-
structible faith in the basic divinity of man it seemed less likely
that the whole of mankind could ever go to destruction. Both men
without equivocation rejected the idea of total depravity that
former ages could not live without, but the "infinite perfectibility"
of man, as Emerson saw it, was perhaps a slower and more painful
but also a surer thing than it was to Franklin. Emerson maneuvers
nature to get behind us and push, so that out of the burning
bush comes not only the still, small voice but also the majesty of
mighty urgings. The Enlightenment made all these things just a
little too easy; revolutions and suffering deepen the insights of
mankind and make them draw on heretofore hidden and untapped
natural resources.

It is well to recall how quite a bit earlier than Emerson that
other preacher, Jonathan Edwards, old Calvinist that he was, had
arrived at a strikingly similar Emersonian God who was also
most definitely a part of nature. Jonathan Edwards had a
European reputation as the outstanding theologian and metaphysician of pre-Revolutionary America. He died in 1758, but not
before his acute mind had mastered and put to use the new
learning from Europe, especially the teachings of Locke and
Descartes. Although Descartes had made a sharp distinction between what to him were the only two substances in the universe—
matter, an extended substance, and mind, an unextended but a
thinking substance—Newton, who knew more about space than
Descartes and was equally religious, held that God too is an
extended substance and that in a literally spatial way things
could be said to exist in the divine mind. In other words, he
identified space and God. Edwards explained, following suit:

"It is self-evident I believe to every man, that Space is necessary, eternal, infinite, and omnipresent. But I had as good speak
plain: I have already said as much as, that Space is God. . . .
We would not therefore be understood to deny, that things are
where they seem to be . . . it is just all one, whether ideas exist
in the divine mind or whether things exist in the same manner

as vulgarly taught." Likewise Edwards digested Locke, particularly that part about everything in the intellect having got there through the door of the senses; but to the five senses of sight, hearing, smell, taste, and touch some English moralists of the day were adding a sixth sense by which men discern right from wrong. Giving this a special twist, Edwards held that to some men by divine grace there had been given a sixth sense by which they perceive virtue as a kind of beauty emanating from the divine excellence of God.

In this way Edwards, the dour New England theologian, managed to sugar-coat even some of the more unpalatable doctrines of Calvinism. "From my childhood up, my mind had been full of objections against the doctrine of God's sovereignty, in choosing whom he would to eternal life, and rejecting whom he pleased, leaving them eternally to perish, and to be everlastingly tormented in hell. It used to appear like a horrible doctrine to me. But I remember the time very well, when I seemed to be convinced, and fully satisfied, as to this sovereignty of God. [He was reading his Bible, I Timothy 1:17. "Now unto the King eternal, immortal, invisible, the only wise God, be honour and glory for ever and ever. Amen."] As I read these words, there came into my soul . . . a sense of glory . . . I thought with myself, how excellent a Being that was, and how happy I should be, if I might enjoy that God . . . forever! After this the appearance of everything altered; there seemed to be, as it were, a calm, sweet cast, or appearance of divine glory, in almost everything. . . . And there has been a wonderful alteration in my mind, with respect to the doctrine of God's sovereignty. . . . The doctrine has very often appeared exceedingly pleasant, bright, and sweet. Absolute sovereignty is what I love to ascribe to God. But my first conviction was not so."

Afterwards Jonathan Edwards, the remote theological precursor of Emerson, spent most of his life preaching cheerful sermons (interspersed with a few others, pretty grim and still notorious), telling how God created the world, yes, for his own glory, but also because like an artist he loved the creation of beauty. The beauty of God's work as displayed in nature fills a large part of what he had to say to his parishioners. His new sixth sense made

him see light, beauty, and sweetness where others saw it not.
Emerson made a point of omitting all the harsh things in the
Edwards credo, but he too constantly beheld the glory that never
was on sea or land and constantly wove just that into the texture
of our planet.

By making the divine a part of nature, Emerson also made it a
part of man. Some such incarnation has been the core of many a
religion. It enabled Emerson to sink the roots of character more
firmly into the earth, and yet retain the heavenly aura. Franklin
never underestimated character. He touched on it again and
again, but almost always in a deft and almost sportive manner.
He wanted to kid us into being good citizens. Emerson lacked
Franklin's levity. As a child Franklin suggested to his father the
more efficient way of saying grace just once over a whole barrel
of salt fish than over each herring served separately. Franklin
was incurably sparse and efficacious and, like many a soberly
practical man before him, insisted that true religion is good works,
and that prayer, if practiced at all, had best be practiced secretly,
making no great show of it. He might have quoted Scripture
in support: "And when thou prayest, thou shalt not be as the
hypocrites are: for they love to pray standing in the synagogues
and in the corners of the streets, that they may be seen of
men. . . . But thou, when thou prayest, enter into thy closet,
and when thou hast shut thy door, pray to thy Father which is in
secret."

"Prayer as a means to effect a private end is meanness and
theft," said Emerson. "Another sort of false prayers are our
regrets." Too often, thought Emerson, prayers "are a disease of
the will," as creeds may be a "disease of the intellect." Don't
gamble with Fortune or try to influence Fortune, said Emerson.
"Most men gamble with her and gain all, and lose all, as her
wheel rolls. But do thou leave as unlawful these winnings, and
deal with Cause and Effect, the chancellors of God. In the Will
work and acquire, and thou hast chained the wheel of Chance,
and shall sit hereafter out of fear from her rotations. Nothing can
bring you peace but yourself. Nothing can bring you peace but
the triumph of principles." Almost musingly Emerson wrote in
his diary of July, 1849: "A feature of the times is, that when I

was born, private and family prayer was in the use of all well-bred people, and now it is not known."

"The dice of God are always loaded." Here Emerson gave a colloquial twist to some ancient Greek words claiming that the dice of the gods always fell aright. This was the ancient doctrine of Nemesis, into which Emerson breathed new life. Things have a way of catching up with you. Murder will out. "You cannot do wrong without suffering wrong." The whole of Greek tragedy emphasized the theme that you cannot cheat the Fates, or get around nature, or make water run uphill. Emerson carries on. Infractions of love are invariably punished; on the other hand, love and you shall be loved. Every advantage has its tax, but there is always an enlargement in the direction of the better. Life keeps on growing. Grow with it. Follow it forward. Woe to the man who lives in his yesterdays. Man is not made to look backward. Keep steeping yourself in the "deep today," which as day follows day covers many lives. Always in the long run nemesis or justice comes out on top of the heap. Of course, to maintain this thesis there is needed a great deal of faith. At bottom it puts man where the old Persians put him long ago, alongside of all the other forces fighting Evil. Man thus conceived is never a puppet, but a self-reliant gladiator.

4. The Divinity of Man

ANYONE WHO BELIEVES that man is in some sense divine has good grounds for insisting on self-reliance. If the individual has access to the creative powers of nature, in the battle of Armageddon we enlist on our side all the deep influences for good already operating in the universe. If these great powers are with us, who can be against us? In this way Emerson reawakens old echoes in a new key. He cements his self-reliance into the bedrock of man's divinity. He gives back to man his natural affinity with the cooperative and creative powers of nature.

In a bold move he unites religion with geology. The earth and the creatures within it have been evolving for a long time. Now he asks his fellow Americans consciously to join this movement. For the flaccid, half-superstitious America, preparing finally to take action on slavery and still looking to the skies for help, this came like a shot in the arm. Don't just sit and wait. Develop reliance in your own judgment and through you will flow the currents of creative energy that have been active since the world began. Emerson's belief in the balancing and supporting action of natural forces had in it nothing of the kismetic, let-George-do-it quality of Orientalism.

Two things are necessary if man is ever to make himself feel more at home on earth: he must learn to tackle his own problems and he must get over the silly notion that he is the babied darling of the universe. Surely help can come from nature, but not in the magical way that many have supposed. Imagine thinking that the sun circles around us as a center—a light hung in the sky just for us! Voltaire in one of his fantastical tales tells of a trip to earth by two giants, one from Sirius and one from Saturn, each giant several thousand feet tall, who question earth pygmies on science and get surprisingly fine, uniform answers, but when they ask about philosophical subjects they get the most contradictory replies. Finally one little man from the earth who was answering them maintained that the stars and the sun had been created just for the human inhabitants of the earth, and the two giants roared with Homeric laughter till our little planet shook.

It is perhaps fortunate that Emerson did not during the peak of his career in the 1830's grasp fully the nature-red-in-tooth-and-claw idea soon to be so forcefully brought home. There is still enough left in him of the sweet reasonableness of the Age of Enlightenment and the Age of Reason to cast a layer of poetry over nature's doings. In essence he was not wrong. His position is the same as that of a doctor probing for a disease which he is going to cure, but before he accomplishes this cure he finds out that the patient's condition was far worse than he thought.

In 1830 Emerson's first wife became seriously ill. He took her south for her health but she died in February, 1831. In 1832 came the difficulties with his church. He left his congregation in Boston because of a difference on the meaning of the sacraments. The Lord's Supper was to him a commemoration, but not a mystic participation. Afterwards he was ashamed to have made so much of this particular issue. For a Unitarian the Holy Communion should not be above reinterpretation. The shift from pulpiteer in one church to a peripatetic lecturer to the whole United States was too broad to pivot on a single item in a creed. The move away from his local church was an enlargement in every way. His audience now became a multitude. Instead of being a local leader, Emerson became, like Franklin, a representative American. Before taking up his new career he sailed for Europe at the end of 1832. In 1833 he returned to America, ready to face the broader outlook. He moved away from Boston, settled in Concord, where he could write and think quietly. He remarried, and settled down to a new life. In a few years he was startling the nation with his "Divinity College Address." Emerson had always been a Unitarian, but this address shocked even some of his broad-minded fellow sectarians.

Ralph L. Rusk, a recent biographer of Emerson, gives illuminating details: "He had unwittingly begun to write the divinity school address years before he was invited to deliver it. Three years before he delivered it he had gone back to Divinity Hall at Harvard and had witnessed 'the best performance' with a heavy heart. A little later he tried to list the defects of Jesus—no cheerfulness, no love of natural science, no kindness for art, nothing of Socrates, of Laplace, of Shakespeare. A perfect man ought to recognize the intellectual nature as well as the moral. 'Do you ask me,' Emerson had written in his journal, 'if I would rather resemble Jesus than any other man? If I should say Yes, I should suspect myself of superstition.' He had nevertheless continued to preach irregularly through most of 1837. Then his pace slackened and he had nearly stopped religious acts. After attending church one Sunday in March of 1838, he had been all but ready to say that he would go no more. 'I ought to sit and think,' he had said to himself, 'and then write a discourse to the American Clergy, showing them the ugliness and unprofitableness of theology and churches at this day, and the glory and sweetness of the moral nature out of whose pale they are almost wholly shut.' But he could hardly have suspected how near he was to carrying out this half-formed purpose."

On March 18, 1838, there is an entry in the Emerson *Journal*: "I regret one thing omitted in my late course of lectures: that I did not state with distinctness and conspicuously the great error of modern society in respect to religion, and say, You can never come to any peace or power until you put your whole reliance in the moral constitution of man, and not at all in a historical Christianity. The belief in Christianity that now prevails is the Unbelief of men. They will have Christ for a Lord and not for a Brother. Christ preaches the greatness of man, but we hear only the greatness of Christ."

He did deliver that divinity speech that very year. He was invited not by the officers of the school but by the senior class. He spoke directly to the graduating class. Afterwards the officers disclaimed all responsibility for his speech. For thirty years Harvard would have nothing to do with him, not officially at least. His own aunt, the gifted Mary Moody Emerson, who displayed so many of the traits of Emerson's own genius and to whom he wrote the letter about Franklin, finally also turned against him and gave him up as hopeless. He was too unorthodox, but since when is it a mark of a great American that he is orthodox? After all, several generations of divines had since the days of the Mathers and Jonathan Edwards been mellowing down the harsh contours of Puritan Calvinism into the milder forms of Congregationalism, Quakerism, and then Unitarianism. But no one so clearly limned the rate of progress as did Emerson in that "Divinity Address" at Cambridge, July 15, 1838:

"Jesus Christ belonged to the true race of prophets. He saw with open eye the mystery of the soul. . . . Alone in all history he estimated the greatness of man. One man was true to what is in you and in me. He saw that God incarnates himself in man. . . . He said, in this jubilee of sublime emotion, 'I am divine. Through me God acts; through me he speaks! Would you see God, see me, or see thee, when thou also thinkest as I now think.' But what a distortion did his doctrine and memory suffer in the same, in the next, and the following ages! . . . The understanding caught this high chant from the poet's lips, and said, in the next age, 'This was Jehovah come down from heaven. I will kill you, if you say he was a man.' The idioms of his language and the figures of his rhetoric have usurped the place of truth; and the churches are not built on his principles, but on his tropes. Christianity became a Mythus. . . .

"Historical Christianity has fallen into the error that corrupts all attempts to communicate religion. It has dwelt, it dwells, with noxious exaggeration about the *person* of Jesus. The soul knows no persons. It invites every man to expand to the full circle of the universe. . . . But by this eastern monarchy of a Christianity, which indolence and fear have built, the friend of man is made the injurer of man. The manner in which his name is surrounded with expressions which were once sallies of admiration and love, but are now petrified into official titles, kills all generous sympathy and liking. All who hear me, feel that the language that describes Christ to Europe and America is not the style of friendship and enthusiasm to a good and noble heart, but is appropriated and formal—paints a demigod, as the Orientals or the Greeks would describe Osiris or Apollo.

"The second defect . . . is a consequence of the first: this,

namely; that the Moral Nature, that Law of laws whose revelations introduce greatness—yea, God himself—into the open soul,
is not explored as the fountain of the established teaching in
society. Men have come to speak of the revelation as somewhat
long ago given and done, as if God is dead.

"The Puritans in England and America found in the Christ of
the Catholic Church and in the dogmas inherited from Rome,
scope for their austere piety and their longings for civil freedom.
But their creed is passing away, and none arises in its room. I
think no man can go with his thought about him into one of our
churches, without feeling that what hold the public worship had
on men is gone, or going. It has lost its grasp on the affection of
the good and the fear of the bad. . . . I have heard a devout person, who prized the Sabbath, say in bitterness of heart, 'On Sun-
days, it seems wicked to go to church.' The Hebrew and Greek
Scriptures contain immortal sentences, that have been the bread
of life to millions. . . . I look for a new Teacher that shall follow
so far those shining laws that he shall see them come full circle
. . . shall see the identity of the law of gravitation with purity of
heart; and shall show that the Ought, that Duty, is one thing
with Science, with Beauty, and with Joy."

We of this day and age who think that a man like Albert
Schweitzer embodies a high Christian ideal find it hard to realize
with how much of a shock Emerson's words came to the pre-
Civil War population of the nineteenth century. That a man like
Schweitzer who patterns his life after the Founder of Christianity
should spend it from free choice in hottest Africa, giving medical
aid to impoverished natives, is something we honor and respect.
Nor should we forget that this versatile man, a medical doctor, a
fine musician, and a great scholar, is also a recognized authority
in the field of historical research on the life of Christ.

Emerson regretfully in his *Representative Men* omitted the
most perfect man of all. In his diary of December 22, 1863, after
he had just read Renan's *La Vie de Jésus*, he remarks that "many
of his contemporaries have no doubt projected the same theme.
When I wrote *Representative Men*, I felt that Jesus was the 'Representative Man' whom I ought to sketch; but the task required
great gifts,—steadiest insight and perfect temper; else, the con-

sciousness of want of sympathy in the audience would make one petulant or sore, in spite of himself." After Renan and Strauss many others wrote Lives of Jesus. Schweitzer in preparing his own scholarly work did a thorough job.

Schweitzer reports: "When I had worked through the numerous 'Lives' of Jesus, I found it very difficult to group them in chapters. After attempting in vain to do this on paper, I piled up all the 'Lives' in one big heap in the middle of my room, picked out for each chapter I had planned a place of its own in a corner or between the pieces of furniture, and then, after thorough consideration, heaped up the volumes in the piles to which they belonged, pledging myself to find room for all the books belonging to each pile and to leave each heap undisturbed in its own place, till the corresponding chapter in the Sketch should be finished. And I carried out my plan to the very end. For many a month all the people who visited me had to thread their way across the room along the paths which ran between heaps of books. I had also to fight hard to ensure that the tidying zeal of the trusty Württemberg widow who kept house for me came to a halt before the piles of books."

Schweitzer borrowed his research books from the Strasbourg University Library which "possessed a practically complete collection of the literature about the life of Jesus, and it had in addition to that nearly all the controversial writings which had been provoked by Strauss's and Renan's Lives." An English translation of Schweitzer's *The Quest of the Historical Jesus* was published in 1911. "The satisfaction which I could not help feeling at having solved so many historical riddles about the existence of Jesus, was accompanied by the painful consciousness that this new knowledge in the realm of history would mean unrest and difficulty for Christian piety. I comforted myself, however, with the words of St. Paul's which had been familiar to me from childhood: 'We can do nothing against the truth, but for the truth.' . . . Religion has, therefore, no reason for trying to avoid coming to terms with historical truth."

A chief point established by Schweitzer is that the historical Jesus firmly but mistakenly believed that the world was coming to an end within the lifetime of those living in his day. "We of today do not, like those who were able to hear the preaching of Jesus, expect to see a Kingdom of God realizing itself in supernatural events." Schweitzer translates the Messianic message into a reverence for life, especially human life as lived by those less fortunate than others. And he translates his beliefs into the sort of actions that speak for themselves.

Many living beings, animal or men, exemplify fierceness, but Schweitzer and Emerson do not. Both emphasize, and in their own lives illustrate, the divine and gentler elements in nature. At one place Emerson tells the story of a monk so gentle that he had difficulty in finding evil anywhere. "It is related of the monk Basle, that being excommunicated by the pope, he was, at his death, sent in charge of an angel to find a fit place of suffering in hell; but such was the eloquence and good humor of the monk, that wherever he went he was received gladly, civilly treated even by the most uncivil angels; and when he came to discourse with them, instead of contradicting or forcing him, they took his part, and adopted his manners; and even good angels came from far to see him and take up their abode with him. The angel that was to find a place of torment for him attempted to remove him to a worse pit, but with no better success; for such was the contented spirit of the monk that he found something to praise in every place and company, and though in hell, made a kind of heaven out of it. At last the escorting angel returned with his prisoner to them that sent him, saying that no phlegethon could be found that would burn him; for that in whatever condition, Basle remained incorrigibly Basle. The legend says that his sentence was remitted, and he was allowed to go into heaven and was canonized as a saint."

When Emerson made a second trip to Europe, 1848–1849, Carlyle took him to see all the slums of London trying to dampen his optimism. Nothing seemed radically wrong to Emerson. Carlyle saw no good in America, or in any other country for that matter except perhaps in Germany. Carlyle became violently anti-American, lampooning our Civil War, and prophesying no good end to this country. Emerson's only answer was that he wished Carlyle would come to America and see for himself. Emerson never lost his admiration for Carlyle, and he used to point to a portrait of Carlyle that he had in his room, saying: "There is a man!"

To Emerson it seemed that nature is not too antagonistic to man. Nature helps us in four ways. He tells us all about this in his book on *Nature*. First of all, nature is a commodity. It supplies us with all we need in order to live. All our useful arts of agriculture, building, and the use of power are built out of what nature supplies. Next, in addition to commodities, it gives us beauty. Hence the ancients called nature a cosmos. "The simple perception of natural forms is a delight." Natural actions are always graceful. "Beauty is the mark God sets upon virtue. . . . Every heroic act is also decent, and causes the place and the bystanders to shine. The poet, the painter, the sculptor, the musician, the architect, seek each to concentrate this radiance of the world on one point, and each in his several work to satisfy the love of beauty which stimulates him to produce."

The third thing nature gives us is language. Emerson has a whole chapter on this. "Words are signs of natural facts." Right means straight; spirit is the wind. We look upon a river and then we speak of the flux of things. So we converse always in figures supplied us by nature. "The visible creation is the terminus or the circumference of the invisible world. 'Material objects,' said a French philosopher, 'are necessarily kinds of *scoriae*' of the substantial thoughts of the Creator, which must always preserve an exact relation to their first origin; in other words, visible nature must have a spiritual and moral side."

Nature's fourth gift is discipline. "In good health, the air is a cordial of incredible virtue. Crossing a bare common, in snow puddles, at twilight, under a clouded sky, without having in my thoughts any occurrence of special good fortune, I have enjoyed a perfect exhilaration. I am glad to the brink of fear." Why fear? Whence the fear? There is something not only beautiful but also stern about Nature: "She pardons no mistakes. Her yes is yes, and her nay, nay." Here Emerson is back on his theme of nemesis and compensation.

"Nature is thoroughly mediate. It is made to serve. It receives the dominion of man as meekly as the ass on which the Saviour rode. It offers all its kingdom to man as the raw material which

he may mould into what is useful." But "all things are moral. . . .
The moral law lies at the center of nature and radiates to its
circumference. . . . Behind nature, throughout nature, spirit
is present . . . it does not act upon us from without . . . but
. . . through ourselves . . . as the life of the tree puts forth new
branches and leaves through the pores of the old." Emerson
stands with a listening ear before this nature that through aeons
of discipline is trying to teach us something or prepare us for
something. Can it be that nature is imperceptibly handing over
the reins of control to consciousness, or is this not a surrender but
an incarnation?

5. Self-Reliance and Character

I	II	III
Give all to love;	Leave all for love;	Tho' thou loved her
Obey thy heart;	Yet hear me,	as thyself,
Friends, kindred,	yet . . .	Tho' her parting
days,	Keep thee today,	dims the day,
Estate, good faith,	Tomorrow, forever,	Stealing grace from
Plans, credit, and	Free as an Arab	all alive;
the muse—	Of thy beloved.	Heartily know,
Nothing refuse.		When half-gods go,
		The gods arrive.

WHAT MANNER of man is this who in the first few lines gives all to love; in the second stanza shows that all the time he has been holding back; and in the third welcomes advance through suffering? There is here an aloof sort of sophistication. Ralph Waldo Emerson, no longer a rough pioneer identified with the crowd yet traveling widely among them, partakes of the scene yet keeps fiercely to his independence. Does he want to turn this entire nation into an America standing free as an Arab?

This is exactly true to the extent that he is urging America to get to know its own deeper possibilities. No servile kowtowing to Europe. In our own domain there dwell real gods. They are in the earth we repossess, and they are in our own breast. It sounds mystical, but not the way Emerson puts it. He made his inspirational words mean something to the semi-isolated Americans of his day. He became a leader, preaching a sort of do-Good, be-Good religion several notches deeper than the deism of Franklin. In doing so he comes to grips with problems Franklin barely touched upon. They all have to do, as Franklin surmised they would, with casting off the dependence of youth and assuming the mantle of adulthood. There can be no effective leadership without a new influx of self-reliance.

The thunderbolt of the "Divinity Address" was heard in 1838. The year before he had been asked to deliver a Phi Beta Kappa oration at Cambridge. This too was an opportunity for which he had been waiting. This address, *The American Scholar,* Oliver Wendell Holmes has called "our intellectual Declaration of Independence." Lowell also found it a remarkable speech: "The Phi Beta Kappa speech was an event without any former parallel in our literary annals—a scene always to be treasured in the memory for its picturesqueness and its inspiration. What crowded and breathless aisles, what windows clustering with eager heads, what enthusiasm of approval, what grim silence of foregone dissent."

In the talk on *The American Scholar,* after remarking that "Man is a priest, and scholar, and statesman, and producer, and soldier," Emerson defined the scholar as "man thinking." In the "distribution of functions the scholar is the delegated intellect." The intellect is nourished by three things: nature, books, and action. Emerson, in his address, comes back to some of the things he had touched on in his book on nature. "Nature is the opposite of the soul, answering to it part for part. . . . So much of nature as he is ignorant of, so much of his own mind does he not yet possess. And, in fine, the ancient precept, 'Know thyself,' and the modern precept, 'Study nature,' become at last one maxim."

"Books are the best of things, well used; abused, among the worst. . . . There is creative reading as well as creative writing." Emerson despises "bibliomaniacs of all degrees" who "instead of Man Thinking," give us the "bookworm." "Books are for the scholar's idle time." Action is better. "There goes in the world a notion that the scholar should be a recluse, a valetudinarian— as unfit for any handiwork or public labor as a penknife for an axe." This could almost be Franklin speaking; Emerson will have none of this either. "I will not shut myself out of this glove of action." "Action is for the scholar subordinate, but it is essential. Without it he is not yet man. Without it thought can never ripen into truth. . . . Only so much I know, as I have lived. Instantly we know whose words are loaded with life, and whose not." These are the sentences that William James underscored in his copy of Emerson. On them he could erect a pragmatism welding action to thought.

"I have spoken of the education of the scholar by nature, by books, and by action. It remains to say something of his duties." Emerson should have said: it remains to say something about courage, for that is what the rest of the address is about, the same kind of courage that he himself displayed in this and in his "Divinity Address." "Mr. President and Gentlemen," perorated Emerson, "this confidence in the unsearched might of man belongs by all motives, by all prophecy, by all preparation, to the American Scholar. We have listened too long to the courtly muses of Europe. The spirit of the American freeman is already suspected to be timid, imitative, tame. . . . Not so, brothers and friends—please God, ours shall not be so. We will walk on our own feet; we will work with our own hands; we will speak our own minds."

It is said that Nietzsche always carried with him a copy of Emerson, but Emerson himself carried with him a copy of Montaigne. Some of his inspiration he obtained direct from Montaigne, who likewise placed man in the animal kingdom yet managed strangely to exalt that human animal. Montaigne had in full measure that worldliness that Emerson aimed at but did not always achieve; and Montaigne had an abundance of almost superhuman insouciance, that devil-may-care, go-ahead self-confidence on which Emerson also took out a patent. A single volume of Montaigne remained to Emerson from his father's library. "It lay long neglected, until, after many years, when I was newly escaped from college, I read the book, and procured the remaining volumes. I remember the delight and wonder in which I lived with it. It seemed to me as I had myself written the book, in some former life, so sincerely it spoke to my thought and experience. . . . I heard with pleasure that one of the newly-discovered autographs of William Shakespeare was in a copy of Florio's translation of Montaigne. It is the only book which we certainly know to have been in the poet's library. . . . Gibbon reckons, in these bigoted times, but two men of liberality in

France,—Henry IV, and Montaigne. . . . His French freedom runs to grossness; but he has anticipated all censure by the bounty of his own confessions. In his times, books were written to one sex only, and almost all were written in Latin."

Now Emerson is apologizing for a Montaigne who outdoes him in frankness, but how he revels in the old Frenchman and how much do the words of Montaigne resemble his own: "I am gray and autumnal myself," Montaigne speaking, "and think an undress, and old shoes that do not pinch my feet, and old friends that do not constrain me, and plain topics where I do not need to strain myself and pump my brains most suitable." Cut these words and they would bleed, remarks Emerson, proceeding to quote a few more of them. "Who shall forbid a wise skepticism," says Montaigne, the darling of all skeptics, "seeing that there is no practical question on which anything more than an approximate solution can be had? . . . Come, no chimeras! Let us go abroad; let us mix in affairs; let us learn, and get, and have, and climb. . . . Men are a sort of moving plant, and like trees, receive a great part of their nourishment from the air. If they keep too much at home, they pine. . . . Let us have a robust, manly life; let us know what we know, for certain; what we have, let it be solid, and seasonable, and our own. A world in the hand is worth two in the bush. Let us have to do with real men and women, and not with skipping ghosts."

Next to Montaigne Emerson probably liked the English best. He admired the character of the English. Emerson's *English Traits* contains an enduring estimate of the American parental stock. The British Empire in 1848, when Emerson was writing about it, had 220,000,000 souls as compared with America's 20,000,000. The English in the middle of the nineteenth century were, as Emerson notes, "exporting a thousand souls a day." The English, firm in their shoes, send out men who stand firm in their shoes. They are great sailors, says Emerson, who found seagoing an acquired taste, like that for tomatoes or olives. The English are an island mixture of seaborne Celts and terrible Norsemen who came in ships. It took generations to turn pirates into royal highnesses, and sea rovers into beefeaters.

Manly, these English—a combination of courage and tender-

ness, as when Nelson, dying at Trafalgar, sends his love to Lord
Collingwood, and then, like an innocent schoolboy going to bed,
says, Kiss me, Hardy, and turns to sleep. (All this is being para-
phrased from Emerson.) Or, take Robin Hood, that gentlest of
thieves, so very English! Emerson goes on and on. Look at those
hundreds of old men, red as roses and still handsome, and what
a lot of land they own too! It is a proverb in England that it is
safer to shoot a man than a hare. Dog, horse, and man—shooting
it out in the hunt; the ancient Persians of today. And what a passion for utility! Everyone has started manufacturing with steam.
Steam itself is almost English. Roger Bacon prophesied that some
day machines would do all the work, and six hundred years later,
machines in Britain have the power of 600,000,000 men. One man
with steam is worth 250 men. Machines produce enough surplus
to keep the whole of England for a year in idleness—which God
forbid: Yet, like Franklin, Emerson with all his fellow feeling for
the English remains American.

"I surely know that as soon as I return to Massachusetts I
shall lapse at once into the feeling, which the geography of
America inevitably inspires . . . that there and not here [in
England] is the seat and centre of the British race; and that
no skill or activity can long compete with the prodigious natural
advantages of that country in the hands of the same race; and
that England, an old and exhausted island, must one day be
contented, like other parents to be strong only in her children.
But this was a proposition which no Englishman of whatever
condition can easily entertain."

The chronic insularity of the English—don't copy it, Emerson
says to Americans, and tells the story of Coleridge, who is said
to have given public thanks to God, at the close of a lecture,
that God had defended him from being able to utter a single
sentence in the French language. An English lady on the Rhine,
hearing a German speaking of her party as foreigners, exclaimed,
"No, we are not foreigners; we are English; it is you who are
foreigners."

One English trait Emerson himself retained unchanged, or
perhaps he with a few choice other Americans even intensified
it, and that was a fierce independence. Ornery as the proverbial

hog on ice, no one could catch and bind him. Age thirty-four, in September, 1837, he wrote: "On the 29th August, I received a letter from the Salem Lyceum, signed I. F. Worcester, requesting me to lecture before the institution next winter, and adding, 'The subject is, of course, discretionary with yourself, provided no allusions are made to religious controversy, or other exciting topics upon which the public mind is honestly divided!' I replied, on the same day, to Mr. W.: 'I am really sorry that any person in Salem should think me capable of accepting an invitation so incumbered.' "

"Trust thyself. Whoso would be a man, must be a nonconformist. . . . Nothing is at last sacred but the integrity of your own mind. . . . A foolish consistency is the hobgoblin of little minds. . . . A great man is come to my house. I do not wish to please him! I wish that he should please me. . . . Nature suffers nothing to remain in her kingdoms which cannot help itself. Self-sufficing, self-relying things. . . . If you can love me for what I am, we shall be the happier. If you cannot, I will seek to deserve that you should. I will not hide my tastes or aversions. . . . I will not hurt you and myself by hypocritical attentions. . . . But so may you give those friends pain. Yes, but I cannot sell my liberty and my power, to save their sensibility."

It is strange that Emerson should note as a trait that both Englishmen and Americans have in common a certain gullibility; occasionally they get taken in. "George of Cappadocia, born in Epiphania in Cilicia, was a low parasite who got a lucrative contract to supply the army with bacon. A rogue and an informer, he got rich and was forced to run from justice. He saved his money, embraced Arianism, collected a library, and got promoted by a faction to the episcopal throne of Alexandria. When Julian came, A.D. 361, George was dragged to prison; the prison was burst open by the men and George was lynched, as he deserved. And this precious knave, in good time, became Saint George of England, patron of chivalry, emblem of victory and civility and the pride of the best blood in the world. . . . In the same way broad America bears the name of a thief, Amerigo Vespucci, the pickle dealer of Seville . . . whose highest rank was boatswain in an expedition that never sailed, yet outsmarted Columbus and baptized half the earth with his unworthy name."

Carlyle, so much admired by Emerson, believed that all history was the biography of the great men who made it. A handful of supereminent individuals were the pivots of history; history being, as Carlyle, the hero-worshiper maintained, what these great men did. In this Emerson did not follow him. Emerson was too democratic to be a hero-worshiper. Emerson too wrote a book, not on great men, but on the USES of great men, as he explained in a first chapter of the book on heroes, whom he called not great, but representative, men. Emerson was critical of all his heroes. But Emerson did say: "The main enterprise of the world for splendor, for extent, is the upbuilding of man." He praised the race, instead of the individual, but he had a specially kind word for the man who was a genius in ability rather than in power. To him a wonderful man, not necessarily a great man, was "better than a thousand kings. One man of genius, and the whole world moves ahead. 'I learned,' said Pestalozzi, 'that no man in God's wide earth is either willing or able to help any other man.' Help must come from the bosom alone." This was the Emersonian version of "Make Something of Yourself!"

However, to the ways in which men can get help from nature should be added this footnote: "When Nature has work to be done she creates a genius. . . . God is rich and many more than one he harbors in his bosom . . . he transmits influences from the vast and universal to the point on which his genius can act. A man's wisdom is to know . . . that the best end must be superseded by a better. I conceive a man as always spoken to from behind, and unable to turn his head and see the speaker. In all the millions who have heard the voice, none ever saw the face . . . what is Genius . . . but a love of the flower and perfection of things, and a desire to draw a new picture or copy of the same? Genius is its own end, and draws its . . . style from within. When genius arrives its speech is like a river. We lead a life of discovery and performance. The sanity of man needs the poise of this immanent force. The doctrine of this Supreme Presence is a cry of joy and exultation."

At one place Emerson speaks of the "terrible aristocracy of Nature." He notices that certain traits "may become fixed and permanent in any stock, by painting and repainting them on every individual, until at last Nature adopts them and bakes them into her porcelain. I affirm that inequalities exist—a primitive aristocracy. The game of the world is a perpetual trial of strength between man and events. The existence of an upper class is not injurious, as long as it is dependent on merit. I enumerate the claims by which men enter the superior class: 1) a commanding talent. It will be agreed everywhere that society must have the benefit of the best leaders. . . . 2) Genius, the power to affect the imagination. Sometimes an extraordinary gift of eloquence. 3) Elevation by sentiment, including self-reliance which is the patent of royal natures."

6. Transcendentalism

EMERSON CALLS his companions and contemporaries transcendentalists, as if he is not one of them himself, and he says some derogatory things about them. "Their solitary and fastidious manners not only withdraw them from the conversation, but from the labors of the world; they are not good citizens, not good members of society; unwillingly they bear their part of the public and private burdens; they do not willingly share in the public charities, in the public religious rites, in the enterprise of education, of missions foreign and domestic, in the abolition of the slave-trade, or in the temperance society. They do not even like to vote. The philanthropists inquire whether Transcendentalism does not mean sloth: they had as lief hear that their friend is dead, as that he is a Transcendentalist." Is he spoofing or is he really dissociating himself from them? He certainly never officially joined them or their enterprises, but he lived with and among them so closely, and his views are so much a part of the general spectrum of transcendentalism, that posterity is practically unanimous in considering Emerson not only a transcendentalist but a prominent one, if not the leader of them all.

He continues: "But to come a little closer to the secret of these persons . . . they are lovers and worshippers of Beauty . . . they are still liable to that slight taint of burlesque which in our strange world attaches to the zealot." There is an airy entry in the *Journal* of October 6, 1836: "Transcendentalism means, says our accomplished Mrs. B., with a wave of her hand, *a little beyond.*" Some did go a little beyond anything Emerson himself was willing to do, such as when they established Brook Farm. In fact, they went beyond Emerson in two directions: some were more utopian and some were more devoted to social problems than he was.

The school of transcendentalists did float just a little above the workaday world. Perhaps that is why Emerson in his heart mistrusted it. Some withdrew from society entirely, as Thoreau did when he went to live in his cabin in the woods. Some established a semiutopian community, Brook Farm, where Hawthorne too lived for a time and then described his experience in *Blithedale Romance*. Others were popular preachers. Many, like Emerson, were writers. The transcendentalists for a short time had a periodical of their own, *The Dial*, of which Margaret Fuller was the moving spirit. A. Bronson Alcott, father of Louisa May Alcott, set up a famous experimental school; George Bancroft, who also belonged, became a historian; and Walt Whitman, an indirect offshoot, paraded Emerson's endorsement of him on the covers of his *Leaves of Grass*. Both Bancroft and Whitman threw themselves into the social politics of the turbulent Jackson era. So did William Cullen Bryant. The loosely comprised band of transcendentalists varied from hermits to fighting editors, and, if the movement is thus broadly construed, Emerson does occupy a place somewhere near the middle. Much as he might try to dissociate himself from extremes to the right and left of him, history puts down the whole movement as centering around Emerson and persists in making the Sage of Concord very much a part of the show.

All had in common that they put their trust in something other than a barren intellectualism, a sort of intuition, and on this more will be said elsewhere, but, offhand, intuition is one of the slipperiest terms in the whole history of philosophy. It is to the credit of the transcendentalists that they in a sense made intuition fashionable. Call it intuition, insight, inner light, or conscience—these people were stout in the convictions to which their emotions as well as their intellects led them. They were a high-minded, vociferous lot, not merely orators, but also reformers. Getting down to the history of the term, Emerson explains: "It is well known to most of my audience that the idealism of the present day acquired the name of Transcendental from the use of that term by Immanuel Kant, of Königsberg, who replied to the skeptical philosophy of Locke, which insisted that there was nothing in the intellect which was not previously in the experience of the senses, by showing that there was a very important class of ideas or imperative forms, which did not come by experience, but through which experience was acquired; that these were intuitions of the mind itself; and he denominated them Transcendental forms. The extraordinary profoundness and precision of that man's thinking have given vogue to his nomenclature, in Europe and America, to that extent that whatever belongs to the class of intuitive thought is popularly called at the present day Transcendental."

Emerson's lucid exposition is excellent and correct as far as it goes, but it is not the whole story. In a way the term "transcendentalism" did originate in a loose interpretation of Kant. Kant is not easy to read. Coleridge and other men, such as Cousin, the French philosopher, in their praiseworthy effort to popularize Kant made it appear that the philosophical giant had indeed exalted intuition into something transcending reason. But this is not, in fact, the case.

The great English thinkers, Locke and Hume, whom Kant endeavored to correct, had in them a strong skeptical vein. When Locke and Hume, so to speak, chopped up all we know into separate sensations, or little unconnected pieces of knowledge, they did a dangerous thing. They not only pushed skepticism to the point of denying certain formerly well-recognized continuities, such as the laws of causation, but they laid themselves open to a powerful counterattack by the idealistic Kant and succeeding German philosophers. By maintaining that sensations, like loose hailstones, pelt the mind Hume woke Kant from his dogmatic slumbers, giving that slow-ripening Teuton the bright idea that the human mind, and the human mind alone, welded ideas together into a universe.

Kant argued that the human mind makes over and connects up the isolated sensations that enter it. This organizing activity of the human mind goes very deep, said Kant. We cast sensations, first of all, into a series of successions, which is time, and next into a three-dimensional continuum, which is space. Time is like the moving point on a line, with the past moment disappearing into the next; and space is a sort of next-to-next in all directions with all elements remaining. This stereo-next-to-next-ness gives us space and its contents. To account more fully for the varied nature of these contents, Kant found that he needed certain modes, better called molds or categories, through which sensations are further connected up. Among these are cause and effect. But the big point in all this is that the mind plays a central role. Hence the resurgence with Kant of a new and powerful idealism, giving the human mind renewed centrality and power.

It has been rightly pointed out that this makes Kant an extremely romantic philosopher. His followers, from Fichte up to Hegel, were even more so. Kant gives an unprecedentedly important task to the human mind. Fichte and Schopenhauer stressed the will as well as the mind; Schelling stressed the imagination, as revealed in the creative faculty of artists; and Hegel finally went the whole length of identifying human thought with cosmic history. Between them, these extreme idealists practically lost sight of the solid earth on which the human animal sometimes seems little more than a puppet. This overwhelmingly idealistic movement, starting in Germany, had resounding echoes in the works of French and English writers, less schooled in the rigid subtleties of logic and more inclined to settle for an unadulterated exaltation of human intuition. Reason, the highest form of intellect, was based on intuition. The lower and more plodding steps of logic they relegated to a lower form of intellect, called the understanding, thus reserving reason for something that with the aid of intuition could take short cuts and surpass all understanding. The net effect was to do more than simply increase the power of reason. It was made into something different, a direct seeing rather than a chain of logical inferences.

It may well turn out that there is room for both intuition and logic; but in the age of Emerson, when intuition first bowed its way onto the American stage, it was hailed almost as a substitute for intellect and logic. This battle between intellect and intuition, logic and insight, is a long and fascinating conflict of which the border skirmishes occurring among American transcendentalists are incidents. As this story continues, the intellect will proceed in its course as a safe guide; but insight, intuition, or imagination likewise will remain as an essential ingredient in scientific thinking. Imagination, unchecked by facts, runs wild, and with this Emerson is in essential agreement. Like all American thinkers, he anchors his creed in practice. He never lets his intuition carry him to extremes. He avoids utopianism. To him life is not an ivory tower, nor all practical politics. His is a middle road. Emerson gives intuition a place, but he does not make it a complete substitute for practical thinking.

America is a land of new beginnings. On a piece of Emerson's land lived Henry David Thoreau. The land had on it a famous pond, beside which Thoreau, the modern Robinson Crusoe, built his hut. Thoreau was good with his hands, and on two occasions the younger man lived for some time in the Emerson household, helping out with practical chores. The two great men got along well together. Absorbing all that Emerson had to say, Thoreau quickly developed a stature of his own. His *Walden, or Life in the Woods* came to be known in Europe and throughout the world as a classic. Thoreau set out to prove something, namely, that we are all too busy with things that do not really count. "The mass of men lead lives of quiet desperation. . . . Anxiety and strain are a form of disease. . . . Most luxuries are positive hindrances."

In March, 1845, Thoreau borrowed an ax and went into the woods by Walden Pond to live. He hewed him a cabin for warmth when summer would change into winter. The rough timbers he shaped up himself. He bought an old shanty for boards. By the Fourth of July the house was ready. He lived there all by himself for over two years, the aim being to prove something—on how little a man could live; and in an account of his stay he tells the reader just how much everything cost, and what he did. The house cost $28.12½, and the first year he grew twelve bushels of beans, eighteen of potatoes, and some peas and corn.

He made his bread, straight from a two-centuries-B.C. recipe given by Cato the Elder. Working about six or seven weeks the first year, he made out fine, and he did even better the next year. In his one-man utopia he had on his desk three limestone ornaments. When he found he had to dust them daily, he threw them

out the window. He did not stay in his hut very much; he preferred the open air. "I would rather sit on a pumpkin and have it
all to myself than be crowded on a velvet cushion."

"I am naturally no hermit," said Thoreau. "I love society as
much as most." During the two years at Walden he had more
visitors than at any other period in his life of similar length, and
he treated all his vistors civilly. If one man came, food was shared;
if twenty came, nothing was said about food, and this he found
no offense against hospitality. He disliked snoopers and beggars.
He kept a few classics lying around and, as befitted a Harvard
graduate, read them in the original. "I love a broad margin to
my life." Best books, he thought, are not read enough. "No wonder
that Alexander carried the Iliad with him on his expeditions in a
precious casket." But mostly he either worked with his hands or
just walked around studying nature, every stick, stone, and plant
of it, together with the animals, in the minutest detail.

He wrote a whole chapter on the sounds one hears at night
when alone in the woods, not omitting the whistle of the train in
the distance, carrying goods to the West beyond. This is the man
who went to jail because he would not pay taxes. This is the
Emersonian disciple on whom Emerson in a funeral address made
one of the sanest pronouncements ever spoken by one American
on another, referring to Thoreau as one "who chose to be rich by
making his wants few" and as one who found more "in one wood
walk, than learned men will find with glass in ten times ten."

Among the whole school of transcendentalists Thoreau is the
anarchist. Thoreau was not an American Indian, but take a redskin
straight out of Cooper, send him to Harvard, but do not let him
lose his sharp eyes and nose or his love of poking around in the
woods, and you get a good facsimile of Henry, the prying hermit.
His father had a pencil factory, but Henry had no use for fac-
tories, for industry, or for government. Yet, the books he wrote,
reflecting his rich inner life, have been gaining steadily in world
esteem until they rank shoulder to shoulder with those of Emerson.

In October, 1840, George Ripley, his wife Sophia, Margaret
Fuller, and Bronson Alcott met at the Emerson home to consider
plans for the founding of the Brook Farm Colony near Boston.
The blueprint of Brook Farm called for not only an educational

establishment of sorts but also a sheltered community where intellectuals could work with their hands to help earn their keep, share each other's company, and as a group escape the evils of industrialization. But anything even remotely resembling a communal scheme congealed the solitary Emerson, who wrote in his diary, "not once could I be enflamed, but sat aloof and thoughtless; my voice faltered and fell. . . . I do not wish to remove from my present prison to a prison a little larger." He explained in detail both his sympathies and his objections; but he decided most definitely against any personal participation in anything as utopian as Brook Farm.

Emerson watched its progress from a safe distance. A shrewd merchant told him it might succeed. Emerson visited Brook Farm. He even took part in a charming sylvan fête. He described it all later as a "perpetual picnic, a French Revolution in small, an Age of Reason in petty-pan." George William Curtis, a resident at Brook Farm for some two years beginning in 1842, remembered Emerson's visits and claimed that Emerson was enamored of the spirit of the enterprise but not of the actual community "in which he saw very plainly all the unconscious drolleries."

Many different persons lived at various times on Brook Farm. Typical were George Bradford, a teacher; Charles King Newcomb, a Catholic; Frank Brown, Mrs. Emerson's nephew; John Sullivan Dwight, who taught music there. Most of them did not stay long. The entire experiment lasted only a few years. Hawthorne was in it for a few months during its heroic period. Hawthorne was thinking then of getting married and he hoped it might help him solve the problem of making a living. His *Blithedale Romance* appeared in 1852. In it Miles Coverdale, a writer, tells of his stay at Blithedale, an experimental community, centering around the somewhat frightening, God-fearing, and excessively masculine prison reformer Hollingsworth. Zenobia, the Junoesque heroine, beautiful and rich, outwardly forceful but inwardly as feminine as Hollingsworth was masculine, moves with fascinating majesty all through the story, until in a surprise ending she drowns herself for love of Hollingsworth, who chose instead the unassertive, demure, but appealing half sister of Zenobia. We do not know she is a sister of Zenobia until toward the end of the book. All through the action she has been a pleasantly awkward little seamstress, desperately worshiping Zenobia and striving by all means to attach herself to her. Hawthorne is writing a novel, not a treatise on sociology, and in the Preface he not only has the usual disclaimer about the characters not resembling living people but he goes out of his way to say nice things about the real people at Brook Farm, whom he liked very much. The novel is in no way a satire on the movement. It merely provides the setting for a quaint romance at the end of which Miles Coverdale (Hawthorne), who throughout the book appears as a writer, confesses to the reader that he too had been all along in love with the little seamstress, Priscilla, but no match for the forceful Hollingsworth who easily got her away from him.

In reality Brook Farm was run by the high-minded Ripleys, as a completely unromantic enterprise, on a rather high intellectual level, with no sex irregularities or aberrations of any sort. It might have been an enlarged cottage beside Walden, only less practical. Hawthorne himself, at the height of the haying season when he is most needed on the farm, prances off for a week's rest in town. To him, as to Emerson, the place had its confining aspects. Most of the work was done by a sturdy farmer they kept on, but even so the enterprise went bankrupt. Emerson was right in sticking to his "smaller prison," from which he could with immunity make steady and frequent excursions up and down the land, lecturing in not-unthrilling fashion to the eager audiences of a pretelephone and preradio age. To Emerson, exploring the West and the North, even the budding metropolis of New York did not seem unpleasing. "For a national, for an imperial prosperity, everything here seems irrevocably destined," he told Margaret Fuller about New York, in words that betokened a world citizen rather than a utopian. "What a bay! what a River! what climate! what men! What ample interior domain, lake, mountain, and forest! What manners, what histories and poetry shall rapidly arise and for how long, and, it seems, endless date! Me my cabin fits better, yet very likely from a certain poorness of spirit; but in my next transmigration, I think I should choose New York."

Transcendentalism has an affinity with Unitarianism, in stressing social service and backing humanitarian reforms. Its preachers—William Ellery Channing, Theodore Parker, Henry Ward Beecher—became national figures, making the pulpit a power in the land. William Ellery Channing (1780–1842), chief spokesman for New England's religion, was referred to by Emerson as "our bishop." Channing's favorite advice was to live in the present and construct for the future. Nature is a revelation of the divine. We know God from our own souls. From the divine within us come the depths of human love. George Ripley quotes Dr. Channing to the effect that "to rob a man of his dignity is as truly to subvert religion as to strip God of his perfection."

Emerson, Ripley, and W. H. Channing, nephew of William Ellery, all resigned from the Unitarian Church, and Thoreau never belonged to it, but Ripley later had a great influence as the editor of the *Christian Examiner*. He had been called the "white hope" of Unitarianism, and one of the influential things he did was to publish translations of European literature. Ripley and his wife, after having poured their lifeblood into the Brook Farm experiment, were in despair when it collapsed in 1847. Imagine Ripley paying off the debts of Brook Farm while at the same time trying to introduce German philosophy into America. On top of that he fought hard against the doctrine of miracles as the only evidence of divine revelation. Miracles were to him undemocratic! They support Authority. Nature is working miracles all the time.

One man who really put into practice what Emerson preached in the "Divinity Address" was Theodore Parker, a Christian minister with a broad social outlook, who for a time carried to new heights the whole transcendentalist movement. He started his busy, crowded life as a poor carpenter and a farmer, and he died before the Civil War got under way. He was largely self-educated, haunting the Boston libraries until he got their contents into his head, mastering twenty languages and working his way upward to become one of the most learned and eloquent preachers of the day, a coiner of winged words, and a true champion of the people. It is reputed that from a speech of his Lincoln learned the phrase "of the people, by the people, for the people."

To Parker the Americans were destined to have a genius for liberty. They dreaded authority. There are two variants of democracy. The motto of the one is: You are as good as I am, so let us help one another. The motto of the second is: I am as good as you are, so get out of my way. Parker also speaks of two literatures: the permanent, which as a rule is superficial, tame, and weak; and the real living national literature in speeches, pamphlets, and newspapers. Literature must be spontaneous, and a thing of native growth. "Religion must be made for man's religious nature, as much as the shoe is made for the foot. . . . To me, the spiritual elevation of Jesus is more convincing proof of his divinity, than the story of his miraculous transfiguration; and the words which he uttered, and the life which he lived, are more satisfactory evidence of his divine authority, than all his miracles, from the transformation of water into wine, to the resurrection of Lazarus. I take him to be the most perfect religious incarnation of God, without putting his birth on the same level with that of Hercules. . . . The miracle question is one of theology, and not of religion."

Parker draws an extensive parallel between naturalism and supernaturalism. He prefers the natural view. "As we have bodily senses to lay hold on matter and supply bodily wants . . . so we have spiritual faculties to lay hold on God, and supply spiritual wants. As we observe the conditions of the body, we have nature on our side; as we observe the Law of the Soul, we have God on our side. . . . We have direct access to Him, through Reason, Conscience, and the religious Sentiment."

To Parker the liberation of American slaves and improved education for the people came to be of more importance than dogmas concerning the Trinity, Eternal Damnation, Miracles, and the Authority of Revelation. He had a famous sermon on the transient and the permanent in Christianity; the transient being like the rain, wind, storms, and sunshine in the weather that changes from day to day, and the permanent being like the laws of nature underneath. Transient are the creeds, confession, doctrines, and dogmas. Permanent is the simple practice of love. The heresies of one age are the orthodoxies of the next. Sects come and go, but the truth shall endure. There was a time when men were burned at the stake for asserting truths conflicting with the Old Testament. The search for the truth he equated with seeking the Kingdom of God, but why the intolerance? "Out of the new sentiments and ideas, not seen as yet, forms of society will come, free from the antagonism of races, classes, men—representing the American idea in its length, breadth, depth, and height, its beauty and its truth, and then the old civilization of our time shall seem barbarous and savage."

Elizabeth Palmer Peabody founded the first kindergarten in America in 1860. For this school, run by Alcott and herself, she wrote out some principles, according to which "Contemplation of Spirit is the first principle of Human Culture." This is not very clear, but perhaps by now enough of the transcendental temper has been absorbed to get an inkling at least of what she meant. Much more illuminating was the excellent way in which her partner, Amos Bronson Alcott (1799–1888), set about organizing a school with the direct object of both entertaining and instructing children at the same time. With all his mildness he was a strict disciplinarian. He aimed to hold the interest of children so strongly that there would be no restlessness or disorder. This was not easy, but Alcott was a genius and a zealot. He also wrote "Orphic Sayings" for *The Dial.* These were pithy but somewhat oracular distillations of the wisdom acquired in a long life of many ups and downs. He regarded the first seventy-eight years of his life as a preparation. It turned out that he still had ten years to go. Early in life, in 1834, he opened the Temple School. It failed. There were scandals. His methods were much ahead of his time. He tried to teach his children elementary biology, including the facts of life. A well-known conservative of the day condemned Alcott's views as "one-third absurd, one-third blasphemous, and one-third obscene." It was difficult in that early day to speak plainly and interestingly to children.

With such opposition Alcott was hooted in the streets and frantic parents withdrew their children from the Temple School. But Emerson rallied to the defense of Alcott. "He aims to make children think, and, in every question of a moral nature, to send them back on themselves for an answer," said Emerson. To Alcott himself Emerson wrote: "I hate to have all the little dogs barking at you, for you have something better to do than attend to them; but every beast must do after his kind, and why not these? And you will hold by yourself, and presently forget them." Another defender said: "The Conservatives are a good party, but they are always the first to stone the Prophets and hale them into the prison of misrepresentation and abuse." He referred to Alcott as a Socrates who preferred to bring out the minds of his hearers rather than to impress on them his own opinions.

George Bancroft (1800–1891), the eminent historian, was well read in German philosophy. He pronounced transcendentalism the discovery of the inner light in man. Cousin called it the divine principle in man. Kant, Schiller, Chateaubriand, Coleridge, Lamartine, and Wordsworth all had the same broad idea: there is something divine in nature. Bancroft himself did not pursue this line of thought. To him, the practical politician and scientific historian, this meant that the day of the multitude had dawned. Culture is not just self-culture. The divine light of genius must penetrate to the walks of common life. Henceforth the masses must be taken into account. Devotion to the cause of the mind is devotion to the cause of the whole of humanity, and assures its progress. Progress does not really arrive until it is diffused through the multitude. Light must get down to the people.

Bancroft, with his insistence that culture must seep down to the people; Emerson, with his lectures speaking to them direct; and Whitman, the poet of the people, endeavoring to speak for them—perhaps all these men have in common the single aim of furthering democracy. John Townsend Trowbridge, a writer of books for boys, in an autobiographical volume shows how Emerson influenced Whitman: "I was extremely interested to know how far the influence of our greatest writer had been felt in the making of a book which, without being at all imitative, was pitched in the very highest key of self-reliance. . . . Whitman talked freely on the subject, that day on Prospect Hill, and told how he became acquainted with Emerson's writings. He was at work as a carpenter (his father's trade before him) in Brooklyn, building with his own hands and on his own account small and very plain houses for laboring men. . . . This was in 1854; he was then 35 years old. He lived at home with his mother; going off to his work in the morning and returning at night, carrying his dinner pail like any common laborer.

"Along with his pail he usually carried a book, between which and his solitary meal he would divide his nooning. Once the book chanced to be a volume of Emerson; and from that time he took with him no other writer. His half-formed purpose, his vague aspirations, all that had lain smoldering so long within him, waiting to be fired, rushed into flame at the touch of these electric words—the words that burn in the prose-poem Nature, and in the essays on Spiritual Love, the Over-Soul, Self-Reliance. The sturdy carpenter in his working-day garb, seated on his pile of boards; a poet in that rude disguise, as yet but dimly conscious of his powers; in one hand the sandwich put up for him by his good mother, his other holding open the volume that revealed to him his greatness and his destiny,—this is the picture which his simple narrative called up, that Sunday long ago, and which has never faded from my memory.

"He freely admitted that he could never have written his poems if he had not first 'come to himself,' and that Emerson helped him to 'find himself.' I asked him if he thought he would have come to himself without that help. He said, 'Yes, but it would have taken longer.' And he used this characteristic expression: 'I was simmering, simmering, simmering; Emerson brought me to a boil.'"

So, while Parker was bemoaning the dearth of good permanent literature in America, Whitman was setting by hand, printing, and presently hawking to reluctant shops a book of stray poems that did turn out to be immortal. He sent a copy of his book to Emerson, and Emerson wrote Whitman a fine letter about *Leaves of Grass:* "I find it the most extraordinary piece of wit and wisdom that America has yet contributed. . . . I greet you at the beginning of a great career." These words Whitman brashly printed in letters of gold on the second edition of his book. This the fastidious Emerson did not like, but Ralph L. Rusk, Emerson's biographer, says that Emerson's letter with the later public use made of it by Whitman, was perhaps "an event of greater importance in the history of American literature than the printing of any other letter has ever been."

The poet of democracy was stirred into life by the magic touch of the philosopher of democracy. John Dewey says: "The coming century, may well make evident what is just now dawning, that Emerson is not only a philosopher, but that he is *the* philosopher of Democracy." Dewey makes Emerson "the one citizen of the New World fit to have his name uttered in the same breath with Plato. . . . We are moved to say that Emerson is the first and as yet almost the only Christian of the intellect." According to Dewey, the final word of Emerson's philosophy is "the identity of Being with Character."

7. Direction of Progress

AMERICAN PHILOSOPHY progresses through Emerson in two closely related directions, both inaugurated by Franklin and both continued by Emerson. One advance is in epistemology and the other in secularization.

The epistemological expansion consists in recognizing that knowledge comes not only from the head but also from the heart. To the head Franklin added the hands, and Emerson adds the heart. In addition to being practical, be intuitive, says Emerson. He is not gainsaying the advantages of practicality, but to the intellect and to practicality Emerson adds an emotional ingredient. The domain of feeling, aesthetic and moral, electrifies knowledge. No one could argue slavery out of existence, or even legislate it away; it had to be fought against. A great moral issue was involved. Emerson welds knowledge to moral issues. This is not a reversal of Franklin, who likewise when the time came joined the fight for freedom, but it is a further advance in the direction of stressing the importance of the heart as the seat of moral courage, and a revealer of what sometimes a man must do.

To put this somewhat poetical phraseology on a more philosophic basis, let us say that Emerson stresses intuition. Intuition furnishes the kind of insight that not infrequently precedes important decisions. The decision taken is then followed by action. Is this use of intuition unreasonable? No, and that is exactly the point. Hand and heart do not contradict the head; they work in line with it. In this broadening of philosophy the intellect is being anchored first in the body and next in the nervous system. This reinforces rather than weakens the intellect. Emerson goes a step further than this by rooting the whole being of man more firmly than ever before in the nature from which he sprang. He does this by identifying some elements in Nature with similar creative and "divine" impulses in man. Thus he not only brings new unity to head, hand, and heart, but reinforces all this by currents coming straight from nature itself.

Closely related is the second advance in the direction of secularization. Ordinarily secularism means attention to temporal and worldly rather than to eternal or heavenly things. Here it means partly just that, but also in part a greater preoccupation with that huge energy complex of hitherto unsuspected magnitude and scope that has come into the knowledge of men since the days of Copernicus, Newton, the geologists, the early evolutionists, and then Darwin. Thus secularization no longer means what it did when the universe, our universe, had not yet absorbed the sky. It now means an enlargement of religion in pace with the expanding world. It means a religion paralleling and spreading out with the new horizons of knowledge and correspondingly effacing former confines. It means an enlargement away from petty sectarian hairsplitting into something of which deism and transcendentalism were imperfect forerunners.

In a 1954 book, *Secularism Is the Will of God*, Horace M. Kallen, a disciple of William James, our next philosopher, gives some modern definitions: "Secularism is the effort to secure . . . through separation of church and state . . . equal freedom and equal safety. . . . Thereby Secularism becomes also the religion of religions. . . . Secularism . . . offers itself as a moral equivalent for the war of faiths. . . . As an article of faith Secularism envisages the miscellany of mankind, in all their irreducible singularities of cult and code and culture and vocation in benevolent and untrammeled communion with one another, and as a free society of free men by means of such communion."

Citing Kallen gets us somewhat ahead of our story in the sense that his secularism represents an idealized end result of what the process of secularization could bring about. It represents one of the ideals implicit in the American idea, and actually embodied in the American political setup. Both Franklin and Emerson were keenly aware of the need of a nonsectarian cooperation which would impart to this country new strength to live up to new ideals. In this respect America is part of a much wider world movement by which mankind relocates its moral bearings in an altered world.

To compare Emerson to Nietzsche seems at first flush far-fetched. Nevertheless, Emerson and Nietzsche have important traits in common. Both write like poets. Both are fired by imagination rather than by logic. Neither of them worked out a systematic body of doctrine. Both are "intuitionists." Both extend the domain of the intellect into the volitional, emotional, and even the irrational depths of man. Nietzsche flouts Hegel's system-building; Emerson derides consistency. Both try to detach men from supernaturalism, Emerson in gentle fashion and Nietzsche violently so. Both are strong individualists. Both, drawing on the whole man, attempt for once in the history of philosophy to get a picture of the human situation that is not distorted by overintellectualization.

On the other hand, although in many ways these two men start out alike, a divergence soon sets in. All we need to do to lay our finger on the parting of the ways between European thought, as put forward by Nietzsche, and American thought, as championed by Emerson, is once more to refer to Carlyle. Although starting out with Emerson, Nietzsche continues very definitely along the lines of Carlyle. Eric Russell Bentley, with his eye on the path entered upon by Carlyle, has written a book called *A Century of Hero-Worship*. He discusses Carlyle, Nietzsche, Wagner, Shaw, Spengler, Stefan George, and D. H. Lawrence—all Europeans. Carlyle's book *Heroes and Hero Worship* goes back to 1840, but Carlyle even then was getting ready to welcome the superman. Carlyle hated the lighthearted eighteenth century; he hated the individualistic French; he despised America; and, to save the world, stood ready to swim in the wake of any new Frederick the Great type of Messiah. While we were fighting our Civil War, which he pooh-poohed, Carlyle came to the passionate defense of a brutish Jamaican governor, Edward John Eyre, a tyrant who openly proclaimed the inferiority of all colored races and used ruthless force to put them down. That way madness lies, but that way Nietzsche also tended to go. "I don't find it easy to believe that little people are necessary," said Nietzsche. Like Schopenhauer, who left money to the police who had put down revolutionaries, Nietzsche felt superior to the herd. Finally came Hitler, Nordic supremacy, and genocide. The Bentley book does not carry the story that far, but it does show the line at which, with Carlyle, Nietzsche begins to diverge from Emerson.

In America men like Emerson and Lincoln saw to it that no hero worship and no genocide got started over here. No aristocracy, blooded or bloody! The parting of the ways hinges, philosophically speaking, on whether you want to save all or only a part of mankind. Shall we sacrifice all for an aristocracy or shall we commit ourselves, come what may, also to the common man? The drift in Emerson and in his transcendentalist brothers is clear. This is democracy or nothing. Emerson faces up to the harder task of cultivating brotherhood. No enslavement, no subservient conformities, no privileged aristocracy. Better to risk stirring up minds than to risk putting them to sleep. By including the common man in our scheme of salvation we reawaken hope in all downtrodden races. Under no condition put your trust in power-drunk heroes!

One German writer, Eduard Baumgarten, who says some perceptive things about American pragmatism, goes off the track when he desperately tries to make out Emerson to be a lover of power. How he grubs around in that little Emersonian "Essay on Power" in an attempt to identify England and America as partners in a joint race for world hegemony. But how pallid are Emerson's pumpings of power out of nature when you look at them in the light of the superman idea. We have had no Napoleon on our back. We simply do not think in terms of world-conquering Alexanders. In Emerson's day puny America was just beginning to put on long pants. No one can read into Emerson the weird ambitions of the pent-up Führers of Europe.

Completely antimilitaristic, almost academic in outlook, Emerson had other worlds to conquer. His kingdom was not that of the soldier. I am not forgetting that Nietsche too in real life was a rather inconspicuous professor of Greek, but the insides of the man were oriented toward destruction. To Europe the separation from aristocratic and from supernatural tutelage came harder than it did to us. America did its weaning more gradually, discarding kings in 1776 and thereafter for a considerable time being compelled to spend itself in subduing the earth in its own back yard rather than in dreaming of world power.

The democratic and the supermanic strains of thought come out respectively in Emerson and Nietzsche. Essentially we are dealing here with the deep roots of the slavery problem, involving the cleavage into aristocrat and plebe. There are three kinds of slavery: the openly physical kind, which it took the world a thousand years to get rid of; the disguised industrial kind, wage slavery, in which for ages the inferior man is given inferior wages—bought off by a token portion of the spoils; and finally there is a third and even more subtle continuation of slavery to which a portion of mankind is conditioned so that they willingly live as faithful slaves, obedient to authority. The manner of bringing about this third kind of slavery, from propaganda to brainwashing, is now coming out into the open. Men who dislike responsibility fall an easy prey to these techniques in the hands of a fiery Führer. Emerson comes out most strongly against such subserviences.

Whether a country can, in a literal sense, exist half slave and half free was settled in our Civil War, but with disguised dictators and sharpened propaganda in the offing, the question of resisting enslavement may come up again. Aristocracies, feigned or real, bent on exploitation, are not giving up as easily as was sometimes thought. The techniques of overcoming sales resistance are being put to new use. Any resistance, even character, can be broken down. The possibilities in radio and television of hidden persuaders have scarcely been touched. This molding of the public mind through every medium of mass communication is something to watch. Franklin used persuasion to good effect in a small and primitive way through his newspapers and almanacs. He stressed concord. Emerson used his pen to advocate self-reliance. He tried to have America set to the world an example of a people who thought for themselves.

In America the two trends of conformity and originality are going to seesaw and sometimes blend. It is unlikely that there will ever be such an out-and-out opposition of beliefs as has existed in Europe and as now exists between the theistic and the atheistic branches of what has turned out to be existentialism. The two forerunners, Kierkegaard and Nietzsche, set the pace. In Europe contrasts are sharper. Nor can profitable analogies be carried much beyond the forerunners. To do so would require too extensive a preoccupation with European philosophy as a whole. It is proper to point out though that American philosophy does to some extent parallel the Western European movement. It is important also to note that Franklin and Emerson do set a trend in American thought from which the five more professional philosophers still to be considered do not depart.

Certainly to the transcendentalist secularization did not connote atheism or even a loss in spiritual depth. Emerson rejects the church. He shocks the orthodox, but not in the blockbuster style of a Nietzsche. Nor does he play brinkmanship with the very outer darkness of despair in the way of a Nietzsche. This in spite of the fact that Nietzsche, like Whitman, was probably set simmering by that Emerson he carried in his pocket.

In the whole movement of American philosophy, carried as far as the Seven Sages take it, Emerson does play a John the Baptist role somewhat similar to that of Nietzsche in the development of Western European philosophy. Just as Nietzsche points to a Sartre and a Heidegger, Emerson points to Santayana and Whitehead. Emerson is a prophet telling us to draw, and draw fast, on new resources. Not only intuition but the whole man with his last ounce of fortitude and wisdom is going to be needed when new challenges, which Emerson only dimly foresaw, are upon us. All agree—and Emerson sounds the note with clearness—that there is never ahead of us the consolation of a sure thing. Get ready for a gamble with fate itself. A pitiless new day is dawning. Train for new urgencies.

If Franklin, like Columbus, had one foot firmly planted in this world, Emerson is there with both feet. He bids us take root firmly and for good. There is a commitment in Emerson such as is not yet found in Franklin. Now we sink or swim, taking a chance on justice here below. That is Emerson's big contribution: a bold anchorage in a mundane world. We have here an irretraceable step toward a religion that, in its main outlines at least, is bound to be secular and toward the exploration of a philosophy that not only is democratic to the core but also so pitiably human as to be almost frightening. No wonder that this frail man had to draw and bid others draw on the last ounce of human self-reliance.

Yet the time comes to all adolescent nations when they must face the responsibilities of adulthood. Is the America of the Emersonian epoch through Emerson catching a glimpse of what it means to come of age? Emerson is a seer who, through his second sight, senses what someday must surely come, and hence his message extends to a mankind statured in a new dimension.

Next to Emerson's significant advance in secularism is his rediscovery of intuition, a kind of deep seeing. Here he is expanding the range of the intellect. He is not a psychologist, but there is a crack psychologist on the way. Our next man, William James, also has things to say about the value of intuition. Intuition is not going to win out over thought. New giants in new logics will have something to say on that subject, but it is well that Emerson definitely bows intuition onto the stage and that William James, with increasing psychological penetration, will further advance our understanding of intuition. We need that glow of intellect surcharged with feeling that in Emerson lights up the world around him. The life of man has in past ages been built up ninety per cent around things invisible to the naked eye, sometimes one hundred per cent, and now that the atoms of the earth are beginning to draw us into their tight embrace, how fortunate that Emerson salvages the invisible through his intuition.

William James:
Primitive Pragmatist

1. Our First Professional

TOWARD THE LATTER part of the nineteenth century, as one of a group of unprecedently gifted thinkers holding forth at Harvard University, William James bent his capable mind to the job of going over the entire American credo from stem to stern. In submitting this staunch craft to a professional overhauling, he did in some sections of it what amounted to a rebuilding job. He put in a more up-to-date engine, streamlined the hull, modernized the interior, painted the outside, and gave the whole contraption a new name. He christened it pragmatism.

James was not too fond of the new name. He thought it would surely be misunderstood. He was right; but it is still a very good name for the Jamesian phase of American philosophy. Many names at first imperfectly hit off the movement they stand for, then become for a time a term of reproach, and finally end up as a sobriquet proudly worn by adherents and routinely accepted by posterity. We have had Methodist, Protestant, dissenter, transcendentalist—dozens of others—and now pragmatist. Coming from a Greek root meaning to do or to act, the noun "pragma" denotes a thing, presumably resulting from action. The whole interior echo of the term fits in well with the American genius for getting things done.

James quite rightly credits the first introduction of the term into American philosophy to Charles Sanders Peirce. James tells how in 1878 "in an article entitled *How to Make Our Ideas Clear* in the *Popular Science Monthly* for January of that year Mr. Peirce, after pointing out that our beliefs are really rules for action, said that, to develop a thought's meaning, we need only determine what conduct it is fitted to produce: that conduct is for us its sole significance." James goes on to say: "This is the principle of Peirce, the principle of pragmatism. It lay entirely unnoticed by any one for twenty years, until I in an address before Professor Howison's philosophical union at the University of California, brought it forward again and made a special application of it to religion. By that date [1898] the time seemed ripe for its reception."

James stuck to the name he got from Peirce, who in turn had got it from Kant, and with considerable personal vigor launched his revamped American philosophy upon the world. After James of Harvard relinquished the tiller, Dewey of Columbia took over. For a number of years both James and Dewey astonished the world with their stout defense of the solid and versatile structure they showed the American way of life to be. They put it forth, not as something novel or revolutionary, but as something of ancient lineage and still good that had been hidden from sight by other and less worthy views which they proceeded to brush away; and when they did so the philosophy stood forth like a new creation.

To many it appeared that James was to American philosophy what Walt Whitman was to American poetry. Certain it is that with James American philosophy bursts forth with an un- mistakable air of its own. If Franklin was our Socrates, Emerson our Plato, then in some sense James is an indigenous Aristotle, or rather he, supplemented by Dewey, make up our Aristotle. Like Aristotle, James had a scientific bias. As Aristotle trimmed off some of the poetic superfluities of Plato, so James soft-pedals some of the transcendental overtones that hovered over Emerson. As Aristotle, before he wrote his *Metaphysics,* launched the logic of his day, so James launched the new science of psychology into its orbit before he settled down to give new shape to a philosophy based on that psychology.

A Boston Brahmin with a Yankee soul, James was accustomed from childhood to weigh American viewpoints against a Euro- pean background. The result is both international and scientific. What he came up with was neither puritanism nor transcen- dentalism nor any religious ism at all. From his *Varieties of Re- ligious Experience* there does not emerge any new sect or movement. Perhaps his great sympathy for abnormal psychology and for wide-open religious experiences of all kinds made him shun anything sectlike or narrow. He interpreted religious experiences as a legitimate part of the much-wider spectrum of both bizarre and ordinary human experiences.

James was becoming conscious of the larger role America was destined to play on the world stage. He was, if anything, more aware than either Franklin or Emerson of how the center of gravity in international thought for a time would shift to this side of the Atlantic. Hence his presentation of the American viewpoint has lost all traces of colonialism. James was no longer even remotely apologizing for what America had to say. In that respect, as Alfred North Whitehead noted, James was not a sectional thinker but a leader who inaugurated a new era for the whole of philosophy. Here was the Voice of America with a ring of leadership broadcasting as one grown-up country to another.

James made it clear that to be a man, help your neighbor, and keep your powder dry were not just pioneer postures, but the ingredients of an attitude basic to needs far beyond those of early American history. James spoke for philosophy in a voice that for all its native charm had an unmistakable air of cultivation. James as a child went to French and German schools in Europe and it was never any effort for him to include the Old World in his purview. His brother Henry became an expatriate. Perhaps Henry James had too much of Europe but William had just enough and not too much. He returned to America for good and took deep root.

At thirteen James in gloves and a high silk hat was walking about the shops of London with his brother Henry, or visiting the Louvre in Paris, or sitting in a studio trying to paint like Delacroix. It may be a source of wonder how William James, who was after all a none-too-robust child born into a fairly wealthy family that traveled a good deal, could have got such a good insight into the rough-and-tumble of American life. One answer was his personal sufferings—both Henry and William were plagued with nervous and other disturbing ailments—

and these sufferings increased their sensitivity. Another was the unusual faculty for empathy which the brothers had. William especially could with astonishing ease live himself into any situation. The environment always struck deeply into his interior.

Ralph Barton Perry, the official biographer of William James, drew a contrast between two American thinkers who, at the end of the nineteenth century, stood at the opposite pinnacles of American thought. One was Royce and the other James. In 1849 a family by the name of Royce set out from eastern Ohio to find their fortunes in California. The father had migrated from England to Canada and thence to the United States. This family in their covered wagon met with inconceivable hardships which, on the part of the mother at least, ricocheted harmlessly off the shield of an impenetrable religious faith. Into this family, with a father who never did find gold in California and became instead an indifferently successful storekeeper, was born Josiah Royce. The mother was determined to get her son educated. She did, but so far as schooling, training, and polish were concerned, Royce was the exact opposite of William James. Both became professors at Harvard. Throughout his life Royce desperately advocated the virtues of a smooth and polished society, while James, who had had every advantage, extolled a rugged frontier life with self-made minds. James, who could belong to any club, was always saying that clubs were not worth a damn, while Royce was hiding his embarrassment in dreams of social elegance. Royce, getting all tangled up in Teutonic metaphysics, spent his life trying to sell Americans a Roycean version of German idealism, while James, the sophisticated New Englander, put the true salt and flavor of America into an indigenous philosophy.

"America," said Santayana, "is a young country with an old mentality." It is "a wise child" with an "old head on young shoulders." America was a transplanted Europe rather than a fresh beginning. It was a rebirth of Europeans among greater opportunities. At any point America could pick up its continuity with Europe. This happened when through William James American philosophy entered solidly into the ranks of world tradition. As Horace Kallen, one of James's disciples, put it: "Among the philosophers of America, William James has no peer in the eyes of the world, whether it be in China or Great Britain, in Italy or Russia, or all the nations of the earth between, men celebrate him not merely as the greatest American philosopher, but as the great philosopher of America."

2. A Remarkable Father

THE MAN WHO really put a foundation under the wide-ranging, easygoing, ever forward-reaching philosophy of Franklin and Emerson was the grandson of another William James, also known as James of Albany. Franklin did not live to see the nineteenth century, but before he died there was fast working his way upward in northern New York this Irish immigrant, James of Albany, who at his death in 1832 left a fortune of three million dollars to be held in trust until the last of his numerous grandchildren was twenty-one. There was more than a touch of Benjamin Franklin about this canny upstater who had a hand in the opening of the Erie Canal and had done well in the real estate, banking, and business world.

In the course of a long life he had three wives and fourteen children. None of his children or grandchildren followed his hints about getting famous in politics or business. They used the family money to get themselves good educations, and Henry, one of the sons of James of Albany, as a boy took some lessons in elementary science from Joseph Henry, later authority on electricity and head of the Smithsonian Institution. Joseph Henry, to show his pupils that hot air was lighter than cold air, taught them to make a type of balloon with lighted torches underneath. One day one of these balloons blew into a neighbor's hayloft with Henry after it, stamping out the flames, but burning his leg so severely that he had to spend two years in bed and have his leg amputated twice above the knee in a day when there were no anesthetics. A cripple for life, Henry, father of William James the philosopher, sought composure in books and in the bosom of his family.

This Henry James the Elder was the man who one day said to Emerson: "I wish sometimes the lightning would strike my wife and children out of existence so that I would suffer no more from loving them." He did love his wife and children very much, but from his deep reading of Swedenborg and his subsequent study of Fourier he got the idea that it was wrong to be too strongly attached to what is yours. His early interest in science had changed to an interest in theological and highly speculative subjects.

When Emerson asked him one day to make a speech before a philosophical club, James asked if it would be all right if he spoke on socialism. "What other subject could you speak on?" asked Emerson somewhat nervously. "I could speak on sin," said Henry James. "Make it socialism," said Emerson. To Henry James the Elder whatever was not socialism was sin.

All of his children revered him, and they always had a feeling that important work was going forward when Father was composing his books. He made no effort to convert his children to his views. Those were things they would decide for themselves when they got older. William James the philosopher always had the highest respect for his father's doctrines, but the father's training was theological, the son's almost exlusively scientific. The accident seems to have heightened the father's sensitivity while at the same time never dimming the vital energy that made such men as Emerson and Carlyle value him as a personal friend. Emerson said of Henry James the Elder that he was "wise, gentle, polished, with heroic manners and a serenity like the sun."

Other personal followers went further. One of them said: "Henry James, the father of Henry the novelist, of William the philosopher, was a mystic of profounder mind than Emerson, an acceptor of his fellow-men with deeper understanding than Whitman, as fearless a scorner of the smug and conventional as Thoreau, and a more conscious plotter of an America that was no echo of an old rhapsody, but a new world indeed, than Poe ever dreamed of."

On his deathbed Henry James the Elder gave terse instructions regarding the funeral: "Tell the minister to say only this: 'Here lies a man who has thought all his life that the ceremonies attending birth, marriage, and death were all damned nonsense.'" It was sometimes hard for the boys to explain to their cronies that their father was not in business and not a regular churchgoer. When the boys asked their father what they had better say, the father in his gentle way exploded: "Say I'm a philosopher, say I'm a lover of my kind, say I'm an author of books, if you like or best of all, just say I'm a Student." This was about as helpful as what he said about his church attendance. In this connection he told his sons to plead for all religions and to say that there was no communion—Catholic, Jew, or Swedenborgian—from which he felt himself excluded.

James the Elder assumed and never for a moment doubted the existence of God as a personal Creator. To him the human individual was nothing. God created the world by stages, first nature, then a redeemed human race, and then a regenerated social order. These stages corresponded to the three realms of body, soul, and spirit. Social democracy was a precursor of the kingdom of God on earth. Man's spiritual development he regarded in terms of an indwelling divinity, but, unlike Thoreau's independence or Emerson's self-reliance, James the Elder's emphasis was on sociality, selfhood through otherhood, in a regenerated mankind.

For Henry James the Elder the whole purpose of nature, God's first product, was to bring into existence a being who can be self-conscious. Then selfhood must be transcended. Anyone who could think of no higher occupation for God than to have God save that person's own personal soul had a pretty low idea of the Almighty. "James," said Joseph L. Blau, who comments on the views of James the Elder in his *Men and Movements in American Philosophy*, "had no patience with any educated person whose view of God was so simple that he could conceive of no better occupation for God than 'literally to bestow divine and immortal life upon that dead, corrupt, and stinking thing' his selfhood." God makes no distinction among persons. God is interested in society. The originating principle of society is the pure and altruistic love of man for man. The aim is the incarnation of God in aggregate humanity. Democracy is social and moral rather than political. Social democracy is the foreshadowing of the kingdom of God on earth.

William James edited and had published in 1885 *The Literary Remains of the Late Henry James*, which contains those works of his father which remained unpublished at his death. In a preface William James said: "Now, the great peculiarity of Mr. James' conception of God is that it is monistic enough to satisfy the philosopher, and yet warm and lively and dramatic enough to speak to the heart of the common pluralistic mind." He characterized it as "an entirely fresh and original contribution to religious thought."

Summing up his own views toward the end of his *Varieties of Religious Experience,* William James says: "Taking creeds and faith-state together, as forming 'religions,' and treating these as purely subjective phenomena, without regard to the question of their 'truth,' we are obliged, on account of their extraordinary influence upon action and endurance, to class them amongst the most important biological functions of mankind. Their stimulant and anaesthetic effect is so great that Professor Leuba, in a recent article, 'The Contents of Religious Consciousness,' *Monist,* xi, 536, July, 1901, goes so far as to say that so long as men can *use* their God, they care very little who he is, or even whether he is at all. 'The truth of the matter can be put,' says Leuba, 'in this way: *God is not known, he is not understood; he is used*—sometimes as a meat-purveyor, sometimes as moral support, sometimes as friend, sometimes as an object of love. If he proves himself useful, the religious consciousness asks for no more than that. Does God really exist? How does he exist? What is he? are so many irrelevant questions. Not God, but life, more life, a larger, richer, more satisfying life, is, in the last analysis, the end of religion. The love of life, at any and every level of development, is the religious impulse.' "

3. The Conquest of Confidence

As a boy William James, the grandson of James of Albany, used to visit the maternal home in the New York State capital where his grandmother lived. She was the third wife of the progenitor of the tribe, and she lived until 1859. By then the fortune had been pretty well parceled out and scattered among the numerous offspring, but there seems to have been enough left to permit Henry and the wife and brood he loved so well to travel back and forth many times between Europe and America. Whether it was this constant moving about, the presence of an erratic and outspoken father, the feeling of not belonging to any particular place, or the absorption from his reading of an Ibsenesque belief in scientific fatalism, William James, in the early part of his life, suffered from great infirmity of the will.

There were also physical troubles. As he grew up James was more and more plagued by backache, eye trouble, indigestion, and insomnia. When the Civil War broke out he was nineteen and, although the whole family was intensely patriotic, there was no thought of either him or his brother Henry enlisting. Two younger brothers did so very promptly later on and made distinguished military careers for themselves. But William spent years persistently dogged by weakness.

Between the ages of twenty and thirty fits of depression kept getting worse and worse. After spells of hard work and genuine accomplishments came periods of low morale when, trembling and spent, he saw the bottom of his own cup of despair. All this in spite of an eager interest in medicine. As an undergraduate at Harvard James did prepare for medicine and easily obtained his M.D. degree. He never intended to practice, but he did use his knowledge of medicine and of psychology to help steady himself. It was not so easy for this physician to heal himself because, as often happens, he was his own worst patient.

He decided to take time out for travel and to find a cure for his ills. Things were pretty bad when he wrote his father from Berlin: "It will be just as well for you not to say anything to any of the others about what I shall tell you of my condition . . . it will only give them useless pain. . . . My confinement to my room and inability to indulge in any social intercourse drove me necessarily into reading a great deal, which in my half-starved and weak condition was very bad for me, making me irritable and tremulous in ways I have never before experienced. . . . Thoughts of the pistol, the dagger, and the bowl began to usurp an unduly large part of my attention."

There were a few more years of intermittent melancholia before there came a turn for the better. Of these years his own son Henry has written: "Bad health, a feeling of the purposelessness of his own particular existence, his philosophic doubts . . . all these combined to plunge him into a state of morbid depression." In his *Varieties of Religious Experience,* James has left us, disguised as an anonymous case, a description of just how he felt when he hit bottom. "It was as if something hitherto solid within my breast gave way entirely, and I became a mass of quivering fear. . . . I awoke morning after morning with a horrible dread at the pit of my stomach, and with a sense of insecurity of life that I never knew before. . . . The experience has made me sympathetic with the morbid feelings of others ever since. . . . For months I was unable to go out into the dark alone. I dreaded to be left alone. I remember wondering how other people could live, how I myself had ever lived, so unconscious of that pit of insecurity beneath the surface of life. My mother in particular, a very cheerful person, seemed to me a perfect paradox in her unconsciousness of danger. . . . I have always thought that this experience of melancholia of mind had a religious bearing. . . . The fear was so invasive and powerful that, if I had not clung to Scripture texts like *The eternal God is my refuge; Come unto me all ye that labor and are heavy laden; I am the Resurrection and the Life,* I think I should have grown really insane."

In 1870, when James was twenty-eight, there was a jubilating entry in his diary: "I think yesterday was a crisis in my life. I finished the first part of Renouvier's Second *Essais*." The French philosopher's emphasis on the will as a means of selecting what we want out of life struck an answering chord in James. He never let go of that insight. He became an apostle of will power, hammering away on the use of the will as Emerson had hammered on self-reliance. In his own *Psychology* the chapters on habit formation are among the most inspiring in the whole range of psychological literature. More jubilation: "Hitherto, when I have felt like taking a free initiative . . . suicide seemed the most manly form to put my daring into; now . . . I will posit life (the real, the good) in the self-governing resistance of the ego to the world. Life shall be built in doing and suffering and creating."

Gone were the dark obsessions. In 1872 his father wrote to his son Henry about William: "Willy goes on swimmingly with his teaching. The students (fifty-seven) are elated with their luck in having such a professor. . . . He came in here the other afternoon when I was sitting alone, and after walking the floor in an animated way for a moment, exclaimed,'Dear me! What a difference there is between me now and me last spring this time: then so hypochondriacal . . . and now feeling my mind so cleared up and restored to sanity. It is the difference between death and life." He never forgot his early struggles with the type of semi-scientific fatalism so characteristic of that period and so masterfully portrayed by Bertrand Russell in *A Freeman's Worship*:

"To every man comes, sooner or later, the great renunciation, by death, by illness, by poverty, or by the voice of duty. We must learn, each one of us that the world was not made for us. . . . The life of Man is a long march through the night surrounded by invisible foes, tortured by weariness and pain . . . one by one, as they march, our comrades vanish from our sight, seized by the silent orders of Omnipotent Death." The litany of nineteenth-century materialism continues: "Brief and powerless is Man's life; on him and all his race the slow, sure doom falls pitiless and dark. Blind to good and evil, reckless of destruction, omnipotent matter rolls on its relentless way; for Man condemned today to lose his dearest, tomorrow himself to pass through the gate of darkness, it remains only to cherish, ere yet the blow falls, the lofty thoughts that ennoble his little day."

Similar sentiments were powerfully portrayed by prominent writers of the day, such as Ibsen and Thomas Hardy. James was well acquainted with these deterministic chimeras, but he lived to work out a way of overcoming them. Thereafter to him that whole oppressive block universe is gone. Instead we have a pluralistic world, a multiverse instead of a universe. No longer is everything inexorably linked in with everything else, with man a helpless cog. Nor does James jump to the other extreme of making man a substitute for omnipotence. Both optimism of the boundless variety and pessimism of the hopeless variety are abandoned for a world that can slowly be made better. Problems can be attacked in piecemeal fashion. Divide and conquer is the motto of the rejuvenated will.

In this gigantic task of improving the world are we entirely alone? This culminating question had also hit the French philosopher Renouvier, and at one point we find James saying: "I am bound to say that my reasonings are almost wholly those of Renouvier." According to Renouvier, God took a partner when he created man. In true French style Renouvier declared himself a republican. He spoke of a republican concept of the world in which the gods are members of a world council. He held that absolute government of the world by divine fiat "is the choice of souls prone to inaction and desirous of seeing everything happen without them, whilst they contemplate and worship. To these must be added the great band of the disabused and the disillusioned." No wonder James spoke of the manliness of Renouvier.

Renouvier did not believe that anything, either matter or spirit, was the absolute king of the world. Forces were struggling with each other for mastery in a world where time is real. Activity of many kinds could be of cosmic importance. Freedom could become a tremendous coalition, not just the struggling of each puny individual. James agreed with Renouvier that in the world there is something really evil, but the world also has in it mighty forces struggling for good. In this attitude James went beyond Renouvier.

Both James and Renouvier made it a central part of their credo that a world part good and part bad could be made better. "Just as Buonaparte declared that the Europe of the future would have to be either Republican or Cossack; so I feel inclined to say," said James, "that the philosophy of the future will have to be either that of Renouvier or that of Hegel." On Kant and the whole German idealistic movement that he started, culminating in Hegel, James never equivocated. "The true direction of philosophical progress lies . . . not so much *through* Kant as *round* him. Philosophy can perfectly well outflank him and build herself up into adequate fullness by prolonging more directly the old English lines." Henceforth James draws freely on the two sources of his philosophic inspiration—the French and the English.

From the English, especially from John Stuart Mill to whom he dedicated his *Pragmatism,* James got much the same sort of help that he got from Renouvier. John Stuart Mill said he could not possibly see in the government of nature anything resembling the work of a Being both good and omnipotent. The power of God was not only finite, but extremely limited. For Mill the struggle between the powers of good and those of evil went on all the time, "a struggle in which the humblest creature can play a part." For Mill a virtuous man could be a fellow worker with the Most High. God offers his help, but at the same time he needs our help. Renouvier, too, was fond of quoting Mill's *Three Essays on Religion.*

Winston Churchill, the American novelist, in his book *A Far Country* put it this way: "Democracy is an adventure, the great adventure of mankind. No adventure is safe, life itself is an adventure and neither is that safe. It's a hazard, as you and I have found out. The moment we try to make life safe we lose all there is in it worth while. We have to leave what seem the safe things; we have to wander and suffer in order to realize that the only true safety lies in development. We have to risk our lives and our souls."

Like the novelist just quoted, James puts a heavy load on human shoulders. He puts some of his trust in the Lord, but not too much. He is a little like his own Western settler of whom he tells an anecdote. It seems one day this early settler from Montana wandering out into the woods, was suddenly confronted by a grizzly bear so formidable that the settler fell to his knees praying: "O Lord, I hain't never asked ye for help, and I ain't agoing to ask you for none now, but, for pity's sake, O Lord, don't help the bear."

A graphic picture of James in the classroom, teaching philosophy, is given by Santayana: "A prophet is not without honor save in his own country; and until the return wave of James's reputation reached America from Europe, his pupils and friends were hardly aware that he was such a distinguished man. . . . He was a sort of Irishman among the Brahmins, and seemed hardly imposing enough for a great man. . . . Even his pupils, attached as they invariably were to his person, felt some doubts about the profundity of one who was so very natural and who after some interruption during a lecture—and he said life was a series of interruptions—would slap his forehead and ask the man in the front row, 'What was I talking about?' But in the midst of his routine of the class-room the spirit would sometimes come upon him, and leaning his head on his hand, he would let fall golden words, picturesque, fresh from the heart, full of the knowledge of good and evil. Incidentally there would crop up some humorous characterization, some candid confession of doubt or of instinctive preference, some pungent scrap of learning; radicalisms plunging sometimes into the subsoil of all human philosophies; and, on occasion, thoughts of simple wisdom and wistful piety, the most unfeigned and manly that anybody ever had."

Later in his life James's summer home in the New Hampshire hills had fourteen doors, all opening outward. His sister Alice thought this house a perfect outward expression of her favorite brother's wide-open personality. James mellowed beautifully. At the age of thirty-six he married and presently had a lively family. But back of the serene and vital philosophy of life that he achieved lay the ten or fifteen years of deadly struggle leading to a final victory which made him a tower of strength to others.

Alice James in discussing her father and her brother William remarked on the striking resemblance between these two men in William's early days. "Though the results are the same, the resemblances," she said, "seem to come from such different nature

in the two; in William, an entire inability or indifference to 'stick
to a thing for the sake of sticking,' as someone said of him once;
while Father, the delicious infant! couldn't submit even to the
thralldom of his own whim." In the daughter's opinion the father
was just plain rebellious, but William at that time had a chronic
infirmity of will. Yet this is the man who later, at the head of his
chapter on habit in his *Psychology Briefer Course,* a book addressed to teachers, could write in his own hand: "Sow an action,
and reap a habit; sow a habit and you reap a character; sow a
character and you reap a destiny."

4. Psychology—Habit and Ego

ACCORDING TO Bertrand Russell, in some ways not at all sympathetic to the Jamesean philosophy: "the best work that has been done anywhere in philosophy and psychology during the [early] present century has been done in America. America, wherever it has succeeded in shaking off slavery to Europe, has developed a new outlook, mainly as the result of the work of James and Dewey."

It is hard to join any conversation about William James without having someone repeat the old saw that his brother Henry, the novelist, wrote novels that sound like philosophy, while William the philosopher wrote books on philosophy that read like novels. Well, it's true. Even the stout two-volume *Principles of Psychology*, a 1,400-page treatise, reads like a warm, personal account. When you get through with the first volume you are glad there is a second; you wish this sound, illuminating, and delightful stuff could go on forever. Among philosophers the only one who approaches him in sprightly tenor and personal wit is old Ben Franklin, the skilled journalist who never allowed himself a dull sentence; but neither he nor Emerson nor even the brilliant Santayana approaches James in the penetrating lucidity and the warm intimacy that radiate from the written page.

In 1878 Henry Holt, the publisher, asked John Fiske to write a book on psychology. Said Fiske: "Let William James do it. He knows more about that subject than I do. He has been studying little else for several years." James was approached and accepted the job. He thought it would take him about two years to finish the book. Instead it took him eleven years, not because he was slow, but because the task, if it was to be done conscientiously, involved a tremendous breaking into new ground. With regard to the long years of work on his great treatise, *The Principles of Psychology,* William wrote his brother Henry James, "I have had to forge every sentence in the teeth of irreducible and stubborn facts."

When the book finally appeared in 1890, it was not only a landmark in psychological science but also an immediate popular success. Ralph Barton Perry, Pulitzer Prize biographer of William James, aptly characterizes this work as an "omnibus" psychology. James welcomed all new and promising trends, from experimental laboratory work in physiopsychology to controlled investigations of so-called psychic phenomena. Psychology cannot afford to omit any facts. James's sympathetic and wide-open mind gave a careful hearing to all manner of marginal as well as to solidly central views. If James were writing today, says Perry, he would recommend that "the tent of psychology should be large enough to provide a place for the bohemian and clinical speculations of a Freud, or the rigorous physiological methods of a Lashley, or the bold theoretical generalizations of a Köhler, or the useful statistical technique of a Spearman." James champions a psychology that moves on, a dynamic and not a static science. He uses a wide-focus movie camera on a broad field of continually changing activities. Also he puts all the old data on the soul back into the hopper and comes up with a new entity: the stream of consciousness.

James the psychologist is a straight extension of James the naturalist. He is the naturalist that Emerson so much wanted to be and, like Emerson, is a very human, almost poetic, type of scientist. Some parts of James sound astonishingly like certain parts of Emerson. In spite of the hardheaded scientific bias which comes out very clearly, he is also a nature poet of almost mystical stripe.

"Philosophers are after all like poets. They are pathfinders. What everyone can feel, what everyone can know in the bone and marrow of him, they sometimes can find words for and express. The words and thoughts of the philosophers are not exactly the words and thoughts of the poets—worse luck. But both alike have the same function. They are if I may use a simile, so many spots, or blazes made by the axe of the human intellect on the trees of the otherwise trackless forest of human experience. They give you somewhere to go from. They give you a direction and a place to reach. They do not give you the integral forest with all its sunlit glories and its moonlit witcheries and wonders. . . . No one like the pathfinder himself feels the immensity of the forest, or knows the accidentality of his own trails. Columbus, dreaming of the ancient East, is stopped by poor pristine simple America, and gets no farther on that day; and the poets themselves know as no one else knows that what their formulas express leaves unexpressed almost everything that they organically divine and feel. So I feel that there is a center in truth's forest where I have never been: to track it out and get there is the secret spring of all my poor life's philosophic efforts; at moments I almost strike into the final valley, there is a gleam of the end, a sense of certainty, but always there comes still another ridge, so my blazes merely circle towards the true direction."

He might almost be writing here of his explorations into psychology. There was always more beyond. Of the interplay between the inner and the outer world James could not get enough. He never lost that semimystical delight in mixing the soul with nature. At the age of fifty-six he described a night in the woods as "a regular Walpurgis Nacht . . . where the streaming moonlight lit up things in a magical checkered play, and it seemed as if the Gods of all the nature-mythologies were holding an indescribable meeting in my breast with the moral Gods of the inner life. The two kinds of Gods have nothing in common. . . . The immense significance of some sort, of the whole scene, if one could only *tell* the significance; the intense inhuman remoteness of its inner life, and yet the intense *appeal* of it; its everlasting freshness and its immemorial antiquity and decay; its utter Americanism, and every sort of patriotic suggestiveness, and you, and my relation to you part and parcel of it all, and beaten up with it, so that memory and sensation all whirled inexplicably together. . . . It was one of the happiest lonesome nights of my existence, and I understand now what a poet is."

Speaking of James, A. A. Roback, historian of American psychology, says: "There can be no question, however, but that he was the foremost psychologist that America produced; and many are prepared to rank him above Wundt." Roback regards the psychology of James as a reflection of the James personality, which was charged with magnetism and charm. James never lost a certain child-impulsiveness. On the night before he was to be awarded an honorary degree at Harvard James showed signs of anxiety lest President Eliot refer to him as a psychologist rather than as a philosopher. Today, says Roback, one is not sure in which field he was best. Every school in psychology with some show of evidence claims him as a leader or at least as the man who first adumbrated their point of view.

The year 1890 was a turning point in psychology. The turning point was James. Ever afterward psychology went in for experimentation rather than introspection. Following James, it has continued to seek allies in physiology and neurology rather than in theology and metaphysics. The two outstanding features of the psychology of William James are (1) that he makes habit the rudder of life, setting the course for both our physical and our mental development, and (2) that he abolishes the static ego in favor of the stream of consciousness.

"All our life," said James, "is but a mass of habits—practical, emotional, and intellectual—systematically organized for our weal or woe, and bearing us irresistibly toward our destiny, whatever the latter may be." And again: "Habit is thus a second nature, or rather, as the Duke of Wellington said, it is 'ten times nature' —at any rate as regards its importance in adult life. . . . The great thing in all education is to make our nervous system our ally instead of our enemy. . . . For this we must make automatic and habitual, as early as possible, as many useful actions as we can, and as carefully guard against the growing into ways that are likely to be disadvantageous."

James connected habit with plasticity, a fundamental property also of certain kinds of matter, invisible and molecular. A plastic structure is weak enough to yield to an influence but strong enough not to yield all at once. Familiar instances in nonliving substances are the clothes that after being taken off retain the shape of the body, a fold in a piece of paper remaining as a crease, water running downhill and carving out a channel. Brain matter is plastic, not to mechanical pressure or to thermal changes from which it is unusually well insulated but to nerve currents. Blood flow and nerve currents are the only two things that get into the brain. Even attenuated nerve currents leave paths. What makes the first path? Probably chance or the way things happen to shake together in an organism composed of varying tensions seeking a balance or level. It is a little like asking what made the first river? The path of least resistance plays a preponderant role both in nature and in human life. Changing those paths is half the history of civilization.

Once a path is made, practice deepens it. Setting the pattern of a nervous network is a little like setting the pattern of a climbing plant. Once it is set, every branch gets thicker. Only the tendrils on the edge remain mobile. The whole system grows in the way it is oriented. Practice perfects and strengthens what is already begun, leaving the way open to learn new things. Habits make things easy. Habit economizes nervous energy. Less effort is needed after each successful try. Habit diminishes the conscious attention with which our acts are performed. The lower centers learn and take over, thereafter performing automatically with little awareness in the higher centers. It is often forgotten that not only the brain but the entire nervous and muscular system can store and utilize information. There is no such thing as an idiotic spinal cord, that is, a cord which remembers nothing. The body is full of places where muscles and nerves have learned their lessons once and for all. We do thousands of things right without knowing how or why. We have forgotten—in the brain, that is—how we learned to digest food and circulate the blood, but we can see the whole process in formation when musical performers play elaborate pieces while talking and thinking of other things. Knitters knit, drivers drive, weavers weave, and blacksmiths forge with the top of the mind off elsewhere or engaged in busy intercourse on other subjects with other minds. James is right in studying the habits of each individual in much the same way that a bartender studies the ingredients of each drink.

The moral implications of habit formation are enormous. There is no hell worse than the hell we fashion for ourselves by habitually shaping our character in the wrong way. The drunken Rip

van Winkle in the Jefferson play excuses himself for every fresh
drink by saying this one doesn't count. Well, he may not count
it, but it is being counted nevertheless. The nerve cells, the fibers,
and the molecules are counting it. They are equally meticulous
in chalking up good efforts. In the nervous system momentum
works both ways.

James's chapter on habit in *The Principles of Psychology* is
reminiscent of Emerson's remarks on heaven and hell right here
on earth. Nature keeps track. With complete indifference nature
both rewards and punishes. Plasticity is a blindfolded nemesis:
the guidance offered is only a permissive sort of guidance. Under
it one can grow strong or go to perdition. The guidance is like
that of a mountain pass: you can either follow it or step into a
crevasse.

In his remarks on habit James asks: why consciousness at all?
We are not conscious of the process of turning food and drink
into bone and muscle, yet the chemistry of it goes on pretty well
without the learning of it from a textbook. Certainly many
complicated physical and neural processes proceed without let or
hindrance in the successful channels established long ago by
endless trial and error. Thank your nameless ancestry! But to
urge that we become once more complete automata is, thinks
James, an unwarrantable impertinence. It is like mending an irregular timekeeper by stopping the clock altogether. Consciousness has helped immeasurably in the evolutionary struggle. It
is a form of increased sensitivity. It is primarily a selecting
agency. Even a lower form of brain helps in making choices.
Extra sensitivity and increased powers of discernment multiply
the number of right choices. Does a seeing man choose to become blind? A farseeing brain can load the dice of fate. Around
this point center some of the deepest insights of philosophy.

Pleasure and pain also come into the picture at a very early
stage. They are not the only two forces in the world, operating
blindly like two balancing weights, as Franklin at one time
thought, but they do range themselves on opposite sides, the
pleasures in general with utility and the pains in general with
the detrimental experiences. For a doctor pain is a signal that
something is wrong. In spite of knowing a great deal about ab-

normal psychology, James does not depart on this point from the general common sense that Franklin also followed. One can get pleasure from bad habits but, as Franklin would say, it doesn't pay out in the end. Both James and Franklin swim in the wake of the utilitarians. They are not devotees of the hairshirt. In this they follow just plain common sense, a trait that will come out again and again in American philosophy. Even the exquisite Santayana glories in the common sense aspects of the metaphysics back of his aesthetic philosophy.

The rules James gives for the establishment of a habit are well known. The first two are taken, as James acknowledges, from Professor Alexander Bain. (1) Launch your habit with as strong and as decided an initiative as possible. (2) Never suffer an exception to occur until the new habit sets and gets to be securely rooted in your life. (3) Seize the first opportunity to act on every resolution you make. (4) Don't preach too much to others or abound in good talk in the abstract; the strokes of *behavior* are what give the new set to character. (5) Keep the faculty of effort alive in you by every day indulging in a little gratuitous exercise.

Here in his psychology James is exhibiting the crutches that he himself used in learning to walk again. As a professor he took a great deal of time out to give popular lectures that were of direct practical help to his audiences. His life was too short to do all the work he had set out for himself. At his death he left some of his deeper studies, embodying his metaphysics, unfinished. But the bold and essential framework of his new philosophy he did erect and it stands for all to see, built on the bedrock of his psychology, with one pillar on habit formation and the other on his concept of the dynamic ego.

"When our country comes to itself . . . when it transmutes into articulate ideas what are still obscure and blind strivings, two men, Emerson and William James, will, I think, stand out as the prophetic forerunners of the attained creed of values." This is John Dewey. He continues: "By common consent James was far and away the greatest of American psychologists. It was a case of James first and no second. . . . Mr. James has been one of the few vital and fruitful factors in contemporary thought."

What a bombshell James exploded when he first turned the

self into a flux! That the external world should be a constantly evolving process was not too hard to take, but our own deepest self also?—that is a different story. Yet in 1904 James said: "For twenty years past I have mistrusted 'consciousness' as an entity; for seven or eight years past I have suggested its non-existence to my students, and tried to give them its pragmatic equivalent in realities of experience. It seems to me that the hour is ripe for it to be openly and universally discarded. To deny plumply that 'consciousness' exists seems so absurd on the face of it . . . that I fear some readers will follow me no farther. Let me then immediately explain that I mean only to deny that the word stands for an entity, but to insist most emphatically that it does stand for a function."

Somewhat the same sort of thing happened in chemistry when early investigators were trying desperately to learn what fire was. For centuries they got nowhere. Some of the old Greeks were sure that fire was one of the four basic elements, along with earth, air, and water, from which the world was made. For centuries fire was regarded as a substance. To quote from an extremely elementary science book: "The reason fire remained a mystery for so long is that men thought it was a substance. They thought it was a sort of luminous hot stuff that poured out of things as they burned. They came near to being right but they were wrong. Fire is not a material substance; it is something happening." Down to modern times men racked their brains to pin down that element of fire. Chemists called it phlogiston and although they tried by every subtle device known to scientific research to catch, measure, or weigh it, they failed. It turned out of course that there is no such thing as phlogiston. Fire is a process.

Burning, or oxidation, may take place at different rates. Life is a very slow combustion. Without oxygen we die. To consider life itself as some sort of process is by this time no longer a shock, but when William James began to apply biological ideas to psychology it was still a revolutionary idea to hold that consciousness was not a substance but a process. Once James grasped it, his stream of consciousness or stream of thought became the pivot of his whole philosophy.

James gave a biological slant to the American doctrine of individualism. In his acceptance of evolution he stressed not the weeding out of unsuitable variations so much as the fundamental fact that nature does have spontaneous variations in all directions. James is the apostle of spontaneity. The world grows; it varies; and so does man. Man is free to grow. What is even more exciting—he can select the variations that he wishes to embed into his stream of consciousness. Our life is made up of things to which we successively and freely give attention. Life is choice. The self is not a substance; it is a line of activity that we succeed in establishing.

A person is a freely built-up and individual stream of life. We have now reached the most original part in the thoroughly American psychology of William James—his denial of the static ego. The originality is not so much in the bare statement as in the way James illuminated the significance of all this. In the bare statement he was only following Hume and others who had metaphysically, rather than biologically, adumbrated a similar view, but in James the whole road moves out from behind the mountain and by looking down we get a clear view of the sharp turn it takes.

Before James psychology was a static science. After him it became a dynamic part of biology. This was not due to James alone, but James will serve, and has earned the right to serve, as a new starting point for psychology. James confirmed beyond all doubt that American psychology, as well as the philosophy of which it is a part, is a living, growing thing.

The human tendency to personification is a pretty deeply rooted way of construing events. It is not as old as the hills but very nearly so. It reached an early height in the days of primitive man. The Bible calls it idolatry. It has not yet been outgrown. "The elusive collar button and the threatening cloud alike still tend to become persons," says W. S. Hunter, a follower of William James. In prehistoric times every minor force of nature was personified. To hit upon a person as the source of your trouble is a quick way of identifying it. It gives you something to get mad at and smash. *Cherchez la femme* or at least blame somebody represents an ancient human tendency. All this because one wonderful day in the long and distant past we learned to see ourself as a person, and then during a long stage in our development we learned to see everything else in our own image. We are a person, the other fellow is a person, and even sticks, stones, storms, and the sun are persons, sometimes quite exalted and terrifying persons. We overdid this business of personifying.

It was long thought that nothing is more certain than that there is within us a unified person. That person even roams about and leaves the body when we sleep. When Descartes tried his famous experiment of doubting everything under the sun he stopped short of his own personality. "*I think, therefore I am.*" And by his own existence he did not mean the existence of his body. He meant the person of Descartes, his personality, his psyche.

Long before Descartes the Greeks, and notably Plato, jumped to a similar conclusion concerning the core of human life. They were the first to call this core the psyche, and they were therefore the first psychologists. In a long tradition, lasting from 400 B.C. to well after the Renaissance, Plato's discovery was never seriously challenged, but in the eighteenth century some skeptical thinkers who were better doubters than even Descartes really got to work on the idea and did a destructive analysis on this famous sacred personality. Locke, the Englishman, started it by removing from the mind its so-called innate ideas. To Plato the soul never dies and was never born. Before entering the body it pre-existed in a world of higher perfections than the present one and from this higher world it remembers much. Reminiscences of this ideal world are often awakened by things we see in this world. It is because we are born with these innate ideas that we are likewise born with a yearning for perfection. Innate ideas give us intimations of immortality, the immortal gods, the perfect configurations of mathematics, and the ideally beautiful forms of art. When Locke took out of the soul all these celestial intimations he left it like a babe with empty hands to be filled by something built up out of sensations coming through the earthly senses. This was quite a realistic comedown from the poetic heights of Plato. It is said that men spoke in poetry before they learned to speak in prose.

Nature too used to be peopled with gods. Now, it so happened that the more men studied nature, not by the theoretical contemplation of the Greeks but by sustained and practical experiments, the more the gods within it tended to disappear. Little by little there was revealed a nature moving along under a type of impersonal law that had little to do with the gods of mythology, their peccadilloes, prejudices, or preferences. Impartially the sun shines and the storms blow on the just and the unjust. Nature became depersonalized. All the naiads, nymphs, and lesser deities, and finally the whole immortal Pantheon, had to withdraw into the realms of poetry.

Such a realistic way of looking at nature made possible a greater control over nature. But within our own bodies the sway of a single supreme personality remained almost unchanged. Over our own inner life a quasi-divine spirit still reigned supreme. All we did and all we were owed its origin and could be traced to this central psyche, also identified with the mind, and when Locke made this mind at birth a blank slate, a *tabula rasa,* he was taking a first step in making it disappear altogether.

For a time, after Locke, it became quite fashionable in psychological and philosophical circles to work out in detail just how a statue with its senses opened one after another to nature could acquire an inside personality like our own. Just as Newton explained the universe by bits of matter and laws of gravitation, so men by analogy explained the mind as a system of sensations integrated by the laws of association. Under such conditions what became of the old-fashioned psyche? One answer comes from Hume, the Scottish member of the skeptical school:

"For my part, when I enter most intimately into what I call myself, I always stumble on some particular perception or other, of heat or cold, light or shade, love or hatred, pain or pleasure. I never can catch myself at any time without a perception, and never can observe anything but the perception. When my perceptions are removed for any time, as by sound sleep, so long am I insensible of myself, and may truly be said not to exist. And were all my perceptions removed by death, and could I neither think, nor feel, nor see, nor love, nor hate after the dissolution of my body, I should be annihilated, nor do I conceive what is further requisite to make me a perfect nonentity. If any one upon serious and unprejudiced reflexion, thinks he has a different notion of himself, I must confess I can reason no longer with him. All I can allow him is, that he may be in the right as well as I, and that we are essentially different in this particular. He may, perhaps, perceive something simple and continued, which he calls himself; though I am certain there is no such principle in me."

"The content of the self," says Boyd Henry Bode, who follows James's ideas, "is furnished by the ideals or interests that we cherish. This is easily verified by observing the way in which we ordinarily refer to the self. Very often, it is true, the self is identified with the body, but this is by no means always the case. If a man says, 'He struck me,' the 'me' in question is clearly the body. But if he says, 'He ruined me (financially),' the 'me' is identified with certain economic interests; if he says, 'He attacked me (in the newspapers),' the 'me' is presumably his reputation; if he says, 'He supported me (in a political campaign),' the 'me' is the political aim to which he aspires."

As William James himself tells the story: "In its widest possible sense, however, a man's self is the sum total of all that he can call his, not only his body and his psychic powers, but his clothes and his house, his wife and children, his ancestors and friends, his reputation and works, his lands and horses, and yacht, and bank account. . . . Its own body then first of all, its friends next and finally its spiritual dispositions, must be the supremely interesting objects for each human mind."

"I am often confronted," says James, "by the necessity of standing by one of my empirical selves and relinquishing the rest. Not that I would not, if I could, be both handsome and fat and well dressed, and a great athlete, and make a million a year, a wit, a *bon vivant*, and a lady-killer, as well as a philosopher, a philanthropist, statesman, warrior, and African explorer, as well as a 'tone-poet' and saint. But the thing is simply impossible. The millionaire's work would run counter to the saint's; the *bon vivant* and the philanthropist would trip each other up; the philosopher and the lady-killer could not well keep house in the same tenement of clay. Such different characters may conceivably at the outset of life be alike possible to a man. But to make any one of them actual, the rest must more or less be suppressed."

Perhaps nothing in the nineteenth century, not even the Civil War, was as important to this country or to any other country as the new work in biology brought to a head by Darwin, who for the first time linked together the development of the human mind and the development of mind in animals. As an ultimate result of his findings psychology underwent a change both in subject matter and in method. Its subject matter used to be consciousness, now it became behavior, especially human behavior as compared with that of other animals. Its method changed from the unique business of introspection to something else that pulled it into line with the other sciences: observation plus carefully controlled experiments. And the backdrop of Dantean and Miltonian theology was changed abruptly to Darwin's magnificently biological canvas, thus silhouetting in an entirely different style the whole performance of psychology.

5. Behavior versus Psyche

FOR HALF A billion years this planet has been demanding of its inhabitants the most varied types of behavior. The sea with its myriad populations speaks a fairly simple language: eat and be eaten. It is said that life began in the sea. Certainly most of us who are not experts on marine biology do not have any adequate idea of the many forms of life that chase and swallow one another in the sea, but we do know that interesting new forms of life arose on the shoreline where living things were gradually coming to terms not merely with water but with earth and air. Gasping, breathing, burrowing, bellowing, climbing, and flying were added to the behavior stockpile in answer to the new requirements.

Mammals still carry the sea or a portion of it in their blood. Land environment is seldom even for one year the same. It varies from season to season and from age to age. Perhaps the ice ages did not much bother some of the denizens of the deep who stayed at home in the sea, but life on land had to learn new ways or perish. Agility, large size, small size, armament, pugnacity, swiftness were all tried. When it is said that we do not know enough about the animal life all around us, forget the fishes, the birds, and all the ordinary four-footed animals, and just contemplate for a moment the world of insects.

Man, as a special tool-using animal, has been on earth in semi-civilized form for perhaps 400,000 years; insects, 400,000,000 years. In terms of generations this means 12,000 generations of human beings as against 300,000,000 generations of insects. Insects have had 25,000 times the chance that we have had to modify the germ plasm and do something constructive with that blind heredity that rules a large part of us all. Three hundred thousand species of insects have been described. About six or seven thousand new species are catalogued every year. Experts guess there are about 4,000,000 species of insects; some say 10,000,000. Nobody knows how many there are. The figures here given may not be exactly right, but they roughly indicate the proportions. They could vary quite a bit and still leave the main point untouched, namely, that there is a vast amount of varied behavior going on around us.

Many insects have completely solved the problem of living. Ant colonies existed long before human beings came, and pessimists say they may go on living after we disappear. They have had a chance to try out behavior patterns available to their size and build until they hit upon what works for them. Compared to ants, termites, and cockroaches we are the shakiest of newcomers. There is only one thing to be said in our favor. What they did we learned to do in one tenth of one per cent of the time. We learn fast. We have discovered how to telescope time.

For that matter, we have recently learned how to beat the insects at their own game. Maybe they can use tools pretty well, but we can use tools better. Insects can turn some of their six legs into tools. One of the legs may have a comb attached, another a pair of pincers to open flowers, others operate legs and mouth together, like needle and thread. Insects have their bits and braces, their hammers and tongs, but we are not dependent upon any single tool or set of tools. We have detachable attachments, whole tool sheds full of them. We keep on making new tools. If skin or scanty fur is not warm enough, we wear clothes or build fires, and in this way master the climate. Through agriculture and stock raising we lick the food problem.

Insects resort to fantastic adaptations to avoid extinction. Half of them are vegetarians, consuming between them every portion of entire plants, and the other half are meat eaters or worse. Sometimes it seems as if they are all monsters, and that we are even more grotesque monsters than they are. Within the past five hundred years we have been enlarging our sense organs. Up to the time when spectacles were invented, about 1350, an eye was an eye. After 1600 we learned to attach to the eye devices that could enlarge objects by several thousand diameters.

Thus we can make out minute things smaller than can be seen by the eye of the smallest insect. Likewise telescopes make our eyes infinitely more intense and farseeing. We can stretch the pupil of the eye 200 inches wide, and peer like a huge giant deep into the Milky Way or, if we like, we can put our two eyes a million miles apart and get a stereoscopic effect.

Dropping a coin in the telephone gives us a voice that shouts across the ocean and ears of such tempered acuteness that a voice can be heard just right, not too loud, not too soft, for a distance of a hundred, a thousand, or ten thousand miles. For hundreds of thousands of years our top speed was 11 miles an hour. When the horse was domesticated it shot up to at least twice that. The bicycle made it 50 miles. The train, the car, the motorcycle, the airplane, and next the rocket have given us the wings of an angel. By now legs and arms are tireless because we have turned their jobs over to machines. This catalogue of how we have been imitating and extending in all directions the behavior pattern of animals could be made much longer. Enough has been said to establish that we can outrun, outfly, and in general outperform any other organism, and since it is behavior or function that determines structure, it may truly be said that by now we are the most grotesque and possibly the most monstrous of animals.

One purpose of this brief and random sketch of animal life and of ourselves as a special kind of animal has been to show that behavior is a broad term, and that in studying human behavior we are studying a small but curious segment of a whole sea of behavior that has been going on all around us for some time. When psychology therefore undertakes to study not the human psyche (for ages thought to be different from anything found in animals) but human behavior, the whole picture changes. James falls in line with Franklin and Emerson, who are trying to bring man back down to earth. Only in James we get with a vengeance an entirely new addition—the animals. His human psychology gets to be comparative psychology. We have had to establish contact with the remote outer spaces of astronomy, with the heretofore unexpected backward reaches of time into an even remoter and obscure past, and now comes this strange new enlacement with the animals. To astronomical and geological there are now added biological vistas.

A new psychology is added to philosophy, and the first thing this psychology does is to tie us with a hundred links to the bizarre animals of today and yesterday. This business of getting to know the world we live in is not as simple as we have all along supposed it to be. But the leadership of our sages is firm. One after another they lead us down fresh lanes, and James, who talks so bravely of trail blazing, is in his psychology leading us down into strings of dungeons.

This newly discovered tie between human and animal behavior has one immediate indication: the aim of all behavior is first of all SURVIVAL. This is worth remembering. Was it not a kind of despair to say that only the soul could survive? Wait a minute! says James in his psychology. Let us take a second look at the whole of human behavior and see whether we may not have lost sight of the main purpose of it all. Human beings have learned how to survive thus far and how to get a great deal out of life. Why not go on that way?

Some of the animals have won their first round against nature and then seem to have come to a dead stop. Is that the best we can hope for? Pay your tribute to monotony and live in the narrow bondage of almost unvarying routine, like the ants and the bees—yes, that is one way, the way that the brainwashings and the "brave new world" seems to be heading for, but even among the animals there have been those that tried other ways, tried nobly and failed. We seem to belong to that kind. We want to go beyond coming to terms. We want to take nature apart and put it together again. We want freedom. We want the whole earth and the fullness thereof, plus what lies beyond.

The history of biology shows us that whenever in the past a species made sudden and tremendous strides—sudden in terms of geology—extinction was near at hand. Certainly it is dangerous to go all out in one direction. Certain fishes get flatter and flatter until they curl up and die. A tail gets to be sharper, turns into a sting, then a hair, and disappears altogether. As the reptiles get bigger they also become more unwieldy. The clumsy dinosaurs of yesterday have all, like poorly designed ships, foundered in the deep. Biological organisms all too often seem to be single-shot affairs. They meet one situation so well that the next, of an opposite variety, completely floors them. Because they found and staked all on one solution they seem to be prohibited from turning around and meeting another problem in a different way. Here is where our lack of specialization helps us.

William E. Burnham in his book on psychology tells the fable of an antediluvian school for all-around excellence, established for the animals, among whom were swimmers, climbers, runners, and fliers. Since the duck had short legs and could not walk very well, they practiced him on walking so long that he forgot how to swim. The eagle was no good at climbing a tree, so they kept trying to make the eagle climb, although he proved that he could fly to the top very easily. This was a demerit because it had not been done in the prescribed way. The ornithorhyncus got a prize because he was good at both running and swimming. But an abnormal eel with large pectoral fins who could run, swim, climb, and fly a little was made the valedictorian.

Julian Huxley calls our slowness to specialize *foetalization*. We remain a sort of semideveloped foetus longer than most animals. One fourth of our life span goes to growing up. And this is significant since it stakes much on teachability. Our next man, Dewey, is going to write whole books on this subject. Meanwhile, all told, we are a curious animal well worth studying, and there is much to be said for studying our behavior in the light of the behavior of other animals. Psychology, especially, has much to gain from this soberingly objective approach. The final question is not: are we superior, but can we survive?

By putting psychology on a naturalistic basis, and by venturing to say that this did not necessarily lead to fatalism or to pessimism, James made a stimulating contribution. But he did more than write a psychology. He took a look at the whole subject of our relation to nature from an entirely fresh angle when he began to discuss the subject of morality.

6. The Moral Equivalent of War

"THE LINE OF least resistance, then, as it seems to me, both in theology and in philosophy," says James, "is to accept that there is a God, but that He is finite, either in power or in knowledge, or in both at once. These, I need hardly tell you, are the terms in which common men have usually carried on their active commerce with God; and the monistic perfections that make the notion of Him so paradoxical practically and morally are the colder addition of remote professorial minds." James, as a psychologist, saw no reason why some form of superconsciousness might not develop elsewhere than in human heads. He frankly admitted that others seemed to have more direct access to this superconsciousness than he himself had, but throughout his life he maintained a warm interest in the investigation of what seemed to others occultism. Some of his scientific colleagues thought he was too credulous on this something more, something beyond the present tentacles of perception, the extrasensorial perception (ESP) of his day. After finishing, in 1902, his marvelous case book on religious believers, James summed it all up by saying: "They all agree that the 'more' really exists; though some of them hold it to exist in the shape of a personal god or gods, while others are satisfied to conceive it as a stream of ideal tendency embedded in the eternal structure of the world."

It is not important that James was human enough to keep a warm spot in his heart for some type of homely religion. It is not important that James was the champion of a sort of American God who is not all-powerful, but a co-struggler in shaping our ends, who welcomes our help as much as we welcome his. All this is perfectly in character and makes him all the more lovable, but what is important is the reverse side of this medallion. Nature is not implacable. It is not that monolithic rock against which all life is bound to knock itself to pieces. What is important is that fatalism has been discarded. James has learned to see the world as a wide-open process—one that does not close on man the gates of doom.

In the old days when a horse broke his leg they shot him. In the same way the materialists of a few generations ago condemned the world. Nothing could be done about it. But now comes James with his idea of the structural plasticity of the nervous system, and it seems to him that the whole world itself has a similar structure. Nature takes on habits, and seems not too hopelessly set in its bad ways. James might very well have got this idea too from Charles S. Peirce, who, as we shall see in the chapter about him, makes a great deal of this idea, but James, instead of analyzing the idea further, seems content to rejoice over it. He is so glad to get out of the slough of despond and back onto a land of some kind of hope that he does not question himself too closely on how he got there.

Nature is not human, but neither is it fiendish. It has its inhuman side, but part of animal life and even inorganic nature seems to be on the side of the angels: a wheat field waving in the wind, seams of heat-producing fuel buried in the earth, the loyalty of a dog to his master, the universal playfulness of young animals and the way their parents cherish them. About the single life nature is indifferent; yet terribly tenacious about keeping the species going. What a glorious invention is sex and how all-pervasive! Yes, nature does have plasticity or a tendency to go in different ways, and not all of its habits are unpleasant. There are thousands of things that James, the jubilator, could now begin to say about nature, but his time was short. He died in 1910, before the big wars started but not before leaving us a trenchant essay on the moral equivalent of war. It was almost the last contribution from his pen. There has never been any better idea than that of James. There cannot be any better. What he recommends is that we work out our warlike propensities by subduing and shaping to our ends that monstrous planet of ours, the earth, our barbarous mother, through whom we have access to the lifeblood of the universe itself. First Franklin wants all men to be scientists, then Emerson would turn them into naturalists, and now James proclaims a holy war of research against nature. Make your nervous system your ally, not your enemy, says James. Now he says treat the world the same way. Make nature your friend, not your enemy. And the point is: it can be done!

Scientists, of all people, realize that war goes on all the time, war against ignorance, war against poverty, war against disease. What has stood in the way of seeing this clearly is the general view that nature is always and everywhere our friend, that it is good to be "natural," whatever that means, and that going contrary to nature is always and invariably bad. This is much too simple and naïve a view of nature. It is like telling a man, Do just what you want to do and you will be all right. Let nature do just what it wants to do and we will be all right. No, No! Both nature and human nature need shaping, and the job is a tough one.

One of the big errors harking back to the days of Roman law is that human life must be patterned on natural laws. Exactly the reverse is often the case. We are born naked, but do we stay that way? From the first day of life the battle begins, a struggle for food, warmth, and shelter. We cannot just let go and be natural. Nature is not human. Perhaps it never will be. Perhaps there must be a rapprochement from both sides. As it is, a man jumping into the ice-cold water to save a child is just as liable to get pneumonia as anybody else. We call a certain powder good for roaches, but the roaches do not think so. And, remember, nature loves roaches too. We forget how very relative to human ends our human world still is.

In nature the species fight each other. Nature is the Old-Woman-Who-Lived-in-a-Shoe. Within the species there is sex and mother love. Within the human species there is all that, plus a cooperation of generation with generation in the heaping up of useful knowledge. It is almost as if men were created to show what really can be done with intraspecies harmony.

And then we spoil it all with war, internecine, fratricidal

war. Man must find, and find quickly, that moral equivalent of war. We have to promote human cooperation. It is our only hope. But when we promote human cooperation it is human life, not universal life, that we are developing. When we select the kindlier impulses of nature as worth following we are not doing so because they are a part of nature. We are doing so for purposes of our own. We are asserting ourselves. We are accepting nature's challenge. We are not blindly following nature. We are striving to lead.

Out of nature's world we can carve a world of our own. We must select, as we select in building our own character. We must develop what we find to hand. We are not born in a ready-made world, nor even in a world destined for some far-off divine event. The whole thing may go to pot. All we have is the raw material out of which we may shape something more lovely than nature has thus far succeeded in shaping.

All this is just a transcription of James. James the biologist turns into James the moralist. But there is a new note of almost natural savagery in his morality, not the savagery of slaughter but the savagery of pitting resolution against resolution. "Man, biologically considered, and whatever else he may be into the bargain, is the most formidable of all beasts of prey, and, indeed, the only one that preys systematically on his own species. We are once for all adapted to the military status. A millenium of peace would not breed the fighting disposition out of our bone and marrow.

"Man lives by habits indeed, but what he lives *for* is thrills and excitements. A deadly listlessness would come over most men's imagination of the future if they could seriously be brought to believe that never again . . . would war trouble human history. In such a stagnant summer afternoon of a world, where would be the zest or interest?

"The plain truth is that people *want* war . . . The born soldiers want it hot and actual. The non-combatants want it in the background. . . . War is human nature at its uttermost. We are here to do our uttermost.

"If now—and this is my idea—there were, instead of military conscription a conscription of the whole population to form a

certain number of years a part of the army enlisted against
NATURE . . . the military ideals of hardihood and discipline
would be wrought into the growing fiber of the people."

Of course, you don't really "fight" nature in the sense of
wanting to annihilate nature, but only in the sense that a man
who has to make a living out of a marginal New England farm
is fighting nature. Nature is immortally tough, and can't be
killed, but she can be explored, and she can make it plenty
dangerous for us as we try to wrest her secrets from her. Here
is true sport, the war of wars. Nature is a challenge. There
is "gold in them thar hills," but you have to dig for it, and if
not gold then uranium, or unlimited power. And while you
dig from time to time look upward, for the air too has in it
Hertzian waves and other things that we can use. We have
already wrested telephones and TV from the air, and that is not
much, you say, but who is putting any limit on additional things
that may be had? Certainly nature is not—that is the one big
point that James is trying to make. We live in a wide-open universe. Already we have bones, blood, brains, and inspiration—
why stop there?

The morality of James is inspirational rather than fully worked
out. Franklin insisted on character built around certain old-
fashioned virtues. Emerson deepened the picture by speaking
of a new kind of self-reliance now needed because our destiny
did not seem to be in the clouds but in a sort of heaven or
hell that we could make right here. Franklin piously left the
way open for "pie in the sky," but the quasi-gentle Emerson
bade us be of sterner stuff. And here we have James, in a
sense, beginning to dot the i's and cross the t's. The kind of
character we need is produced by habit formation. We get
inspiring details on how we can get habits on our side. Then
we learn that nature too is not so dead and hopelessly obtuse
as those old Puritans had thought who with Bunyan wanted this
world to go up in flames. Nature is our treasure trove. Here
lies our future. And what James says about the moral equivalent
of war is no more than just another hint: Mortals of the world,
unite! Pit yourself against the universe. There is a foeman worthy
of your steel, and the booty may be enormous.

7. Radical Empiricism

BETWEEN SPURTS of magnificent health and intermittent exhaustion James worked slowly ahead. After completing his 1,400-page psychology he girded himself for another similar effort in philosophy. But somehow he never pulled it off. He made brilliant beginnings, but, like Emerson, he was beguiled into giving popular lectures and then turning these lectures into books. But these were popular books, and not the deep solid effort that James felt was needed to put the new philosophy on its feet.

"I actually *hate* lecturing," exclaimed James in 1908, "and this job condemns me to publish another book written in picturesque and popular style when I was settling down to something whose manner would be more *streng wissenschaftlich,* i.e. concise, dry, and impersonal. My free and easy style in *Pragmatism* has made me so many enemies in academic and pedantic circles that I hate to go on increasing their number, and want to become tighter instead of looser. These new lectures will have to be even looser; for lectures must be prepared for audiences; and once prepared, I have neither the strength to rewrite them, nor the self-abnegation to suppress them." Two years later he died, still in the midst of brilliant skirmishes defending such comparatively shallow epigrams as "the truth is what works."

Let me not be misunderstood. I am not saying that a case cannot be made out for finding out what works, but the question is, whether in that case we should label our goal the truth. Is it the truth we are after or is it something that works? When a doctor diagnoses his patient's disease correctly and says that the patient has cancer, that is not the whole thing he is after. The truth is that the patient has cancer, but what the doctor wants is to get around the truth and cure the patient so that it will no longer be true that the patient has cancer. When we look for what works we are not just looking for the truth. James was inclined to get confused on this point. Dewey set him straight, and so did Peirce. They claimed that in his *Will to Believe* James was getting further and further away from his own philosophy and in so doing endangering the whole structure. Like the great Irish fighter that he was James enjoyed the ensuing battle, which often engendered a lot more heat than light.

The whole matter is easily straightened out if we remember that we may often be justified in adopting a belief *as a working hypothesis* when the truth of it has not yet been conclusively proved. There is more to it than that, but the man to straighten us out here is Peirce, not James. James was not a logician like Peirce, but James was right in the part that imagination can play in the framing of an hypothesis that later may turn out to fit the facts. Suppositions do play a part in scientific thinking, but to fight for unproved hypotheses just because we can't find the facts is to turn back the clock. James's excuse was that sometimes action was called for when there was not time to wait. There he had a point, but the point was a practical, not a scientific, one. The fact that quarterback decisions are sometimes necessary does not perforce make them right or true decisions. All this amounts to is that sometimes we have to take a chance.

Back of James's delight in defending a guess at the truth lay his warm, impulsive, and intuitive nature. As has been shown, James was fond of Renouvier, and James lived long enough also to read Bergson. He was almost equally fond of Bergson, and never allowed himself to say a word against Bergson who, it is well known, was inclined to reject intellect and rely on intuition instead. The emphasis here is on the word "instead." Bergson substitutes intuition for intellect. James never went that far, but neither did James succeed in working out a clear statement of just how intuition is related to the intellect. James did have a little more to say on this, as we shall see later, but for complete clarification it is necessary to wait until we get to Whitehead.

Enough that James in some of these things points to the region where others will find a path.

The strong points in James's philosophy which sometimes he calls not pragmatism but radical empiricism are three. First of all, James stressed relations. Offhand this means nothing at all, but in the light of an entirely new logic of relations by Peirce, the protopragmatist whom James draws upon, it gets to be significant. Anyway it is a good piece of metaphysics. Secondly, James fought the bifurcation of nature into the two separate worlds: of the scientist, on the one hand, and of the man in street, on the other. This too becomes more meaningful when we see what Whitehead later is going to do with this. Finally, James with rare insight, after rejecting the static ego, shows how it is possible for one portion of nature to get to know another part. This was a flash of pure genius because it showed how one could breach the wall between spirit and matter that heretofore had held these two so irretrievably apart. James brings about a pioneer union between spirit and matter.

These three points are enough to show that James was on the right track, and that if he had had the time he might have gone considerably further in giving more or less complete form to that bright new philosophy that he was seeking to establish.

Locke was the first to put real stress on the historic distinction between primary and secondary qualities. Colors, sounds, tastes, and smells, when we think of them as qualities of a substance, are secondary, that is, they are less inherent in the substance than certain other qualities. After all, part of the smell and taste is in us. It seems to be a contribution of the senses. On the other hand, extension, shape, and mass are really primary. Here Locke is beginning to put up a fence between the world outside and the inner world of the senses.

Science, says Locke, deals only with the primary qualities of figure, motion, and extension, or in more modern terms, vibrations and electrons. Somehow Locke begins to give the impression that only the primary qualities are real and the secondary ones illusory or subjective. Many a good scientist, following this lead, has proceeded on the assumption that he and his brother devotees by studying electromagnetic waves were studying the only world that really exists, thus widening the gulf between himself and the man of common sense. Locke's error aids and abets man's universal love of abstractions. Just as certain medieval mystics were happy to escape into a world of theological abstractions, so many a modern scientist is happy to escape into the abstract world of mathematics which Plato also found so pleasing.

Let it be said immediately and emphatically that James does not hold by this famous bifurcation of nature. He was much too human and too wise to concoct a philosophy with no room in it for sunsets or symphonies, for the cry of a child or the song of a bird. Yet he was also too good a philosopher not to tackle this problem in true professional style.

James was fond of identifying his philosophy with "the great English way of investigating a conception." With Bacon, Locke, Hume, and Reid he has many deep agreements. He ranks himself of their school. Hence the empiricism of radical empiricism. These men were all empiricists or believers in experience. Experience and empiricism come from the same Greek root meaning to try out. But James does more than parrot these empiricists. He supplements and extends their views. He makes empiricism more thorough. Hence he ventures to call his view a radical empiricism.

The English empiricists accept sensations but reject the relations between sensations, thus giving romantically inclined Germanic thinkers an opportunity to ascribe profound organizing powers to the human mind in uniting or categorizing these loose sensations. The English thinkers, says James, should have seen that the connections or relations come to us right along with and at the same time as the sensations, thus neatly sidestepping the German device. These relations or connections, the binding tissues of life, are not "links forged by reason" but themselves immediate sensations.

According to James, we receive "a feeling of *and*, and a feeling of *if*, a feeling of *but* and a feeling of *by*, quite as readily as . . . a feeling of *blue* or a feeling of *cold*." These connectives are what turn the loose pieces of experience into the stream of experience. As James puts it, "Relations of every sort, of time, space, difference, likeness, change, rate, cause, or what not, are just as integral members of the sensational flux as terms are, and . . . conjunctive relations are just as true members of the flux as disjunctive relations. This is what I have called the 'radical empiricist' doctrine in distinction from the doctrine of mental atoms which the name empiricism suggests."

Thus James classes himself with the great empiricists or believers in experience of English tradition, but submits their views to a major emendation which incidentally puts steam and motion into the whole scheme because it changes it into a dynamic process. To him experience is a steady flow or stream, a flux which goes on quite independently of whether we with our senses are there or not. We are lucky if we can survive amid this stream. It is our business to learn to select from it what we need for our own separate whirlpool.

At one time in his life James taught for a few months on the West Coast. One evening in San Francisco deep philosophical discussions ranged far into the night around the person and the views of William James. Among those present was Eric Temple Bell, the eminent California mathematician. Later that day came the famous earthquake. Encountering William James in the morning after the quake, safe and sound amid the ruins, Bell asked James what he thought now of those profound discussions that had so excited everybody the night before, and the disheveled James, looking at the flames and the still-trembling earth, replied: "Words, words, words, nothing but words."

Bell, the remarkable author of numerous scholarly but readable books on mathematics, is one with James in denouncing the type of romantic idealism for which he reserves the special name of numerology. No one outdoes Bell in his reverence for mathematics, but ever since the time of Pythagoras some people have been led to believe that the world is nothing but numbers. Extreme idealists resemble numerologists. All of us show an inclination toward numerology when we fall in love with simplified schemata and maps because they are so clear. We forget that no map can catch and hold the whole of nature. No matter how marvelously beautiful and intricate thought patterns may be, in the end they do not encampass life. Always there are emergents not entrapped by the cunningest of symmetries. The danger then is (1) we make the world conform to the beautiful and unchanging dogma or (2) we forget the world altogether and seek a personal escape into the world of dreams.

To abstract from the fullness of life and then to consider these abstractions fuller and richer than life itself has always been a human failing. It is a case of the green grass grows far away. Not content with exaggerating the worth of these abstractions we give them exclusive reality. Essence then precedes existence. If this tendency goes to extremes in any one individual, we recognize it as an aberration.

The normal type of human being, the type that admittedly has mastered the art of survival, sees things first and then gets ideas. But there occurs also a less usual type who gets ideas first and then sees things. In extreme or alcoholic cases the things are out and out hallucinations. Among primitives, men who see visions of what is not there may sometimes be accounted soothsayers or prophets. They are so different from normal people that as specially gifted persons they are given protection. At other times they may be stoned or otherwise put to death because they are just too queer. As a matter of fact, in nature any group of organisms which persistently saw visions instead of daylight facts would quickly in the normal course of events be wiped out. When men in certain historic periods pay too much attention to abstract and apocalyptic visions, the only thing that saves mankind from following them over the brink is a good thick dose of common sense.

Along these lines there are two errors that occur outside of the madhouse because they fall within the realm of what is considered fairly normal conduct. One is committed by the romanticists, who equate human and universal history. This opens the road to mass egotism. The other error is committed by the fatalist, who folds his hands, keeps his head in the clouds, and lets the world go by. If the fatalist is articulate he may pride himself on his stoicism or even preach defeatism or despair. Between the two extremes of romanticism and defeatism there sometimes seems to be no middle road. But there is, and at this point James comes forth with something that is neither a foregone fatalism nor an unjustified romanticism, but just plain hardheaded study of the interaction between man and his environment. Man is important and the world is important. The interaction between them is the real process of living.

This interaction breaks down the fence between the individual and his environment. As long as the ego is static and the world a show, solipsism stands just around the corner. Like St. Augustine, man can speak only to God. But now by hard and painful lessons man discovers the many new bonds that tie him to a little whirling planet, to a long process of geological ages, and to a vast host of lower but equally struggling creatures caught up in the same net, and it behooves him to work out a more mundane philosophy. The first thing is to drop the bifurcation. This will not be gone into further here because it is the basic preoccupation of a very great philosopher discussed later on. What James has to say on this subject is sound but elementary.

But also in James, as part of the effort to bridge the gap between man and nature, the knower and the known, we find that his view of the dynamic nature of consciousness and his view of the significance of relations dovetail together to give us the nub of a new epistemology. If consciousness as a substance is abolished and consciousness is made something else, what becomes of man, the thinking reed, the knower who knows? Here James has hit upon the theory of a neutral stuff in turmoil that constitutes the world, a single underlying ingredient that can play the double role of hammer and anvil, eater and food, knower and known. The same bit of pure experience can function now as the knower and next as the known. There is no impassable gulf fixed between the two. Nor between spirit and matter. Here truly philosophy is only just now undertaking some magnificently new beginnings.

William P. Montague, who heard James lecture, puts his finger on the origin of this newly unifying view. "Just as one and the same point can be a member of two or more intersecting curves, so, as William James pointed out (for the first time, I believe, in a college class which I attended in 1898), can one and the same object be a member of the independent order of existence and at the same time and with no disruption of identity be also an object of experience. By accepting such a view of the matter . . . we can escape bifurcation or epistemological dualism without falling into either idealism or panphysicalism."

For James, as for Edwin G. Boring and other eminent psychologists of pragmatic persuasion, consciousness itself is a relation, a movable and fluctuating relation between the living organism and its environment. Consciousness, as James says, is a function. It is not an object, it is not static, it is a relation. So is truth.

8. Facing the Situation

WHEN WHITEHEAD, the eminent mathematician and philosopher, took the place at Harvard University formerly occupied by William James, what did he mean by saying that James inaugurates the era of modern philosophy? It was not like him to say nice things just to honor a former occupant of his post. Whitehead was well informed on the march of philosophy both here and in Europe, and he in all probability meant exactly what he said. Scholars have heretofore made Descartes the first of the modern philosophers, but as time goes on they may stand corrected.

Future historians may consider that the modern age did not begin till 1900. This makes 1600–1900 the age of transition between the medieval and the modern age. We then get ancient, medieval, transitional, and modern, making Descartes the first postmedieval or the first transitional philosopher. Only with Einstein, nuclear physics, atomic power, and the exploration of outer space does the modern age begin.

Relativity with its strangely dislocating dimensions sounds the opening note of the modern age, to be followed almost immediately by the finding of the Heisenberg uncertainty principle at the very heart of things. It was because Whitehead was such an undisputed authority on all these matters that he could look a little deeper than others into the significance of what William James was adumbrating.

Since the days of Descartes there has been much painful growth. American philosophy begins with the first of three major disenchantments. Franklin first brought home to us what it meant to have the world decentralized and dwarfed by the joint machinations of Copernicus and Newton. Emerson also felt this but was more concerned with the second disenchantment, by which the span of human civilization became the tickings of a few late seconds on a timeclock that had been going for geological ages, producing this and countless other worlds. The biblical 4004 B.C. lost all its significance against this new unrolling of the scroll of time. It gave Emerson his chance to relocate the Day of Creation into the Present and to speak in a new way of Mankind in the Making.

It might seem as if the new facts concerning the age of the earth, summarized in Lyell's *Geology* of 1833, had ladled out a big enough dose of disillusionment to last mankind for some time, but worse was still to come. The facts of evolution had not yet been brought home to us. This was done by the humble but indefatigable Darwin whose *Origin of Species* appeared in 1859. What the Newtonian heavens were to Franklin, and the slowly developing geological ages of earth were to Emerson, the evolution of man, as pinpointed by Darwin, was to William James. William James began his career as an illuminator of evolution by lecturing on Herbert Spencer. Gradually he departed more and more from the vague generalities of Spencer by substituting for these the vivid realities and concrete instances set forth by Darwin.

So long as it was the heavens that exploded or the earth that suddenly grew incredibly old, man could in a measure retain his calm. But Darwin was the first to tamper definitely with our own pedigree. Other philosophers of the so-called modern age, even the mighty Kant, somehow always exempted the human race. Kant began with some strong scientific interests. He originated a nebular hypothesis around 1750. In his old age, in an essay on anthropolgy, he even hinted that man could have developed from an apelike creature; but it did not sink in. Much, much more spadework was needed before even the most scientific of men were really forced to face their ancestors.

But after another hundred years of cumulative research the whole thing burst wide open in the 1860's. We made a third major advance into disenchantment. The human race joined hands with the animals. To Aristotle women and slaves were in a sense lower animals that did not belong or that could not be built into a man's world except as accessories. That view was remedied, but the animals remained until yesterday the burden bearers of mankind or the objects of the hunt, whose flesh we ate without compunction. Then along comes William James, the philosopher of Darwinism, and first professional propounder of a sort of relativism in philosophy. The biological facts of evolution and the stream of life, embracing the animals, has to be absorbed by philosophy. And now we begin to get for mankind a new and truly modern outlook, characterized first and foremost by a deracination of which William James had felt the full effect.

Mankind so completely uprooted must either perish or seek a new beginning. To Whitehead the whole cosmos is a continual series of perishings and new beginnings, and that is why he pitched upon James as a pioneer who first fashioned a Noah's Ark in this new and swirling world.

In one of his lectures on the subject of Great Men and Their Environment, before the Harvard Natural History Society, James starts out by expounding the ancient view that all things hang together. This is still the view, among others of Herbert Spencer, but James next asks himself what is it that makes one century in the world's history so different from another, and one period in a nation's history so different from the next, and his answer is: "The difference is due to the accumulated influence of individuals, of their examples, their initiatives, and their decisions. The Spencerian schools replies: The changes are irrespective of persons and independent of individual control. They are due to the environment, to the circumstances, the physical geography, the ancestral conditions, the increasing experience of outer relations; to everything, in fact, except the Grants and the Bismarcks, the Joneses and the Smiths."

This way of tying up the fall of a sparrow with what happens in the Milky Way seems to James a myth. It fails to distinguish the two cycles of causation, a remote and a proximate one. "It was the triumphant originality of Darwin to . . . discriminate between the causes which originally produced the peculiarity . . . and the causes that maintain it after it is produced. . . .

Separating the causes of production under the title of 'tendencies to spontaneous variation,' and relegating them to a physiological cycle which he forthwith agrees to ignore altogether, he confined his attention to the causes of preservation, and under the names of natural selection and sexual selection studied them exclusively as functions of the cycle of the environment."

Pre-Darwinian evolutionists mixed the two causes. Lamarck and Spencer made the environment everything. The giraffe lengthened his neck by continually stretching up to get the leaves. "Darwin's first achievement was to show the utter insignificance in amount of these changes produced by direct adaptation, the immensely greater mass of changes being produced by internal molecular accidents of which we know nothing." Next, as James points out, Darwin asked: "Is the environment more likely to preserve or to destroy him, on account of this or that peculiarity with which he may be born? In giving the name of 'accidental variations' to these peculiarities with which an animal is born, Darwin does not for a moment mean to suggest that they are not the fixed outcome of natural law. . . . The great mechanical distinction between transitive forces and discharging forces is nowhere illustrated on such a scale as in physiology. Almost all causes there are forces of *detent.*"

The point is that we must accept the great men of history as data, just as Darwin accepted his spontaneous variations. A great man gives direction. What he does is like the decisions we make every day in our own lives. Whether a young man enters into medicine or business depends on some decision. Thereafter one road is closed. Nations the same way. "Every painter can tell us how each added line deflects his picture in a certain sense." Mr. Spencer attacks the great-man theory of history because he says it is vague. James does not agree. To him it is vague to invoke the zodiac to account for the fall of a sparrow. It is much better to look for Cock Robin with his Bow and Arrow. Many regions physically alike produce different nations. In mental life the genius of discovery depends entirely on the number of random notions and guesses which visit the investigator's mind. In short, Spencer overlooked chance; James stresses it. And this gives the world its novelty, a novelty of which even James himself by no means yet seizes the full import.

Darwin's stress on chance ties right in with the roots of James's philosophy which he called an empiricism "because it is contented to regard its most assured conclusions concerning matters of fact as hypotheses liable to modification." An empiricism is not a closed system. It is no more closed than experience itself is closed. It can be emended. It is a self-correcting system. Hence others can carry it on. At another place he calls it a "radical" empiricism "because it treats the doctrine of monism itself as an hypothesis. It does not dogmatically affirm monism." And anyone who does not affirm monism is a pluralist. Thus vanishes Spencer's monism in which everything hangs together with everything else.

"The difference between monism and pluralism," says James, "is perhaps the most pregnant of all the differences in philosophy. *Prima facie* the world is a pluralism; as we find, its unity seems to be that of a collection. . . . After all that reason can do has been done, there still remains the opacity of the finite facts. The negative, the alogical, is never wholly banished. Something —call it fate, chance, freedom, spontaneity, the devil, what you will," James finds is always left over. Quoting P. B. Blood, a gifted writer, James says the universe is "wild,—game-flavored as a hawk's wing." For James reason itself "is but one item in the mystery."

"The stronghold of the deterministic sentiment is the antipathy to the idea of chance. . . . I have already told you that 'chance' was a word I wished to keep and use. Let us then examine exactly what it means, and see whether it ought to be such a terrible bugbear to us. I fancy that squeezing the thistle boldly will rob it of its sting. . . . The sting of the word 'chance' seems to lie in the assumption that it means something positive, and that if anything happens by chance, it must needs be something of an intrinsically irrational and preposterous sort. Now, chance means nothing of the kind. It is a purely negative and relative term. . . . All you mean by calling it chance is that this is not guaranteed, that it may fall out otherwise."

This is just one other instance where, as James says, "Pragmatism unstiffens all our theories. Theories thus become instruments, not answers to enigmas, in which we can rest." Pragmatism is a method, an attitude, "the attitude of looking away from first things, principles, 'categories,' supposed necessities; and of looking towards last things, fruits, consequences, facts." Here we have it exactly. What James is describing is the method by which science operates, employing it piecemeal to parts of that pluralistic world that James looks upon as a collection. James is the first in this country to generalize into philosophy the methods of science. These methods themselves are not new, but in their wider application they are distinctly and devastatingly new.

Christiaan Huyghens in a Preface to his *Treatise on Light* (published in The Hague, Jan. 8, 1690), says "I wrote this Treatise . . . twelve years ago. . . . There will be seen in it demonstrations which do not produce as great a certitude as those of Geometry, and which differ therefrom, since the Geometers prove their Propositions by fixed and incontestible principles. Here the principles are verified by the conclusions to be drawn from them. . . . It is possible to attain thereby to a degree of probability which very often is scarcely less than complete proof. This happens when things correspond perfectly to the phenomena which experiment has brought under observation, especially where there are a great number of them; when one can imagine and foresee new phenomena which ought to follow from the hypothesis which one employs, and when one finds that the facts correspond to our prevision."

Thus in proposing to base philosophy on the methods of science James picks out a horse that has been in the racing business for a long time and has been steadily forging ahead. It is pretty safe to bet that James's philosophy is going to score additional wins. The name of that horse is Chance, but with determinism we had no chance at all.

James is in line with the modern trend of enlisting in the

establishment of a philosophy all the resources of man, not just his intellect. An animal caught in a trap may have to use his teeth to bite off a leg. Keeping even a tame rabbit in a room brings out latent tendencies. He begins to gnaw the legs off chairs, revealing the rodent part of him. The human situation has taken one desperate turn after another, and may take still more. So let us face the situation with everything we have, using, so to speak, the full human armamentarium. Franklin adds the hands to the head; Emerson, the heart; and now James teaches us how to use the entire nervous system. We must draw on that basic habit-building propensity that has served us so well before the head came into prominence, and that we may need again.

In this connection when it comes to discussing what kind of knowledge is furnished by "direct acquaintance with" James has some excellent *aperçus*. He distinguishes it from knowledge about, or inferences. Inferences are the business of the head, but what is this other direct knowledge, so beloved by Bergson, with which James also is flirting? In his *Tigers of India* James says: "There are two ways of knowing things, knowing them immediately or intuitively, and knowing them conceptually or representatively. Although such things as the white paper before our eyes can be known intuitively, most of the things we know, the tigers now in India, for example . . . are known only representatively or symbolically. . . . Exactly what do we *mean* by saying that we here know the tigers? . . . A great mystery is usually made of this peculiar presence in absence . . . I hope you may agree with me . . . that in representative knowledge there is no special mystery, but only an outer chain of physical or mental intermediaries connecting thought and thing. *To know an object is here to lead to it through a context which the world supplies. . . .*

"Let us next pass on to the case of immediate or intuitive acquaintance with an object, and let the object be the white paper before your eyes. The thought-stuff and the thing-stuff are here indistinguishably the same . . . and there is no context of intermediaries or associates to stand between and separate the thought and thing. There is no 'presence in absence' here, and no 'pointing' but rather an allround embracing of the paper by the thought." Here we have *scire, wissen,* and *savoir* replaced by *noscere, kennen,* and *connaître.* James notes that this "is less purely intellectual than the other." When a blind man touches an object his nervous system speaks to him directly about it.

James does not give us a full epistemological analysis of these two types of knowledge, and his immediate successors are inclined to rule out intuition, as a formal and separate source of knowledge, altogether, but Whitehead with full analytical apparatus comes to the aid of William James. In fact, that is one of the reasons—his grasp of intuitive knowledge—why Whitehead makes so much of James. He supplements James here, as others do elsewhere; so much is this the case that, before the story is over, the primitive pragmatism of William James is going to be like City Hall; it is going to have a whole city built around it.

Meanwhile the main points made by James are: (1) He keeps in all the facts; it's a thick world or nothing. (2) He breaks down the barriers between thoughts and things; the old Cartesian dualism here has its first encounter with the demolition squad. (3) Franklin is amply confirmed in his tendency to judge by deeds and not by words; results, survival values, are what count. (4) Emerson's hell and heaven here below is given its psychological foundation. (5) The way is open to a metaphysics and an ontology along lines set up by James.

John Dewey:
Promethean Instrumentalist

1. Cultural Heredity

PHILOSOPHERS CAN BE quite upsetting. Because they bring in new and disturbing views, they get under people's skins. One of the very first of them, Socrates, was accused of causing juvenile delinquency, and was forced to drink the hemlock. One of the very latest, John Dewey, was accused of the same thing. Although he lived a long time, it was fortunate that he died before they could get the cup to him.

Nowadays, when only half of us go regularly to church, it is no longer too dangerous to attack the church, nor do we any longer expect too much from the church. But the schools are different. We still go to school. Every one of us at one time went to school, and our children are all of them in school right now. Anyone who tampers with the school system is twisting our arm.

Some people blame crime on the home and some on the school. This pits the parents against the teachers. Obviously the teachers are in the minority. They get to be the scapegoats. We pushed the job of educating our children onto them, and what happens when they fall down on the job? Do we then take the children back and educate them ourselves? No, we continue to vituperate the teachers, especially their leader, John Dewey. William James had a soft spot in his heart for teachers and educators, but John Dewey somehow managed to become their patron saint, and all the sins of the teachers now fell on his head. We shall come back to Dewey the educator, but in this sketch we look at him first as a philosopher. Like Socrates, he taught youth by having something to say to them. What did John Dewey say?

First of all, he said that the brain is an instrument for biological adaptation. He was not called an instrumentalist because he played an instrument in the band, but because, as a philosopher,

he considered the brain, not primarily a receptacle but, like the
eye and the hand, a tool to help us stay alive. He told the young
to use their brains not for cramming or for prestige but for getting ahead and keeping alertly alive. Here he might have been
taking a page right out of Franklin, but he had also read James,
and so he looked at the brain as a biological organ. Like Franklin and James, he had a bias toward science. A synonym for instrumentalist is experimentalist, with an eye to experiments which
are the chief preoccupation of the scientist. Dewey preferred
that term. He tried to avoid calling himself a pragmatist, although, broadly speaking, all three terms stand for the same point
of view.

In the Preface to his *Logic* Dewey says: "The word 'Pragmatism' does not, I think, occur in the text. Perhaps the word
lends itself to misconception. At all events, so much misunderstanding and relatively futile controversy have gathered about
the word that it seemed advisable to avoid its use. But in the
proper interpretation of 'pragmatic,' namely the function of consequences as necessary tests of the validity of propositions, *provided*
these consequences are operationally instituted and are such as
to resolve the specific problem evoking the operation, the text
that follows is thoroughly pragmatic." After this paragraph he
leads into his *magnum opus*, and incidentally in this paragraph
he has given the reader a sample of his exact and logical style
which lacks some of the airy graces but none of the cogency of
James. Dewey is harder to read than James, but his thinking is
tight and his mind is strong.

Dewey agrees with Franklin, Emerson, and James that man
is primarily a doer. No one can sit still, do nothing, and survive.
Even the loftiest contemplation does not, as Franklin might say,
boil any parsnips. The brain is built to enter into a chain of action. It is a central link. The brain stands between the incoming
message and the outgoing response. To think means to receive
messages and transmit orders. It means coupling stimulus to action. No thought is completed until it has found an outlet in action. Thinking is an essential part of human behavior. Dewey
forged an unbreakable bond between thought and action.

It all went back to some basic, fairly recent, discoveries in neurology. Sir Charles Bell (1774–1842), a famous surgeon, found that muscles did not convulse when he not only touched but cut posterior nerve roots coming from the spinal cord, while a mere touch of the anterior roots caused convulsion of the muscles. He concluded that certain nerves transmitted orders to the muscles; others did not. This was one half of the discovery that there were two different kinds of nerves, motor and sensory. Later François Magendie (1783–1855) completed Bell's researches by lifting the incoming nerves with his scalpel and proving that they transmitted the sensations inward. Between the afferent and efferent nerves lay the spinal cord, on top of which is mounted the brain. Johannes Müller, in 1831, confirmed and brought together the Bell-Magendie discoveries. Here, then, we have an Englishman, a Frenchman, and a German all working together to establish a clear-cut picture of what later got to be known as the reflex arc, tying up the brain with the nervous system, and making it not just a receptor but also a transmitter. A message comes in and is switched to the appropriate muscles for the needed action.

As early as the 1830's it was known therefore that the nervous system has reflex arcs, some of them built in before birth, causing instinctive responses to stimuli. Between the nerve ends of the two types of nerves there may be a synapse, a spinal cord, or a brain. It need not come as a surprise that some sixty years later it became clear that in some sense the whole brain could be considered as a nodular enlargement of the top of the spinal cord. To us who are accustomed to telephone exchanges it appears as a commonplace idea. William James imported from Germany a very fine psychologist, Hugo Münsterberg to run the experimental psychological laboratory at Harvard. One of the first things Münsterberg did was to write extensively about the reflex arc. Pavlov in Russia was showing how reflex acts in animals could be conditioned. Food makes saliva flow in a dog. Always ring a bell when food is brought, and presently the ringing of the bell alone will cause the saliva to flow. This conditioning of responses is of immense significance to education, from the training of animals to the teaching of men. Some Russian psychologists of that early day stopped talking about psychology and spoke of reflexology instead. In America, following Pavlov, behavioristic psychology leaped forward. To all this John Dewey paid close attention. The approach to his philosophy is through the door of behavioristic psychology.

James's *Psychology* was published in 1890. In the *Psychological Review* of July, 1896, Dewey had an epoch-making article on the reflex-arc concept. In this article he reviewed and criticized current concepts of the reflex arc, not to do away with the idea but to strengthen it. He thought that not enough had been made heretofore of the homogeneousness of the whole combination which links stimulus to action. "The sensory stimulus is one thing, the central activity, standing for the idea, is another thing, and the motor discharge, standing for the act proper, is a third." What he wanted was that each of the three should be considered just a division of labor in the single task of adapting the organism to its environment.

Dewey referred to an illustrated discussion of the stimulus-reflex problem given by James. At the beginning of his *Principles of Psychology* James had two line cuts of a child stretching out its hand to touch a lighted candle. Said James: "We have a baby before us who sees a candle flame for the first time, and, by virtue of a reflex tendency common in babies of a certain age, extends his hand to grasp it, so that his fingers get burned." Here James had a picture of nerve currents, one going in from the eye and another going out through the hand. "If this were the baby's whole nervous system . . . we should have no alteration in his behavior, not matter how often the experience recurred. . . . But we know that 'the burnt child dreads the fire,' and that one experience usually protects the fingers forever. The point is to see how the hemispheres may bring this to pass." There was a second picture showing additional lines going from the reflex arc also to the hemispheres of the brain. The burning experience left a trace in the brain. James loosely called this trace an idea. Next time the child reached for the candle, that burning trace was reanimated. "The grasping will be arrested in mid-career, the hand drawn back, and the child's fingers saved."

It is this situation that Dewey discussed in the 1896 article. The ordinary reflex-arc theory had been fully accepted by

1896, but it still had in it survivals of the metaphysical dualism first formulated by Plato: sensation (mixed), idea (psychical), movement (physical). The S-R (stimulus-reflex) situation was still composed of separate and distinct segments, one of them mental and the others not. This, thought Dewey, made it too jerky and too obscure. It was a single and continuous coordination, the whole thing being circular, a change in a system of tensions, with the three elements nothing more than divisions of labor. The elements were distinctions not of existence but of function. A hen by touching the eggs with her breast triggers the brooding impulse. A chick sees the yellow kernel of corn, and, presto, picks it up and swallows it. The whole thing is a swift performance which soon gets to be an established habit. Human beings are always forming habits of this sort. A man turns from his bed, his feet hit the floor, and he starts walking. The true units of psychology are habits. The whole S-R operation is a single act. The knowing is a part of the doing. Repeated acts become habits.

When the child got burned it had a problem. The brain helped the child to solve that problem. Further details on how the brain was brought to undertake that function make up a good part of Dewey's work in philosophy.

Dewey may be considered a continuation of James. It is said that the Scottish philosopher Hume woke the German philosopher Kant from his dogmatic slumbers. After having read Hume, Kant did some vastly original work of his own. In the same way Dewey woke up after reading the two-volume work on psychology on which William James had spent eleven years, and in this psychology Dewey found a new beginning for his own work.

There are therefore two Deweys: one before he read James and the other after he read James. Darwin more than any other single man influenced James, and in Dewey this same influence continues. In Dewey the biological ideas of Darwin are further incorporated into philosophy.

Artificial breeding by which a rather colorless type of pigeon was changed into a number of almost fantastic varieties was one of the things that set Darwin to thinking that species were not fixed. They could be changed. The doves remained doves, but different doves. Dewey applied this basic idea to the human spe-

cies. Human nature too could be changed. This was the idea that
began to come out strongly in what James had to say about habits.
Human habits were not easy to change but it could be done.
Dewey considered the brain as an instrument for changing (and
improving) the human species.

After James had finished his psychological masterpiece he
wanted to do something equally grandiose for philosophy. It was
too late. It would have taken another lifetime to build up a philosophy from his psychology, but providentially Dewey appeared on
the scene. He took up where James left off. Dewey did get to
write that big initial volume that James felt was needed to get
the new philosophy on its feet. If the kind of thinking set forth
in the pragmatism of James was to prevail, the whole methodology of philosophy had to be made over. This Dewey tried
to do.

The work of Dewey is not just a continuation of the personal
views of James. James, like Darwin, stands not so much for
anything personal as for the extension of the methods of science.
To incorporate into human knowledge the new facts of biology
was the aim of Darwin. To deepen the methods of philosophy
by making them more biological was the aim of James. In this
Dewey followed him. The whole movement reinforced by these
two men was the movement of science, and the way they reinforced it was to build the new facts of biology into their
system of philosophy.

Modern geneticists, of whom Theodosius Dobzhansky is a
good example, distinguish two kinds of evolution: cultural and
biological. Biological evolution occurs when traits are transmitted by the genes; in cultural evolution the same thing happens by teaching and learning. Every man has two heredities:
biological and cultural. The changes brought about by biological evolution take many generations. Dobzhansky speaks of a
"widespread misapprehension that biology considers the genes
to be isolated from the environment and unchangeable by
external agencies. Nothing can be farther from the truth." There
are "mutant genes or mutations, and mutations are regarded as
the raw materials from which evolutionary changes are com-
pounded—by natural selection, by the process of sexual repro-

duction, or by other agencies." The agencies that produce these mutants, and then allow some of them to survive, operate with extreme slowness but they do operate.

In the other type of evolution the changes are not so slow. "The biological uniqueness of man lies in the fact that the human species alone has evolved culture. . . . Cultural evolution was added to biological evolution, just as biological evolution was superimposed upon the evolution of matter, cosmic evolution." Dobzhansky points out the basic difference between the two types of evolution: "Acquired cultural characteristics are transmitted; acquired bodily characteristics are not." It takes time for nature to turn a Pithecanthropus into a Homo sapiens; it also takes time to produce an educated man from an untrained child, but much less time, because in cultural evolution acquired characteristics are transmitted direct from father to child or from teacher to child.

In the lifetime of each individual there occurs that cultural evolution. In some it goes further than in others. It used to be thought, not so long ago, that only a few superior men could really be educated. Now education (at least a modicum of it) extends to all men. It is this cultural evolution, the part of evolution that operates by education, that fascinates Dewey. It is his one great preoccupation. In that broad sense Dewey is the philosopher of education.

"The second American revolution," according to Mortimer J. Adler and Milton Mayer, who mentioned it in their *Revolution in Education,* began on "July 28, 1868, when the Fourteenth Amendment to the Constitution enfranchized every male citizen." They point out that "in less than fifty years, from 1840 to 1883, school attendance increased 520 per cent. . . . In one decade alone, 1870–1880, illiteracy was cut in half. . . . For all the preceding centuries . . . no man had dreamed of an age in which all men would be citizens who had to be educated. . . . Never before have the men who thought about education had to think about educating a whole people."

There is a latent optimism in all this. One reason Darwin's doctrines seemed alien is because they introduced us, if not to a nature "red in tooth and claw," at least to a nature that varied spontaneously and impartially in all directions. If not giving mankind the cold shoulder, nature at least was showing man no partiality. Is this bad or is it good? It looked bad that acquired characteristics could not be inherited—the school of Lamarck could not believe it; they differed with Darwin on this point. But now it turns out that there is a way in which acquired characteristics can be passed on from father to son. One generation passes them on to the next—through education.

Nothing was more natural than that someone, early in the game after evolution had been accepted, should study with fresh insights this human way of passing on acquired characteristics through education. Animals cannot do it. We can. It was Dewey who made this new domain his special province. He became the specialist on cultural heredity.

The optimism latent in cultural heredity has a direct bearing on democracy. If education can spread to the ranks, there is hope for a government "by the people." It is hard to do anything about the genes, but something can be done about habits, perhaps even nature's habits. Through this newly opened door Dewey walks onto the scene.

2. The Green Mountain Boy

DEWEY LIKES to think of the human animal as a busy beaver who can and should go to almost any lengths, working day and night, to make the world a better place to live in. There is a sense of urgency and bustle about him. In this he is directly in line with his three predecessors. All give the impression of youthful energy and the pressure of a big task ahead. This is a contrast to the contemporary philosophers of Europe, who belong to different countries and do not have the feeling that there is a mighty nation back of them with a lot of steam of its own. All of Dewey's mentors, especially James and Emerson, feel they are speaking to a youthful and promising America. Dewey is the first to get a taste of world wars, but he retains his democratic zeal. There is no feeling that we have now been cut to ribbons and that it is time to throw in the sponge.

Franklin started a kind of strenuous and practical religion of civic improvement. He stressed that men should be judged not by sectarian beliefs but by what they could do in their new environment. In the New World, he found, we get along better if we fight less about religion and concentrate more on being good neighbors and on helping each other, which, incidentally, sounds very much like going back to a simpler and earlier religion of good deeds plus character formation. Then along came Emerson with very much the same idea except that he went a little further. What he said was that Franklin's system of looking at what you do and how you act, rather than at what you believe in the way of religion, is itself a kind of religion. And here comes the clincher: this new religion is exactly the kind of religion we need in a world where we can no longer stake our main hopes on the hereafter, but in which we have to make our own heaven or hell right here. Hence, too, more stress on character than even Franklin had given, for it is character that tips the scales between heaven and hell. A man must live with himself during his whole lifetime, so don't have it on your conscience that you did not do your best.

In William James we get more of the same. The strenuous note has not abated. Emerson had begun to stress the inner as well as the outer life, hinting that in this secularized form of religion it was more necessary than ever that a man have guts. How he strove, in the face of an ancient and crumbling metaphysics, to build up our self-confidence! William James did the same, basing his advice on personal experiences. He had felt the world rising up against him, and he told us exactly how he "overcame" that overwhelming anxiety of doom. James put a psychological foundation under the New World attitude of bustle and self-reliance. James showed that biologically this attitude was perfectly sound.

Now along comes Dewey, sharing with James the belief in a wide-open world, and taking up the problem where James left it. James was overconcerned with the individual. Dewey redresses the balance by stressing joint effort; and the best way to strengthen such joint effort is to raise the level of every participant by heightening his intelligence through education. In this he harks back to Franklin's attitude. Like Franklin he believes that the mind is an instrument for changing our environment for the better.

In Max Eastman's *Heroes I Have Known* the hero as a teacher is John Dewey. Max Eastman, one of the many who knew Dewey personally, contributes graphic glimpses of the man. Dewey, who believed in and practiced physical exercise, remained throughout life surprisingly agile and unaging. He astounded natives by swimming in a lake in wintertime. At the age of ninety in Key West in Florida he still got around to cocktail parties, absorbing sunshine and spreading homely good cheer.

He was an American boy who grew up in Vermont, keen for personal education, yet aware that it was not necessary at any stage in a man's career to go to Germany for postgraduate work. His instincts were right. He wished to remain ruggedly American. At Johns Hopkins, where he went after graduating from the University of Vermont to get his Ph.D., he ran into George Sylvester Morris, a teacher well versed in Hegelian philosophy. Morris took Dewey with him to the University of Michigan, where Dewey got his first job at $900 a year. Morris was a greatly beloved teacher. Dewey remained under his spell until he encountered the still greater influence of William James.

As professors go, Dewey rose very rapidly. After being assured on all hands that teaching philosophy was not a promising career, he moved in 1894 to the University of Chicago at $5,000 a year, and soon inveigled William Rainey Harper, who was better at getting money from other people than at giving it away himself, into increasing his salary to $7,000. Dewey had quite a family by that time. Three children were born during the stay at Michigan, and three more in Chicago.

Dewey's early life falls neatly into two ten-year periods: 1884–1894 at the University of Michigan (with one year out at the University of Minnesota); 1894–1904 at the University of Chicago. Thereafter he went on to an even longer career at Columbia University. The year he was at Minnesota (1888), George Morris died, and Dewey was called back to head the department at Michigan, putting him in line for an even more important post at Chicago. Twice the Deweys under tragic circumstances lost a child. While traveling with the family in Italy the two-and-a-half-year-old baby Morris died. Dewey never ceased to think that this baby, named for his favorite teacher, was the brightest child ever born on earth. Later another child, Gordon Chipman, contracted typhoid fever on the ship from Montreal to Liverpool when the family was on another trip to Europe. Again the loss of this child at the age of eight was a great blow to both parents, and when Dewey rejoined his family in Venice, they adopted an Italian boy, Sabino, of about the same age as the child they lost.

The general picture that emerges of Dewey is that of a family man not averse to having his children sprawl all over him while he petted them with one hand and wrote philosophy with the other, meanwhile keeping an eye on a highly successful experimental school full of other people's children at Chicago. Dorothy

Canfield Fisher says: "John Dewey's theories of education were evolved and written with one of his children climbing up his trouserleg, and another dipping his finger into the inkwell on his desk." She implies that this sturdy unsentimental Vermonter would perhaps rather die than say it direct, but that all his actions did say: I love children.

This befits the man who wrote the American Declaration of Independence for children, yet it would be entirely wrong to consider Dewey primarily as a father and an educator. He was a hardheaded, wide-ranging philosopher. Sidney Hook says: "Dewey carries with him traces of his Vermont social environment, not as memories but as habits, deep preferences and an ingrained democratic bias. Vermont shows itself in his simplicity of manner, his basic courtesy, freedom from every variety of snobbishness and matter-of-fact respect for the rights of everyone as a human being and citizen. His simplicity, directness, and complete lack of self-consciousness put even the shyest person at ease. His intellectual humility is so profound that it might seem to be the pose affected by a great man, were it not so obviously sincere—his sense of humor is beautiful, although a little unpredictable. A dry chuckle, a grin, a twinkle that lights up the whole face are its premonitory signs."

Dorothy Canfield Fisher, who has written a whole book on the *Vermont Tradition,* says that "the Vermont tradition is based on the idea that group life should leave each person as free as possible to arrange his own life." Vermonters are a fiercely unregimented lot. They love to disagree. Money to pay for Dewey's postgraduate education at Johns Hopkins came from the small savings bank account of an aunt. "The Deweys are Burlington people. I never knew them personally, never met John Dewey till he was an old man. But from our folk tradition, I am sure that Burlington neighbors thought the aunt was only 'acting sensible.' . . . That's what money's for, child." "The Vermont ideal," Mrs. Fisher continues, "is to treat people who work with their hands with as much, and as little, and the same kind of pleasantness as anybody else . . . the motto of noblesse oblige infuriates us." In other words, if a neighbor's roof catches fire, you help him extinguish the flames, and you are not sniffish about it. The only reason you help him is because your own roof is not at that moment on fire, and, if it were, and the situation were reversed, he would do the same for you.

Porteus, the sociologist, who made a study of Australian aborigines, remarks at one place that missionaries thought it strange that none of the natives said thank you when they were starving at Christmas time and the missionaries handed them food. These aborigines, constantly on the move hunting small and timid wild animals, have no property, no domesticated animals, they have not even invented the wheel, still living as they were in the Stone Age, but even to them it seemed perfectly natural that in time of need men share their food. This is not worth saying thank you about.

In that characteristic part of America known as Vermont, no one "orders" anybody. According to Dorothy Canfield Fisher, a Vermonter never "works" for anybody, he is just helping him out. "The Vermont farmer has a lot of folkways to avoid a drill-sergeant's way of issuing commands. He can say, 'What say we get the upper field plowed this morning?' Or, 'How'd it be to cultivate the corn while the good weather holds?' 'When I got up this morning, I said to myself, it's about time to get, etc., etc.' Admiral Dewey, born and brought up in Montpelier, at a great moment in history said politely, 'You may fire when ready, Gridley.' What is there so remarkable in that?" John Dewey was a "plain farmerlike old fellow," some of whose books "have been translated into Arabic, Swedish, Spanish, Czech, Chinese, French, Danish, Italian, Hebrew, Portuguese, Turkish, Hungarian, and Japanese—too many languages to list. . . . The New York Times calculated that at the time of his death his published works must have totaled a thousand . . . three hundred of these works were written after he 'retired' at the age of 70."

His father was a storekeeper, not above making up a showcard with a rhymed paraphrase on it to help him sell his own brand of coffee: "Lives there a man with soul so dead, Who never to himself has said, Give me to wet my daily bread. A cup of Dewey's coffee." His mother was a serious, warmhearted, well-read Vermont girl from a liberal family, but who later came under Evangelical influences and then got into the habit of asking her three stalwart sons embarrassing questions, such as: How do you stand with God? The big boys, playful as hound dogs, always treated her with great gentleness. The house was too big. Rooms were rented to students from the University of Vermont. To these Mrs. Dewey was as motherly as she was to her own boys, always offering them cups of hot chocolate and wedges of pie. She invariably had time to talk, and did not necessarily rush out for needle and thread every time she saw a rip in a young man's coat.

As to when and how Dewey wrote his philosophy later on when settled in a very busy life, it is perhaps overlooked that at Columbia Dewey had a desk within a stone's throw of his classroom, right in the hall, with a typewriter on it. After classes he stalked thither to tap out undisturbed the flow of measured thought that school and family contacts engendered in his brain. In his classroom he was much too polite and too gentle to impose his own views on his students. Almost it seemed as if he was always hoping to learn something from them instead. Any question anyone put to him was listened to with patience and answered in carefully considered detail. No one was ever brushed off. The great pedagogue took his own students very seriously. His inquiring and sympathetic mind could easily be led into bypaths far from his scheduled lecture. In his classes he went to any length to help the plodding student, being well aware that the bright ones got more out of his books. Therefore when the bell rang, and the voice of the lecturer stopped, the typewriter started clicking.

Dewey had not the eloquence of James, any more than Aristotle had the polished style of Plato. Was Aristotle's influence any less because his thoughts have come down to us in the form of crabbed lecture notes? There is something about the art of clear thinking that blasts its own way. The power to sustain singlehanded a truly cogent inquiry is so rare that the performance stands out like a Parthenon or a Taj Mahal.

Dewey made it a point to lecture not only at home but also abroad. He even toured and talked in Japan, China, and Russia. Thus his was a philosophy that flowed across national frontiers.

In spite of this his philosophy remained as American as jack rabbits and corn meal. In giving Dewey a degree in 1930 the University of Paris described him as "the most profound and complete expression of American genius."

The reason there is a certain amount of neglect and mis-understanding of Dewey and other leading American thinkers is not that these thinkers worked in out-of-the-way corners. As James was long the glory of Harvard, so Dewey was for many years a shining light at Columbia. It is just that, like the Greeks of old, Americans are inclined to take their original thinkers for granted. Just as the first appreciations in America of William James were reflections of what people abroad were saying about him, so now when we are beginning to see that other nations too can boost their scientific education to a point that puts us momentarily to shame, it is likely that what Dewey stood for in the way of promoting scientific education may come to be better understood. His significance will perhaps sink in.

Another reason why we neglect Dewey's own works is that they are hard to read. It is easier to take some one else's say-so on Dewey. Unlike Franklin, Emerson, and James, Dewey is not a stylist. However, there is one thing that he has in common with that old incomparable stylist, Plato himself, and that is that he can hang on to an argument. No one who reads Plato's *Dialogues*, not just one or two of them but the whole magnificent bunch of these intellectual swordplays, can fail to note that Plato had an unusually strong mind. This brain belongs to somebody who delights in human thought. One gets exactly the same impression from reading Dewey. Always he knows just where he is headed, and he burrows through till he reaches daylight. Like Plato, he seems above human turmoils, yet keenly aware of them. Bertrand Russell, not overly sympathetic to Dewey's style, after struggling through *Experience and Nature,* says: "It seemed to me after several rereadings to have a feeling of intimacy with the inside of the cosmos that I found unequalled. So methought God would have spoken had He been articulate but keenly desirous to tell you how it was."

Justice Holmes hit Dewey off in the same vein: "I would not miss the opportunity to express the profound respect for Professor Dewey that I have drawn from his writing. It seems to me that his insight into the movement of the universe as it shows itself to men goes to as high a point as has ever been reached by articulate speech." Jane Addams thinks that "although Dr. Dewey is not easy to read, nor, in the Chatauqua sense, a popular lecturer, through the conscious use of his luminous mind he has made over for thousands of people the connotations of the very word philosopher."

What was there so different about Dewey's philosophy? Perhaps Joseph Ratner, compiler of the Giant Modern Library volume of excerpts from Dewey's philosophy, puts his finger on it: "But for a philosophy which encompasses every important intellectual and cultural activity to end, as well as begin, with the world of everyday life is altogether novel, an achievement unique in the history of thought." Ratner is forgetting William James, who also did that very thing; in fact Dewey is an extension of James, and it is quite characteristic of American philosophers that they do not get too far away from everyday living.

"A belief in intelligence and in individuals fully themselves and freely sharing their lives—this is an old and a deep strain in the American tradition," says Irwin Edman: "Dewey restated it in terms of a machine age." A similarly simple definition of American thinking as exemplified in Dewey we owe to James Harvey Robinson: "The chief function of philosophy as Dewey sees it, is to show us how to think and talk in a profitable manner conformable to the information we now have (which should constantly be increased) about ourselves and our world." Dewey was born in 1859, the year Darwin's *Origin of Species* was published, and he died in 1952.

3. The Quest of Certainty

To THE Greek philosophers, seeking a first foothold in human speculation, Dewey gives prolonged scrutiny. Their views prevailed until almost yesterday. In a profoundly revealing analysis Dewey spans the two thousand years between us and them, showing how their quest differed from ours. No one brings out with quite the crushing force that Dewey does, how the Greeks craved one single thing—certainty. The Greeks themselves and, since the days of the Greeks, almost all mankind has been engaged in a quest for certainty. In a changing world the Greeks looked for something that did not change. They looked at the changing world and in their mind's eye saw a single underlying substratum. Thales thought it was water. Others came out for air, or earth, or fire; Empedocles, for all four which by Democritus were simplified to atoms from which all elements were made up. Thus the world was anchored in something firm. Occasionally a man like Heraclitus messed things up by saying that if the earth is fire then the whole world is constantly consumed. Everything being in a flux there is only becoming, not being. But his stripe did not win the day. Out on top came men like Parmenides and Plato, who declared for the eternal and the changeless.

For two thousand years now, says Dewey, we have been under the spell of that dominant Greek attitude which identified knowledge with what was stable. The real world for Plato was the world of ideas. Aristotle made them forms. All through the Middle Ages men never stopped trying to find a firm rock to which they could cling as to a refuge. Aristotle became the official philosopher. In a convincing way Dewey argues that even today all idealists and many realists still follow the Greek pattern of searching for a certainty that never changes. Dewey's philosophy comes in monolithic blocks and this thesis of a former quest for certainty is one of them. He presents this thesis in tremendous detail. About all one can do is paraphrase the central argument. There is no possible doubt about its drift. Dewey considers the switch from a quest for certainty to the acceptance of a changing world one of the great events in human civilization.

At bottom this part of Dewey's philosophy is a critique of Greek and medieval abstractionism. Men substituted a simplified map for the varying landscape. They lived with their eye on that map, dreading the wicked world, ready, like Bunyan's Christian, to flee the wrath to come.

The spectator's view of knowledge and a preference for the changeless go hand in hand. To Plato the philosopher is a spectator who watches the fray. Slaves do the work. The philosopher is a gentleman of leisure thinking high thoughts. Certainty he finds where the Greek mathematicians found it, in the realm of eternal, immutable Being. The knowledge of things that change is bastard knowledge, mere opinion. Real knowledge is of Being. Euclid's geometry and Aristotle's logic are both based on this static view of knowledge. It need hardly be said that this view goes directly counter to the American view that thought is action. However, this modern view has not yet permeated our bones, and the next point that Dewey makes is that science itself is still in a transition stage.

Modern science, which emerges with Galileo and Newton, is still more than a little imbued with that same hankering after immutable Being. In spite of the fact that Newton found in the calculus that he invented an effective means of engaging in the detailed study of motion without first stopping or killing it, the revolutionary and philosophical significance of his laws of motion did not sink in. However, in the two hundred fifty years succeeding Newton, constituting the transition age, acceleration, restless energy, and relativity have more and more come to occupy the center of the stage, obsolescing the Platonic and medieval preference for static certainty, and at the same time upsetting deeply rooted habits and attitudes. The spectator view was a very comfortable one. It began by ignoring slavery and sidestepping many of the real problems of democracy. Escapism ran riot. Pampering human helplessness, some of the extensions which Christianity built on top of Platonism ended by giving up altogether the world of the flesh. It left to a supernatural agency the task of transplanting man into a glorified world. The same trend, changing the factors, has occurred in other religions stressing transmigration or nirvana.

The scientific version of otherworldism is to look askance at the changing and variegated secondary qualities that mean so much in the personal life of each of us, and to stress instead, as the only genuinely real things, those ghostly dancing electrons. This view tries to look at what electrons ARE and not what they DO. It seeks a Being back of the Performance. The average man feels uneasy in the presence of science because, in spite of its magical gifts in the way of technical improvements, science takes away the common world. The scientist, like the medieval mystic, disbelieves his own eyes. Now that is all right up to a certain point. The man in the street knows by now that the sun does not really rise in the east, but he also knows that the sun gives him a sun tan and grows his grain. What, pray, is the metaphysics back of all this scientific activity that makes our daily living so much more comfortable and at the same time smashes all our outmoded otherworld dreams as it threatens us with the vast silences of death and doom?

Here Dewey and all the Seven Sages form a solid phalanx in refusing to pamper men any further. This is a stern world. It puts us on our mettle. The present world is not hopeless, and there can be joy in striving to make it better. They bring us back to our rightful task here on earth. They—especially Dewey —cast before our feet a mighty challenge to make over the world. Is this sheer arrogance or does it make sense? Should we give way to despair and anxiety, disdaining a thorough examination of how malleable the world may really be? Let us at least get interested in what works and what does not work. Does leaving everything to fate work? Does it work to say that nothing any man can do can possibly make a difference? Even a worm does something. He turns up the soil and quite unconsciously helps man with his crops. There is certainly something a much more highly gifted animal such as man can do, and this is Dewey's point. Philosophy is a reconstruction.

Dewey, James, and Peirce all say: Get off the spectator's bench and join in the fray to make the world a better place to live in. Who knows how far we may go? Do not overstress ideologies—any more than our forefathers did in the days of the American Revolution. It is our business to try to get earthlings of contrary views to work together. Men of different outlook can learn to work together, as our own thirteen original colonies abundantly proved. In Dewey we get a continuation of these early beginnings. He champions a far-reaching method of inquiry in which science and philosophy join hands.

Modern science takes seriously the study of change. Newton's world of billiard-ball atoms, separated in space and time, ruled by unchanging mathematical laws, endured for two and a half centuries. Now it is crumbling. Newton was still operating on the Greek formula of a search for the eternal and immutable. Einstein reinstated change. He shifted the emphasis from the theoretical structure itself to an operational basis calling for laboratory and experimental testing of that construction.

In the old view what you begin with had to contain all that follows. Hence those elaborate cosmogonies. Instead, Dewey, interpreting the new view, would have us begin with the gross and macroscopic world of the senses and then institute a controlled inquiry. This inquiry is a continuing affair. It centers about events, not objects. More events are happening every day. There are discoveries, new insights, and fresh correlations. Our stock of verified information keeps growing. Each new success gives the key to still others. We are committed to a philosophy of experimentation. Some say that this is like a study of perpetual motion, a contradictional absurdity. Naturally a static world would be easier, but we do not live in a static world. It is easier to plan a graveyard than to direct the traffic at Times Square, but must things always be easy?

What we are doing in these paragraphs is to give a free paraphrase of Dewey's ideas regarding the quest for certainty, in which he sets up an illuminating contrast between the ancient and the modern world. It is admitted that he does not give us an easy philosophy. Challenging tasks confront mankind, and there is no certainty of success. Gone is the comfort of eternal verities, maintaining that what was true yesterday is true also today.

And here Dewey comes to another point: the solutions of one age are not necessarily the solutions of the next. At one time it was perhaps a good thing that men learned and practiced the warlike arts. At least there were decisions of some sort and the decisions were not fatal to mankind. The hydrogen bomb has changed this situation. Slavery was at one time a blessing. It was better than killing prisoners of war. Perhaps slavery was the only way in which habits of work could become ingrained. After the collapse of the Roman Empire, which after all was an extension of the Greece of Alexander the Great, we may have needed a period of stabilization, lest we disappear altogether. But what is good for one period is not necessarily good for the next. Babies do not lie on their backs all through life. Mankind, too, matures. Rules and regulations for an agricultural world do not necessarily apply to an industrial world. The atomic age is different and needs a different philosophy.

All this is well and good, but are there not even in a changing world some principles that remain always the same? Does change have any meaning except against a background of stability? The answer would be no if the Aristotelian logic of substance and attribute still held in a dynamic world. Dewey himself started life as an adherent of the logic that culminated in Hegel, who in a seesaw dialectic offset Being against Becoming. Dewey dropped all these shackles when he became a convert of James. Shedding his Hegelianism, Dewey became an experimentalist, adopting the methodology of experimental science. Science, long wedded to invariants, has recently had to admit that *everything* is relative. Change means something even if everything changes. The things which in a static world were supposed to stay as firm as the Rock of Gibraltar now turn out to be assumptions, or man-made points of view of relative import. Even principles, basic principles, including laws of nature, slowly change. This is an age in which even the law of gravity gets a new interpretation.

In practice we are quite accustomed to dealing with entities that never seem to be for two consecutive minutes quite the same—a little child, for example. Were the people of the Middle Ages unaware that the world is dynamic? They knew that everything seems to sprout from a seed and change from the day it is born. But here Aristotle, the virtuoso and unparalleled maestro of logic for two thousand years, had a trick up his sleeve. The acorn being an oak *in potentia*, the substance or gist has been there from the start, only the form changes. His logic permitted a sort of preformationist evolution. The real revolution in modern thought has been the rejection of Aristotelian in favor of a functional logic. More about that when we come to Peirce and Whitehead, but Dewey made a beginning. It is not substance but function that scientists study today, and no one has done more than Dewey to get that spirit of science out of the laboratories and into public life. Science is problem solving, and problems are not limited to those encountered in a laboratory. This section deals with the quest for certainty but it dovetails with a later section on the theory of inquiry in which Dewey rewrites the technique of human thinking in terms that make it applicable to modern social problems. Dewey sees unlimited possibilities in the scientific method, and to blame Dewey for our present unpreparedness in scientific education is like blaming the sun for putting out your reading lamp.

Sometimes in reading Franklin, satisfying and many-sided as that delightfully worldly sage can be, one wishes for a little less glibness about some of those deeper beliefs that Franklin passes over so lightly. "I believe I shall, in some shape or other, always exist. . . . The Scriptures assure me that at the last day we shall not be examined on what we thought, but what we did." And that self-penned epitaph—in which he refers to himself as "an old book, discarded, yet the work itself shall not be lost, for it will appear once more, in a new and more beautiful edition, corrected and amended by the author"—is sheer poetry.

So along came Emerson, as delightfully, if less flippantly,

sweeping away altogether an external heaven and hell and, like Franklin, urging men to make the most of themselves here and now. Franklin said: Trust in God, and keep your powder dry. Emerson said: Give all to love, but keep yourself free as an Arab from your beloved; but he too is still too much of a poet, as is James, when he joins Emerson in a witches' Sabbath of enjoyment of nature at the end of which he understands what a poet is. Compared with these, Dewey, the dour Vermonter, is a sobering philosopher, always in shirtsleeves, and never, even for a moment, donning a kimono. And yet Dewey does not supersede or even negative these men; he merely supplements them in a way called for by the times. Retaining the practicality of Franklin, the deep fervor of Emerson, and the scientific bent of James, Dewey girds himself to face a nature having in it no ministering angels other than such as we can be to each other. Man stands alone on a self-made platform of shifting principles. Does this mean that he negatives all optimism? Does he abolish the hopefulness of his predecessors? By no means. They have been preparing the human mind for just this situation into which Dewey is the first to look from the depths of two world wars.

As life gets more complicated, so do the tools by which we deal with it. But does the automobile abolish the wagon? Does not a truck do what a wagon used to do and do it better? Men struggle with the transportation problem, and when we now fly things by freight, no one should say that the oxcart stands condemned. It stands improved. "Sixty years ago you told us that atoms were hard, indivisible, and unbreakable, made perfect in the beginning of things, and persisting in unworn perfection ever since. Today you tell us that atoms are loose structures which can be very easily broken. . . . Your accepted theories of one generation are abandoned in the next: how can I be sure you are right this time?" This is E. N. da C. Andrade, a renowned physicist, speaking, trying to reconcile lay readers to the swift changes in modern science. The answer, as Andrade so forcefully points out, is that science does not claim finality. When the jet takes the propellers off the planes, we are still only tinkering with our wagon. The world keeps moving and science tries to keep up. Brains keep on absorbing, heeding, and learning things they paid no attention to before. We discard, with regard to atoms, a theory scarcely sixty years old, as we discarded one by Democritus which was over two thousand years old. And yet, even these oldest views are not so much annihilated as just made over and rendered more adequate. When a child's shoulders grow broader, his coat must be enlarged. Dewey calls philosophy a constant reconstruction.

"I sometimes think that the entire inwardness of James's personal and philosophical being was his warfare against absolutisms and all that they imply," says Horace Kallen in a piece written in commemoration of William James, and in the same way Dewey fought these same absolutisms. He refused to close his system. Revisions must be expected and welcomed when they come. James uproots the whole of past psychology to make room for a dynamic view of human consciousness. Dewey similarly uproots the static universe. Does this rob us of our security? Does a spinning world, streaking through space, amid the other whirling dervishes of an expanding universe, disturb our daily walk? Go to the ant, thou sluggard in thought, or to the bee flitting from flower to flower, with no thought for the morrow, and keep at it as they do.

Aristotle identifies first philosophy or metaphysics with theology or a knowledge of the heavenly bodies which are gods. These give us the realm of first reality, the realm of true being, quite different from the realm of change. But now Aristotelian physics along with his metaphysics has gone into the discard, and we tackle a world of constant change. Dewey prepares the way for this. He does not give us a metaphysics. Santayana will start that and his successors will continue it, but Dewey gives us the methodology of thinking in the new way, and the root of it is that instead of dealing with static schemes or even with substances we now deal with changing problems. Even to formulate these problems is difficult, but Dewey gets the new formulations off to a good start. Setting up new oracles at Delphi, we force nature to give us the answers.

For us existence precedes essence. This is going to require a logic of change, and Dewey is prepared to provide us with one. What we get in Dewey is the end of the worship of certainty and the beginning of a logic as well as a metaphysics of change. This means the acceptance of an unfinished world, not all present even *in potentia* at the beginning, and not predetermined by any means even now. The new gospel is that in the shaping of this world man can have a hand.

4. The Social Element

DEWEY IS a big man who thinks along big lines, and who presents his thoughts in monolithic blocks which, put together, constitute the solid framework of his philosophy. There are no brief summaries in Dewey. There is no short cut to his system. His views are presented in somewhat ponderous volumes each of which constitutes, so to speak, a wing of the entire structure. There is, however, one all-pervasive feature of Dewey's thinking to which no single large volume is dedicated; I am referring to the social element in his thinking.

The nearest he comes to giving it a separate volume is in his *Individualism, Old and New*, published in 1930, after the first war and with the depression coming on. First one world war and then another with a depression between have confirmed in Dewey a tendency, exhibited from the start, of never thinking of an individual in isolation or apart from his fellow men and the large movements that sometimes like a tide engulf the individual. Dewey speaks of "the tragedy of the 'lost individual.'" Individuality "is not something complete in itself, like a closet in a house or a secret drawer in a desk, filled with treasures that are waiting to be bestowed on the world." Dewey stresses that individuality "develops into shape . . . through interaction with actual conditions."

Something new has been added to the outlook of philosophers since James, who died in 1910, gave voice to an ardent personal individualism. An ineradicably social outlook has been forced upon mankind by the sweeping events that followed 1910. "We may then say," says Dewey, "that the United States has steadily moved from an earlier pioneer individualism to a . . . tendency to combination in all phases of life." It is not just wars and depressions that have forced individuals into new and tighter combinations but it is our whole economy. "Anthropologically speaking," says Dewey, "we are living in a money culture." It has been a long day since we were a nation of isolated farmers and small villages. Dewey speaks of the "dominant corporateness." "At present the 'socialization' is largely mechanical and quantitative." People are herded together, caught in the coils of factory systems and the great enterprises of transportation and communication. Socialization not only proceeds normally but gets out of hand as when men are swept into armies or lashed by depressions.

"Because of the bankruptcy of the older individualism, those who are aware of the breakdown often speak and argue as if individualism were itself done and over with." In the face of new social conditions, self-assertion of the pioneer type is unavailing. "What is the effect upon the self-respect of the large classes of men and women who periodically, once in so often, find themselves in large numbers thrown out of employment, and find that they have to beg, not for charity, but for even a chance to do work . . . ? The undermining of confidence in oneself, of respect for oneself, the undermining of faith or belief in the world and in others . . . is I think impossible to overestimate. When people find that they cannot do things that they are capable of doing, the attitude that comes toward the world is either one of impotence or enfeeblement, or else one of bitterness and hostility."

Dewey can no longer consider the problems of the individual without taking into account the social element. Anyway the whole trend of the man is to think in terms of the entire nation or even of world movements. Large vistas preoccupy him as when he compares the static quality of the entire ancient and medieval world with modern dynamism. In this he differs from the narrower intensity of James. In fact one might say that just as James turned the personal ego from a static substance into a dynamic flow of individual consciousness so Dewey does just that to the whole world. Today the dynamism of a universe of vast energies, by penetrating the consciousness of the people on this little planet, is bringing about mass movements and mass responses. The tight web of communication, the swiftness and ubiquity of travel, the heightened awareness of others, is making hermits, monasteries, and voices crying in the wilderness extinct. That new and all-pervading social element speaks out from every page in Dewey. This makes Dewey primarily the philosopher not of individual problems but of social reconstruction.

I think, though, there is another reason, which began to operate early in Dewey's career, that accounts for much of his bias toward construing personal problems in social terms. A close friend of the Deweys in the Ann Arbor days when Dewey was at the University of Michigan was George H. Mead. Mead had just taken his first job there as an instructor of philosophy. Like Dewey, he was a devotee of James. In fact for a while Mead tutored the James children. He was so enamored of James that he had to go to Harvard to do his postgraduate work under him. George Mead accompanied Dewey to the newly founded University of Chicago, where they worked together like soulmates. In Chicago they lived in the same apartment house. The children of both families for a time grew up together.

Although Dewey left to go to Columbia, Mead stayed on at Chicago, where he died in 1931. James speaks fondly of the "Chicago school" of Mead and Dewey which is doing such good work in pragmatism. At Chicago Mead was a beloved and greatly revered teacher, but such a brilliant talker and so continually revising his own ideas that he never got around to publishing very much, but after his death students and colleagues collected enough material from Mead, chiefly lecture notes, to make four books.

In a biography of Dewey written by his daughters there is an account of the close relationship of the Deweys and the Meads. "The older children of the two families are nearly of an age and close family friendships were quickly established, the Deweys visiting the Castle home in Honolulu from which Mrs. Mead had come. The Meads remained the closest friends of the Deweys, even after the removal of the Deweys to New York, until their deaths. Since Mead published little during his lifetime, his influence on Dewey was the product of conversations carried on over a period of years and its extent has been underestimated."

Between these two men there was established in a sense a division of labor. Mead was working backward from James into social psychology in a way that fascinated Dewey. The results of Mead's highly original researches into the social origins of self-consciousness were taken over *in toto* by Dewey and incorporated into his basic thinking. To continue with the description given by Dewey's daughters: "Mead's scholarship, especially in the natural sciences, was much greater than Dewey's. In the years of his association with Dewey, Mead's principal interest was the bearing of biological theories upon scientific psychology. . . . Mead had also developed an original theory of the *psychical* as the state occurring when previously established relations of organism and environment break down and new relations have not yet been built up; and, through inclusion of relations of human beings with one another, a theory of the origin and nature of selves. Dewey did not attempt a development of these special ideas, but he took them over from Mead and made them a part of his subsequent philosophy."

Mead's discovery of "the origin and nature of selves" is worth looking into more closely because it is the basis of Dewey's stress on the social element in knowledge and in the development of the individual. Mead believes with James "that the diameter of the self waxes and wanes with the field of social activity." Learning is not a mere conditioning of reflexes. Mead agrees with Freud "that we do our thinking with minds that have already an organized structure which determines in no small degree what the world of immediate and reflective experience shall be," but, again, this is not a mental organization in the sense that Kant supposed, but rather in the sense that rational conduct grows out of impulsive conduct. Behavior arises from impulses or congenital tendencies to react in a certain way. These impulses are not merely biological, but also social in character. Organisms are always seeking and interpreting or reacting to stimuli. We are by nature active. Just as an ox may be said to endow grass with the character of food, so thought may be said to endow certain parts of the world with meaning.

Mead with his biological training was inclined to think that it was not our upright gait, our prehensile hands, our flexible vocal powers, or even our gigantic cortex, but rather the fortunate combination of all of these which gave each of us a self apart from our fellow men to recognize as our very own. When man became self-conscious he crossed a barrier that has stopped all other animals. A horse standing forlornly in the rain does not think, "Here am I, a poor horse, out alone in all this weather." The bees in a busy hive do not think, "What clever little fellows we are!" Animals have done much, but they have never accomplished that peculiar twist of becoming reflexively aware of their own individualized existence.

We ourselves managed it not through hard work but through play—almost accidentally, as it were. In the great long-ago of prehistory there were social games in which there were gestures, cries, and finally an individual consciously playing a part. No one has ever described this debt that the self owes to others, his playmates and companions, in quite the detailed and convincing way that Mead managed to do it. Everything we are we owe to our fellow men. The soil in which a self first sprouted is that common ground of primitive communication between us and our fellow men. Without communication there is no awareness of self. Without others there is no self. Other animals occur in droves just as we do, they vocalize and gesture, yet we are the only ones who have developed an inner organization, poetically referred to as "man's unconquerable soul." Within that group of gregarious, chattering animals which constituted our remote ancestry sounds were for a long time just animal cries, significant only in the effect they had on others, like the crowing of a rooster or the warning cry of the mother hen. Then came a stage in which protoman began to look upon himself too as a member of the audience. This is the stage to watch. Once he learned to talk a little, he was bound also to start talking to himself, which is another name for thinking.

According to Mead, the conversation of gestures is the intermediate step between impulsive behavior and language. "Gestures become significant symbols when they implicitly arouse in an individual making them the same responses which they . . . arouse . . . in other individuals." It is a fortunate circumstance that we can hear our voice the same as the other fellow does. We cannot see our facial gestures as well as he can, but we do hear our own voice. Meanings emerge in social experience just as colors emerge in seeing. "Conscious communication develops out of unconscious communication within the social process; conversation in terms of significant gestures, out of conversation in terms of non-significant gestures; and the development in such fashion of conscious communication is coincident with the development of minds and selves with the social process."

The self is built up of the attitudes which others take toward our acts. Taking and understanding the attitude of the other fellow builds up a composite self of your own. Understanding others is something we have to keep on doing. We have here an interaction resembling teamwork in a ball game. Discipline of self follows naturally when we understand the role of the other fellow. "There is neither 'I' nor 'me' in the conversation of gestures; the whole act is not yet carried out, but the preparation takes place in this field of gesture. Now, in so far as the individual arouses in himself the attitude of others, there arises an organized group of responses, and it is due to the individual's ability to take the attitudes of these others in so far as they can be organized that he gets his self-consciousness. The taking of all of these organized sets of attitudes gives him his 'me'; that is, the self he is aware of."

"It is often assumed," said Mead, "that democracy is an order of society in which those personalities which are sharply differentiated will be eliminated, that everything will be ironed down to a solution where everyone will be, so far as possible, like everyone else. But of course that is not the implication of democracy; the implication of democracy is rather that the individual can be as highly developed as lies within the possibilities of his own inheritance, and still can enter into the attitudes of the others whom he affects. There can still be leaders, and the community can rejoice in their attitudes just in so far as these superior individuals can themselves enter into the attitudes of the community which they undertake to lead."

It is easy to see why Mead and Dewey form a single school and why Dewey incorporated Mead into his own thinking. According to Mead: "The world in which humanity lives today, especially in the western world, is as different from that of the 18th century as were two geological epochs." And the end is not yet. Mead calls his views "social behaviorism" and, like Dewey, correlates his thinking closely with the scientific method of research. "Scientific method has no vision . . . of a perfected order of society, but it does carry with it the assumption that the intelligence which exhibits itself in the solution of problems in natural science is of the same character as that which we apply or should apply in dealing with our social and moral problems; that the intelligible order of the world is akin to its moral and social order because the same intelligence which enters into and controls the physical order . . . deals with the problem of human society. . . . Society gets ahead, not by fastening its vision upon a clearly outlined goal, but by bringing about the immediate adjustment of itself to its surroundings, which the immediate problem demands . . . We are at home in our own world . . . not by inheritance but by conquest. . . . It is a splendid adventure if we can rise to it."

In this way both Mead and Dewey get from biology back to modern science in general and to the modern democracy based on the methods of industry and science, but the remarkable achievement of Mead, taken over by Dewey, was the way in which, like a paleontologist, he reconstructs from scraps of information pertaining to our very early biological development, the birth of the human self and of the present-day reflexive self-consciousness. Later on from Peirce, another thinker who greatly influenced Dewey, and from Chauncey Wright will come further details on the semantic origins of human thought. Meanwhile it is easy to see how much it is from Mead that Dewey gets his inclination to stress the social element in human thinking.

5. Why We Think

THIS IS NOT the title of a Dewey book, but he does have one, *How We Think*, and another, published in 1938, called *Logic, the Theory of Inquiry*. Of the latter book he says: "This book is a development of ideas regarding the nature of logical theory that were first presented, some forty years ago, in *Studies in Logical Theory;* that were somewhat expanded in *Essays in Experimental Logic* and were briefly summarized with special reference to education in *How We Think*." Here, then, are Dewey's mature reflections on the function of human thought.

It is another one of those solid slabs of concatenated insights that go to make up the Dewey philosophy. Dewey's analysis of inquiry is central to his philosophy, as it is to the whole of the American philosophy that has been developing in Franklin, Emerson, and James, and is now reaching a further stage of completion in Dewey. *The Theory of Inquiry* is a profoundly biological interpretation of human thinking. It explains how we think, but much more deeply disturbing and equally lucid is his explanation of why we think. This "why" goes to the heart of the matter. We think in order to survive.

Anyone who imagines that any one of these philosophies, or that American philosophy as a whole, is superficial makes a big mistake. They are deadly serious. For that same reason these philosophies are not easy. There are no glib solutions. No confrontation that forces man to face his true situation can possibly be superficially optimistic. At best we get an inspiring challenge; at worst there is no hope at all. What we learn from the biological turn which American philosophy begins to take in James and continues to pursue in Dewey is that at one critical juncture in

213

his biological career man faced a choice. It was as if a wayfarer were held up by a brigand who demanded: Money or Your Life, only this demand was: Think or Die. We had to learn how to think in order to survive.

Thinking is not easy. Thinking is problem solving, and in order to solve problems you must first of all face them. That alone is sometimes almost impossible for a human race that has resorted as extensively as we have to fables and evasions. Not that these evasions have not been helpful. To some creatures nature gives long legs and long ears, to some triggered wings, so that by swift flight and artful dodges they may avoid destruction. Others seem built to turn around and fight. Fighting, again, is of two kinds, based on strength or cunning. Cunning seeks out the weak points in the enemy and overcomes him by superior strategy as well as resolute opposition. David's slingshot and the Trojan horse are but two of hundreds of gimmicks by which human guile brought victory, but the biggest single gimmick ever invented is thought itself. We did not begin to use it until we had to.

In Dewey's analysis of scientific thinking it will later become very clear that imagination has played a preponderant and by now carefully controlled role in constructing hypotheses. But imagination can also become a magnificent organ of flight. Leonard Woolf, the historian, gives a good account of how in the beginning mankind overplayed the imagination. As he reconstructs the story, two or three hundred thousand years ago through some fortunate change in diet or climate (or through a chance partaking in games, as Mead suggests) man broke "the iron bonds of animal immutability." He invented symbols and learned to use what we now call his imagination. The question is if man did succeed in waking up from the thoughtless trance in which animals played around, why did he stay so long in that primitive state? The answer is that primitive man awoke from animaldom and then almost immediately fell right back into a trance, a different kind of waking sleep in which he was, so to speak, hypnotized by his own imagination. He received the gift of second sight, and then immediately mistook the world of the imagination for the real world. The big mistake was his utter and childlike belief in magic. Even today we have done little more than make a start at substituting science for magic.

Primitive man interpreted the entire world in terms of his free-floating visions. Later we shall see how symbols make this possible. For almost three hundred thousand years man was terrorized by his imagination. The result now seems to us like a nightmare. Everywhere were spirits and demons, and the chief business of life became the art of cajoling, bribing, placating, and sidestepping these arbiters of human destiny. False beliefs can become very powerful. Indeed, according to Woolf, only false beliefs can be given the sanctity of absolute truths. "All absolute truths are false beliefs and all false beliefs tend to develop into absolute truths." That is the only way we can protect them. A true belief is always a steppingstone to something else. A false belief flatters us. True beliefs are real attempts to face reality. Woolf's exposition may smack of overstatement, but it puts into bold relief the use of the imagination as an organ of flight. This can be carried just so far, until the whole of humanity begins to prepare itself not for this world but for an entirely different world of their own fancying. From these hallucinations we are now in the painful process of recovering. One item in the recovery is to see that this wrong use of the imagination is an entirely NATURAL mistake, discovered just in time so that we can recover from it.

It must be remembered that in the primitive world the insane were not kept segregated as they are today. Recognizing insanity for what it is, and making provision to segregate the insane, has been a big step forward. Even so, an occasional, outwardly harmless, madman still catches the imagination of the multitudes, leading them sheeplike into mass insanity. A Führer or a Duce is simply the old savage back on the throne. The speeches of Mussolini and Hitler were full of appeals to primitive passions. Once these are aroused, reason and tolerance become criminal offenses. These men rearouse the sleeping savage mind within us all. Get the herd stampeded and we all go together because we hate to be separated from the warmth and approval of the herd.

Woolf analyzes Hitler's *Mein Kampf*, a Teutonic version of

Mussolini's message, and finds complete prototypes in parts of
Frazer's *Golden Bough.* The fundamental trait is anti-intellectual-
ism. The drift is toward the old magical cycles of prehistory. The
recent aberrations in Germany and Italy were a process of de-
civilization. These were backward steps on the long bridge between us and the animals. The training of children, under modern
and ancient dogmatisms, is very like the training in obedience and
conformity given primitive children. Anthropologists, among them
Denison in his *Emotion as the Basis of Civilization,* make it very
clear that there can be no group adherence without a unifying
emotion, and since these emotions are transitory, there must be
frequent ceremonies aimed at keeping these emotions alive.
Logical demonstration alone does not transform a truth into a
belief, especially not to a primitive mind; it takes emotional
dramatization. Emotion alone gives a sense of reality. It was the
function of primitive ceremonials to transform imaginings into
strong beliefs. Primitive men do not merely imagine that they
are all descended from a certain totem, say a bird, but they feel
this to be true. They feel their unity with the totem. That bird
sitting up there on the bough is me. This kind of logic antedates
the law of identity. It has by now been pretty well analyzed by
anthropologists. Lévy-Bruhl calls this early law that preceded the
logic of fixed identities the law of participation. Men participated
in the life around them before they learned to THINK about it.

It is because of this long back history of the development of
human cogitations that an exposition such as Dewey gives, an
exposition on an entirely naturalistic basis, still seems to us
strange. We do not yet understand that thought is a tool. Both
signs and symbols are tools. Man is a tool-using animal. Franklin
told us that much. Man has specialized in the making and using
of tools, and among his most recent tools are signs and symbols.
These are our highest and most ingenious tools, as the most
humble and lowest tools are the built-in physical limbs and organs
we share with other animals. Unless these appurtenances help
us to survive, they are a detriment, and no better than the heavy
carapace that sunk the primitive giant lizards.

Perhaps our native complement of tools, thanks to our upright gait and other accidents, gave us a slight edge on the other animals. It left our hands free for gestures and manipulation. Picking our ancestry from among the warm-blooded animals made our size just right. If the lungs had had to give oxygen to the rest of the body direct, we could never have become bigger than a mouse. That is one of the troubles with insects. Circulating oxygen via the blood stream allowed us to grow enough cells for muscle, bone, cartileges, and some left over for nerves and brain. The brain and the larynx turned out to be superbly useful, especially the brain on which the sounds made by the larynx impinge.

Our supersensitive brain turned out to be a wonder organ. Animals respond to the harshness of nature by thick coats of fur, huge bones, flapping wings, and a thousand other devices. We copy them faithfully, but reserve the seat of honor among our tools to signs. There is nothing mysterious about a sign. A sign is a part of an event. Using a sign is a trick by which a part is taken for the whole. In playing hide-and-seek a smart child knows that he need see only a tip of a finger to know where a person is. A dog hears the car coming up the gravel driveway and dashes out to greet his master. All of us, men and animals alike, recognize thousands of signs, signs of rain, signs of good weather, signs of enmity, and signs of friendship.

No animal can brave the hazards of locomotion, introducing himself rashly into a succession of different environments, without developing the capacity for responding to signs of danger. Passage from light to dark, wet to dry, hot to cold, solid to gaseous, all have to be in some sense prefigured and prepared for. So what happens? Animals develop external senses by which they see, hear, and smell at a distance a bewildering array of different objects. There are additional senses pointing inward. Animals know not only when night changes into day but also when the stomach is empty. The inner senses, not located in any one spot, signal hunger, thirst, warmth, cold, discomfort, tickling, pain and other things that chart the interior as other senses do the outside world. How much of life is a business of paying attention to signs few of us ever stop to think. We are as oblivious of the significance of signs as a fish is of sea water. Yet God help the animal that does not feel hunger cramps when food is needed. Heaven is denying that creature a sign.

To learn to use signs we do not need much of a brain or any brain at all. Photo-, chemo-, rheo- (running water), stereo- (contact) tropisms guide the lowly snail. In our muscles we have a kinesthetic sense which sometimes operates when we walk automatically in the dark at night to a switch and turn it on without any fumbling, or when with no forethought we throw a piece of paper at an angle straight into the wastebasket—couldn't do it again, if we tried! The ability to recognize and to act on signs, even barely perceptible ones, is a highly developed physical business. Sometimes there is a delay in the response to the original sign. The length to which this delay can be stretched without erasing the sign is taken as a measure of the intelligence of animals. All intelligence is based on some kind of retention. Train animals to recognize that food is coming from some opening with a light above it. Keep changing the light to different openings. The animal will always make for the proper goal. Now put out the signal light and hold back the animal with your hands. Let him go and see how long he will remember which opening had the light above it: rats 1–5 seconds; raccoons 10–25; cats, 16–18; dogs, 3 minutes; a child 1½ years old, 20 seconds; 2–3 years old, 50 seconds; 5 years old, 20 minutes; a gorilla, 2–3 hours; but a grown-up human being beats them all; and whether these figures are exactly right or not, that is the point. Man has further tricks so that he never forgets—he can write things down.

That a stimulus should keep going after it hits you is no more mysterious than that a billiard ball keeps going and sets another going, or that a match can light a fire. Things do keep going. No one pushes the planets around. A sign too is a very simple thing recognized by nearly every form of life. The use of symbols, however, goes beyond the use of signs. The step taken when signs become symbols was not entirely clear to James. It was clear to Dewey. But before going on to Dewey's very clear exposition of how we think, it will pay to rehearse almost in words of one syllable that important step which men took in advancing from signs to symbols. A sign is not a symbol. A symbol is a specially useful kind of sign, our own invention, and not found among the animals. When the teacher of Helen Keller, that remarkably well-educated deaf-mute, helped her to spell out on the fingers of one hands *w-a-t-e-r*, while holding the other hand under a stream of water, something happened in the brain of Helen Keller. In a flash of insight she got the idea that these letters in that succession were the name of a substance. They were not the same as water, but a symbol of it. She immediately became wild with a desire to learn the names of other things. This symbolizing is a wonderful game. This naming of objects is something to which every child, but no animal, attains. It is a significant event in human history. The story that when Adam in Paradise had nothing much else to do he was given the task of naming all the animals is a flashback to the importance of this early discovery of giving names to things. Adam's successors saw to it that by now there is a name for everything under the sun.

A symbol is an artificial sign. Watson, the psychologist, has a story of a man who did not want to talk. He disdained words and carried about with him a whole array of ordinary utensils to indicate his needs. He spurned the handy substitutes now in universal use among men; and a mighty convenient thing it is to carry practically the whole world of objects invisible and weightless right in your own head.

A sign may be part of a chair, but a symbol for a chair is not part of the chair. It is an arbitrary sign, an invented one. Then just as things get connected up with one another so do their signs or symbols. In language we systematize a set of very remote signs. We manufacture a flock of arbitrary signs for different objects and then begin to manipulate the symbols instead of the objects. The results are spectacular!

A symbol is an uprooted sign. Animals have to wait until they get a sign from some object. We make the mountain come to Mohammed. We pluck a sign from its stem and use it all by itself when the object to which it refers has passed out of our horizon. This is the origin of that second-sight business known as memory and imagination. We have developed enormously our capacity for retaining these arbitrary signs. This is the origin of all literature.

When plants achieved mobility, they, so to speak, turned themselves into animals. When animals achieved symbols they, so to speak, turned themselves into human beings. A human being is an animal manipulating symbols without having to refer them in each instance to their place of origin—a talking animal, in other words. Today we speak of man as an *animal symbolicum* rather than an *animal rationale*. If intelligence is measured by the length of time a sign is retained, we are by far the most intelligent of all animals, and that is perhaps why we have been successful in subduing all the other animals. Our symbol retention is not a simple storage resulting from throwing all our symbols together higgledy-piggledy into a heap. Symbols are signs so arranged as to be subject to instant recall. When we can manipulate our symbols so that they give us results with objects outside, then we are thinking logically, and that is what Dewey's "logic" is all about.

Not waiting for signs to come to us haphazardly, but growing them in gardens, so to speak, was somewhat analogous to what happened when our remote ancestors discovered that animals did not have to be hunted. Keep the young and raise them yourself. When hunters became herders civilization leaped ahead, although Dewey at one place reminds us that hunting habits remain deeply rooted. He traces back to it even the scholar's research and perhaps man's whole search for truth. Similarly at one time in prehistory it was found not necessary to walk your legs off to find stray patches of edible plants. Gather the seeds and grow them. No animal was smart enough to copy us in these matters. The origin of agriculture and the domestication of animals are basic discoveries analogous to the one by which signs are separated from their objects and made to multiply like seeds. The thing is so huge and yet so simple that we miss its significance. It is all so commonplace by now that along with herding and farming we forget how fundamental and important the invention of language has been to the human race.

Long, broad, between, over, under are words every bit as good as *tree, dog,* and *man.* Once signs represent not merely objects but also the relations between them and the things objects do, we can by means of these detached signs get a picture-story. To a child, four dots in a row, the first a little bigger than the others, means a train. We are all highly gifted caricaturists. From the merest hints we get a picture of a situation or an action. As a result we can pocket and relive whole sections of our lives, environment and all.

These are not pictures in the sense that the shadow of a horse or even the drawing of a horse on a piece of paper is a picture. A symbol need in no way resemble what it stands for. All we need is a one-to-one correspondence between each word and the object, relation, or action it represents. Then we are not merely naming things but telling stories. Pretty soon we are telling stories and making pictures that we like better than the real thing. The word "tree" may seem to us more pregnant with significance than any specific tree we may encounter, since it stands for them all. Somebody may draw a picture of a tree, or tell us of a tree, that we think quite perfect. It catches the tree at just the right moment with the evening sun upon it and keeps it there, immortalizing the best aspects of the tree or by associating it with sentiment turning the tree into a moment of glory. Imagination is the name we give to this business of creating and holding before us a duplicate, it may be a glorified duplicate, of the real world.

Needless to say this can also become a highly dangerous business in sending us after mirages instead of what is really there. Broadly speaking, mankind is now in that sober stage where it is reducing to manageable order that twin world of signs and symbols with which, whether we like it or not, we are going to be saddled to the end of our days. Once we have these things they are so useful that they can never be thrown away. Every now and then some genius comes along—D. H. Lawrence, for example—with the message to reunite with nature in the old close way still practiced by the animals. But it is of no use. Life is more than just an intensely emotional experience. We have lost our careless innocence. We are committed to conquering, exploring, not just enjoying the earth. A complete man embraces both the joys and the dangers. We wish to bend to our will the forces of the world, and we wish to enjoy not only what lies at our feet, but to seek out and savor the fullness of that world.

In order to do that we have first of all not to silence but to curb the imagination. This world of our imagination must not be permitted to ride us like a nightmare. It must be trimmed down to match what is really there—a painful process because it means giving up some of our dreams. The hypotheses furnished us by fancy must be rigidly subjected to verification. The imagination must be disciplined so that it can really help us, not to flee but to face and to control realities. The whole movement of pragmatism is an attempt to bring Pegasus, Mythos, Chimera, and other winged steeds back to pasture and to put them under harness. It may sound prosaic but it happens to be necessary, for ideals, no matter how wonderful they may be, can destroy as well as help us. Our next man, Santayana, will endeavor to teach us how to laugh a little at our own ideals and hold them no less dear.

Thought must be tied up with action. Thinking is incipient action. This brings us right back to Dewey's extremely sane hints on how to think and why we think. "Persons do not just think at large," says Dewey, "nor do ideas arise out of nothing. Go through your own experience and you will not find a case where thinking started up out of nothing . . . follow the thread far enough and you will find some situation that is directly experienced, something undergone, done, enjoyed, or suffered, and not just thought of. Reflection is occasioned by . . . this primary situation. It does not merely *grow out* of it, but it *refers back* to it. Its aim and outcome are decided by the situation out of which it arose. The function of reflection is to bring about a new situation in which the difficulty is resolved."

Dewey gives a simple case: "Suppose you are walking where there is no regular path. As long as everything goes smoothly, you do not have to think about your walking; your already formed habit takes care of it. Suddenly you find a ditch in your way. You think you will jump it (supposition, plan); but to make sure, you survey it with your eyes (observation), and you find that it is pretty wide and that the bank on the other side is slippery (facts, data). You then wonder if the ditch may not be narrower somewhere else (idea), and you look up and down the stream (observation) to see how matters stand (test of idea by observation). You do not find any good place and so are thrown back upon forming a new plan. As you are casting above, you discover a log (fact again). You ask yourself whether you could not haul that to the ditch and get it across the ditch to use as a bridge (idea again). You judge that idea is worth trying, and so you get the log and manage to put it in place and walk across (test and confirmation by overt action).

"If the situation were more complicated, thinking would of course be more elaborate." But Dewey emphasizes that the "two limits of every unit of thinking are a perplexed, troubled, or confused situation at the beginning and a cleared-up, unified, resolved situation at the close . . . In between, as stages of thinking, are (1) *suggestions*, in which the mind leaps forward to a possible solution; (2) an intellectualization of the difficulty or perplexity that has been *felt* (directly experienced) into a *problem* to be solved, a question for which the answer must be sought; (3) the use of one suggestion after another as a leading idea, or *hypothesis*, to initiate and guide observation and other operations in collection of factual material; (4) the mental elaboration of the idea or supposition as an idea or supposition (*reasoning*, in the sense in which reasoning is a part, not the whole, of inference); and (5) testing the hypothesis by overt or imaginative action."

"*The function of reflective thought is, therefore, to transform a situation in which there is experienced obscurity, doubt, conflict, disturbance of some sort, into a situation that is clear, coherent, settled, harmonious.*" Dewey italicizes this whole paragraph. It is hard to miss the point that thinking solves specific problems and should be pinned down to that. The stress is on the testing of each hypothesis. If you can't or won't test an hypothesis, you are playing with a dream.

In his *Logic, The Theory of Inquiry* Dewey goes into all this in a manner that is detailed enough to satisfy any academic standard. What he does is to go over every paragraph of Aristotle's logic for a translation of all its meandering and turnings into the corresponding minutiae of modern scientific investigation. But the gist of it, the large hinges on which the whole discussion turns, are in the few paragraphs given above. About the only other large new thing that he adds is that toward the end he stresses that thinking is a *social* process. Dewey remarks that "C. S. Peirce is notable among writers on logical theory for his explicit recognition of the necessity of the social factor in the determination of evidence and its probative force. The following representative passage is cited: 'The next most vital factor of the method of modern science is that it has been made social.'" This widens the field of inquiry to include social as well as personal problems. Dewey differs from James in stressing the social rather than the personal aspects of thinking.

It is overwhelmingly important that we should be willing to have the results of our thinking tested by others. Let others check it also, is the motto of the scientist. This cuts off monomanias at the root; it curtails emotional bias; and it makes agreement rather than argument the arbiter of what is going to stand. Let the facts decide. Always there have been in life a multitude of homely facts on which most men agree. We all know enough to get in out of the rain. There is a whole realm of common sense, filling the daylight hours, that sensible men don't fight about. Most of these things are easily tested, and have been tested thousands of times. No one is going to fight about whether water boils at 212 degrees or freezes at 32. The variations for different air pressures have all been worked out; other liquids have been investigated for their boiling points—these and a million other data we look up in a reference book and do not fight about. This whole body of "warranted assertions" (Dewey's name for truth) has achieved social acceptance. The business of science is to add more territory to this area of social agreement.

Dewey developed his logic along the lines of a technique for solving social and personal problems, not along metaphysical lines. The kind of logic that we mean when we speak of the logic of events, or of mathematics as a type of logic, was not Dewey's specialty. Later in life Dewey agreed that his subtitle, Theory of Inquiry, should have been used by itself rather than insisting on calling his book primarily a Logic. Peirce, who had more feeling for the new scope about to be given to logic, called Dewey's work an excellent introduction to logic, but not logic itself. It was the genetic aspect of human thought, how it arose, and what its function was in a practical way that interested Dewey most. Hence his theory of inquiry, with its social overtones, has a direct bearing on ethics. By far its most important implication is that the scientific man, or any man who pretends to be scientific in his thinking, cannot sidestep questions of morality. The clear way in which he proceeds to work this out is one of Dewey's major contributions to philosophy. Dewey did indispensable spadework in laying the foundations of a naturalistic ethics.

6. An Earth-bound Ethics

THE CENTRAL IDEA in the ethics of Dewey is a simple one. It is most plainly put in the New Testament question, Luke 14:28: "For which of you, intending to build a tower, sitteth not down first, and counteth the cost, whether he have sufficient to finish it?" An entire ethics can be built around the disparity of ends and means. Dewey does it. His contribution to ethics is another of those well-worked-out solid sections of his philosophy that stands firmly on its own foundation. The gist of it is in a short article of sixty-seven pages, *Theory of Valuation,* which he wrote for the International Encyclopedia of Unified Science, and which was published in 1939. A more plodding approach, thoroughly psychological, is found in *Human Nature and Conduct,* first published in 1922, and issued in 1930 as a volume of the Modern Library.

Trouble in any situation starts when the means do not fit the ends. No one today builds towers, but the homely illustration applies equally well to a house. You have twenty thousand dollars to build a house. Now what sense does it make to start building one that costs two hundred thousand or two million dollars? Worse still, set your heart on a castle in Spain, all fitted out with a fairy princess and liveried servants, something not only beyond your means but beyond everyone else's means. The very essence of magic is that means are disregarded. Clap your hands, a genie appears, and the castle is built overnight. That is how things happen in *Arabian Nights* or Disney Land, but not in real life. The first thing to do in laying the foundation for an ethics is to take a good look at the world we live in.

There is much more in this simple maxim of counting the cost before you build a tower than appears on the surface. It telescopes a dozen ancient and modern international proverbs counseling elementary prudence from the Greek, Nothing to Excess, down to the Yankee, Look before You Leap! It adds a fourth type of excellence to the ancient trio of truth, goodness, and beauty, that fourth quality being fitness or efficiency, that exact adaptation of means to ends, with no waste motion, that characterizes the professional performance. It is a quality that appeals to practical inventors and ingenious people everywhere. Americans, like the Greeks, can sit for hours watching professional games. Is there here a kind of perfection that is different from truth, goodness, or beauty, and that in a way combines them all?

Dewey with his tenacity for the practical claims that implicit in this maxim is the stubborn fact that means and means alone justify the end. Keeping your eye on the means operates like a moral Occam's razor that first of all shears off all impossible ideals. It lays the ax at the roots of all counsel smacking of the magical. No chasing of rainbows! No falling in love with beautifully worked out decalogues! It is so easy to say: Don't do this, don't do that. Most moral precepts consist of don'ts. All these wonderful precepts—does anybody ever keep them? Are they just pious platitudes? The Decalogue has been with us for thousands of years. Thou shalt not steal! Various other don'ts and some do's, such as, Love your neighbor as you love yourself, but very little on the means to arrive at these goals. It is so easy to set up a code or pass a law and even to provide penalties and hire enforcement officers, yet stealing still goes on. As for enforcing love, everyone knows it can't be done. The real nub of morality is in finding the means, knowing how, implanting the inclination. No wonder that Dewey, before he gets much further, goes right back to what James also stressed, human habits. But before he does so, he has something more to say about useless hypotheses.

Thinking in a vacuum with action indefinitely suspended is the normal activity of a madhouse. The fact that thinking normally leads to action, that it is justified only when it suggests the right action, and that action should not be separated from thought, enables us to get down to solid earth also in the field of ethics. The farmer who does not believe in artificial fertilization, or in using chemical fertilizers, or in any one of a number of new suggestions, should not prevent his neighbor from trying them out.

Maybe the neighbor is taking a chance, maybe he isn't. If his crop is doubled, the prejudice against that brand of fertilizer is sure to die out. If the fertilizer is a poison, that too will make everything clear as day. If communism cannot work, why worry about it? Don't just preach capitalism, find out how to make it work and it will sell itself. We are all human beings looking for the right way to promote human happiness. We can learn from each other, and what we need to learn is the means to attain ends the desirability of which no one disputes.

Historically, specific sets of values have arisen from trying to keep in power a certain privileged group. Now do not pretend that that is not really what we are trying to do. Good is good-for-something. If good means good for the chosen few, let us look that squarely in the face. If your ethics means looking out only for yourself, the first one to know it and to condemn it will be your neighbor. If good means good for the whole human race, then if things go wrong we all hang together, but it gives us a clue as to selecting and rejecting certain means. If the sole aim of man is to glorify God, then nothing else matters. What Dewey counsels in the face of remote ends is to be wary of them all. Stick to your immediate problems. Some of these remote ends are like the castles in Spain. And yet so often man has achieved the apparently impossible. Ah, yes, but never without first considering and perfecting the means. There is only one road you can pave with good intentions, the rest need something more solid. All progress has been by finding and promoting the means.

And by "means" it is intended to imply not to get a thing done just any old way but to get it done just right. "Don't overeat!" means eat just right. Eating cannot be cut out altogether nor does eating mean stuffing, it means something between the two. That every virtue represents a happy medium between too much and too little is a discovery as old as Aristotle, but the modern contribution to this ancient doctrine, emphasized by Dewey, is that by studying the means one can find the end. Ends are not just picked out of the blue. This has always been the stumbling block in ethics. Where do we get our models? Plato said we got them by reminiscence from a former perfect world whence comes the soul. Aristotle more or less left it at that; at least he believed in perfect and permanent forms that came from somewhere, and that lasted pretty well up to Darwin's day. Darwin gives us the true origin of species—variations in all directions from which a selection is made. This necessitates a revision of ethics. That too becomes a selection of possibilities—not hopeless demands, but possibilities. This is the gist of the new evolutionary doctrine that means must be considered in the determination of ends.

The means must lie within the realm of attainment. This is not so great a limitation as at first sight it might seem to be. Means are like steps in a staircase. Don't try to step from the bottom to the top step. Take them one by one and you get to the top from which you may build a new staircase. The caution is against omitting the intervening steps. Nature seems to progress in the same way—by little steps—until, given time, the ameba becomes an eagle and the eagle an aviator. All alike are products of the same process. Do not underrate what can be accomplished by studying, and utilizing, the means at hand.

Man's best building blocks are habits. In this Dewey agrees with James. He begins with a consideration of such deep habits as eating and breathing. It is obvious that these are habits that no one can dispense with. It is also clear that they are ways of using and incorporating our environment. It is unrealistic, in any study of habits, to separate a man too far from his environment. You cannot separate a man's body habits from his surroundings. In the same way do not separate his mind habits from the world. To do so leads to a belief in magic. Human habits cannot be changed by magic. Dewey uses the illustration of trying to correct wrong posture. Straightening up once or twice is not enough. We straighten up and fall right back into the old posture. It takes effort, continuous effort, to get into a new habit. Does it help to tell a drunkard that he should learn to drink water instead of whisky? These wrong habits are not easily dislodged. All human endeavor in bettering ourselves and the world we live in is tied up with ways and means.

Some good habits have been learned very early. They are so useful that we never drop them. We all learned how to walk and talk. To recognize shapes and to distinguish colors are other things learned so early that the process has been forgotten. Children learn these things as babes when they feel a round ball over and over and keep looking at it. These habits no one wishes to change. Problems arise when we get equally deep-seated habits that we do wish to change. Psychoanalysis deals with some of these on the assumption that getting to know how we learned or acquired these habits may help us to unlearn them. It is like unteaching ourselves some of the early principles that have become part of us and the acquisition of which has been forgotten.

Dewey thinks it may do some good to try a flank movement. Think of the immediate next step, not of the remote end. Looking at the remote end may make you dizzy or paralyze you. Concentrate on the means. The hard drinker who keeps thinking of not drinking gets nowhere. He must find some positive interest as a substitute for that negative goal. The idea is to do something else instead. Take a step in a different direction and keep your eye on where you are putting your feet.

Life is a system of habits, most of them deep-seated and indispensable, but some of our habits are still on the growing edge. A tree is alive at the tips of the roots and the tips of the branches where the leaves are. The trunk cannot be changed except by slow accretions through these tips. The interpenetration of old and new habits in man is called character. Dispositions are habits, although disposition is a misleading word, as it suggests something we can't do much about. A disposition gets to be a predisposition, that is, a way of acting that we gladly indulge whenever we get the chance. The trick is to acquire the right predispositions. Acquired predispositions and aversions have everything to do with character.

To say that motives alone count is to miss the point entirely. You cannot in this life take the will for the deed. Whole systems of ethics have been built on the idea that good will is more important than actual doing. Kant had his ethics turn on purity of motive. Unfortunately motives are seldom one hundred per cent pure. Character is speckled. If we make motives and moral intentions too prominent, nothing on earth seems good, and we are back at the business of stressing total depravity. Kant lands himself on that spot where, again, a real heaven and hell are needed to give people their just deserts. Only in a magic world can good intentions serve as counters for good deeds. On this earth we have to practice through trial and error the business of learning to be good, that is, acquiring character.

Wide uniformities of settled habits are called customs. Customs come out of the past and are continued blindly. But mechanization is not all there is to habit. Sometimes customs must change, as when an ice age sets in. Then we have to start sifting our habits into intelligent and unintelligent habits. Fortunately outward conditions usually change gradually, and we can build up new habits slowly.

Consider how language grew up. Men did not first of all intend to talk nor did they first of all invent a perfect grammar. They just started grunting, squeaking, cackling, crying, and talking came as an ultimate refinement. Grammar, like Topsy, just grew. Models for language came after language was established. Nor was language taught man by a mythical perfect speaker, an all-knowing linguist who spoke all languages perfectly and was a master of the grammar of each. Ethics is in the same boat. It was not handed down on tablets. What holds good of language holds good of other human institutions. The authority for good conduct, the standards of it, come from life itself. You say: Why live? That is your problem, and most people are perfectly content to live, the only question is, How? More intelligently or less intelligently? Customs are a first rough attempt to make life somewhat intelligent so that it will last longer and have less friction. In psychology too we must begin with the facts of habit and custom. Do not begin with a separate realm of psychic force. If you do, you will end up by pitting this force against the other forces of life, the unconscious against the conscious, the will against the deed, and you will get in deeper and deeper.

Dewey makes much of impulses. An impulse may be a warning. Nature sometimes hands out premonitions. Impulses are pivots upon which a reorganization of activities may turn. Impulses are precious things. They may give new directions to old habits. Some should be carefully nurtured and kept alive to become the basis for a new habit. Neither innate ideas not an empty wax tablet is the correct picture of the human mind. Keep one eye on deep-seated bodily habits and another on the environment. Mind is the growing edge between these two. Impulses can become organized. In a sense human society is always starting afresh. This is in the sense that new adjustments are possible, and impulses are often the harbingers of just such an adjustment.

We can gradually remake ourselves. Even old habits can be changed. The unformed activities of childhood are the best material for this. Childhood and youth offer the great opportunities. That is the real meaning of education. Hence too Emerson, an eternal youth, throws consistency to the winds.

There is little progress as yet in making behavior a product of intelligent guidance. We have depended on heroic individuals, on wishful thinking, on chance catastrophies, instead of on continuous reconstruction. Nations need not, like persons, grow old, but they do. It is custom and not the nation that senesces. Rigid moral codes become outmoded. There are impulses to change them but the impulses go unheeded or are suppressed. Moderns sometimes oscillate between periods of wild impulse and strict conformity. But the great inertia of life is custom. We exaggerate the fixity of instincts. Even animal instincts are less fixed and unalterable than is supposed. To Aristotle it seemed that slavery was rooted in human nature. To us it seems that war is. The wage system seems equally inevitable. We miss the lessons of history and prehistory with their discarded forms. How deeply rooted is private property? Must human beings always exploit each other? Does it take personal profit to keep men at their tasks? Incentives and motives need to be re-examined. Man needs more study of himself. "In learning habits it is possible for man to learn the habit of learning. Then betterment becomes a conscious principle of life."

Why must there be just one motive? Must man do everything either for profit or for pleasure? Many activities are per se pleasurable. Nor is man naturally averse to serviceable action. He is not only a craftsman, but also a sportsman, artist, adventurer, administrator, and speculator. Some say self-love is everything. Some say there are two forces: egoism and altruism. Some say three: greed, fear, and glory. Some say sixty. Then, again, fat sociological volumes trace everything back to the single instinct of imitation. Others say all ethics rests on developing our scant stores of sympathy. Other bold spirits, especially recent psychologists, carry all back to sex or love of power. Hobbes long ago made fear the sole motivation. Plato divided man into three levels of society, each group, like rabbits, seeking their own carrots: merchants, appetite; soldiers, ambition; lawgivers, rationality. Some say everything is self-preservation.

In all this the fallacy is obvious. In every case the end is treated as an actuating cause. Strange how intelligent men are trapped by so obvious a fallacy. Rust, thunder, lightning, and nitric acid are no more real than fear, anger, and rivalry, but it is wrong to think of these special emotions as generating forces. Don't think of them as forces at all. Psychic force is a myth.

Habits end up with no thought intervening at all. Habits do not by themselves stop and think. It takes a shock or a block of some sort to loosen them at all. Sometimes some inner voice gives us a warning. We have that fleeting impulse to change a habit. Catch that impulse, for it may mean a new beginning. Once that happens we face a problem, and the time has come to use that new invention of problem solving. Impulse, plus effort, plus everything that Dewey and James can teach us on habit formation may lead to the kind of self-improvement that makes for character.

The hard things to do are the little steps that lead to big results. Stop fighting! If the human animal solved the one problem of how to get along without future wars, mankind would take such a spurt forward that many other things might become easy. New ideals would come within reach. It is not a high ideal to get rid of poverty, but we have never succeeded in doing it. The purpose of thought is action that leads to results. Our thoughts on ethics are still too wishful. It is wrong to found an ethics on feelings alone. In the end comes the counting of the cost and the calculation of ways and means. On that area of ways and means ethics too should concentrate. Dewey is in line with his philosophical forebears in stressing deeds, not words.

7. The Religious Sentiment

It would be grand if the sections of Dewey's philosophy dealing with art and religion were as complete as certain other sections. In these fields he had basic insights and made some sound beginnings, but he did not get around to working out fully either his aesthetics or his metaphysics. In art, for one thing, he lacked a clear-cut theory of intuition. With James he recognizes two kinds of knowledge, the direct acquaintance with and the knowledge about, but Dewey was disinclined to call the former knowledge at all. All his detailed work was done on the second type of knowledge, the discursive type, based on language. Dewey says:

"A certain ambiguity in words has played a very considerable rôle in fostering the doctrine of immediate knowledge. Knowledge in its strictest and most honorific sense is identical with warranted assertion. But 'knowledge' also means understanding, and an object, or an act . . . called *apprehension*. . . . Just as, after considerable experience, we understand meanings directly, as when we hear conversation on a familiar subject or read a book, so because of experience we come to recognize objects on sight. I see or note directly that *this* is a typewriter, *that* is a book, the other thing is a radiator, etc. This kind of direct 'knowledge' I shall call *apprehension;* it is seizing or grasping, intellectually, without questioning." Here Dewey puts the word "knowledge" in quotation marks. He does not consider this knowledge, but something more like eating or grasping—direct appropriation.

Then in his *Art as Experience* Dewey keeps hammering away at the idea of immediacy. "It cannot be asserted too strongly that what is not immediate is not esthetic." Art is an immediate delight in something in nature that answers to the inner man and causes us to vibrate like a tuning fork. Here Dewey is laying the ground-work for a theory of art corresponding somewhat to the immediate knowledge denied above. This whole matter of the two kinds of knowledge and the relation between them will not be cleared up until we come to Whitehead. The failure to think this through until he came to perfect clarity prevented Dewey from explaining art as fully and as clearly as he might have. In aesthetics we get better guidance from Santayana and Whitehead.

In art we come face to face with creation. Likewise all reli-gions agree on the necessity for some kind of creation. Either nature itself or someone must do something creative with nature, and generally the someone who does that is supernatural or divine. That he can do so is his talisman as a god. He bends nature to his will. Is man in some small sense divine? Does he get his greatest enjoyment, that particular lift into a seventh heaven, from exerting even a modicum of creative force?

Dewey speaks of the power of choice. "When we begin to choose, we have entered upon a road that has not yet come to an end." We enter a realm of adventure. For Dewey there is no such thing as a religion in general, but there is an attitude which can be characterized as religious. Some say that this religiously tinged experience is the ultimate basis of religion itself. With this Dewey does not agree. There is no definite kind of experience marked off as religious, but there is a religious quality that may belong to different kinds of experience, aesthetic, scientific, or political.

This separation of the religious from a religion is not easy to effect. It is sometimes an adjustment, an accommodation, to con-ditions which cannot be changed. It may be passive submission, yet more than a mere stoical resolution to endure. Dewey says that it is the claim of religions that they effect this generic and enduring change in attitude, but that he himself would like to turn this statement around and say that whenever this change takes place there is a definitely religious attitude.

There is in human experience sometimes a sudden orientation that brings with it a sense of security and peace. It may be pro-duced by devotion to a cause, by a passage in a poem, by philo-sophical reflection, as in the case of Spinoza. The connection between imagination and the harmonizing of the self is closer than is usually thought. Mostly such reconciliations are attributed to a supernatural or, as with James, to a subconscious source. It is a conviction that some end should be supreme over conduct. Such moral faith is not easy. When a professional man acts in the spirit of his calling he is controlled by such an unseen ideal, the kind of steadfast confidence that moves mountains.

What is wrong about such idealisms is that they convert the high faith in action into a system of beliefs about antecedent reality. Here too Dewey would reverse the attitude. The essentially UN-religious attitude attributes human achievement to physical nature alone, whereas it is Dewey's view that when we work with nature the divine in us grows stronger. We are parts of nature. Faith in the continued disclosure of truth through directed cooperative human endeavor is more religious in quality than is any faith in a completed revelation. Identification of the ideal with a Being outside of nature refuses to see that other possibility of an ideal that may have its roots in natural conditions. This is the position of Santayana, as it is of Dewey. Ends have power in human conduct. Aims and ideals that move us are generated through imagination. Imagination, a human achievement, is one of the components of the process of creation.

These considerations may be applied to the idea of God, or to the idea of the divine. There are conjunctions in nature and in society that generate and support ideals. "It is this ACTIVE relation between ideal and actual to which I would give the name of 'God.' The striving we find in fellowship, friendship, love and growth thus comes to a head. There is nothing mystical about this. One reason why personally I think it fitting to use the word 'God' to denote that uniting of the ideal and actual which has been spoken of, lies in the fact that aggressive atheism seems to me to have something in common with traditional supernaturalism. Militant atheism is also affected by lack of natural piety." Dewey will have none of it.

Matthew Arnold's conception of a power not ourselves is too narrow. These powers operate within as well as without. We need more than an external Jehovah. It was wrong to put the values prized in religion into a supernatural realm for safekeeping. Formerly religion permeated all the customs and activities of the group. Most of us have forgotten what it was like. This change has been the greatest change in history since religion began. The conflict between church and state had something to do with it. We are no longer just born into a church and fated to stay there. The supernatural has oozed away. Secular organizations replace it. There is now a personal choice, and this choice may amount to a dedication. "To achieve this faith and élan is not an easy task."

It is impossible to ignore the fact that historical Christianity has been committed to a separation of the sheep from the goats, the saved from the lost, the elect from the mass. Spiritual aristocracy has tainted the church. The escape has been into a theological sphere in which we rejoice that God will punish the wicked. We can gloat over the vengeance that shall be his. This does not heal the wounds caused by white supremacy or by the smugness of belonging, without merit of our own, to the elect.

It is unfortunate that the religious factors of experience, so clearly set forth by Dewey, have been textured into an extranatural or supernatural structure. In *Treasure Island* there is a terrible pirate with one leg who gets about on his crutch with the dartlike celerity of a huge bird. He moves around faster and more suddenly, certainly more ominously, than an ordinary mortal. Moreover, the detachable crutch is a lethal weapon. The man, like Terror personified, permeates the book. In this way institutionalized religion, using the supernatural as a crutch, has terrorized mankind, forgetting that the supernatural was a crutch, which, when we learn to walk again, we do not need.

8. To Live Is to Learn

THROUGHOUT ALL the major chapters of Dewey's philosophy runs the theme song of the importance of education. The condemnation of dogma in his *Quest for Certainty* is a plea for having education deal with the problems of today. His stress on the social element in life brings out how much we can learn from and teach each other and how valuable is the sharing of life. His logic is not so much a logic of the rules of thought as an analysis of the learning process through problem solving. His ethics puts before mankind a vast task of educational reconstruction. Even the religious sentiment, as it is felt by Dewey, is an exalted partaking in the creative task of reconstructing the world. It is this insistence throughout on the importance of education that makes his work a landmark in American philosophy.

James, in the last chapter of his *Principles of Psychology*, published in 1890, showed insight in betting on Weismann rather than on Lamarck. Darwin himself had not been too sure about the biological inheritance of acquired characteristics. James was right in holding that in biological heredity acquired characteristics were not passed on. James was right also in pointing unerringly to the modifiability of human habits, as the basis of that other nonbiological, but cultural, heredity which can be transmitted. To open up more widely than even James did this bright aspect of human heredity was the distinguishing feature of the philosophy of John Dewey. James, in his personal life and in his philosophy, got away entirely from the prevalent view of his day that heredity meant doom. He did this by discovering the human freedom of choice. This hopeful revelation of man's reshaping both himself and the world through science and through education is continued by Dewey. In this he is the spokesman of a deep-seated American faith that has come out thus far in each of its leading philosophers.

The first thing Dewey stresses is that this passing on and this enrichment of human culture applies to every human being. Greek civilization, wonderful as it was, was based on slavery. All the higher reaches of culture were for the privileged classes. The name of Dewey is associated first of all with the wiping out of these class distinctions. Education is something that applies to everybody. The Greeks were wrong in beginning to channel it only to freeborn individuals who did not work with their hands. Next, the transmission of culture applies to every human trait. Learning begins at birth. Culture is handed down as a whole by initiating the young immediately into the ways of the elders. Children learn to speak the language of their parents. On language float all the other mores. What genes are to biological heredity, words and language are to cultural heredity. Not only words but gestures and habits are copied. Just how the child does all this and just how the adult world manages to get all its ways passed on is the gist of what is meant by education. It is a mistake to identify education too closely with the schoolroom. Education was going on effectively long before schools were invented.

However, today there is so infinitely much more to transmit than there used to be that the school has developed as a sort of aid to overburdened parents. This new aspects of things—schools as an arm of democracy—gives the whole matter of education a professional twist. The Roman father in the early days still had powers of life and death over his large family, which included the slaves, and just as government when it takes over the family task gets into a host of new problems, so the teachers taking over from the parents run into new situations. Education, like government, gets to be a separate profession. Its importance is measured by the habit parents now have of entrusting to teachers the most precious possession they have, their own children. Plato saw the beginning of these important relations between education and government, and today these relations are a paramount problem of modern society. If teachers fail, what can parents do about it? This has become of crucial concern, not only to parents but to governments looking for manpower. Manpower today is measured in a huge variety of special skills, in other words, man-power is brainpower. So everything revolves around education. In addition to all this Dewey makes philosophy itself, that culminating spearhead of human advancement, in essence nothing but more and more self-education of mankind through the increase of knowledge.

"Instrumentalism means a behaviorist theory of thinking and knowing. It means that knowing is literally something which we do . . . the operations of knowing are . . . natural responses of the organism." According to Dewey, education "may be treated as a process of accommodating the future to the past, or as a utilization of the past for a resource in a developing future. The former finds its standards and patterns in what has gone before." Dewey seeks an "interaction of native activities with the environment which progressively modifies both the activities and the environment." There is a large place in democracy for the "widening area of shared concerns." These are the merest hints, giving at most a very inadequate sample of how slowly, methodically, and carefully Dewey develops his views on education as a type of reconstruction. As an educator Dewey comes at the tail end of a long movement. The evolutionary outlook started long before Dewey. Many obviously needed reforms were instituted before Dewey appeared on the scene. Long before Dewey had anything to say on the subject, many educators opposed vindictive punishments, regimentation, drilled memorizing of dates, dogmas to be learned by rote, and the whole idea of mental faculties which, like muscles, were to be strengthened by exercises not necessarily useful in themselves.

It was Horace Mann who had his fight with Boston schoolmasters over their sixty-five whippings a day in "a representative school of 400 children." He won out at least in principle well before the day of Dewey. The idea that children were by nature wicked and corrupt was discarded with Calvinism even before Emerson, who backed Alcott in his experimental school of an early day. Franklin put on record his deep resentment of the floggings he got when his own brother was teaching him the printer's trade. Early reformers in education from Comenius to Pestalozzi, household words in the history of education, had done their work. No one wants to turn back the clock to the day of the oxcart before the voice of any educational reformer was heard in the land.

Two or three decades before Dewey, Colonel Francis W. Parker, first at Quincy, Massachusetts, and later at the Cook County Normal School, developed educational methods displaying enthusiasm for childhood and a deep faith in humanity. Miss Lelia E. Patrick wrote a book on the Quincy methods in 1885. Froebel and his kindergarten methods were firmly entrenched before Dewey. These methods tried to extend education beyond the three R's. Dewey criticizes Froebel's theory of child activity as an unfolding. Both stress child activity and close living with the teacher, but Dewey made it creative living, not just an unfolding, and he stressed that education meant learning from adults. Then there were the Herbartians who around 1890, also before Dewey's time, brought to America what they learned in Jena about first arousing an interest. Tie up new things with the old apperceptive mass, the things already there. Dewey had a different idea. Interest is related to effort. All animals make an effort at adaptation. Both the child and the adult are biological organisms built to learn how to fit into conditions on this earth. Man, unlike the animals, sets varied goals and must learn how to choose. This takes attention and effort, but no child is inert. The child is already active; now try to make him intelligently active. Coercion only makes him choose the lesser of two evils, and the fact that you can pound the multiplication table into some children does not mean that it is best taught by punishment.

A child has interests. "These interests are neither to be humored nor repressed," says Dewey. "To humor them is to substitute the transient for the permanent. The interest is always the sign of some power below. The important thing is to discover that power. To humor interest is to fail to penetrate below the surface, and its sure result is to substitute caprice and whim for genuine interest."

"As one relates this condemnation of humoring childish whims with present-day attacks on Dewey for humoring childish whims, one hardly knows whether to laugh or cry," says William H. Kilpatrick. Caricatures of all new methods by angry parents who probably still use a switch in their own homes and believe in training children as dogs are trained abound and get pinned on Dewey. According to Dorothy Canfield Fisher, "The only thing to say about the grotesqueries occasionally attributed to Dewey's educational ideas is to ask urgently of every person who hears this kind of gossip that he read and study one of John Dewey's own books. The lack-witted nonsense which perhaps you disapprove of in Dewey's educational ideas you will never find in any statement from his own pen. That nonsense comes from people who have no idea what he is talking about, and he is not the first great 'leader of humanity' (as the Belgian Encyclopedia calls him) who has been misrepresented by his less intelligent friends."

Criticism from those who know reveals no great differences from Dewey, and certainly no lack of respect for him. Thus in an article published in the *Saturday Review* of February 21, 1959, by Robert M. Hutchins, it might almost be Dewey talking when we hear Hutchins say: "If our hopes of democracy are to be realized, every citizen of this country is going to have to be educated to the limit of his capacity." Dewey was wrong when he said: "President Hutchins calls for liberal education for a small, elite group, and vocational education for the masses. I can think of no idea more completely reactionary and more fatal to the whole democratic outlook." Can Hutchins have changed his mind? In the same way when Hutchins says: "If life is learning, and I think it is, and if our object is to become a community learning together, education ought to continue throughout life." This again might be Dewey talking.

Mortimer J. Adler and Milton Mayer published in 1958 *The Revolution in Education.* The "revolution" in this book has nothing to do with the methods instituted by reformers but with the appalling new task confronting us now that we have to educate the entire youthful population. Presumably this book represents a point of view opposed to that of Dewey, but when differences are discussed, the authors bend over backwards in letting Dewey state his own case. One is reminded of how Franklin became a deist by reading a book against deism. No one is going to emerge from this book with anything but a healthy respect for Dewey and he may even stop being an Adlerite. The authors sift things down by a series of dichotomies, the first of which is aristocrat-democrat. No one today is going to vote for aristocracy, so we come next to a division of the democrats into realist-idealist. The realist urges different kinds of education. The idealist hopes that this can be avoided. Perhaps, opines the realist, by the age of twelve tests can indicate where the youthful candidate stands and among which of five groups he should be put: humanists, scientists, artisans, executives, or laborers. Such a realist is not to be confused with the aristocrats ruled out above who do not believe in education for the masses. The realist believes strongly in equality of opportunity. He just thinks that many cannot make the grade.

On the other hand, the idealist condemns differentiation across the board. In Europe only the rich, speaking by and large, keep on going to school, which means wasting such talent as may exist among the poor. The idealist is against relegating the masses to vocational training. One such idealist is Sidney Hook, who considers "vocational education conceived as job-training . . . the greatest threat to democratic education in our time." John Dewey also is on the idealist side when he says that to give the majority of children "an education conceived mainly as specific trade preparation is to treat the schools as an agency for transferring the older divisions of leisure and labor, culture and service, mind and body, directing and directed class, into a society nominally democratic." He considers vocational, preprofessional education during the period of basic schooling undemocratic.

To quote again from the Adler-Mayer book: "Chairman Lewis Strauss of the Atomic Energy Commission points out that between 1950 and 1960 the Soviet Union will have trained 1,200,000 new scientists and engineers and the United States 900,000. 'If the crisis in education is not met,' says Admiral Rickhover, 'we will be in danger of losing the Cold War by default.' Are we to curtail liberal education because the Russians do? The realist says, Yes. The idealist, recognizing that the question is, at bottom, political, argues that we lose the Cold War by default if we expand vocational education at the expense of liberal education. Liberal education and it alone, he says, is education for freedom." From the book one gets the impression that Adler and Mayer are prepared to desert the democratic realists and, with Sidney Hook and

Dewey, go over to the democratic idealists. This leaves a final dichotomy of the democratic idealists into traditional-modernist.

First from the democrat and the aristocrat both parties select the democrat; next from the realist and the idealist both select the idealist, so all that is left is to choose between the traditionalist and the modernist.

The traditionalist holds that the liberal education of the past is still good, and should now be given to the many instead of to the few. Since the number of working hours per week has fallen from 70 in 1850 to 40 now, and since the 40-hour-a-week man produces six times as much as his ancestor working twice as long, the great problem is to prepare for this increased leisure. There is now talk of a 32-hour week. With so much leisure everyone should get a liberal education. Unfortunately the educational system is still overwhelmingly vocational instead of humanistic.

Both the traditionalist and the modernist deplore narrow job training, but the traditionalist wants no mixing of the liberal and the job training. The modernist does, and wants the two placed on more of an equal footing. The traditionalist sticks to an exclusively liberal training, but the modernist says that that is an anachronism. He too wants every child to have a liberal education, he cannot exclude concern with the vocational aspect of life. John Dewey says: "A truly liberal, and liberating, education would refuse today to isolate vocational training on any of its levels from a continuous education in the social, moral, and scientific contexts within which wisely administered callings and professions must function." Integrate liberal and vocational education at every level! But how?

One suggestion is to include instruction in the historic backgrounds of the vocations. This Dewey advocates. "An education which acknowledges the full intellectual and social meaning of a vocation would include instruction in the historic background of present conditions; training in science to give intelligence and initiative in dealing with the materials and agencies of production; and study of economics, civics, and politics to bring the future worker into touch with the problems of the day and the various methods for its improvement. Above all, it would train power of readaptation to changing conditions so that future workers could not become blindly subject to a fate imposed on them."

What does the traditionalist want to do? Certainly we need lawyers, doctors, and above all engineers. A single liberal education can be carried just so far. At some point men switch over into the professions and into a thousand specialties. All agree that the start of the education should be liberal. Is the fight merely about at what point the switchover occurs? All agree that the liberal course should have in it some science and that the professional courses should not neglect cultural aspects. Is the fight merely about the degree of admixture of the two?

It is easy to see that these schools are not so far apart as they look. It is also easy to see that just as God is on the side of the strong battalions, so time is on the side of the kind of education that gives us quickly the scientists, the physicists, and the engineers we so desperately need. Here Dewey is with the modern trend, since, like Franklin, he is a convinced advocate of the scientific method.

The traditionalist stands for the reflective rather than the investigative or experimental method. He denies that modern science is exclusively modern. He speaks of scientism rather than of science. He holds by philosophy rather than by science, although he has to admit that the chief exponent on the other side is a philosopher. "John Dewey is clearly the founder of the [modernist] movement." Modernists began as reformers about 1900. The traditionalists did not appear until about 1930 "in a social situation characterized by the boom of the late 1920's and its subsequent collapse—a situation marked by moral cynicism, political indifference, and a preoccupation with the biggest, the shiniest, and the newest marvel of material production." It included, Adler notes, a protest against scientism. When the criticism against "scientism" got under way "Dewey himself in 1938 repudiated extreme 'progressivism' as a misunderstanding and over zealous application of his educational philosophy."

The rock-bottom difference between traditionalist and modernist continues to be the meaning of the scientific method and of science itself. Says Dewey: "We differ profoundly from their belief that the evils and defects of our system spring from excessive attention to what is modern in human civilization—science, technology, contemporary social issues and problems." The traditionalist makes more of the past, the classics, and the great tradition of the church. His is the perennial philosophy. What was good remains good. On this Dewey comments: "Our adverse criticism of the philosophies of the past are not directed at these systems with respect to their connection with intellectual and moral issues of their own time and place, but with respect to their relevancy in a much changed human situation."

"Motivated, perhaps, by polemical considerations," say Adler and Mayer, "the traditionalist accuses the modernist of being nonscientific as regards the nature of reality. . . . True, experience is a process in time, true, too, the world is a world of change and changing things. But the world has permanent as well as mutable characteristics. As the traditionalist sees it, the modernist's exclusive reference to experience reduces all reality to process." Having said this, Adler and Mayer proceed to speak in this volume as if Whitehead is on their side of the fence, and Dewey on the other. This is not the case. Whitehead, of all men, stands pre-eminently for the view that reality is a process. Although Whitehead is a great humanist and a great mathematician, which Dewey was not, he stands shoulder to shoulder with Dewey and James in considering reality, not as a perennial substance but as a constantly changing and creative flux. In fact, along educational lines, as we shall see, Dewey gets powerful support from Whitehead. In bringing the whole question down to a matter of which philosophy we want, Adler is entirely right, but in the matter of philosophy all we can do is to let the American philosophers speak for themselves. It will be found that all the Seven Sages travel with remarkable unanimity along much the same road. Even Santayana, coming up next, although classed strongly on the side of the humanists, is no exception.

Toward the end of a 1958 book, *John Dewey in Perspective,* George R. Geiger makes a spirited attempt, in a sense, to "rehabilitate" this philosopher. The author, following Dewey, asks for a commitment to the "Promethean way of life." "In Prometheus seizing fire from the gods we have the picture of a Maker, a technologist, a transformer. We have the symbol of continuous and responsible reconstruction of man's world. We have at the same time the sign for sacrifice and risk, since Prometheus was bound. Here is a view of man and of nature which offers a challenge as searching as any that human genius has ever called forth. It offers a promise, too, since Prometheus was finally unbound."

George Santayana:
Spiritual Materialist

1. Normal Madness

THE PHRASE IS Santayana's. George Santayana, almost an exact contemporary of John Dewey, was born a few years later than Dewey, 1863 instead of 1859, and died in the same year, 1952. His life spanned as Dewey's did, the same mad, two-world-war period which introduced the atomic age, and reflected even more deeply than that of the native Vermonter the disturbing turmoils of that age. In a sense he fled from them. Santayana's life falls into two separate cycles, one fifty and the other forty years in length. During the first of these cycles he viewed the world from a vantage point in America, during the second from a scholar's asylum in Europe. Both cycles were equally productive. He was a footloose, unwearied worker. Born in Spain, educated in America, and dying in Rome, unmarried, unattached, he liked to refer to himself as a deracinated man or, less dramatically, as a wandering scholar who made the world his home. In bearing and in personal punctiliousness he was about as different from Dewey, the family man, as could possibly be imagined, yet in his philosophy he dovetails into Dewey, his views falling into the same broadly naturalistic pattern, Dewey stressing the malleability and Santayana the indifference of nature.

Both Dewey and Santayana were greatly occupied with Greece. Santayana breathed the spirit of Plato and Aristotle but his accent was American. With James too he had a close affinity. His thoughts were quite as independent, original, and unconsciously American as those of James, with that same slightly offbeat and untamed quality that James also savored. Like James, he sought for ways to manage the world so as to give himself time and opportunity to enjoy it to the full, adding, if possible, to its aesthetic fillip. This men can do by building islands of "normal" mad-

ness within the senseless deliriums of geological ages with atoms
for a heart. For, make no mistake about it—this is a mad, mad
world.

The cosmos, for all its apparent order, when you look underneath is alive with unleashed energy. Those far away and misty
galaxies that look so peaceful, if you could walk up to them you
would see that they are studded with dramatic exits and en-
trances. Stars are born and die. Suns last for aeons and then
suddenly their place knows them no more. Violent explosions
occur in the heavens. What happens? Do they turn into whirling
corpses, stark and cold, some still tied to a glowing twin, or do
they just give up their souls in a last burst of dissipating energy?
Physical astronomy is still a new science, but the more it is studied
the more it turns into cosmogony. Eventually we may know how
it all arose and how it all keeps going. Some stars, like our own
sun, certainly are centers of fiery upheaval, flames shooting outward from the rim millions of miles into space. Within its interior
tremendous nuclear explosions are as natural as breathing. Possibly through these shuddering rages of concatenated atom split-
tings this huge monster renews its life-giving energy, which even
as far away as the earth we sometimes feel as a scorching heat.
Nevertheless, this fiery mother nourishes satellites of the most
varied types. Other suns have other planets; in fact, there are billions of suns; this thing staggers the imagination.

Our own planet teems with life. Each of the myriad forms of
life on this planet has its day in court. Some forms of life go
under, some survive. Nature, if you call nature the sum of it all,
seems callously indifferent or indulgently tolerant—whichever
way you like to put it—to vast experimentation. The most dis-
parate self-centered vortices of life, large and small, spawn under
her tent. Each independent whirl of energy tries for a time to
maintain itself. No one type prevails. None gains dominance,
unless you can call our own recent and rapid climb up the bean-
stalk a dominance. In this vast multitude, of which humanity is
a member, each component pits itself against the enormously
gregarious impartiality of nature, which in its deepest essence
seems to be an uneasy congeries of self-sustaining madnesses.

Come to think of it, why should one form of life prevail over any other? Are we right in not being nice to the tuberculosis germs that feed on our lungs? Have we an exclusive right to life? Why should men have dominion over the beasts of the field, slaying innocent oxen for food, snaring and baiting at will any form of fowl or fish? It is easy to put down on paper a claim that the maker of the universe gave us that right. If elephants could write, they would do the same. Our own systematized delusions are particularly well worked out, but other forms of paranoia in other animals, not having words like ours, are as stubbornly maintained. The other animals do have actions which speak louder than words, and we reply with equally ferocious actions which have thus far enabled us to win out over all other animals, as well as over poisonous plants and fungi.

But the point here is not that there are many different madnesses, pitted against each other, but rather that within each specific manifestation of madness there are other extreme and plainly suicidal forms of madness. Let the cosmos be, all told, not only infinitely greater than we thought but also infinitely more fierce—on this point Emerson stands corrected—yet there seems to be at least a spark of nurturing sanity within all this ghastly horseplay. Some win out. A prize is offered. What is the secret of survival? Normal madness—as opposed to gluttonous insanity? Yes, says Santayana. To paraphrase his exposition from the *Dialogues in Limbo:* Belief in the imaginary and desire for the impossible are extreme or abnormal madnesses, but conventional sanity is a normal madness, like love in youth or religion among the nations. Two protecting deities, Punishment and Agreement, daily remove the maddest. The good work of punishment heals and harmonizes the worst of fellows. Before dying in the arms of Punishment madness may be mitigated and tamed by Agreement. All get a brief chance to learn from experience. Migratory fowl are well informed about Egypt without ever having read Herodotus. Agreement weaves bonds. In friendship madness is tempered by Agreement. Madness is natural, and, like all things natural, it loves itself and lives in harmony with nature.

Because madness is inconvenient to society, men call it contrary to nature. But nothing can be contrary to nature; and that a man should shriek, or talk to the air or to a guardian genius at

his elbow, or should kill his children and himself is not contrary
to nature, but only to the habit of the majority. You may therefore, without scientific error, praise madness or deride it. Every
nation thinks its own madness normal and requisite.

The intoxication of life is the first cause of its appearance.
What madness to assert that one collocation of atoms or one conjunction of feelings alone is right or better than another. Also,
suddenly to renounce all madness is to miss the truth about madness. Wisdom is the evanescent madness, which lets the dream
continue but no longer lets it deceive. We have here been paraphrasing Santayana.

Santayana's normal madness in his *Dialogues in Limbo* is put
into the mouth of Democritus, the atomist, also known as the
laughing philosopher, who in this Santayana whimsey claims that
he can smell a man's philosophy. As a hound by the scent can tell
a fox from a boar, so Democritus can smell out the man who has
the right philosophy, which is something, of course, not so different from what Democritus himself is sold on. The Stranger
enters the imaginary dialogue between Democritus and Alcibiades
by announcing that he is a disciple of Democritus. I knew it, says
Democritus in effect, but do you know why I am superior? And
then he goes on to answer this question himself.

It is because no dreamer can know the truth, not even about his
dream, except by waking out of it. If you spin one dream to
explain another, how will you ever get out of the labyrinth?
Though I am alive, says Democritus, and must behold appearances, I am sane and know reality. Democritus has waked out of
his dream. Life is the quintessence of madness.

At this point the Stranger in the dialogue, who is none other
than Santayana himself, feels that he should make a contribution,
and he tells the story of Autologos. It is a story about a child, a
botanist, and an old woman. A child named the flowers by names
of his own invention; the rose he called beauty; the jasmine,
pleasure, and so on. The botanist let him do this, although he
knew the real names of the flowers and although he had told the
child that flowers have no souls. Then along comes an old woman
who with her pruning knife cuts off everybody's head, flowers,
child, and botanist included. The old woman is the goddess Diké,

the same one that Democritus called Punishment, and the botanist was Nomos, or Agreement, and the child was Autologos, or innocent illusion. After all this talk about Madness, Aristippus, another of those present, is all for raising immediately an altar to Madness. Dionysius, who has joined the parley, agrees. After all, says Dionysius, my business is to fill the votaries with a new frenzy of worship. The whole discourse is summed up as an apology for illusion and a proof of its necessity. "The young man who has not wept is a savage, and the old man who will not laugh is a fool."

The best way to get a perspective on Santayana is to consider him one of the small brotherhood of scientifically oriented thinkers who try to reconcile the rationality of science with the zeal of religion. Edward A. White in 1952 wrote an excellent book, *Science and Religion in American Thought,* in which he analyzes the work of four men who discuss in detail the so-called "warfare" between science and religion. All of them are "biased," if you want to put it that way, in favor of science, yet not one of them thinks there is any real conflict between science and religion. This applies to John William Draper, Andrew Dickson White, John Fiske, and David Starr Jordan, all of whom have written books on this subject.

All this is put on a much wider footing by Santayana, who wastes no time going over science in detail. Instead he accepts the entire methodology and all the established results of the separate sciences, lumping them together under the term "materialism," which in the bright lexicon of Santayana is not necessarily a dirty word. In Santayana, incomparable stylist and poet, we have a self-confessed "materialist" who wrote a set of five books advocating the spiritual life, and later wrote another set of five with the exactly same purpose. Is this a stunt, or do we have here the beginnings of a broader formulation of man, the spiritual being, as a product of nature? This is not a scientific technician making out a case for the deeper values of religion, but a poet and a thinker to whom the very essence of life on this planet is summed up in what he calls its spiritual values.

Santayana differs from the other apologists of science in having a different background. The others were Protestants, but Santayana approaches the subject of man's higher life from a Catholic inheritance. All this, as we shall see in the next section, he acknowledges quite candidly. To an astonishing degree Santayana remains Catholic or universal in his tastes and predilections. He fundamentally dislikes Puritanism; and Protestantism he sideswipes as a pre-Christian, heathenish approach, tainted with commercialism. It may be that five hundred years from now Santayana will be put down as an allegorizing Catholic remarkably true to the central tenets of his inherited faith and one of the first to put on a solid and nonmystical basis the legitimately spiritual aspirations of mankind.

2. An American Don Quixote

IN THREE SMALL volumes, leisurely written by Santayana toward the end of his life, we get comments on the people he knew, on his family, and on the genesis of his philosophy. Everything Santayana wrote, no matter when or where, was literature in a finished style inimitably his own. The poet, the critic, the philosopher in him could always, as in these autobiographical notes, produce a polished story, highly readable, and giving insight into the inner life of a truly solitary soul. For the bare facts of his early life and ancestry here are a few paragraphs in shortened form but in his own words:

"Both my father and my mother's father were officials in the Spanish civil service in the Philippine Islands. My father had studied the country and the natives, and had written a little book about the Island of Mindanao; he had been three times around the world in the sailing-ships of the period.

"It was in Madrid in 1862, where my mother had gone on a visit intended to be temporary, that my father and she were married. He had been an old friend of hers and of her first husband's, and was well aware of her settled plan to educate her children in America, and recognized the propriety of that arrangement. . . . My mother returned with her Sturgis children to live in the United States and my father and I remained in Spain. The education and prospects which my father, in his modest retirement, could offer me in Spain were far from brilliant; and in 1872 he decided to take me to Boston, where, after remaining for one cold winter, he left me in my mother's care and went back to Spain. I was then in my ninth year, having been born on December 16, 1863, and I did not know

257

one word of English. . . . I picked up my English by ear
before knowing how it was written: a circumstance to which
I probably owe speaking the language without a marked foreign
accent.

"Like my parents, I have always set myself down officially
as a Catholic: but this is a matter of sympathy and traditional
allegiance, not of philosophy. My mother, like her father before
her, was a Deist: she was sure there was a God, for who else
could have made the world! But God was too great to take
special thought for man: sacrifices, prayers, churches, and
tales of immortality were invented by rascally priests in order
to dominate the foolish. My father, except for the Deism, was
emphatically of the same opinion.

"Thus, although I learned my prayers and catechism by rote,
as was then inevitable in Spain, I knew that my parents regarded
all religion as a work of human imagination: and I agreed, and
still agree, with them there. But this carried an implication in
their minds against which every instinct in me rebelled, namely
that the works of human imagination are bad. No, said I to
myself even as a boy: they are good, they alone are good;
and the rest—the whole real world—is ashes in the mouth."

From the first volume of his autobiography, *Persons and
Places, The Background of My Life*, emerge vivid relatives and
equally vivid reactions from the boy thrust into the American
world at the age of nine. At one point he says, "I had a spontaneous feeling that life was a dream." This Spanish refrain,
"La vida es sueño," runs through his whole life, not rendering the
pictures he saw any less real, but as an under-the-surface channel
to some deeper life current. In Santayana the New and the
Old World mix quite smoothly, but the inner core of him got to be
entirely American. The hidalgo and the Americano in him on
occasion sing a plaintive song, but the solid challenges of fate
he meets cheerfully head on. No Spaniard is namby-pamby.
We keep on liking Don Quixote even when he is fighting wind-
mills.

Nevertheless, rightly or wrongly, Santayana says of himself,
"I have never been adventurous; I need to be quiet in order to
be free." Thinking of his father, Santayana remarks: "The

Spaniard is an individualist. He distrusts everything and every-body, even his priests and his kings." The father, who ended up practically a hermit in the small town of Avila, Spain, thought oxtail soup, as the English ate it, "fit to resurrect the dead." Spells of dysentery undermined his courage, but on his death bed he asked for extreme unction and a chicken.

Santayana's mother was of Catalonian origin. Her father, a disciple of Rousseau, left Spain when Napoleon came in 1823. Later he went to Glasgow, gave Spanish lessons, and learned English. This explains how Santayana's mother could be born in Glasgow, Scotland, and yet be ultra-Spanish. Her father next went to Virginia, whence he was appointed consul at Barcelona. After the consulate at Barcelona lapsed, he obtained what he thought would be a lucrative post in the Philippine Islands. It turned out to be a small position in an out-of-the-way place where he died, leaving the future Santayana's mother to make her way back to Manila where she met and married George Sturgis. Eight years later Sturgis died. His widow, who had had five children in seven years, was expecting another child when she arrived in Boston. Out of the children of the first marriage three survived. George Santayana was the only child of the second marriage. His mother prized what the Sturgis family stood for, security, but she was far from well off. Only later did things ease up somewhat, but Santayana was never anywhere near wealthy, especially in the early days. The Sturgises, formerly merchant princes, were rapidly falling on evil days. Only one still had an important business in London, but he was a remote figure. Santayana tarries with the different uncles, but gives a whole chapter to "My Sister Susana," a half sister who later married a Spaniard and moved to Spain, welcoming George as a visitor. His father read English perfectly but could not speak it. When George was still young, Susana took the little boy in tow and began to teach him English. He also spent some months in a kindergarten with very young children where without embarrassment he learned to speak good English.

From age eight to sixteen he went to a Latin school which was cheap and free. He learned Latin easily but had difficulty with Greek. He left the school with honors, but "in reality, I remained there as I remained at Harvard for 25 years, a stranger at heart." He was much interested then and later in architecture, especially of churches. Walking was his only form of exercise. At seventeen Santayana's philosophy was pretty well formed. He was convinced of the "steady march of cosmic forces which we may, in a measure, enlist in our service, and thereby win the prize of life without laying any claims to dominate the universe, either physically or morally." This was a comparatively mature, though a very ancient, conclusion. He had also become keenly aware of the uncertainty and blindness of human opinion. To him Emerson and Lucretius are the only ones who speak of nature in the right way.

James impressed Santayana as a medical man. In the lectures of James, pragmatism appeared in its negative form as scorn of everything pretentious. He also remembered the love James had for lame ducks, which later took the form of breadth of mind. James detested any system of the universe that excluded romantic surprises. Death MIGHT open new worlds to us, not what religions predict but something at once novel and natural. Santayana agreed with James that Spencer's evolution was a tangle of loose generalities. Santayana also speaks of Spinoza, "lessons from whom in several respects laid the foundation of my philosophy." He liked the way Spinoza spoke of "God or Nature," and his remark that the mind of God resembles the mind of man as the Dog Star resembles a barking animal. "I regard Spinoza as the only modern philosopher in the line of orthodox physics, the line that begins with Thales and culminates, for Greek philosophy, in Democritus." Conclusion: morality is something natural.

The second biographical volume, *The Middle Span,* opens with Santayana in Germany. He never learned to speak German well. He liked the music, the uniforms, and the beer. He listened to Paulsen, who lectured on Greek ethics and then on Spinoza. He heard Ebbinghaus condemn James for not thinking through the *Will to Believe,* and he comes to the defense of James, calling him "no draught-horse patiently pulling the scientific barge along a placid academic canal," but rather "a red Indian shooting the rapids with spasmodic skill and elemental emotion."

He never liked German philosophy and later wrote a vitriolic condemnation of German idealism as leading to egomania.

A string of fugitive, miscellaneous pleasures is not happiness; happiness resides in imaginative reflection and judgment. Epicurus renounced most of the ordinary pleasures for the sake of peace, equanimity, and intelligence. Santayana could not take a doctor's degree in Germany, where he felt too much at loose ends. He went back to become a resident graduate student at Harvard. "On my return to America in 1888 I at once consulted Royce as to my thesis for the doctorate, and suggested for a subject the philosophy of Schopenhauer, because Schopenhauer was the German author that I liked most and knew best. The wise Royce shook his head. That might do, he said, for a master of arts, not for a doctor of philosophy. Instead he proposed Lotze. . . . My dull thesis on Lotze was duly accepted, and I was told that I was the most normal doctor of philosophy that they had ever created. . . . I wish now that my thesis might have been on Hegel; it would have meant harder work, and it would have been more inadequate, yet it would have prepared me better for professional controversies, and for understanding the mind of my time. Lotze was stillborn, and I have forgotten everything that I then had to read in him and to ponder. I liked Hegel's *Phänomenologie;* it set me planning my *Life of Reason.*"

Santayana stayed on at Harvard, first as instructor, then as assistant professor, and finally as a full professor, a slow climb, since Eliot disliked Santayana because he was a humanist and not enough of a specialist. Santayana considered himself only an indifferent success at Harvard, speaking of the Harvard years as a "period of somnambulism." If so, during that sleepwalking period of his life he wrote one of the masterpieces of American philosophy, the five volumes of the *Life of Reason.* At the close of his last lecture, before he retired in 1911, his class rose and cheered him for twenty minutes.

The years 1904–1906 he spent abroad, the first as a sabbatical year in Italy and the East, the second at Paris as an exchange professor at the Sorbonne. Many vacations and exciting hours were spent in England. Ninety per cent of his memoirs are

given to asides about his philosophy and to reflections on relatives
and friends. These volumes often read as if they were preliminary sketches for the novel he wished to write and finally
did write in 1936, *The Last Puritan.* Santayana found it hard to fit
himself into any prescribed routine. "Never having been in army,
nursery, or an Evangelical family. . . . I saw at once that I
was unfit to live under a free government where other people
voted as to what I should do." Spain is described as "grandeur
without luxury," and England sometimes as "luxury without
grandeur." When asked why he did not marry, Santayana
answered that he wished to be free and did not intend to live
always in America. He avoided rich women, not that he had
any fault to find with them, but "a man who has been torn up
by the roots, cannot be replanted and should never propagate
his kind. I was not a believer in what my religion, or any
religion, teaches dogmatically; yet I wouldn't for the world have
had a wife or children dead to religion. Some bury as deep
as possible the fact that they were born Catholics or Jews.
But I am not a man of that stamp. I have been involuntarily
uprooted. I accept the intellectual advantages of that position,
with its social and moral disqualifications. And I refuse to be
annexed, to be abolished, or to be grafted onto any plant of
a different species."

In the last volume of his reminiscences, *My Host the World,*
Santayana speaks of a change of heart he underwent at thirty.
He quotes Dante's: "Drop false hopes, the seed of tears, and
listen." He decided then that being a student, preferably a
wandering student, was his real vocation in life. He also quotes
Goethe: *"Ich hab' mein Sach auf Nichts gestellt."* "I was driven
from the temporal to the eternal, setting my heart on nothing
. . . I lived my philosophy." In a chapter on his old age in
Italy, he explains that he desired solitude and independence.
"I like to be a stranger myself, it was my destiny." He did not
club up with other strangers. He found an old book on Walks
in Venice, and following it started to talk Italian, at first with
a modernist priest who had translated some of his works; later
he became proficient enough to be eloquent in Italian in a
limited way.

Santayana claims he never enjoyed youth as thoroughly as he did old age while writing *Realms of Being, Dialogues in Limbo,* and *The Last Puritan.* These, of course, he wrote in English. They are thoroughly American in spirit, and by this time he had an eager audience in America. Nothing to Santayana is invincibly young except spirit. "In fine, I opened my eyes on the world with the conviction that it was inhuman: not meant for man, but habitable by him, and possible to exploit, with prudence, in innumerable ways: a conviction that everything ever since has confirmed. . . . The great master of sympathy with nature, in my education, was Lucretius . . ." He goes deeper than the romantic naturalists. "Not only aesthetically but dynamically, as felt by Lucretius, nature to me is a welcome presence; and modern progress in mechanical invention and industrial luxury has excited joyously my materialistic imagination, as it did prophetically that of Bacon." Santayana also speaks of the love of employing leisure in small mechanical occupations, and admits that often in life he "sipped at the rim of the plutocratic cup."

Santayana took the early war between the United States and Spain in his stride, grieving only that the pitiful weakness of Spain had now been revealed to the world. The two great wars were to him monstrous adventures in enthusiastic unreason. To the terribly disappointed old man it seemed that the contemporary world had turned its back on any desire to live reasonably. A home, a family, a chosen trade, and freedom in practicing it—the proletariat knows pretty well what the fundamentals are—but instead the world chooses war. Santayana hated militarism, egotism, conceit, and any attempt to reform mankind by misrepresenting their capacities and their place in the universe. This zeal for *bouleversement* is no merely ancient or medieval delusion; it persists today. Cervantes wrote his *Don Quixote* aiming to destroy the silly romances of his day and succeeded only in writing a still greater romance himself, the prototype of all future novels. Santayana, a disillusioned romantic, succeeded only in presenting in his own philosophy a grander and more enveloping romance than any he derided.

Baker Brownell, a student of Santayana's at Harvard, contributes a physical portrait. "While Royce would loaf in the doorway before class, a cigar in his mouth, his great white head lolling to one side, and James would flit in and out along the hall on some business or other, Santayana would come to class and then go away, and that was all. He had no periphery there outside of the class room. Once on his way down the hall, he paused before the bronze, seated Emerson for whom the hall is named. He looked at it a moment and turned to me standing nearby. 'How do you like it?' he asked me; and to my rather indefinite reply, he said, 'The upper part is all right, but those shanks are too prominent.' I walked on with him to Phil 10; it is the only time I saw him dally outside of the class room.

"He was a dark, gentle looking man, unobtrusive, medium sized. He was quietly dressed, neither arty nor academic, and usually, as I remember, wore fastidious, faintly trans-Atlantic black. Within his quietness one discerned a distinguished manner, grace, reticent pride; and he had beautiful eyes. He was bald, rather tragically so, we students thought, but he had a handsome and philosophic beard that later gave way to more handsome though less philosophic mustaches without a beard. His lectures were quiet, gently spoken. He rarely paced the stage. Usually he sat in his chair, his musing hands, before him, gave his lecture or carried on a leisurely class discussion, and when the bell rang, stopped. Certainly the so-called enigma and evanescence of his philosophy was not personal flightiness or whim. It was, if anywhere, in the natural texture of his thinking."

Santayana was in America from 1872 to 1912; thereafter he lived in Europe, mostly in Rome. Baker Brownell thinks Santayana left just at the wrong time. "He missed in America the brilliant movement in poetry that began with the founding of *Poetry, A Magazine of Verse*, in 1912, the year he left, but I am not sure that his tradition-tinted literary values would have been congenial to it anyhow. Sandburg, Frost, Masters, Lindsay, Stevens, Jeffers were just coming into the sunlight. He missed most of the new American dancing and wild music, the bands, the jazz, a massive Dionysian folk movement that would have influenced him even in his resistance. He missed much of the modern architecture and its drive towards cleanness and functionalism. Frank Lloyd Wright that year had just published his architectural designs in Germany. The Progressive rebellion against the old line interests burst forth that year and has continued intermittently down through Wilson and the second Roosevelt. But these liberal vitalities in the arts and in society might well have left him cold even had be been here. His own vitality was of another sort."

3. The Unfinished Symphony

EACH MAN, we shall find, carries the basic American philosophy a little further. It is a great mistake to consider it finished even today. It is folly to criticize William James, the exponent of pragmatism, as if in him the whole movement of American philosophy came and went. He fits into the movement, occupying his niche and nobody else's. He merely set it going along certain broad directional lines already clearly laid out by the American genius of Franklin and Emerson.

Then came Dewey, who built it out still further on the social side. Even so, Dewey also still left the structure very incomplete. Dewey greatly advanced historical logic, implanting it firmly in the scientific method, but even here what he gives us is only an extensive introduction. He tells us how we think, how the mind works in solving a problem, but he tells us very little of the logic embedded in the structure of reality. Why are and must things in a sense be thus and so? Others will begin to square off on this problem. Dewey, as yet, has almost no metaphysics. Before that part of philosophy can be built up, we need some bold speculations on ontology, the science of being. These we begin to get from Santayana.

Not too many historians of philosophy have tried to show how American philosophy hangs together. Most of the accounts, no matter how long, soon become too complicated and do not succeed in setting forth clearly the main directions in which American philosophy is tending. One of the better, clear and short accounts comes from William Savery of the University of Washington. This does not carry us very far, but it gives us light on two essential points. Published as a comment on Dewey's philosophy in *The Philosophy of John Dewey,* edited by Paul

Arthur Schilpp (1951), it covers not only Dewey but the whole field thus far.

A good way to differentiate American philosophy, thinks Savery, is to pick out one or two main lines in which it departs from conventional philosophy and strikes out into fresh pastures. One of these advances occurred in the account of what we mean by truth. There have been only two significant theories of truth in the whole 2,500-year range of the history of philosophy; one of these is the correspondence theory of truth, as held by common sense, by Aristotle, and by the Scholastics, and the other is the coherence theory of truth, as held by Spinoza, Kant, Hegel, and others.

The correspondence, or copy, theory makes truth a copy or reproduction of the real thing. An idea corresponds to its object. Just how does not matter so much, but ideas in some way resemble or stand for things. In the other theory the emphasis is on the way ideas hang together as a consistent whole. In the coherence theory what we get is something on the model of mathematics, where there are no internal contraditions and where the whole constitutes a beautifully coherent system. If it is logically consistent throughout and has no parts flatly con- tradicting other parts, we may have hit upon the truth—at least we have something consistent with some sort of being. The coherence theory went along fine until some men voiced the awful suspicion that perhaps all we were doing was to build up a theory of what things might be or even of what we would like things to be. Is the world itself really so coherent? James, for one, makes a great point of saying that it is not.

For twenty-five hundred years these two theories, either the one or the other, have ruled the roost. Now comes a new theory of truth. Truth is connected with action. Very roughly speaking, the truth is what works and what gets established. We might call it the survival theory. When James first roughly sketched it out in the crude form of "the truth is what works" he certainly got himself into a lot of trouble. Things stood a little better when Dewey took the new ideas in hand, laying down what amounted to a new theory of induction. It will become still clearer when we hear what Peirce, the master logician, has to say. As Savery puts it: "Peirce led to James and James to Dewey and the result was the inductive and experimental theory of truth. It is the now famous theory of pragmatism or instrumentalism. According to this the original of truth is verification and its most extended meaning is verifiability. . . . It is . . . a curious thing that it was in unphilosophical America that an inductive theory of truth came into being." James "made it clear that the truth of a conception is to be determined by its prediction of future experiences." This inductive theory of truth leads directly to the operational theory of truth held by prominent physicists and mathematicians such as Bridgman, Eddington, and Brouwer. Logical positivism too is an offshoot. And Santayana, as Savery puts it, is a "sidestream overhung with the magical beauty of essences." We shall see that Santayana is much more than that, but it is well to stress early Santayana's delineation of essences.

The second thing that all American philosophies have in common is that they start with common sense and never throw out the thick everyday world in favor of the thin abstractions usually associated with philosophy. American philosophies are pluralistic rather than monistic. One hint as to how the world may be pluralistic and still have some sort of unity is supplied by Savery when he calls the views of James, Peirce, and Dewey concatenism. The world is a chain of interlocking links. James stressed this sort of jointed overlapping. Concatenism is a middle way between monism and such completely isolated separation of small parts as we get in Leibnitz's monads. This hypothesis of a concatenated world Savery regards as the most important invention of philosophy since the middle of the nineteenth century.

The stuff of the world is natural events—according to Dewey and James, neither physical nor mental. James speaks of a neutral substance that can go either way. Dewey makes mind and matter different characters of natural events, matter expressing their sequential order and mind the order of their meanings when they enter certain connections and dependencies. Both James and Dewey make consciousness denote an awareness or perception of meanings. Consciousness has a great deal to do with perspectives. A positivist knows only perspectives and their connections, but a realist (and all the men encountered thus far, including Santayana, are realists) believes in a massive background to our perspectives which cannot be ignored and within which our perspectives are projected.

This massive background is the thick world, an external world into which we shoot our perspectives. We have a direct experience of these manifold, shifting perspectives of which each living human being is a center, but behind and beyond, joined in some way, is the existential world in which we are all so deeply implicated. Dewey is not a materialist, since for him life and mind emerge from something simpler, but Santayana plainly makes matter the matrix from which all else emerges. If he had made his essence basic he might have been a monist, but, no, all these eternal essences are grounded in the existential world. This makes Santayana, too, a realist and a pluralist. But Santayana is much more than that.

It is as if thus far all the makings of a huge Oriental carpet had been brought together but no one had started the actual weaving. There were the colored threads, the design, the loom, all the materials and the instrument and even a sketch as to how the design could be worked out, but no one had set about making the rug, which, come to think of it, is a truly happy and exciting task. In reading Santayana you feel that he is making the rug. This Ishmael uprooted from Europe, thrown into all the gears and meshes of American life, and then back again to Europe is not an outcast. Of all people he is at home in this world, and no more afraid than his father was of sailing leisurely around it several times, learning how to live, and how to get the most out of the process of living, which he considers a sort of creative business, like a silkworm spinning its cocoon. Above we loosely called it a carpet. At any rate in Santayana we get a man quietly at work picking out the beautiful strands all around him and weaving them into a Life of Reason.

It is hard to explain the restful quality of Santayana. Gone is the fevered rush. This man, like Cardinal Newman, has finally found the truth—had never left it, as a matter of fact—and he is at home, giving you quietly the meaning of it all. In Santayana there is a wealth of constructive detail about the good life such as is found in no other philosopher. It is impossible to imagine a happier resignation and a more calmly exciting task (if one can use terms which don't seem to fit together) than the one that this man is engaged in. Perhaps it is peace rather than restfulness that Santayana has found. Peace on earth and good will to men is exactly what he preaches, except that he is not preaching it so much as just doing it, as best he can, and enjoying it.

In Santayana we get a curiously satisfying sketch of what it means to lead a spiritual life. It is in human life the transition from grossness to fineness, from baseness to nobility, from aimlessness to concentration. It is hewing to the lifeline. It is enjoying the charm of the unfinished quality of it all. Always there is more, much more to do. The vistas remain exciting. We are told that when the Lord had created the earth and the heavens he looked upon his work and saw that it was good. Santayana is a man who walks with delight in the footsteps of the Lord. Joining the other American philosophers, he revels not in abstractions but in the palpable, polychrome world of sunsets and flowers and of human beings lovelier than flowers.

4. The Life of Reason

"I STAND IN philosophy exactly where I stand in daily life,"
says Santayana. "My philosophy is justified . . . by the facts before every man's eyes; and no great wit is requisite to discover
it. . . . A philosopher is compelled . . . to plunge *in medias
res*. . . . If he begins in the middle he will still begin at the
beginning of something . . . he would reach origins or elements
only at the end of his analysis." Santayana explains that he is
not beginning with first principles, because such principles,
if discovered at all, are found only after they long have been
taken for granted, and employed in the very investigation which
reveals them.

"I am not concerned about make-believe philosophies, but
about my actual beliefs. . . . Philosophy is nothing if not honest.
. . . To me experience has not a string of sensations for its
objects. . . . Experience, at its very inception is a revelation of
things . . . it is a mere prejudice to suppose that experience
has only such categories as colour, sound, touch, and smell . . .
far more primitive in animal experience are such dichotomies as
good and bad, near and far, coming and going, fast and slow,
just now and very soon. . . . Belief in substance . . . is the
voice of hunger. . . . It is as if Substance said to Knowledge:
. . . I should not have been so cruel as to give thee birth, if
there had been nothing for thee to master; but having first prepared the field, I set in thy heart the love of adventure."

The trouble with beginning to quote Santayana is that it is
hard to stop quoting him. Whether he caught it from James or
not, he has some of that same breathless quality. There is a lure
in his pages that draws you on. In the five books of his

Life of Reason we get the inner flowering of Santayana's life at Harvard. After he left the United States he wrote another five books, equally fascinating, *The Realms of Being*. How the Realms and the Reason differ from each other can be put into a sentence. In the books on Reason we get close-ups; he moves around with his camera and gives a bewildering variety of shots all expressing his own personality; while in the Realms he moves further away, you get an aerial view, vaster vistas, you see the plan.

Reason in Common Sense, the first of the five books begins, as simply as can be, from right where you stand. We are born into a world already pretty fearfully and wonderfully put together. Adaptation of life to its surroundings has long been carried on by irrational and even unconscious processes. In the passion of love, an irrational instinct, a man gets something to live for, a mate, a momentary madness that has method and is going to develop into a life of reason. To lead a life of reason is to fall in love with the good, but first of all a man has to learn to distinguish excellence from trash.

To deny that pleasure is good and pain evil is a grotesque affectation. Here Santayana follows Aristotle. A man who prefers to inflict pain on those he loves is a fiend. Thus at the threshold of reason there is a kind of choice: the soul adopts the body's aims. In saying this we are using the language of common sense, and that is a good way to start out. Reason, taking the side of the body, enters into a partnership with the world and begins to be respected there. The first task of intelligence is to represent the environing reality. Thus intelligence intertwines itself with experience. Thought is a form of life like nutrition, generation, and art. Aristotle took for granted that reason would side with the body in seeking happiness.

And now comes a modern touch, slightly departing from Aristotle. Reason thickens life. It does not and should not abstract from life, for if it does, it gets away from life and may climb into realms of its own from which it cannot get back to earth, and then ceases to be useful. Take the simplest mental operation on sensible data, the process of counting. To be aware that a second stroke is not the first, I must retain something of the old sensation. Repetition becomes cumulative. Primitive man with face raised to heaven encounters brightness. Presently the sun is a god. What is conceived to support the physical qualities becomes a vital force. The mind gives us a sense of acquaintance with a certain field of reality. Knowledge is a recognition of something absent; it is a salutation, not an embrace. Repeated recognitions become objects. Thus the notion of an independent world is born, a conception of reality—the first flight of reason. The genial discovery that all of nature makes one system is the Magna Charta of the mind. This unification of nature is only a beginning. God existed in man's apprehension long before mathematics and even before the blue vault of heaven. For long, every morning there was a new world with the same fool to live in it, but the animistic view puts mind among nature. Mind dwells in the world. The inner or personal world is at first a poor remnant, probably most evident in dreams.

Concomitantly there is the discovery of fellow creatures conceived to share the same thoughts and passions in a nature personified also in gods and devils with feelings like ourselves. Aristotle and others made too much of the generalizing process. They ignored the primary fictions. We should not. The origin of ideas involves CONCRETION rather than ABSTRACTION. Whitehead is going to make much of the hint that Santayana here throws out. The mind makes the world not thinner but thicker, with more of reality in it. Remember that the mind includes the imagination. The mind does not deny common sense. Philosophy is not opposed to common sense. It gets along with common sense and deepens it. On this Santayana is most emphatic in his *Scepticism and Animal Faith* from which the thoughts given above are taken.

For all of his wonderful essences Santayana is in the thick of pragmatic philosophy. Never for a moment does he forget biology. A supreme good, or an abstract good, is a good for nobody, a dialectical superstition. Zeal for such shibboleths inhibits the exercise of intelligent choice. Such a single fixed goal assumes a fixed and universal human nature, belied by evolution. Human nature is a variable in which the ideal of one age has no authority over the ideals of another. Reason, as a

function of human nature, cannot be indifferent to the good
and evil of each passing day. Human nature is variable in the
sense that the steam engine has varied greatly since its invention, but it, and even the electric motor, is still built around
the same basic idea—a force in nature harnessed to help the
human arm. The living mind cannot surrender its rights. Man
is a biological creature learning to use its mind. It is a commonplace of the schools that to form abstract ideas is the prerogative
of human reason. But do we attain truth by making a silhouette
of our experience? Santayana refuses to be wafted into the whorls
of abstract thought. His feet are on the ground and they stay
there. Creation is a work of life, and the method that brings
order out of chaos is called intelligence.

Mankind can never surrender its animal nature. If it does it
perishes. Man represents the universe that sustains him. It is
noteworthy that utopias are inane. Mortality has its compensations: one is that evils are transitory, and another is that better
times may come. The life of reason has a natural basis, but has
in the ideal world a creative and absolute authority. To give
a general picture of human nature, thus conceived, is the aim of
his next book *Reason in Society.* The main principle is that nature
carries its ideals with it, and that the progressive organization of
irrational impulses makes life rational.

Love has an animal basis, but an ideal object. To make the
origin of love divine and its object natural is to reverse the
truth. The love that to the naturalist is a thin veil, and a prelude
to the self-assertion of lust, becomes thus a noble and immense
inspiration. Human reason lives by turning the friction of material forces into ideal goods.

In nature plants bloom and die, a vital rhythm from blossom
to seed and back again, like the seasons. When love is finally
consummated, it feels a profound impulse to welcome death.
This is Santayana's version of the death wish; he quotes Goethe:
*"Lachend lass' uns verderben! Lachend zu Grunde geh'n. Ende
in Wonne, Du ewig Geschlecht!"* Animal love is deserving of
more sympathetic treatment than Western poets have given it.
The joy of gazing on the face of the beloved, of following or
being followed, of tacit understandings and avowals, of flight,

conquest, and surrender, make bright pages in the thin biography of many a soul. The darkness which covers this passion is one of the saddest consequences of Adam's fall. Public opinion often condemns what is in itself perfectly innocent. When chastity begins to seem holy and perpetual virginity an absolute ideal, man throws away the very elements needed to make something higher.

If women are rarely seen and ordinarily not spoken to, there may be love at first sight. Not to believe in love at all is a sign of great dullness. The lover worships from the heart and beholds that what he worships is no low being, but an ideal form essentially eternal and capable of endless embodiments. This makes life ideally relevant to generation. Whenever this ideality is absent, and the lover sees only what all others see, there is no bewitchment; no divine shaft has pierced the heart. Love is a true natural religion. The loftiest edifice needs the deepest foundation. A man who has truly loved will not recant his essential faith; he will keep his sense for the ideal and his power to worship. All these are Santayana's thoughts.

Love is but an overture whereby passion settles into possession, courtship into partnership, pleasure into habit. A child, half mystery and half plaything, comes to show what has been done and to make its consequences perpetual. Life narrows down to one mortal career. The family is one of nature's masterpieces. Parents are a memory for children; children a vicarious immortality for parents. To be born half-made is an immense advantage provided by being born into a family. It is difficult to think of any substitute for family which in the balance of nature might not dry up affection, and make man worse. One substitute for a family might be that mothers alone should be the guardians of children and sole mistresses of their houses, with husbands taking only pecuniary responsibility, making a stable home for the children, and leaving marriage to be dissolved at the will of either party. Women's emancipation, even so, might well prove the opposite of what is intended, so that they would have to take all over again to the arts of seduction to regain their lost social position. Family life in Western nations is still bungling, painful, and unstable; and the evils of prostitution, adultery, and divorce, together with unhappy marriages, still prevail.

As the state grows the family weakens. In Europe we get democracy paralleling individualism. Under Rome Asiatic provinces flourished when peace existed, tyranny offering many protections. But the military class never allows peace for long. To fight is a radical instinct. To knock a thing down stirs a deep delight in the blood. Barbarism has its pleasures. To call war the soil of courage and virtue is like calling debauchery the soil of love. Discipline is one of the few virtues of war, but war tries to do good by doing harm. To find joy in another's trouble is not unnatural, but it is wicked; to find joy in one's own trouble is incurable madness. It is a question whether the virtues of war—animal courage, discipline, and self-knowledge—together with gaiety and enthusiasm, could not be cultivated by more harmless occupations. Santayana suggests sports as a liberal form of war stripped of its compulsions and malignity. Also, if two or three powerful governments of the day could get together (this was written before UN) and enforce the decisions of some international tribunal, they would render war impossible —it is as simple as that. Many solid achievements in nature come through dumb perseverance along simple lines.

Santayana has a kind word for Plato's timocracy (long *i*), which Santayana calls a government by men of merit, instancing the Roman Church where people are born equal but grow unequal. A modern form of timocracy would give all a chance to develop their full capacities and allow scope to proved leadership. Promoting worth unites the advantages of many forms of government, avoiding the abuses. Montesquieu based democracy on virtue.

Reason is a principle of order. Order arises wherever an organic equilibrium naturally establishes itself. Consciousness establishes order by seeing nature from the point of view of ideal interests. Between his constant somatic feeling and his social relations a man has to find his life. The highest form of vanity is love of fame. But what good is it to Vergil that boys still read him at school? To wish at all cost to be immortal is to identify ourselves with truth, which in Santayana is a fundamental confusion of essence with existence. Less wide than fame, there is the comradeship of men of the same breeding or profession, a limited recognition. Friends should be young together. Such an ideal socius may lead away from friendship to hero worship or out-and-out idealization, as Achilles in Homer and Jesus in Christianity. Religion, art, and science are the chief spheres in which ideal companionship is found. It remains to traverse these to see how the life of reason flourishes there.

In his third book, *Reason in Religion,* Santayana gives us his conception of how religion may be an embodiment of reason. If that happens, the God to whom depth in philosophy brings back men's minds is far from being the same God from whom a little philosophy estranges men. As it is, each religion, likely as not, contradicts another religion, but the attempt to speak without any particular language is not more hopeless than the attempt to have a religion that shall be no religion in particular. Every healthy religion has a marked idiosyncrasy, a surprising message, a bias, its own vista on the world. But, although religions are many, reason is one. Perhaps the common element is that religion is a second life, directing man toward something eternal. The word "eternal" has a special meaning in Santayana, who speaks of all essences as eternal. The eternal is a recurring, man-made handhold in the flux, like spikes in a mountainside for climbers. Many things are eternal, as opposed to being within the changing flux, as we shall see in studying Santayana's essences. Whitehead used the same terminology. It would be an approximation to say that the eternal is an ideal, and the ideal in turn a fiction that is true because it works, but the approximation begins to go in the right direction. It is going to take all the skill that the extremely skillful and imaginative Santayana can muster to make clear to us what he means by his ideals grounded on a natural basis. The chief argument for them is that there can be no other. It's Hobson's choice.

Religion pursues rationality through the imagination. Like poetry it is wrong when it arrogates to itself literal truth and moral authority, neither of which it possesses. Poetry never pretends to literal validity, but improves the world by imagining it improved. Religions are better or worse, not true or false. Worship is earlier and nearer to the roots of religion than dogma is. To be given the choicest morsel, to be praised, to be blindly obeyed, could happen to anything with power, god or demon, making man and the power he fears almost natural enemies, living a sort of politic peace. Of course, this can shade off into acts of thanksgiving, acts grateful rather than calculating, and then the god may become a farseeing friend.

As sacrifices express fear, prayer expresses need. Prayers, also magic, are not necessarily a substitute for work. We may need just a little help over and above what we ourselves can do. Hebrew positivism turned into a religion of redemption, tribal unity leading to an exclusive devotion to Jehovah, denying finally even the existence of other gods. Someone stumbled on the idea that Jehovah favored only the righteous, God became moral, and assigning a magic value to morality gave a moral value to religion. Thinking themselves a chosen people with a unique and only God—no people had such pretensions before—was an arrogance by which the Jews rendered themselves odious to mankind. Had not the Jews taught Christians and Moslems the same fanaticism, the nature of religion would not have been falsified among us and we should not now have so much to apologize for.

Santayana gives a poetic account of the Christian epic. There was a great, immortal King who had existed from all eternity but who in the fullness of time decided to create human beings in his own image. The start is very like the Epic of Gilgamesh. The beings springing from a single specimen began their career about 4000 B.C. To aid man, nature sprang into being. The first man was made out of clay; the first woman was fashioned from one of his ribs; but into them was breathed the spirit of life.

They were placed in an orchard where they often saw the immortal King, its owner, walking in the cool of the evening. The Great King suffered his creatures to multiply and to own the earth. They could eat of the fruit of every tree save one. Incited by a devil, the creatures of the King transgressed this single prohibition and were banished from the orchard, with a curse on their heads, the man to live henceforth by the sweat of his brow and the woman to bring forth in pain. However, the Great King, lest the work of his hands should wholly perish, promised to redeem some of Adam's children. Noah was saved from the Deluge, Lot from Sodom, Isaac from sacrifice, Moses from Egypt, the captive Jews from Babylon.

Final redemption was to come ultimately through a descendant of Eve, the Son of man who would also be the Son of the King, and whose foot would bruise the head of the serpent (the devil). For this reason a tribe was set apart to keep alive the memory of the promises of the King. The rest of mankind, abandoned to its natural depravity, sank deeper and deeper, into crimes and vanities. The Flood, a general punishment, from which only Noah and his family were saved, permanently weakened nature. Men now lived only seventy years. Weather remained perverse. Herbs and roots lost their original potency and stronger food had to be furnished to man by the flesh of other animals. Natural man continued ferocious and bloodthirsty.

There were now two parties or cities in the world. Augustine called them the City of Satan and the City of God. The latter was composed of the saints to be saved, many of them humble people. In the second fullness of time salvation was to come, not as the carnal Jews had imagined it, in the form of an earthly restoration, but through the grace earned by the death of the Son of the King. This legalized the salvation of the elect who otherwise together with the rest of the world would merit and receive eternal damnation.

The conflict between the two Cities will fill the ages until the day of reckoning when those who had believed the things of religion to be imaginary would behold with dismay the King visibly coming down through the clouds from heaven, the angels blowing their alarming trumpets, all generations of the dead rising from their graves, and judgment without appeal passed on every man. Thereupon the blessed would receive eternal bliss with their King and Master, and the wicked everlasting torments with the devil whom they served.

For many centuries this epic was to the European world what Homer had been to the Greeks. Santayana makes rather a sharp distinction between classical Christianity and Protestantism, a Teutonic religion which is anterior to Christianity and may survive it. Proponents of the early gospel met Pharisee and Puritan with biting scorn. Protestantism does not. It is convinced of the importance of success and prosperity. Contemplation seems to it idleness; solitude, selfishness; and poverty a dishonorable punishment. It is righteous, regarding married and industrial life as godly; it is sentimental; its ritual is meager and unctuous. It expects no miracles, it thinks optimism akin to piety, and regards ambition as a moral vocation. It does not believe in renunciation. Its benevolence aims at raising men to well-being. Its devotees are attached to the Old Testament. It is a religion of a race, young, wistful, and adventurous. In countries formerly pagan this new paganism is now flourishing.

Twice in history, in the Stoics and in the Protestants, we get a dissolution of mythologies. The dissolution of both Greek and Christian mythology ended in pantheism. From the age of the Sophists to the age when paganism finally disappeared took a thousand years. Religions do not disappear when discredited; they are replaced. Perhaps today science is replacing religion.

Santayana has a special chapter on "The Belief in a Future Life" in which he stresses "the eternal quality of ideas and validities." "A future life, on the contrary, is a matter for faith or presumption; it is a prophetic hypothesis regarding occult existences. This latter question is scientific and empirical, and should be treated as such." In other words, it requires evidence. "The mass of this evidence, ancient and modern, traditional and statistical, is beneath consideration; the palpating mood in which it is gathered and received, even when ostensibly scientific, is such that gullibility and fiction play a very large part in it." The necessity for considering the future and the fear of death are the real reasons for the stubborn belief in immortality. If hereafter I am to be the same man improved I must find myself in the same world corrected. Were I transformed into a cherub or transported into timeless ecstasy, it is hard to see in what sense I should continue to exist. The results might be interesting in themselves and might enrich the universe; they would not prolong my life nor retrieve my disasters. That another life, to supplement this one, must closely resemble it makes the magic of immortality disappear. Adequate incentive to virtue was once thought the chief business of a future life. Today such rewards are not considered a rational basis for virtue. May not men live for their children, their art, or their country?

Nature in a sense has solved the problem of perpetual motion in the stars. Besides, there is a kind of immortality in the seeds, little successive explosions of further editions. Hence a strong impulse to reproduction. Nature, in denying us perennial youth, has at least invited us to become unselfish and noble. Here is one of those pointers to spirituality. Living in the spirit is immortality right here. There is an escape from death open to man; memory is the first stage; this is the start of reason; then some vision of truth, some self-forgetful satisfaction becomes a heritage that moment transmits to moment and man to man. "Apprehension, which makes man so like a god, makes him in one respect immortal; it quickens his numbered moments with a vision of what never dies, the truth of those moments and their inalienable values."

Reason lifts a larger or smaller element in each man to the plane of ideality. No man is wholly immortal. If nature has added intelligence to animals, it is because they belong together. Intelligence is a natural emanation of vitality. If eternity could exist otherwise than as a vision in time, eternity would have no meaning for men in the world, while the world, men, and time would have no status in eternity. Santayana explains more fully than Emerson ever did what it means that heaven is within us and in what sensible manner we can, by garnering spiritual riches, begin to feel more at home on earth.

A discussion of *Reason in Art* is postponed for consideration later with another book of his, *The Sense of Beauty,* and other things that Santayana wrote on art, in which subject he of all American philosophers should have a message. His *Reason in Science* closes the series.

Science is still young. Religion has had several turns at the wheel, but science has had only three hundred years in Greece and three hundred years in modern times. It miscarried in Greece from too much rhetoric. Nevertheless, in starting afresh in modern times it is building on what has been done in the past. Today two powerful trends are helping science onward: evolution and physics, the latter in the form of an almost immaterial idealism

similar to what prevailed in a primitive way at the time of
Pythagoras.

"Laws . . . possess only a Platonic sort of Reality. They are
more real, if you will, than the facts themselves, because they are
more permanent, trustworthy, and pervasive; but at the same
time they are, if you will, not real at all." Here we are back to an
old question: Which is the more real, matter or form? The
answer is that both are real, but incommensurably so. We are
dealing with different modes of Being. This is one of the fundamental insights of Santayana. He is here entering upon metaphysics by differentiating "incommensurable" modes of being. He
will return to this in full force in his later *Realms of Being*. At
this point it illustrates a fundamental trait in this philosopher: his
honesty. He does not use his great skill as a writer to befuddle
the reader. Always he pursues his subject to a clear-cut conclusion. This you can either accept or reject, but what a relief that
Santayana himself never hedges. The ribs of his logic shine
through all his fine raiment.

Even during our waking hours we shuttle continually between
worlds of fact and fancy. Man has developed tremendously his
faculty for dreaming. A Spaniard can dream wide awake with
his feet on the ground; rub on some Yankee ingenuity and you
have Santayana, with that clear insight of his on how fact and
fancy interlock. This too is the great problem of science. How
can we keep fruitful hypotheses coming? It takes men of imagination to think them up. These flashes of insight, sometimes so
fugitive, come out of the blue, and they seem to come only to men
with a spark of genius. Yet a hypothesis by itself is nothing; with
it must come at least a glimpse of some crucial experiment that
can be used to test it. It is like bringing the sperm and the egg
together. Do not hang on to unfruitful and unverifiable hypotheses. That is where the honesty comes in.

Mythologies play a big part in the world. There have been
some monstrous mythologies. There were long periods in history
when almost any story seemed a good story, and, in a sense, a
story no matter how fantastic is better than blank stupidity. Any
excuse is better than none at all. "Our troubles come from the
colossal blunders made by our ancestors (who had worse ances-

tors of their own) . . . blunders which have come down to us in our blood and in our institutions." These mistakes get to be an entangling mechanism in themselves. We are caught in the machine. And most men do not mind it. The machine has become as real or more real than anything else on earth. The only way to come from out our dream is to get an electric shock from the earth itself. Men can dream of flying till kingdom come, but nothing happens until someone, no matter how clumsily, gets busy on airplanes. These are improved, and today, thanks to science, men are flying.

"If you are in the habit of believing in special providences, or of expecting to continue your romantic adventures in a second life, materialism will dash your hopes most unpleasantly, and you may think for a year or two that you have nothing left to live for. But a thorough materialist . . . will be like the superb Democritus, a laughing philosopher. His delight in a mechanism that can fall into so many marvellous and beautiful shapes, and can generate so many exciting passions, should be of the same intellectual quality as that which the visitor feels in a museum of natural history, where he views the myriad butterflies in their cases, the flamingoes and shellfish, the mammoths and gorillas." This could be Emerson speaking. "Materialism has no contempt for mortal sorrows. . . . The mechanical world is not dead or ugly . . . nor unreal. . . . Nature is not as cruel as a theology which assigns a whole portion of humanity to perpetual torture with none of the blessed anaesthetics that are so merciful a part of nature.

"The passion for a large and permanent population in the universe is not obviously rational. What matters is quality. A reasonable and humane demand to make of the world is that such creatures as exist on it should not be unhappy, and that life, whatever its quantity, should have a quality that may justify it in its own eyes." That nature should have mind in it is no more wonderful than that a foot should make a footprint. Remember that the footprint does not make the foot. Similarly the mind does not make the world. On this point Santayana is an uncompromising realist. Mind is epiphenomenal. Santayana does not hesitate to turn on Dewey and James when in his opinion they get to be too romantic about what the mind can do. Santayana is not a reformer. Vice versa, Dewey turns on Santayana for his lack of social sense. Each of these men supplements the other. They are not of opposing schools, but each finds his treasures in a different locus. In the house of the universe, too, there are many mansions.

It is a feat of true philosophic import to find a whole new realm of essences in which a very deep part of man can learn to be at home without stultification. However, this is no place to sum up. There still remain to be examined the *Realms of Being,* the basic idea of which Santayana may have obtained from Schopenhauer, the pessimist, who found in art the one solace and refuge of man. A shade of *dolce far niente,* or at least a dislike of strenuosity, may be needed to heighten that delight in beauty that is also the mark of Plato. What is fascinating about Santayana is the way he hooks his "essences" into the universe, more firmly and more clearly than do his predecessors. In Santayana we get into metaphysics in a way that neither James nor Dewey could accomplish. It still does not have the finished touch that a greater knowledge of mathematics could give it, but let us leave that for Peirce and Whitehead. Santayana gives us the best possible, and the most readable, introduction to this indispensable study of the different kinds of being that go to make up the world.

In his *Life of Reason* he makes only a beginning. He gets no further than some profound remarks on ideation. The mind makes objects objects. A certain arrangement of sticks becomes a chair. A chair is something we can sit on, and that is what this arrangement of sticks means to us. Our whole life is tenanted by objects charged with meanings. Even animals begin to inject meanings into what they encounter. Grass is not just grass to an ox, it is food. Here we are beginning to get into the entrails of pragmatism. Thought is interlaced with what we do in a way so intricate that the ramifications have not yet been fully explored. One general conclusion reached by Santayana at this point is that science, by its very tendency to replace religion, is going to be of great help in tracing the deeper roots of this broader philosophy that includes feelings as well as intellect.

5. The Realms of Being

"There is no more bewitching moment in childhood than when the boy, to whom someone is slyly propounding some absurdity, suddenly looks up and smiles. The brat has understood. A thin deception was being practiced on him, in the hope that he might not be deceived, but by deriding it might prove he had attained to a man's stature and man's wit. It was but banter prompted by love. So with this thin deception practiced upon me by nature. The great Sphinx in posing her riddle and looking so threatening and mysterious is secretly hoping that I may laugh." And Santayana laughs. But much more than just a momentary insight precedes the bright smile that is the philosophy of Santayana. The youth who became a philosopher had to go through a protracted period of hard thinking.

There are four volumes devoted to the Realms of Being: (1) The Realm of Essence, (2) The Realm of Matter, (3) The Realm of Truth, and (4) The Realm of Spirit. There is also an introductory volume: *Scepticism and Animal Faith,* published in 1923. The volumes on Essence, Matter, Truth, and Spirit appeared during the years 1927 to 1940. Compared with the *Realms,* some have thought the *Life of Reason,* published 1905–1906, to be a *Jugendarbeit.* This is not the case. Much too much is made of the difference in points of view between these two major works, the so-called shift from activity to contemplation. There is no real shift—only progress in depth. In the *Realms* we get a well-sketched-out ontology, or Science of Being, a real addition to what went before in all of American philosophy and a real addition also to Santayana's own *Life of Reason.*

To arrive at his ontology Santayana invented a new method.

285

Much is made in Europe of a new method first set forth by
Edmund Husserl (1859–1938) in his *Logische Untersuchungen*
(1901–1902). Husserl is the father of phenomenology. The philosophy called phenomenology is arrived at by a new trick of considering first of all just everything that comes to mind, holding in
suspense any question of whether any one thing is more real than
any other. Ideas, dreams, fancies, facts, the whole jumble, is just
to be looked at with no preconceived notions or prejudices about
which of them is real. Husserl coins many new terms for the
various facets of his philosophy, but the process of suspending
judgment he calls "bracketing." He "brackets" certain considerations, setting them aside for the moment, while he studies appearances. What he brackets is first of all every other philosophical
doctrine, and secondly he brackets the question of existence. We
may have three things: a horse, a picture of a horse, and a dream
about a horse. Now do not get hung up on the question of which
of them is real. Bracket all that. Consider merely what is before
the mind.

This new method of approaching philosophy is not exactly
skepticism, nor is it common sense, nor is it deduction or induction; it is a special artifice by which everything is put afresh into
a single hopper, and out of this at the end will come some new
classifications. In Santayana we get the American version of this
special technique, and we get it couched in books that are infinitely more readable than the German volumes (even in translation) of Husserl. Whether Santayana owes anything to Husserl
is doubtful. The two methods have some striking similarities, but
Santayana's way of tackling the question of Being was in all like-
lihood an independent invention. The times called for a new
approach, and Santayana himself calls his own phenomenology
a species of skepticism.

Skepticism as the starting point for a philosophy has been tried
many times before, as when Descartes doubted everything except
his *cogito ergo sum*. There have been men who thought they
were better doubters even than Descartes, and Hume was one
of them, but Santayana as a skeptic can outdo even Hume. In
none of these cases does the resulting philosophy seem to have
suffered from the original doubting. Santayana claims that his

systematic doubting, roughly equivalent to holding everything in suspense, led him to the discovery of the realm of essences. Essences do not have real existence. They have being but they do not exist, as do most of the other things in nature. Possibly this means nothing more than that they do not grow wild. They are like a plant in a pot. The pot is the human head. They grow only in human heads. Possibly they are more than that. It is a question whether essences occur outside of human heads. Some say they do, and it is easy for us to think that they do; in fact, to make essences the most important things in the world. All types of phenomenology, including Santayana's, lead to a distinction between existence and essence.

Santayana claims that if he really tries hard he can doubt almost everything; and having achieved that stage of utter submission to doubt, he then, like a true Catholic, accepts certain things on faith, which in his case he calls animal faith, because man shares it with the animals. "The last step in skepticism is now before me. I shall deny the existence of everything, and abolish the category of thought altogether. Belief in the existence of anything, including myself, is something radically incapable of proof, and resting, like all belief, on some irrational persuasion or prompting of life." For the thorough skeptic it is true that he himself lives and thinks, but to establish that truth he must appeal to animal faith. If he is too proud for that and simply stares at the data, the last thing he will see will be himself. Santayana therefore has a faith, but he picks the most simple faith around, the one shared with all struggling, unreflecting humanity, as well as with the animals.

"That external things exist, that I exist myself, is a faith not founded on reason but precipitated in action. . . . Knowledge . . . is belief . . . in a world of events. The belief is native to animals." Or in slightly different words the original articles in the animal creed are "that there is a world, that there is a future, that things sought can be found, and things seen can be eaten. . . . While life lasts this faith must endure . . . it is the expression of animal vitality. . . . It is involved in any pang of hunger, fear, and love. It launches the adventure of knowledge." In resorting to animal faith Santayana avoids beginning with certainties.

Instead he begins with certain assumptions that men have in common with the animals.

Thus far we have three things: doubt, animal faith, and essences. "The principle of essence is identity. . . . Essences are infinite in number. . . . So nature resprouts in us. Essences spring up inexhaustibly. They surprise even an omniscient God." Essences are numerous and varied, but, remember, they do not exist in the same way that matter does. "Essences are all the being that could ever be—the potential." Essences even go beyond anything that may ever have existed, or could, so far as we know, exist. There is almost no limit to the play of the mind. No one ever saw a unicorn, but people have imagined them and a million other picturable and nonpicturable fancies. "Mind comes to enrich the essence of the world, not to reproduce it."

A projection of essences back into existences leads to a falsification or a "bifurcation" of nature. Does Santayana here coin this famous word of which Whitehead is later to make so much? In a bifurcated world two irreconcilable streams flow side by side or, even worse, they intermingle, to the great confusion of us all. "But the essences given to the spirit are forms of imagination and thought; never essences of things." Introjecting essences as false counterparts of things leads to those deep bifurcations (soul and body) that alienate us from existence.

Santayana is very emphatic that "no essence can be the origin of anything: not even of another essence, much less of any fact." "Essences have the stamp of indelible multiplicity and of eternal individuality. Poetry and music lie as deep in the realm of essence as any logic. The realm of essence is the playground of even greater freedom. Essence is an eternal invitation to take form." Essence and existence are two modes or realms of being. It is also abundantly clear that for Santayana existence comes first. For this reason over and over again he calls himself a materialist. Matter is the matrix.

A fourth item to be added to doubt, animal faith, and essences, is intuition. "The acquaintance with essence I call intuition." We intuit essences. Sometimes he calls this contemplation. "We can also approach them through contemplation: sometimes sense itself distinguishes essences from facts as when I suspend action, or continue it automatically, while my thought is elsewhere, absorbed in the image and arrested there. Beauty bursts upon me and the reins drop from my hands. . . . The beautiful is a great liberator of other essences. . . . Stop living and acting, and instead be God and float on self-created essences. . . . In play at the beginning it is seen how happily essence and matter conjoin. If the play life of childhood can be restored to the soul there is great happiness . . . the whole thing is fun."

No philosopher who adds intuition to logic is going to have an easy time of it. Any enlargement of philosophy beyond the conventionally intellectual is going to break into new ground. If philosophy is to include the whole man, we need gifted pioneers, like Santayana, who can loosen up stilted phraseologies to delineate new boundaries. Few have done this with the same degree of delight that is found in Santayana. To him these new explorations are not sweat and blood but just plain fun. Put Santayana down as a philosopher who never wears a hairshirt.

Some more things that essences are not: "An essence then is no abstraction, no unrealisable generality, but an actual aspect which anything can wear, determining its nature, or revealing it to an attentive mind. . . . An essence is not a mental state, a sensation, perception, or living thought; it is not an idea, as in British philosophy, but only in the Platonic or graphic sense of being a theme open to consideration. Mental facts are not units either in nature or in logic; they are subdivisions made by psychologists. The repetition of events is impossible, the recovery of essences is easy. This dyad, though I give it a learned name, is something the cat has when it misses one of its two kittens. . . . Finally essences are not constituent parts of things. But appearances, which are essences, are the qualities of things for experience. These ulterior questions, however, cannot arrest the impetuous dogmatic instinct which asserts things to be what they seem and to exist in the very terms in which they appear. The stones would laugh, if they got wind of this human assurance."

The realm of essence, then, is one mode of Being. Santayana labors mightily to delineate it, but do not expect from Balboa a complete chart of the Pacific. The realm of essence will receive further clarification from an examination of the other realms, but the main thing is that we have here a fresh adventure into ontology. Santayana next takes up the Realm of Matter, but it makes things simpler if the other two Realms of Truth and of Spirit are looked at first. In a way truth and spirit are subdivisions of the essences. The real polarity is between essence and matter; these stand at the opposite ends of the scale.

Santayana uses the word "truth" in the sense that it bears in ordinary conversation. In this matter, as in many others, he follows common sense. Truth is "that segment of the realm of essence which happens to be illustrated in existence." This plainly makes the realm of truth one part of the realm of essences, but it also raises some fascinating questions, such as, why do some essences "get exemplified" or ingress among existences and others not? "By the truth I understand the complete ideal description of existence." Suppositions contrary to fact transcend the truth. Santayana is inclined to say cavalierly that truth does not enter into the fields of mathematics or logic at all. What is necessarily logical is not necessarily true. Does logic help us to see why certain things are or can be true? Logic and mathematics have "contacts" with truth. Santayana uses the word "contact" as if truth were an ocean into which you could dump certain essences—those that can swim. On contact with water (existence) they get wet. Truth adheres. This of course is an oversimplification, but it is one of the many graphic attempts that Santayana makes to see clearly in this new field of realms of being.

"In general it is fabulous to represent phenomenology, or the drama of ideas, as the motive force in history. Phenomena are inert results, aesthetic figments, while derivation of events is a natural flow of nature." This is a slap at German idealists of the Hegelian stamp. Santayana is never going to allow ideas or essences to run the show. He is a realist, not an idealist. The genesis of things is in matter. "Logic when turned into metaphysics spoils both physics and logic." "There are no necessary truths. Logical propositions may be necessary, and some of them true. But truth, being a radiation of existence, is contingent. Existence decides what shall be true."

The point Santayana makes very strongly, almost in defiance of his Spanish blood, is that the whole world is not just imagination. No man of common sense would ever think it was. But there are different modes of being with different grades of reality. Thus far we have three: existences, essences, and truth. In his differentiation of truth Santayana follows the pragmatic path. The criterion of truth is pertinence to action and implication in the dynamic order of things. Primitive imagination attributes power to wishes, but that is superstition. Ideas are not true because they are clear, but often become clear because true. Mind does not completely fit nature, and possibly still would not fit if it were radically changed. At the bottom of Santayana's thinking is his unalterable conviction that mind, especially the human mind, is not at the heart of nature. We live in a world not made for us, but of which we can make something. The world is possibly deeply inhuman, but for all that not necessarily unfit for human abode. We can make it habitable. Look how different cities are from the forest primeval. Essences help. A clear idea of what is meant by truth also can help. The great question to Santayana is not whether we can make over the entire world but whether we can make something of our own lives. Can we make our own lives more humane and beautiful? is his first question, and in that sense he is a profound humanist. Also Santayana is in line with Dewey rather than with James in holding that man does not make the truth.

Truth can be tragic, and the existing world "fatally determines the truth about itself. . . . Existence, as it generates truth, may also generate beauty or goodness, but not with the same pervasiveness. They are more accidental than truth, arising only at certain junctures, whereas truth rises by automatic radiation from every region of fact. . . . To reduce the truth to coherence is to deny truth, and usurp that name for a certain comfort and self-complacency is mere thinking." Here the coherence theory of truth is discarded in favor of the pragmatic conception with certain overtones. "The only belief I myself entertain because I find it irresistible, is the belief in a realm of matter, the expectation of persistence and order in a natural world. But the realms of truth and essence are in quite another case. They are not proposed as objects of belief, but as conceptual distinctions and categories of logic, in which nature can be described." In that sense Santayana can speak of truth as a part of the realm of essences, and as eternal and unchanging since only one description fits the facts.

Nothing infuriates a man more than to be contradicted in the convictions he learned with care and on high authority until they became central to his thought. All this usurpation of truth by convention only goes to show that the greatest deceiver of mankind is man. The animals are mortal without knowing it, and doubtless presume in their folly that they will live forever. Man alone knows that he must die; but that very knowledge raises him, in a sense, above mortality by making him a sharer in the vision of eternal truth. This does not mean that he has to love the truth.

Hatred of truth is seldom mentioned, yet it is commoner than the love of truth. Mostly we like truth because we need information for practical purposes. Note that a child will protest and be inwardly wounded if a story once told him is told differently the second time. His little soul has accepted that world and needs to build on it undisturbed. Love of what we know and hatred of what we do not know are incorrectly identified with love of truth. What we love is our safety, our thoughts, our illusions, and our confidence in habit. Fear of being deceived is again a love not of truth but of safety. There can be no peace in delusion. We wish to be armed to face the obdurate facts and our pride recoils from the confusion of finding ourselves mistaken.

There is no reason why we should love the truth but sometimes we do. Nature breeds life, life is everywhere aflame with love, and should not relations radiating from human life shed some love on to the realms of truth and essence? Love is, biologically, an emotion proper to generation. The joy proper to all vital functions in their perfection counts for something. Thus love of truth can become a form of worship. What mystics call the truth is something beyond truth. Life may transcend truth, but here we approach the realm of spirit.

Before understanding what Santayana means by spirit there

must be some grasp of what he means by psyche. Santayana distinguishes psyche and spirit in a way that is reminiscent of an orthodox doctrine which holds that during gestation the vegetative soul is replaced by an immortal one. The psyche is something like a vegetative soul, the center of the unconscious unity of an individual life. The psyche belongs to the realm of matter. Many forms of life get along very well without self-consciousness. What mysterious *principium individuationis* guides the lowly plant or the one-celled animal in its way through life? For this Santayana coins the term "psyche." Spirit is something higher and definitely human.

At one place Santayana calls the psyche a trope, which is a mode of substance, a habit established in matter. "Events have a form as much as things have. An event is a portion of the flux of existence, a sequence. . . . I will give a separate name to the essence of any event, as distinguished from that event itself, and call it a trope." The flux can be measured only by tropes which repeat themselves. Men and women of the world are sometimes quick to divine what is going on; this imaginative insight makes use of tropes and can be turned into scientific channels. Simple tropes called laws exist in which a tremendous amount of detail is suppressed. Laws are not forces which run things; they are forms. There is in law no relation of cause and effect and no assurance that law is constant. Into the class of laws and other tropes falls the psyche. There is a sense in which it is true that every man is a law unto himself. He has a character according to which he does things. He has a psyche that seems to push him along in grooves already established. Spirit is a broader term. When the psyche reaches the stage of becoming self-conscious, as happens in man, there is new scope to living, and we get into the realm of spirit.

"Spirit is not a substance with a life of its own; it hates, it fears, it loves, it inquires, it feels perplexed and forsaken. It is merely the psyche become conscious. Better thus than that it be condemned to grow, work, and die without ever loving anything ideally, or knowing its own *raison d'être*." The treacherous notion of a disembodied spirit is completely disavowed. In opening his book on the realm of the spirit Santayana warns the reader not to expect tidings from a spirit world. Spirit is not substance. Spirit is not a potentiality, not a seed, not a power. "It is not even—though this touches more nearly its actual character—a grammar of thought or divine Logos, predetermining the structure of creation and its destiny. That would be in the realm of truth."

Santayana gives a glossary. The body is a closed system of vital tropes. The psyche is a self-sustaining and reproducing pattern or structure of an organism, conceived as a power, a mythological notion. All natural organisms have psyches. The soul is the same thing as a psyche looked at morally from within—also called a self or a person. Spirit is awareness, revealing world and self; other names are attention, feeling, thought, or any word that marks the total difference between being awake or asleep, alive or dead. "The only possible way for a spirit to create is to imagine." But what a power that is! The one great evil that spirit encounters is distraction. Distraction dissipates and destroys the creative impulse. A Garden of Eden where all was health, safety, and abundance would only evoke an animal placidity, into which spiritual joy might break at rare intervals. Spirit is essentially a culmination, and perfect happiness a quality to be attained occasionally in natural life, not in another nonnatural life beyond. To say we belong by nature to a different region is simply contrary to fact.

Life and beauty may be renewed in perpetually other shapes. The soul too much concerned about immortality is not spirit, but animal psyche, a principle of natural impulsive life. There are innumerable incarnations. The Christian view that the number of incarnations is limited to two is an impoverished beginning. The heavenly kingdom has already come. Spirit triumphs in childhood, in laughter, in understanding, in moments had by sage and saint. It is by understanding the world, not by quitting it, that we get liberation. Health and knowledge, nothing more, is requisite for liberation from distraction by the flesh, the world, and the devil.

Sometimes Santayana, completely forgetting that he is a naturalist, speaks like a true believer. Having freedom to what shall we devote it? Freedom is preliminary to union with what?

The answer is the Good, the Socratic Good both utilitarian and spiritual. The harmony of natural goods becomes a spiritual good called the beautiful. The Good is a harmony to be established, an influence to be felt, an inner transformation to be experienced. Socrates and Plato were right in making the Good, not the universe or even the truth, the goal of life, attainment of which is happiness. Moral unanimity or fellowship with the life of all substances in so far as these support or enlarge his own life is the actual Good. Let us have no fabulous universes!

Essence, matter, truth, and spirit are not separate cosmological regions, separately substantial, and then juxtaposed. They are all meant to describe a single natural dynamic process. They are all realms of being. This is an ontology. "In regard to my intended allegiance to common sense, I confess that in several important matters I have not been able to maintain it." This he blames on human language. It is hard to explain a complete ontology in words of one syllable. It is too much like trying to explain Copernicus by sticking to expressions like "the sun comes up in the east." You have to become somewhat technical, but as little so as possible. Matter and spirit are not two worlds. There is only one world, the natural world, and only one truth about it; but this world has a spiritual life possible in it, which looks not to another world but to the beauty and perfection that this world suggests, approaches, and misses. "On this point, although I am perfectly willing to stand alone, I rather expect that posterity may agree with me."

Does God exist? The answer is Yes, but what we are really asking is whether the reality signified by the notion of God, if we understood that reality better, could still bear the name of God, or had better be designated by some other word. This is at bottom the whole question in dispute between atheists and theists. It is a question of terminology. At another place Santayana says that to worship an infinite Being as good or sublime, and to make a God of it, inverts the moral order. There would be better excuse for worshiping matter, since it is matter that feeds and kills us, and these are the function that popular religion first attributes to the deity. But to worship essence, which can do nothing, merely because it is infinite and ineffaceable would

be a refined madness, fortunately not likely to prove contagious
when its true object is understood.

The divine element especially incarnate in human existence
is spirit. St. Paul often speaks of Christ dwelling in him as if
this were a spirit dwelling in him. "There is an analogy between
Christian theology and my ontology, but it must not be pressed:
the one is dogma, the other a language—based on analysis and
meant only to render articulate the dumb experience of the
soul." Santayana continues: "In Realms of Being I am endeavour-
is only to distinguish the TYPES of reality that I encounter.
Theology could not possibly be true unless revealed miraculously;
and I presume that most of my readers would agree that
miraculous revelations are creatures of the heart. Religion itself
sometimes calls its dogmas mysteries and its creeds symbols,
as if admitting the difference in kind between imagination and
truth."

In the Realms of Being we have Santayana the artist at work.
He is giving himself four large vistas to contemplate. The prime
realm of course is matter, and that Santayana should assume this
is the most important thing about his philosophy. By giving
matter the undisputed primacy Santayana saves himself from an
idealistic metaphysics. Thus his ontology is grounded in a
realistic metaphysics. In another sense he is not really providing
us with a metaphysics at all, because he sticks to faith in essential matters, animal faith, but a faith nevertheless. With that
faith he allows himself certain great artistic liberties in delineating
three magnificent realms of essence, spirit, and truth. Like
Moses, he climbs Mount Nebo and gets a good look at the
promised land.

The deepest thing in Santayana is his commitment to the
reality not of matter but of time. His philosophy along with
those of the other men thus far considered is a temporal philosophy. Change is real. But he does say something very vital,
and something considerably more elaborate than anyone else has
said, about three other realms which do not exist in the sense
that matter exists, but which are nevertheless terribly important to us. As befits a humanist he does not stint these human
values. Our business is to create an artistic world of our own.

Santayana gives his version of such a tripartite world, and every part of it, even our truth, has poured over it the magic of beauty. The next section will take up Santayana's analysis of beauty. His ontology is a marvelously pregnant aesthetics. He gives us an ontology but not a metaphysics. It will take someone more fully trained in mathematics than Santayana to give us that, but meanwhile Santayana does some vastly original work and pushes philosophy ahead in the sector of aesthetics.

6. Art and Life

THERE IS A creative streak in nature and it comes out in us. It also comes out in the rest of nature, and thus there are in effect two streams of creative effort, one originating within and the other outside of us. Both interest Santayana, but it is on the stream from within that he concentrates. First of all, art is not just an individual matter, it can be, and it always starts as, a joint or community effort. One illustration is furnished by the medieval cathedrals. Human beings jointly created not only these cathedrals but also what they stand for.

"Mythology and theology are the most striking illustrations of this human method of incorporating much diffuse experience into graphic and picturesque ideas; but steady reflection will hardly allow us to see anything else in the theories of science and philosophy. These, too, are creatures of our intelligence, and have their only being in the movement of our thought, as they have their only justification in their fitness to our experience."

Our entire culture is as much a part of us as leaves are part of a tree. The fact that some of it is unconsciously created does not make it less ours. "What are the celestial gods, the nymphs, the fauns, the dryads, but the definite apperceptions of that haunting spirit which we think we see in the sky, the mountains, and the woods? We may think that our vague intuition grasps the truth of what their childish imagination turned into a fable. But our belief, if it is one, is just as fabulous, just as much a projection of human nature into material things; and if we renounce all positive conception of quasi-mental principles in nature, and reduce our moralizing of her to a poetic expression of our own sensations, then can we say that our verbal and illusive images are comparable as representations of the life of nature to the precision, variety, humor, and beauty of Greek mythology?"

The greatest imaginative creations, according to Santayana, "have not been the work of any one man. They have been the slow product of the pious and poetic imagination. Starting from some personification of nature or some memory of a great man, the popular and priestly tradition has refined and developed the ideal. . . . The devotion of each tribe, shrine, and psalmist has added some attribute to the god or some parable to his legend; and thus, around the kernel of some original divine function, the imagination of a people has gathered every possible expression of it, creating a complete and beautiful personality, with its history, its character, and its gifts." These communal efforts are similar to those of Shakespeare creating a Hamlet. "The Christ men have loved and adored is an ideal of their own hearts. . . . The Virgin Mary, whose legend is so meagre, but whose power over the Catholic imagination is so great, is an even clearer illustration of this inward building up of an ideal form."

Whether pagan, or Christian, or creative conceptions still to come, Santayana's point is that these joint creations exceed in holding power anything an individual can do. "No poet has ever equalled the perfection or significance of these religious creations. The greatest characters of fiction are uninteresting and unreal compared with the conception of the gods; so much so that men have believed that their gods have objective reality." No one can visit the island of Delos even today and take a look at what remains of those serried and varied temples without getting some inkling of what they used to mean to people, any more than he can enter the Chartres Cathedral without some participation in the spirit of the builders.

Man tends to spiritualize his environment, and the forms that that environment then takes are little more than crystallizations of a creative ferment that comes close to being life itself. The first thing that strikes one about the views that Santayana has of art is the breadth and the scope of them. It is in his aesthetics, his theory of art, his notions of beauty that his entire philosophy comes to a head.

When Santayana started teaching philosophy at Harvard he was urged to take up a specialty. "I was a kind of poet. I was alive to architecture and the other arts, I was at home in several languages: 'aesthetics' might be regarded as my specialty. Very well: although I didn't have, and haven't now, (1945) a clear notion of what 'aesthetics' may be, I undertook to give a course in that subject. It would help to define my status. I gave it for one or two years and then I wrote out the substance of it in a little book: *The Sense of Beauty*." This was the first book published by Santayana. It appeared in 1896. A new Dover edition, in paper covers, was issued in 1955. It has become a small classic in its field. In it he first speaks of the materials and the form of beauty, and then of art as a means of expression. This dry, academic outline gives no notion of the almost quaint beauty of this little volume with its rich vein of thought and its multiplicity of illustrations. It must have been thrilling to listen to Santayana because what he tried to do was to awaken the aesthetic powers of his students.

The outline and the definitions are not the important items. Santayana does not attach much importance to any "flip" definition of beauty, not even his own. Aesthetics is concerned with human value. "In appreciation, in preference, lies the root and essence of all excellence. Or, as Spinoza clearly expresses it, we desire nothing because it is good, but it is good only because we desire it. . . . Values spring from the immediate and inexplicable reaction of vital impulse, and from the irrational part of our nature." It is the preponderant stress that Santayana gives to that deeply buried tangle of Freudian roots within us that gives him his fundamental setup. His philosophy is like a water lily floating on the water, drinking in the sun but drawing sustenance also from below. In fact, in Santayana the subconscious, the irrational, and the prehistoric parts of man more than ever begin to count for something in the shaping up of the final structure. Philosophy before him did not pay enough attention to these elements. If for his insights Franklin draws on astronomy, Emerson on geology, James on biology, Dewey on culture, Santayana goes deeper than Dewey into the unconscious roots of our culture. This, in spite of the fact that Santayana nowhere features the unconscious or makes a special study of it, any more than Emerson does of geology. The point is that Santayana unquestioningly accepts and takes for granted the overwhelming importance of our material roots with all that they imply in the way of irrationality and caprice. His unique achievement is to found spirituality, the whole ethereal realm of it, on materialism. And he does it the hard way. "I might have taken refuge," says Santayana, "in that half-poetical language to which I am not disinclined, and might have called the realm of matter simply nature." He could have called himself a naturalist or have disguised his materialistic bias in any one of a number of ways; but he didn't. In fact, by now, when we know that matter can be turned into energy and vice versa, the term Santayana chose has an obsolescent, slightly antiquated, sound. Yet what he means by it is perfectly clear.

Art gives to matter a form more humanly propitious. It is the almost haphazard imprint of mankind upon the world. It differs from plain utility somewhat as spontaneous fantasy differs from stark purpose. Man is spontaneously active. Children don't just sit and stare. They run about and play. Adults too run, dance, sing, sculpt, and paint often for the sheer fun of it. Hands, tongue, ears, and eyes all have art extensions. "Language especially is like a cobweb that might catch a fly." "Man's simian chatter becomes noble as it becomes symbolic." Art cooperates well with the roving, forward-marching, and restless element in spirit. Something in man welcomes a change in fashions. Man is an idol-making and an idol-smashing creature.

"The value of art lies in making people happy, first in practising it, and then in possessing the product. . . . A rational pursuit of happiness . . . would embody that natural piety . . . mourning death, celebrating love, sanctifying civic traditions, enjoying and correcting nature's ways. . . . Art is simply an adequate industry that helps render the world pervasively beautiful. . . . Art is an achievement, not an indulgence. In industry man is servile. . . . In action itself his medium is often treacherous. . . . In science he is an observer. But in art he is at once competent and free; he is creative. . . . Nothing is more delightful than genuine art. . . . Thus the emergence of

arts out of instincts is the token and measure of nature's success
and of mortal happiness."

In making our own heaven on earth, man's conscious and unconscious ways of making his own life beautiful are central. In
his early book on the sense of beauty Santayana ventures on the
definition that beauty is objectified pleasure. This has been attacked, among others by Dewey, who in his basic view on art
differs very little from Santayana. Dewey saw in this definition
remnants of antiquated psychologies. He interpreted this definition as meaning that aesthetic quality does not belong to the
object but is projected into it by the mind. This slightly idealistic
interpretation is not what Santayana had in mind, for like
Dewey he makes man very much a part of nature. Dewey and
Santayana are not as far apart as might appear. Art, as Santayana
makes very clear, deals with the part of the world that we can
change over nearer to our heart's desire, and only that part.
Dewey, as is also well known, is inclined to be more optimistic
than Santayana. Dewey often talks as if man can pretty well
change the whole world; hence the significant title of his book, *Art
as Experience. All* experience can be art; whereas Santayana says
some experience can be art. On what art is and what art does
the two agree remarkably well. The criticism of Santayana's
psychology is not a serious one, since both men are alike in being
confirmed naturalists. Santayana is not a Hegelian who "objecti-
fies" his thoughts in the world any more than Dewey is. "Objectified" pleasure, as the term is used by Santayana, could just
as well mean pleasure of such a degree in objects that in be-
holding them the beholder identifies himself with the object.

Both Dewey and Santayana wipe out the distinction between
fine and industrial arts. Both interpret art in the widest way. Both
insist on immediacy in the art experience, and Santayana has
no prejudice against the use of the term "intuition." Later on
Whitehead, who puts to further use so much of what he finds in
Santayana, is going to make this intuition a standard part of
the knowledge process, thus wedding art to science more closely
than even Santayana succeeds in doing. According to Santayana,
"Whenever the golden thread of pleasure enters that web of
things which our intelligence is always busily spinning, it lends

to the visible world that mysterious and subtle charm which we call beauty." The passion of love has close relations with beauty, for "it is precisely from the waste, from the radiation of the sexual passion, that beauty borrows warmth. . . . When love lacks its specific object, when it does not yet understand itself, or has been sacrificed to some other interest, we see the stifled fire busting out in various directions. One is religious devotion, another is zealous philanthropy, a third is the fondling of pet animals, but not the least fortunate is the love of nature, and of art; for nature also is often a second mistress that consoles us for the loss of a first."

All subjects, even the most repellent, when the circumstances of life thrust them before us, can be observed with curiosity and treated with art. Art does not seek out the pathetic, the tragic, or the absurd. Agreeableness of presentation may be mixed with the horror of the thing. The mixture of artistic presentation saddened by truth is pathos. In various ways the mind can be brought to contemplate with pleasure a thing which, if experienced alone, would be the cause of pain—a conflagration may be called an evil, still we may be delighted by a blaze. A child might watch a shipwreck with fascination, not understanding the calamity. There is also *Schadenfreude*. We all smile when Punch beats Judy. Santayana's discussions of art are replete with interesting details. Byroads are fully explored. His main position, however, is never obscured; everywhere art makes an alien world more human.

Works of art are monuments to moments of inspiration when we see ourselves in a favorable light and the world not too different from us or, at worst, something that we could overcome. The final sentence of Santayana's classic, *The Sense of Beauty*, assures us: "Beauty is a pledge of the possible conformity between the soul and nature, and consequently a ground of faith in the surpremacy of the good."

7. A Reasonable Morality

SANTAYANA SPEAKS OF three stages in ethics: prerational, rational, and postrational. In ethics you lay down the rules, in morality you carry them out. Morality to Santayana means the practice of ethics.

Do not underestimate prerational morality. Prerational morality, that is, morality of some sort as a practice of furthering life, is established almost the moment life begins. This morality becomes your own personal morality when you begin to distinguish yourself from others. The more you are aware of yourself the more you get involved in your relations to others. There is here a shift from survival of the tribe to survival of yourself *and* the tribe. Thereafter morality may run the gamut from complete egotism to complete self-sacrifice. Santayana abhors both extremes. In fact the big problem in ethics is to lay down a scheme that will avoid both extremes and still be a pulsating morality with real life in it.

"A certain amount of egoism is normal and natural to every biological organism," says Santayana, "but egotism is evil." The *t* makes the difference. What Santayana condemns in egotism is the "ultra-romantic and ultra-idealistic" method of "looking for reality in your own breast." He is thinking of the philosophic position of Hegel and of the political position of a man like Hitler. Santayana has said some scathing things about German idealism. Although "self-assertion and ambition are ancient follies of the human race . . . to take what views we will of things . . . and then to declare that the things are mere terms in the views as we take them" is outright insanity. "Nothing can be an object of knowledge except some idea of the mind. . . .

In focussing . . . through the lenses and veils of sense knowledge arises," says Santayana, paraphrasing Kant, but "to arrest our attention on these veils and lenses and say they are all we know" is something "only a maniac would do." It is like mistaking specks on your glasses for birds in the sky and then building on the arrangement of these specks an entire ornithology.

And what are we to say when men infect each other with these myopic madnesses so that whole nations get banded together in widespread and devastating destruction? Why make the state a huge idol? Santayana singles out Fichte as a whipping boy. "That a State, even when on the point of making war, should solemnly assert its love of peace and its aversion to conquest, is nothing; for in the first place it must needs make this assertion and so hide its real intention if it would succeed in its design; and the well-known principle *Threaten war that thou mayest have peace* may also be inverted in this way: *Promise peace that thou mayest begin war with advantage.*" This is Fichte speaking, but to put the state above good and evil, to make it an end that justifies all means, is the kind of irrationality that is not only antisocial but also against life itself.

Santayana discusses heathenism and pictures it as exemplified in a bull. "What the red rag is to this brave creature, their passions, inclination, and chance notions are to the heathen. . . . The bull, magnificently sniffing the air, surveys the arena with the cool contempt and disbelief of the idealist, as if he said: 'You seem, you are a seeming; I do not quarrel with you, I do not fear you. I am real, you are nothing.' Then suddenly, when his eye is caught by some bright cloak displayed before him, his whole soul changes. His will awakes and he seems to say: 'You are my destiny; I want you, I hate you, you shall be mine, you shall not stand in my path. I will gore you. I will disprove you. I will pass beyond you. I shall be, you shall not have been.' . . .

"So exactly . . . the heathen soul stands bravely before a painted world, covets some bauble, and defies death. Heathenism is the religion of will. . . . Judaism and Christianity, like Greek philosophy, were singly inspired by the pursuit of happiness . . . on earth if possible . . . or, in the last resort, in a different life altogether beyond the grave. But heathenism ignores happiness, despises it, or thinks it impossible. The regimen and philosophy of Germany are inspired by this contempt for happiness." Some of these things were written in the heat of passions aroused by World War I, but when World War II came Santayana republished his *Egotism in German Philosophy* without changing a word in it. It still seemed to him to hold good. Since then more decades have rolled by, and Germany for the greater part at least has realigned itself with democratic nations. If Santayana were still alive he might continue to apply his strictures unchanged to any totalitarian state founded on a dialectic developed from Hegel.

Those who find anywhere in Santayana overtones of fascism are on the wrong track. No one has more unequivocally condemned the egotism of dictators and the unbearableness of a tyrannical state. Nor do his occasional scornings of a democracy led by mediocre figures and deciding issues by a majority vote warrant the conclusion that he condoned fascism. The kind of government he preferred is made very plain in his remarks on timocracy which have already been considered. Nor does his very latest book written after living in Europe through the wars indicate a change of mind.

This book, *Dominations and Powers,* offers nothing essentially new. It does present an interesting rearrangement of his basic classifications. This time he calls them Orders. First comes the Generative Order, which is the Realm of Matter all over again. But then comes something slightly different. With two world wars freshly in mind, he calls the second the Militant Order. When in 1912 Santayana ran away to Europe he jumped from the frying pan into the fire. The world wars hit Europe much harder than they did America. Hence the Militant Aspect of humanity gets new consideration. The third Order of Society is the Rational Order, and here we are back again on the safe ground of the Life of Reason.

Dominations and Powers with the subtitle *Reflections on Liberty, Society and Government* was published in 1954, two years after Santayana's death. The preface to this book is dated February, 1951. Dominations is for Santayana a bad word. Powers may be beneficent and are not condemned. If anything, this last book is a reutterance of Santayana's great love of freedom. It opens with a description of childhood as a long cramped period from which at adolescence the individual flees as a bird from a cage. The restraints of parental and school authorities bit deeply into Santayana's flesh. And so do all restraints, especially tyrannies. His was a free spirit, chafing under the compulsions of society. The one thing that his swansong most resembles is a thinly disguised apology for his running away. His views have not changed. He still lashes out with some of the old indignation, this time against militancy.

"The moral inspiration of communism is brotherly, pacifist, ascetic, and saintly. Christianity was originally communistic, and all the religious Orders continue to be so in their internal economy and discipline. It is built on tenderness, on indifference to fortune, and to the world, on readiness for sacrifice, on life in the spirit. It cannot be militant. But what is now called communism is more than militant, more than a doctrine and a party bent on universal domination; it is a conspiracy. It is ferociously egotistical, and claims absolute authority for the primal Will of a particular class. This class, far from embracing all mankind, does not include all the poor, not the fundamental rural population that traditionally till the soil and live on its products, but enlists only the uprooted and disinherited proletariat crowded into modern industrial towns, with the politically inspired unions of sailors, miners, and railwaymen . . .

"Originally the American colonists breathed independence and individuality, religious and political, at the same time feeling confident of their vocation and ability to grow rich and to save their souls with none but divine guidance. Their zeal for democracy had a political root also in their Protestantism. They remembered the revolt of their kinsfolk in the old country against ecclesiastical and royal despotism, and against landlords. . . . The Russian democracy on the other hand has been dominated by conspirators, themselves perhaps dominated by ideologies. Personal ambition and apostolic zeal were inextricably blended in the leaders; and while they were not without a certain congenital or mystical sympathy with 'the people,' they remained essentially politicians. . . .

"In spite of this diversity of origin, I think that the two kinds of democracy may generate similar regimens. Both aspire to be universal; and under either of them, if absolutely dominant, mankind might become safe, law-abiding, sporting, and uniform."

In venturing on a bold comparison between the two leading democracies of the middle of the twentieth century Santayana is straining at his leash in a direction away from the ivory tower. He remains perfervent on the subject of absolute liberty, which to him is "the primary aim of life." On page 237 of his *Dominations and Powers*, 1954, he prints in capital letters the eternal law of liberty that nature has engraved also in the heart of man: "THINK AS YOU LIKE, SAY WHAT YOU THINK, DO WHAT YOU CHOOSE." Yet the highly civilized Santayana is not pleading for a return to savagery. It is merely that he has a skin supersensitive to bonds. He wants freedom and diversity. He shies away from uniformities. He is a man looking for a kingdom not yet of this world.

What we clearly get out of all this is that Santayana unqualifiedly condemns the sort of idolatry that would sacrifice not only happiness but the very lives of individuals to the state. Do not put up an ideal of some sort—any sort, for that matter— and then sacrifice yourself and others to it ruthlessly. Santayana points to a danger in ideals. There are in ethics two great commandments: Put life first, and, secondly, enhance it. This rules out any complete disregard of life, whether of your own life or that of others. "The root of all morality is animal bias; and to renounce that bias would be to renounce life."

Life comes first. Without life no happiness. Mass suicide or any kind of suicide is not the answer. Ethics must not renounce life, but further it. Our gods must be with us, not against us. When Xenophanes held that if oxen had gods their god would be an ox, he was expressing a profound insight into deification. Our own gods must be human gods. Men make gods and in turn their gods make them. The Great Stone Face, inscribed on the mountain, continues from morn to night to shape the conduct of beholders. That is how ideals operate. Sometimes gods turn into devils; the power that should enhance annihilates.

Then we must smash our idols. Even the Old Testament prophets knew that this had occasionally to be done.

The guiding beacon is the furtherance of life. If the gods demand human sacrifices, look them in the face. If they want to save only a few men and let the rest perish, keep on looking them in the face. There is something wrong here. When Prometheus, who was himself a god, stole some of the fire from Zeus, the head god, and gave it to mankind he kindled the wrath of Zeus, who chained him in perpetuity to a rock where the vultures could tear at his entrails. Prometheus, who had brought civilization to mankind, stood by his guns. He would not admit having done wrong. Man needed help and he helped him. In telling this first story of a Savior of Mankind the Greek tragedians voiced some of the best things ever said on human ethics. Prometheus was reminding Zeus not to be a tyrant. He was doing more than that; he was defying Zeus to do his worst. Power is not everything. Men have a right to happiness. The Fates could overthrow Zeus, and there would be a deliverer (Hercules), the Savior of Mankind. Right is above might. Santayana says: "Any actual God would need to possess a religion of his own, in order to fix his ideals of conduct and his rights in respect to his creatures or rather, as we should then be, to his neighbors." Santayana speaks of something "deeper than nature and higher than God."

Prerational ethics is on the whole pretty sound. It avoids extremes. At this stage in the world of human morality we find the judgments of Mrs. Grundy, the aims of political parties, the commands of the religious authorities, special revelations of duties to individuals, and all systems of intuitive ethics. Prerational ethics may not be clearly formulated, but prerational morality is vigorous because it is sincere. Santayana points out that it gets expressed in the numerous proverbs of folk wisdom. "Make hay while the sun shines. A stitch in time saves nine. Honesty is the best policy. Murder will out. Woe unto you, ye hypocrites. Watch and pray. Seek salvation with fear and trembling, and *Respice finem*. . . . A bird in the hand is worth two in the bush. *Carpe diem. Ars longa, vita brevis.* Be not righteous overmuch. Enough for the day is the evil thereof.

Behold the lilies of the field. Judge not, that ye be not judged.
Mind your own business. It takes all sorts of men to make a
world." These maxims work both sides of the street. Some
counsel foresight, others practicality. Some counsel boldness,
others caution. In the prerational stage of morality man has a
varied assortment of goods. That is the weakness of prerationality
—no harmony—the precepts cancel each other.

A rational morality needs a more nearly perfect self-knowledge.
A completely rational morality, thinks Santayana, has never
existed in the world and is hardly to be looked for. But noble
attempts were made by the Greeks to rationalize morality. "In
lieu of a rational morality, however, we have rational ethics;
and this mere idea of rational morality is something valuable."
A sketch of rational ethics was "founded by Socrates, glorified
by Plato, and sobered and solidified by Aristotle." Rationality
in ethics "consists in accepting any estimation which any man
may sincerely make. . . . What he really esteems is what ought
to guide his conduct; for to suggest that a rational being ought
to do what he feels to be wrong, or ought to pursue what he
genuinely thinks is worthless, would be to impugn that man's
rationality, and to discredit one's own. . . . More even than
natural philosophy, moral philosophy is something Greek: it is
the appanage of freemen." The Socratic ethics is compacted in
equal measure of sincerity and courtesy. "Each man is autono-
mous and all are respected. . . . Rational ethics . . . formu-
lates a natural morality." It differs from artificial systems, such
as observance of the Sabbath, in having a broader basis and in
being more complete.

"If pleasure, because it is commonly a result of satisfied instinct, may by a figure of speech be called the aim of impulse,
happiness, by a like figure, may be called the aim of reason.
The direct aim of reason is harmony. . . . Happiness implies
resource and security; it can be achieved only by discipline.
. . . Discipline discredits the random pleasures of illusion, hope,
and triumph, and substitutes those which are self-reproductive,
perennial, and serene, because they express an equilibrium maintained with reality. . . . Morality becomes rational precisely by
refusing either to accept human nature, as it sprouts, altogether

without harmony, or to mutilate it in the haste to make it harmonious. . . . When Socrates and his two great disciples composed a system of rational ethics they were hardly proposing
practical legislation for mankind. One by his irony, another by
his frank idealism, and the third by his preponderating interest
in history and analysis, showed clearly enough how little they
dared to hope."

Whatever occurred after them is postrational morality. "Pessimism and all the moralities founded on despair, are not prerational but postrational. . . . These systems are a refuge from
an intolerable situation: they are experiments in redemption.
. . . Postrational morality thus constitutes, in intention if not
in fact, a criticism of all experience. . . . It is an effort to subordinate all precepts to one, that points to some single eventual
good. For it occurs to the founders of these systems that by
estranging oneself from the world, or resting in the moment's
pleasure, or mortifying the passions, or enduring all sufferings
in patience, or studying a perfect conformity with the course
of affairs, one may gain admission to some sort of residual
mystical paradise; and this thought, once conceived, is published
as a revelation and accepted as a panacea."

Santayana discusses Aristippus and the Cynics, Epicureanism
and Stoicism, all the Neo-Platonic views, and Christianity. "Christianity is thus a system of postponed rationalism, a rationalism
intercepted by a supernatural version of the conditions of happiness. . . . Poverty, chastity, humility, obedience, self-sacrifice,
ignorance, sickness, and dirt may all acquire a religious worth
which reason, in its direct application, might scarcely have found
in them; yet these reversed appreciations are merely incidental
to a secret rationality, and are justified on the ground that human
nature, as now found, is corrupt and needs to be purged and
transformed before it can safely manifest its congenital instincts
and become again an authoritative criterion of values. In the
kingdom of God men would no longer need to do penance,
for life there would be truly natural and there the soul would
be at last in her native sphere."

On the whole, it is opined, there is no real advance in this
view. Christianity, in becoming theological and otherworldly,

cuts its own moral taproot. It makes what is done on earth relatively unimportant except in its relation to the next world, thus laying the ax to the tree of human life on earth. In common with other postrational systems it is too pessimistic. In what is by some construed as an ignoble attempt to save the individual soul, it gives up all real attempts to save this world. As some very early theologians plainly saw, by saving a portion of mankind at the expense of the rest it violates the principle of human solidarity also known as brotherhood.

At one point in *The Dialogues in Limbo* Santayana has it out with Socrates. Santayana, disguised as the Stranger, tells Socrates, whom he meets in Limbo, that in a later age Socrates instead of drinking the poison might have cultivated sanctity. In effect he twits: better a living saint than a dead hero. "After all," he tells Socrates, "were you not yourself constrained to turn away from this world and lay up your treasure in heaven?" To which Socrates replies: "No, no: how should a plain man like me, plodding and carnal, desire the life of a god or dream of ever enjoying it? . . . To heaven I never looked for a refuge from the earth, or to a second native land: I saw there an eternal pattern to which men might always point, and after which they might religiously fashion their earthly lives and their human republic." At the same time Socrates exclaims: "Death is not an evil, but vileness is; and when vileness is cultivated for the sake of life it renders life vile also. I thanked the gods when I was alive for having been born a Greek and not a barbarian, and now that I am dead I thank them that I died in time, lest I should have become a Christian."

Santayana is here skirting some of the ultimate questions on ethics. It is easy to draw from his discussions not three final conclusions but three suggestions as to the direction in which he is developing this vital subject of ethics: (1) The distinction he makes between ethics and morality suggests a pragmatic criterion. An ethics on paper is easy; the question is does it work? (2) The Promethean illustration lacks the ultimate sting because a god cannot die. For an immortal not to give in to another immortal is after all a somewhat theoretical problem. Most solutions of human problems deal with limited situations and

often center around that very matter of determining limits.
(3) If life is valued in terms of life and life enhancement
(preservation and growth), we get into one of those circular
situations similar to the one in which we say that everything is
in motion and that even rest is relative. Santayana pushes
Socrates into a corner on this when he makes Socrates veer in
the direction of evaluating life in terms of vileness and nobility.

The determination of limits, however, often has little to do
with the study of what is between them. One might study ovals
and realize that too flat an oval gets to be a line and too
round a one might become a circle, still leaving the study
of ovals as a legitimate subject. Human life is undoubtedly
the segment of a spectrum, shading down at the bottom into
animal life. We have lost our taste for being just animals.
Perhaps we aspire to be gods, and it is this end of the spectrum
that is open. Santayana, along with others of the American
school, insists that this end be left open. Do not assume too
hastily with pessimists that a wailing wall is the only thing that
we can face. Dewey with his suggestions of step by step attempting goals within our means and Santayana with similar
counsels of moderation are beginning to set a pattern. This pattern is more optimistic than the one provided by the parallel
movement of existentialism in Western Europe, although Santayana has this in common with certain of the existentialists
that he has written a novel.

Philosophers who seek to embrace the whole of man, not just
his intellect but also his muscles, his nerves, his blood, and
his entrails, may need a broader canvas. Spinoza's attempt to put
human emotions in the form of a geometry was not too successful. Both Santayana and Emerson burst out into poetry, and
Santayana wrote in addition *The Last Puritan.* Mario suggests
in the epilogue to the novel that "there is a better philosophy
in it than in your other books." This is not true. Anyone who
tried to get Santayana's philosophy from his novel instead of
from his other books would find thin pickings. Nor is the novel,
as its title might suggest, a study of Puritanism. Santayana has
little sympathy with Puritanism, but he has a lot of sympathy
with Oliver Alden, the hero of the book. There is a deep fellow

feeling for Oliver that stays there throughout the book, so much so that the reader cannot but suspect that in many ways Oliver is a delineation of Santayana himself. Certainly he is more Santayana than the ever-so-witty but superficial Mario or the infinitely refined but weak and oversubtle Peter, and never, never could he be the Lord Jim of the book, half pagan and half scoundrel.

Yet somehow Oliver is not Santayana. For one thing he did not have the vitality of Santayana. Perhaps for that reason the author had to kill off Oliver young. Oliver dies in a stupid accident which occurred after the war was over, before he had lived a life anywhere nearly as full as even his own father had. Oliver harbored some tremendous frustrations that also bothered Santayana, and these put him very close to the dislocated and eternal stranger that Santayana felt himself to be. Twice Oliver is on the point of marrying a perfectly wonderful woman. There were two such women, each almost a perfect mate. The merest shift in adjustment could have issued in a happy marriage, allowing normal growth, but no, always on the edge of a perfectly normal physical intimacy Oliver holds back. Is it just the Puritan in him? Time and again the main character is chided for not being able to be natural, and in that sense Oliver is a study in Puritanism, but a very sympathetic one. Oliver was enormously rich. He had many admirable traits. One gets the feeling that he was too much for Santayana to handle with complete success.

Yet the novel is a fine and an unusual one. It has been compared to *Moby Dick,* to *The Education of Henry Adams,* to *Marius the Epicurean;* but somehow the characters in Santayana's book are better chiseled out and the whole plot has a more modern flair to it. Perhaps Santayana merely used this novel to round out his picture of man as a stranger here below who nevertheless has no other place to go. As in certain existentialist novels, the weakness of characters is better portrayed than their strength. We learn more of Santayana the man, but it cannot be said that the novel adds significantly to his philosophy.

Existentialism is a European philosophy. None of the seven American philosophers have a direct connection with this movement, but in reading Santayana, and sometimes in reading James, one is strongly reminded of the parallelism between their views and those of the existentialists and their slogan that existence precedes essence. There is no question that in Santayana too existence comes first. The thick world of daily existence rather than the thin world of abstractions remains the starting point and center; this in spite of the fact that Santayana makes essences the high concern of the spirit. Nowhere does he put essences first. Spirit is rooted in matter. He never reverses this primacy in the sense that he makes man a spiritual rather than in nature and origin a material being. Spirit, the flower of our being, has its genesis in matter, the matrix of all life.

The peculiar fascination of the Santayana philosophy is its dexterous manipulation of the alternate themes of materiality and spirituality. It is clear, however, that this is an area on which more remains to be said. Meanwhile Santayana and Dewey open up anew the question of how far man can humanize the world. Certainly there have been many changes made in the island of Manhattan since it was bought from the Indians. Man changes the face of the earth. On the whole globe he impresses his own image, and now he is reaching into outer space. But how far can he go? The other way to put this is: Just where is man going to be thwarted?

Santayana, with the others, wants to leave the door to the future wide open. Meanwhile he better than the others prepares us for accepting this earth as our home, and its exploitation as our job. His profound analysis of the creative element in all religions, with the further suggestion that science itself is the accepted religion of the day, marks him as an advanced humanist. His philosophy bridges imagination and thought. His real spadework was done in establishing a new ontology, implanting in solid soil the roots of man's spirituality. On this he is going to get powerful help from Peirce, a less famous philosopher, who died long before Santayana did and whose work remained for a time unknown.

Charles Sanders Peirce:
Trail-Blazing Logician

1. Light under a Bushel

FRANKLIN AND EMERSON filled their own shoes. Each of them, singlehanded and without help from anybody, traced in forceful outline a growingly distinctive way of life, Emerson continuing where Franklin left off. In the hands of James and Dewey this same way of life became a more and more powerful American philosophy, attracting attention also in other countries. But as this philosophy in James and Dewey buckled down to cases the going got tougher. To be original in setting up a vast philosophical structure required some very hard thinking. From this neither James nor Dewey shied away, but at certain junctures they were glad to get some help from an eccentric genius who remained in the background.

No one who has read James and Dewey can have failed to note that time and again they gesticulated to a shadowy figure behind the academic scenes, thanking him for suggesting some of their leading ideas. So did Josiah Royce get help from the same source. James acknowledged that he got his main position, and even the name of his philosophy, from this mysterious stranger. Dewey relied on him for some of his crucial points of departure. That shadowy figure with the fertile brain, that power behind some of the bolder strokes of James and Dewey, that intellectual master who stood ready to forge whole wings of the framework of American philosophy was Charles Sanders Peirce (rhymes with terse).

While James and Dewey were working away in their respective high posts at Harvard and Columbia, Peirce with no high post at all was getting them to develop some of his own best insights. They ungrudgingly admitted their indebtedness to him. James even tried to draw Peirce out of the shadows. Dewey leaped to his defense when someone, as he thought, misinterpreted Peirce. "Users of Peirce's writings," said Dewey sternly, "should either stick to his basic pattern or leave him alone." Meanwhile both James and Dewey were themselves doing pretty much what they liked with some of Peirce's brain children. James did so quite freely, but the more he departed from Peirce the more he poured his own reflected glory over the obscure Peirce. Dewey was more scrupulous, especially in handling definite opinions, but Dewey followed Peirce only part of the way. There is more of Peirce beyond and beneath Dewey than Dewey could or cared to bring out, but both James and Dewey did use large portions of Peirce in the constructions of their own philosophies. Dewey wrote a logic which he thought fairly complete, but which Peirce regarded only as a wonderful piece of genetic psychology, serving admirably as an introduction to a new logic still to be built. On this logic Peirce himself spent most of his time.

"Among philosophers of the recent past," says Thomas A. Goudge, professor of philosophy at the University of Toronto, "who are making an impact on contemporary thought, a foremost place must be given to Charles Sanders Peirce. During his own lifetime (1839–1914) he was neglected and unknown. Today [1950] he is almost a vogue. The reason for this change of status is that between 1931 and 1935 six large volumes of his *Collected Papers* were published. These quickly revealed to students what his own age failed to appreciate, that Peirce was a thinker of the first magnitude. The result has been a steadily mounting interest in his ideas, and numerous publications have appeared which bear witness to his influence. Recently there has been formed 'The Charles S. Peirce Society,' whose object is to promote study and development of his philosophy in its manifold aspects." All the men who used Peirce considered him a grabbag from which they could pick what items they needed. Valuable items remained behind. Why did Peirce not write his own philosophy? What kept this original mind dammed up? Thereby hangs a tale almost as miraculous as that of the loaves and fishes. How come that men could take parts of him and feed multitudes and that Harvard University could thereafter come along and publish basketfuls of leftovers?

These leftovers have been eagerly pounced upon by clever professors of philosophy who each in his own way have tried to reconstruct Peirce. During his lifetime Peirce found no Boswell. After his death he found almost too many. These books that are appearing criticize Peirce and at the same time enhance his reputation. Usually such a post-mortem growth in a philosopher is a sign of real substance in the man. It happened to Spinoza, to Socrates, and to others. The more the published fragments of Peirce are dug into by eager interpreters the more we see that James and Dewey were right in regarding Peirce as a first-rate thinker. Alfred North Whitehead sums it all up in a few words: "Peirce was a very great man, with a variety of interests in each of which he made original contributions. The essence of his thought was originality in every subject he taught." [1a]

Only Peirce did hardly any teaching. Once for five years, as a part-time instructor, he gave some courses at Johns Hopkins. Mostly he just wrote. Like Charles Darwin, he buried himself for a large part of his life in the country. Here Peirce spent his time writing snatches of about four masterpieces at a time. Darwin almost did not get around to writing his own masterpiece but was prodded into activity when Wallace began to publish identical theories. Peirce was not similarly prodded. The grand schemes he was working on were never finished. They stand there in his eight volumes (two more were added in 1958) as parts of an incomplete edifice, but what a structure! It embraces the whole of modern science as so many new beginnings. Perhaps Peirce himself is the only one who could have given a more finished form to what he wrote, but perhaps also he never intended that the structure itself should be finished. It cannot be finished. Philosophy does not stop; all Peirce tried to do was to put it on the right track.

As we examine the niche that Peirce is now beginning to oc-

[1a] The short quotation of Whitehead on Peirce here given does not appear in Whitehead's works but in a letter he wrote in 1945 to Frederic Harold Young. Although Whitehead knew of Peirce, regarded him highly, and in his own philosophy shows marked resemblances to Peirce, it is unlikely, as we shall see later, that Whitehead had extensively studied Peirce or was directly influenced by him.

cupy, one reassuring fact immediately asserts itself. None of the five men who have thus far spoken up for American philosophy was a mathematician, but Peirce, like his father before him, was an eminent mathematician. This gives his whole philosophy a new tang.

In this day and age, when more has been done in mathematics in the past one hundred years than in all the preceding centuries together, we need a mathematician sensitive to this whole area of fast-developing knowledge. When Einstein and other leading cosmologists are drawing on mathematics as never before, we need for philosophy a spokesman who is well versed in mathematics. So few philosophers are. Well, Peirce was a highly trained philosopher-mathematician, and so was Whitehead. Our last two sages more than make up for any deficiency in this respect from which American philosophy may thus far have suffered. Charles W. Morris, himself a foremost exponent of a pragmatic type of philosophy, makes it plain that in his opinion in the American movement James was the psychologist, Dewey the educator, Mead the sociologist, and Peirce the logician. We might add that Santayana was the artist or aesthete of the movement, and Whitehead pre-eminently its metaphysician. Morris points to many other lesser men, such as Ames, Tufts, Moore, and Lewis, who contributed ideas to a philosophy that is still in formation, but the man who struck out boldest of all and who laid the metaphysical foundations was Charles S. Peirce.

Somewhere Peirce, in thinking of Kant, enumerates what he considers the seven qualifications that any philosopher should have in high degree. These are (1) ability to discern what is before one's consciousness, (2) inventive originality, (3) generalizing power, (4) subtlety, (5) critical severity and a sense of fact, (6) systematic procedure, (7) energy, diligence, persistency, and exclusive devotion to philosophy. Many men have not been slow to point out that these were exactly the qualifications that earmarked Peirce himself. Above all he was original, and persistent in his blind devotion to philosophy.

Bertrand Russell, not overly sympathetic to pragmatism, says: "Peirce's pragmatism . . . is a very different doctrine from those of James and Schiller and Dewey, and one not open to the same criticisms. He has, in fact, two doctrines, not mutually inconsistent, one as to what truth is, the other as to how we discover it. He gives . . . two definitions of truth. One of them, quoted by Dewey, says: 'Truth is that concordance of abstract statement with the ideal limit towards which endless investigation would tend to bring scientific relief.' The other, not quoted by Dewey, says 'Truth is the universe of all universes, and is assumed on all hands to be real.' Pragmatism, for Peirce, was only a method; the truths which it sought to discover were absolute and eternal. He did not believe in the supremacy of action over thought . . . for to say that we live for the mere sake of action, as action, regardless of the thought it carries out, would be to say that there is no such thing as rational purport. . . . Peirce was a man of tremendous energy, producing a multitude of ideas. . . . He reminds one of a volcano spouting out masses of rock, of which some, on examination, turn out to be nuggets of pure gold."

James Feibleman, sympathetic to Peirce, who has as a matter of fact written one of the best books [1] about him, says: "Peirce is rapidly beginning to be acknowledged as the greatest of American philosophers, as a system maker worthy to rank with the best that Europe has produced. He is in all probability destined to become the source of a native philosophical tradition, the classic philosopher who will give America its self-respect by making it intellectually a thing of its own apart from its debt to Europe. He may thus appear to future historians as the focal point, the origin and very center, of the American culture, which must always remain related to that of Europe yet which could contribute something of its own to the world and thus be independent of the European tradition."

Because Peirce himself never pulled his own system together or presented it for publication, men who try to do this for him end up with astonishingly similar yet in some ways different interpretations. This is because some do not accept all of Peirce.

[1] James K. Feibleman, *An Introduction to Peirce's Philosophy Interpreted as a System* (New York: Harper and Bros., 1946).

Thus Justus Buchler wrote a fine book [2] on Peirce in which he threw out all the metaphysical speculations of Peirce and concentrated solely on what Buchler considers the solidly scientific parts of Peirce, which he called his public empiricism. "Public empiricism is, I think, a point of view essentially sound. It is a considerable advance over nineteenth-century positivism and the great tradition of British empiricism, and it is an original product at the same time that it synthesizes the best in three—Locke, Reid and Kant—whom Peirce admired most among modern philosophers." Ernest Nagel, the eminent logician, in a foreword to the Buchler volume, credited Peirce with two fundamental insights: "the recognition of the central rôle played by symbols or language in human behavior and knowledge; and the recognition that human knowledge is an achievement of biological organisms functioning in social contexts."

A more complete reconstruction that comes off very well is that by Professor Goudge,[3] quoted above. Goudge does not throw out the metaphysical parts of Peirce; he merely subordinates them, as does another "reconstructionist" of Peirce, the English scholar W. B. Gallie. Goudge undertook to interpret Peirce's thought in terms of a basic conflict which he believed it exhibited. Thus he was able to survey Peirce's main ideas without brushing any of them aside as "unrepresentative." Goudge considered Peirce's "sudden popularity" as springing "from the remarkable anticipation in Peirce of themes that are in the foreground of current philosophical discussion. Such subjects as the foundations of logic and mathematics, semantics, induction and probability, phenomenology, chance and determinism in nature, evolutionary metaphysics—all are dealt with in the *Collected Papers*. Moreover, much of the exposition has a freshness, originality, and penetration which cannot fail to impress the reader. No matter how widely he may differ from Peirce's conclusions, he is bound to be stimulated by the new avenues of reflection opened up, and by the unusual perspectives in which

[2] Justus Buchler, *Charles Peirce's Empiricism* (New York: Harcourt, Brace and Co., 1939).

[3] Thomas A. Goudge, *The Thought of C. S. Peirce* (Toronto: University of Toronto Press, 1950).

ancient problems are viewed. Even the language used has a surprisingly contemporary ring. Part of the tragedy of Peirce's career lay in the fact that his thinking was so far in advance of his own time. He had, indeed a twentieth- not a nineteenth-century mind."

Gallie,[4] the British exponent of Peirce, in his Penguin volume on the American philosopher, gives a hundred and eighty pages to what he considers the basic views of Peirce, and sixty to his "metaphysical ideas." His volume, although the shortest of the books on Peirce, is not the easiest to read, because, among other things, he tries to give a fairly detailed account of Peirce's logic. It makes no attempt to be popular, but he does try to overcome European prejudice against accepting seriously this American philosopher. He warns the reader that pragmatism is not just colonial hogwash. "Harvard, the nursing ground of the movement, was in the second half of the last century a cultural center at least the equal of Oxford and Cambridge; it had long and deep, if somewhat narrow, intellectual traditions of its own, and in the opinion of Charles Darwin it contained enough brilliant minds in the 1860s to staff all the universities of England. Nor were the founders of Pragmatism in any sense intellectual backwoodsmen: Peirce and James—and the same can be said of the best of their Pragmatist successors—thought and wrote as men profoundly steeped in European culture and with a lively awareness of the best contemporary movements in European thought. Peirce in the 1870s and the 1880s was teaching logic on lines which were eventually to reach Oxford some sixty years later, while James, as Professor of psychology, was facing the main philosophical problems that arise from that subject with a freshness of vision and a mastery of all relevant detail which no British philosopher has ever commanded. . . . British critics of Pragmatism have concentrated their attacks on the writings of James and his disciples, neglecting, or treating only at second hand, Peirce's original statement and later developments of his Pragmatist principle."

Professor Manley Thompson, of the University of Chicago,

[4] W. B. Gallie, *Peirce and Pragmatism* (Baltimore, Md.: Penguin Books, 1952).

presents a reconstruction with special attention to Peirce's own hints on what books he intended to write.[5] We do get here a little better idea of what Peirce's own books might have been like had he finished them, but, as in most reconstructions from diffuse material, too much of the scaffolding is left. Results are clumsy. Peirce himself could write very well. After all he did write and have printed some seventy-five papers and twice as many book reviews. Some of his papers on mathematical subjects are marvelously finished, clear, and easy to understand. With his architectonic ability, it is a thousand pities that he was never given the facilities, the encouragement, and the stimulus himself to finish his *Guess at the Riddle* or his *Grand Logic*. As it is, all the men who write books expounding his system are of real help in bringing into focus the materials now scattered throughout the eight volumes of his literary remains. As condensations they give the ordinary reader some idea of what these valuable thoughts of Peirce were all about.

Perhaps as valuable as the reconstructions are the carefully made selections now beginning to appear, two of them in paperbound volumes. One of these by Professor Buchler,[6] cited above, does not in the selections slight the metaphysics of Peirce. The other, equally satisfying book of excerpts, is by Philip P. Wiener, a close student of the whole philosophic movement of which Peirce is a part. This volume, called *Values in a Universe of Chance*, contains new material on the life of Peirce.[7] Such biographical material is still very hard to get. Someday perhaps someone will prepare an adequate biography of this neglected philosopher. In his personal life there are many unsolved riddles. There is also in existence an earlier, hard-cover book of excerpts from Peirce including valuable early articles and a good introduction by Morris R. Cohen, as well as a supplementary Essay by John Dewey. This volume, published in 1923 by Peter Smith, bears the intriguing title *Chance, Love and Logic*.

[5] Manley Thompson, *The Pragmatic Philosophy of C. S. Peirce* (Chicago: University of Chicago Press, 1953).

[6] *Philosophical Writings of Peirce*, selected and edited with an Introduction by Justus Buchler (New York: Dover Publications, 1955).

[7] *Values in a Universe of Chance, Selected Writings of Charles S. Peirce*, edited, with an Introduction and Notes by Philip P. Wiener (New York: Doubleday Anchor Books, 1958).

Perhaps the most readable of the single books on Peirce is the one by Feibleman. This has more unity and swing to it of the sort that Peirce might have given to a single volume on his thoughts if he had lived in happier circumstances and had had access to the books, the income, and the audience that he should have had. The miracle is that Peirce did as much writing as he did and that men like Feibleman can make such a detailed and sympathetic presentation. Best of all for the serious student are Peirce's own works published posthumously by the Harvard University Press. Unconnected and abrupt as some of these fragments are, among them it is not hard to find gems of completeness and hundreds of brilliant paragraphs. All his notes are here beautifully printed and, what is more, are indexed by subject. The volumes—whole stretches of them —are not at all hard to read, and somehow the message of the man comes through better from his own racy outcroppings. He has a genius for coining apt and unusual words, and although everybody wishes he could have written finished books, in one way these notes with their constant revisions are curiously satisfying. Most men print books in their youth, followed by later books, each modifying the preceding volume. In Peirce all the thoughts of a lifetime are put into one continuous stream of thought eight volumes long. The man is there all the time, laboring away, and one can almost see him, perhaps writing with alternate hands. It was said that he could do just that, write equally well with both hands, and even write a question with one hand while answering it with the other. In the volumes of notes Peirce continued updating and revising his thoughts as he went along.

2. From the Yard to the Garret

WHEN THE GREEKS wanted to lampoon a philosopher they depicted him as a stargazer who fell into a well. On the comic stage it was always good for a laugh to see how a man searching the skies, unbeknownst to himself zigzagged off the beaten path, into a hole at his feet. Today an occasional philosopher still does just that. The genius becomes so preoccupied with the big things in his mind that he gets into trouble at home and in the office. Neither his wife nor his boss cares much about what guides the stars in their courses; both want the stargazer to pay more attention to the little day-by-day practical things that count.

Peirce too was one of those uncompromising geniuses who start life with every advantage and then somehow get sidetracked. It is not a case of taking to drink or going down the primrose path, but more like the inventor who rides a hobby to death, or like Socrates who prefers to talk in the market place and then gets Xantippe down on him. Peirce had a number of distractions and one of them was writing down the thoughts that kept coming into his head. It is hard to see just why he failed to make a living, but the fact is that starting life as a carefree youth, sauntering in the Harvard Yard with his father, an honored professor of mathematics at the school, he did nevertheless as an old man have to hide in a garret from his creditors. From the proceeds of a small legacy left him in middle life he made a down payment on a large rambling house in an out-of-the-way place in Pennsylvania. What attracted him was the spacious attic into which, after it was fixed up, he had visions of gathering his disciples and teaching them. The visionary's disciples failed to materialize; the people at Johns

Hopkins, where he had done a little teaching, refused to send him pupils even if he promised to leave the house to Johns Hopkins. After many years money and time ran out—so he rigged up a rope ladder, and when creditors came he pulled up the rope ladder after him and was not at home, except to himself in his garret outsitting the inconvenient callers while he scribbled on a tablet. He died, uncomplaining, attended by his devoted wife, also ill, after Peirce himself had been supported for years on a mere pittance from friends or on what came in from writing occasional book reviews or articles for a philosophic dictionary. When he could get them, in the last years of his life, he took small doses of morphine to keep down the pain from a progressive cancer. What he worried about was not being able to continue work on the logic that so needed doing. The vision in the heavens still entranced him as he fell into the well.

Charles Sanders Peirce (1839–1914), a few years older than James and outliving him by four years, had, as Frederic Harold Young, who gathered some facts on his life, put it, "an intellect masculine in its boldness and sweep, vast in its learning, austere in its self-discipline, and comparable to that of Leibnitz in its combination of mathematical, logical, scientific, and metaphysical powers." He was the second son of Benjamin Peirce, a Harvard professor of mathematics and astronomy. When Charles Sanders Peirce was seventy years old he reminisced almost garrulously about his family and his father: "My father was universally acknowledged to be by far the strongest mathematician in the country and was a man of great intellect and weight of character. All the leading men of science, particularly astronomers and physicists resorted to our house; so that I was brought up in an atmosphere of science. But my father was a broad man and we were intimate with literary people too. William Story, the sculptor, Longfellow, James Lowell, Charles Norton, Wendell Holmes, and occasionally Emerson, are among the figures of my earliest memories. Among them I remember the Italian Gallenga, who went by the name of Mariotte. The Quincys we also knew very well, but not the Adamses. My mother's father had been a Senator in Washington. But his weak lungs having obliged him to retire, he set up a law school; and in that way

I used to see some of the most eminent of the political people, such as Webster. Bancroft had been very intimate with my mother's family, as in his old age he was a great friend of my wife here. I used occasionally to see him; and Lothrop Motley was one of our friends.

"My father had strong contempt for certain men whom he considered shams, and among them was Charles Sumner, who was, I must say, one of the absurdest figures of vanity I ever laid eyes on. Among the lawyers I remember Rufus Choate, Judge Story, etc. Another figure of my childhood was Emerson's friend Margaret Fuller (Countess Ossoli). I was brought up with far too loose a rein, except that I was forced to think hard and continuously. My father would sometimes make me sit up all night playing double dummy till sunrise without relaxing my attention."

J. J. Sylvester, another eminent mathematician of the day, considered Charles a greater mathematician than his father. On long walks with his father, it was about the father's problems and not the son's that they talked. Both loved mathematics and philosophy. At fourteen Charles started reading books on logic. At sixteen he entered Harvard. Here he ignored the regular work, doing just enough to get by, but kept up his growing preoccupation with logicians and philosophers. He soon got deeply into Kant, and his father helped him by pointing out "lacunae in Kant's reasoning which I should probably not otherwise have discovered." Charles adored his father. He deeply digested the lessons in critical thinking. Said Charles, "The best thing for a fledgling philosopher is close companionship with a stalwart practical reasoner."

Charles also trained his powers of sensory discrimination, and in this too his father seems to have been with him. Charles was tremendously interested in the feeling as well as the intellectual side of life. As a freshman he read the German Schiller, who stressed the primacy of feeling in life. Charles prided himself on being an expert wine taster. He strove for the superlative in both feeling and thought, but he was not built to be a mystic. The capacity for feeling did not get in the way of a keenly analytic brain. In fact nothing got in the way, but the fact that he had the feelings, and expressed them, may have helped to make the course of his life more difficult.

Professor W. B. Gallie says of Charles's father: "Benjamin Peirce was primarily an applied mathematician, but the originality of his mind was perhaps best shown in his *Linear Associative Algebra*, the opening sentence of which, 'Mathematics is the science which draws necessary conclusions,' shows an approach far in advance of current conception in America, and indeed in Europe. The main lines of Peirce's intellectual development were laid down by his father's teaching." How gaily Peirce started out his career as an undergraduate at Harvard appears from the notes on the first twenty years of his life published in the Harvard Class Book of 1859:

1839. September 10. Tuesday. Born.

1840. Christened.

1841. Made a visit to Salem which I distinctly remember.

1842. July 31. Went to church for the first time.

1843. Attended a marriage.

1844. Fell violently in love with Miss W. and commenced my education.

1845. Moved into new house on Quincy St.

1846. Stopped going to Ma'am Sessions and began to go to Miss Wares—a very pleasant school where I learnt much and fell violently in love with another Miss W. whom for distinction's sake I will designate as Miss W'.

1847. Began to be most seriously and hopelessly in love. Sought to drown my care by taking up the subject of Chemistry—an antidote which long experience enables me to recommend as sovereign.

1848. Went to dwell in town with my uncle C. H. Mills and went to school to the Rev. T. H. Sullivan where I received some lessons in elocution.

1849. In consequence of playing truant and laving in the frogpond, was taken ill. On my recovery, I was recalled to Cambridge and admitted a member of the Cambridge High School.

1850. Wrote a "History of Chemistry."

1851. Established a printing press.
1852. Joined a debating society.
1853. Set up for a fast man and became a bad school boy.
1854. Left the High School with honor after having been turned out several times. Worked at Mathematics for about six months and then joined Mr. Dixwell's school in town.
1855. Graduated at Dixwell's and entered College. Read Schiller's *Aesthetic Letters* and began the study of Kant.
1856. Sophomore. Gave up the idea of being a fast man and undertook the pursuit of pleasure.
1857. Junior. Gave up the pursuit of pleasure and undertook to enjoy life.
1858. Senior. Gave up enjoying life and exclaimed "Vanity of vanities!"

These frothy notes skip lightly over his involvements with philosophy, advanced mathematics, and aesthetic feeling. They do not mention his "boxing bouts" with Chauncey Wright in philosophy or his classmate Frank Abbot whose views he was later to defend. There is no indication that he thoroughly mastered Kant, learning both editions of the *Critique of Pure Reason* inside out and by wrangling with Wright and his father, getting things straight, so that in the very year he graduated we find he left notes in which the main landmarks of a mature philosophy are already clearly outlined.

In these notes he projects vast schemes of thought, but never a word about the Civil War then breaking over his head. His father had taught him how to close his mind to certain things while concentrating on others. This he seems to have done with a vengeance. His mind entered in the pathway of the great thinkers and it was not easy for him to come to earth. If he did come down he did things awkwardly, distractedly, intemperately. The blind spot for current events was bad enough, the scorn for phonies which he got straight from his strenuous father did not make things any smoother, and the concentrated wrangling on high things, combined with man-of-the-world posings must have made Charles one of the "beatniks" of the day. After remarking that "to be social is one thing, to be gregarious is another," he announces concerning some writing of his: "My book is meant for people who *want to find out;* people who want philosophy ladled out to them can go elsewhere. There are philosophical soup shops at every corner, thank God!"

Peirce, a gay and high intellectual, is not fooling around. Life is short and he wants to find out. Spread out on his every page, there is a sort of deadly intent to get to know, and no patience at all with humbug.

Here is a young man with his head permanently in the clouds. William James said in a letter of September 16, 1861: "In last year's class there is a son of Professor Peirce, whom I suspect to be a very smart fellow with a great deal of character, pretty independent and violent though." In these biographical paragraphs on Peirce there is no attempt to make out that Peirce was easy to live with or that people did not find him hard to get along with. Geniuses are proverbially porcupinish. To be thoughtful in small matters, to be forgetful of self, to be attentive and always polite, look for these things in a politician or in a good executive, but not necessarily in a thinker. To paraphrase Emerson, when "God lets loose a thinker upon the world" there is bound to be trouble, and some of it lands on the thinker's own head.

Immediately after graduation Peirce, who was trained in science, went off to the wilds of Louisiana to do some surveying. Then in the summer of 1860 he came back, and took six months with Professor Agassiz to study his method of classifying the sciences. This he needed as a cornerstone in his system of thought. The idea of a basic classification of the sciences, as a kind of map of the field of knowledge, always stayed with him. He also took a job with the U.S. Coast and Geodetic Survey with which in one connection or another he remained sporadically at work for some thirty years. Peirce says: "I was educated as a chemist, and as soon as I had taken my A.B. degree, after a year's work in the Coast Survey, I took first six months under Agassiz in order to learn what I could of his methods, and then went into the laboratory. I had had a laboratory of my own for many years and had every memoir of any consequence as it came out; so that at the end of two or three years, I was the first man in Harvard to take a degree in chemistry *summa cum laude.*" This was a master's degree in 1862. "But I had discovered that my only very unusual gift was for logical analysis. I began with German philosophy."

Of his marriage to his first wife, Melusina Fay, Professor Gallie reports: "He had married, at the age of 23, a Miss Melusina Fay, a society lady who in her later years was very well thought of in Harvard circles. But for whatever reasons, the marriage proved an unhappy one. Peirce's wife deserted him in 1876, and he divorced her on grounds of desertion seven years later. There seems to be little doubt, however, that although legally the wronged party, Peirce was himself to blame in this unfortunate affair; the divorce caused a rift between him and his own brothers, and almost certainly affected his chances of obtaining later in life the kind of teaching post which he desired and deserved. In 1884 Peirce married again; and his second wife, a French lady, survived him. He had no children. . . . The personality disclosed in Peirce's writing is an almost wholly attractive one; perhaps it is a slightly eccentric personality, but it is pre-eminently sunny, high-spirited, generous, and robustly self-confident . . . entirely free from academic jealousy and from personal assertiveness; in controversy he is always the fairest, indeed most chivalrous of opponents; and although his best writings contain plenty of punch they show not the slightest trace of swagger. Witty, arch, enthusiastic, magnanimous, occasionally fanatical in pursuit of his own most difficult ideas or in his assaults on the doctrines of others, but in the main sanely and even severely self-critical. Peirce the writer stands in most extraordinary contrast to what is generally reported of Peirce the man in society."

Max H. Fisch and Jackson I. Cope in a note commenting on Peirce's life at Johns Hopkins, published in Wiener and Young's *Studies in the Philosophy of Charles Sanders Peirce,* say that Harriet Melusina Fay (1836–1923), published under the name of Melusina (or Zina) Fay Peirce, and that her writings are an overlooked source for Peirce's political views. They also hint that there may be a disguised allusion to her in Peirce's own words: "Many a man has cherished for years as his hobby some vague shadow of an idea, too meaningless to be positively false; he had, nevertheless, passionately loved it, has made it his companion by day and by night, and has given to it his strength and his life, with it and for it, until it has become, as it were, flesh of his flesh and bone of his bone, and then he has waked up some bright morning to find it gone, clean vanished away like the beautiful Melusina of the fable, and the essence of his life has gone with it. I myself have known such a man." Melusina, or Melisande, in the folklore of French romance is condemned every Saturday to become a serpent from the waist downward. She begs her husband never to see her on that day. Perversely he does see her, and she is now obliged to leave her husband and wander like a specter till the day of doom.

At age thirty-four, on November 25, 1875, Peirce wrote a letter to Daniel C. Gilman, President of the newly established graduate school at Johns Hopkins about his qualifications in logic and how he might be suitable to teach it. In his letter he warned about two things, the first being that he could not relinquish his job at the Coast Survey, which still required his guidance although it did not take up too much of his time, and: "The second is a very painful matter upon which I dislike to speak at all, and of which I will say the least possible. It is that I have been for a number of years in disagreement with my wife, not having lived with her for a long time, and not having even seen her for over a year; and the reasons for this on the one side and on the other will, I hope, never be known. It is however certain that we shall never live together again. This is a fact to which you will naturally give a weight, should you seriously consider inviting me to Baltimore."

For ten years after graduation from Harvard, with his troubled married life getting under way, with a job of sorts in the Coast and Geodetic Survey, assigned for most of the time as an assistant computer to his own father at the Harvard Observatory, with his head full of schemes about his own slowly developing and vast philosophy, how did Peirce look to others? Toward the beginning of 1869, when Peirce had been out of school ten years, William James wrote concerning Peirce to his brother Henry: "The poor cuss sees no chance of getting a professorship anywhere, and is likely to go into the Observatory for good. It seems a great pity that as original a man as he is, who is willing and able to devote the powers of his life to logic and metaphysics, should be starved out of a career, when there are lots of professorships of the sort to be given in this country, to 'safe,' orthodox men. He has good reason, I know, to feel a little discouraged about the prospect, but I think he ought to hang on, as a German would do, till he grows gray." That same year William James again wrote to his brother: "I heard Charles Peirce lecture yesterday . . . on British Logicians. It was delivered without notes, and was admirable in matter, manner and clearness of statement. He has recently been made assistant astronomer with $2500 a year. But I wish he could get a professorship of philosophy somewhere. That is his forte, and therein he is certainly *très fort*. I never saw a man go into things so intensely and thoroughly." Then three years later, as a bit of gossip, he told Henry: "Charles Peirce and wife are going to Washington again for the winter and perhaps for good. He says he is appreciated there. He read us an admirable introductory chapter to his book on logic the other day."

On one of Peirce's trips to Paris in connection with his scientific work on geophysics he fell in with Henry James. In 1876 Henry James wrote to his family: "The only man I see here familiarly is C. Peirce, with whom I generally dine a couple of times a week. He is a very good fellow—when he is not in ill-humour; then he is intolerable. But as William says, he is a man of genius, and in such in the long run, one always finds one's account. He is leading here a life of insupportable loneliness and sterility—but of much material luxury, as he seems to have plenty of money. He sees, literally, not a soul but myself and his secretary." William wrote to Henry: "I am amused that you should have fallen into the arms of CSP, whom I imagine you find a rather uncomfortable bedfellow, thorny and spinous, but the way to treat him is after the fabled 'nettle' receipt: grasp firmly, contradict, push hard, make fun of him, and he is as pleasant as anyone; but be overawed by his sententious manner and his paradoxical and obscure statements—wait upon them, as it were, for light to dawn—and you will never get a feeling of ease with him any more than I did for years, until I changed my course and treated him more or less chaffingly. I confess I like him very much in spite of all his peculiarities, for he is a man of genius, and there's always something in that to compel one's sympathy."

Peirce had two opportunities to tie up with a university. The first was with Johns Hopkins, just then starting out to be something new in the way of a graduate school. Both Peirce and his father championed the idea that a university was first of all a center for the advancement of knowledge and, secondly, for teaching. This new emphasis on research was exactly what was aimed at by the new school slowly and carefully being built up by President Gilman, to whom, as has been noted, Peirce had sent a letter of application. Gilman gave him a part-time instructorship that did not involve severing his connections with the Survey. In other words, Gilman tried out Peirce in a minor job, but when it came to making a permanent appointment Peirce was passed over in favor of G. Stanley Hall. Fisch and Cope in their account of Peirce at Johns Hopkins say that the "five years Peirce taught logic to graduate students, about half of them from the mathematics department . . . was the most distinguished and creative teaching any university has ever had in logic, and Peirce's students were brought to a level of original achievement which has never been rivaled. The chief monument of the quinquennium is the volume of *Studies in Logic by Members of the Johns Hopkins University* which appeared in 1883. This volume was intended to inaugurate a series, and others would doubtless have followed if Peirce's appointment had continued."

One of the members of Peirce's first class at Hopkins was Christine Ladd, later known as Mrs. Christine Ladd-Franklin. She said: "Peirce had all the air . . . of the typical philosopher who is engaged, at the moment, in bringing fresh truth by divination out of some inexhaustible well. . . . No effort was made to create a connected and not inconsistent whole out of the matter of each lecture. In fact, so devious and unpredictable was his course that he once, to the delight of his students, proposed at the end of his lecture, that we should form (for greater freedom of discussion) a Metaphysical Club, though he had begun the lecture by defining metaphysics to be the 'science of unclear thinking.'" Such a club was formed and had its first meeting on October 28, 1879.

All this was in the early days of Johns Hopkins when Gilman was feeling his way toward making this the greatest graduate school in America. At the opening of Johns Hopkins in 1876 Thomas Henry Huxley had given a famous but rather scathing address on the importance of scientific education. The year 1876 was the hundredth anniversary of the founding of America, and for Hopkins to have the famous evolutionist give an opening address caused quite a stir. From conservative quarters there was criticism that at the opening of the university Huxley had been included but prayer had been omitted. President Gilman got many letters, one of them saying: "It was bad enough to invite Huxley. It were better to have asked God to be present. It would have been absurd to ask them both." Gilman felt that the university had a reputation for impiety to live down. So when G. Stanley Hall came along, a man with a Ph.D., which Peirce did not have, and moreover a man with seminary training, conservative, safe, and a born promoter, it is easy to see why Gilman chose Hall. As if to drive the matter home Hall in his opening address remarked that "the new psychology, which brings simply a new method and a new standpoint to philosophy, is, I believe, Christian to its root and center. . . . The Bible is being re-revealed as man's greatest textbook in psychology." Peirce could not compete against this sort of thing.

After 1884, the last of Peirce's five years of intermittent lecturing at Johns Hopkins, came another chance for a job at Harvard, but unfortunately Peirce had had a fight with the Harvard Trustees about the way Professor Royce had treated Francis Ellingwood Abbot, who long ago had been an undergraduate classmate of Peirce's. Abbot in 1885 had published a book on *Scientific Theism* of which Peirce thought very highly. Peirce always maintained that it was this book which converted him to the view that scientists should be realists, not nominalists.

This became his own doctrine, for which he gives full credit to Abbot.

Abbot became a Unitarian clerygman and, like Emerson, resigned from the church but retained an interest in writing. The book on theism held that science is founded on a system of self-existing, self-determining, objectively real relations. This objective reality of relations was taken over by Peirce. William James also made much of it. In fact, Abbot won European recognition for his book, and during a year when Royce was absent on sabbatical leave Abbot was asked to lecture in his stead. This was in 1887, and when Royce came back, whether from jealousy or because he did not like Abbot's rejection of idealism, Royce launched a vicious attack on Abbot, questioning both his competency and his scientific standing. Abbot fought back. There were lawsuits. Peirce got into the fray by demanding that Royce apologize to Abbot. Royce won out. Abbot was disgraced. Abbot wrote one more book and then committed suicide on his wife's grave. In his pocket was a brief note saying that the work begun in his college days was now finished. That work had to do with the establishment of a positivistic religion based on evolution, possibly a remote outcome of early discussions at Harvard with friends including Peirce.

Peirce's intervention in the Abbot affair got him into President Eliot's books as a troublemaker. Charles W. Eliot had been confirmed as president of Harvard in spite of what James called "his great personal defects, tactlessness, meddlesomeness, and disposition to cherish petty grudges"; and, as James was to say in later years, Peirce had "dished himself at Harvard by inspiring dislike in Eliot." Nevertheless, James wrote to President Eliot as late as March 3, 1895: "Now I want to propose to you no less a person than Charles S. Peirce, whose name I don't suppose will make you bound with eagerness at first, but you may think better of it after a short reflection. . . . The better graduates would flock to hear him—his name is one of mysterious greatness for them by now—and he would leave a wave of influence, tradition, gossip, etc. that wouldn't die away for many years. I should learn a lot from his course. Everyone knows of Peirce's personal uncomfortableness; and if I were president I

shouldn't hope for a harmonious wind-up to his connection
with the University. But I should take that as part of the dis-
agreeableness of the day's work, and shut my eyes and go
ahead, knowing that from the highest intellectual point of view
it would be the best thing that could happen for the greatness
of the Philosophical Department. It would also advertise us as
doing all we could, and making the best of every emergency;
and it would be a recognition of C.S.P.'s strength, which I am
sure is but justice to the poor fellow. I truly believe that the
path of (possibly) least comfort is here the *true* path, so I have no
hesitation in urging my opinion. . . ." Eliot answered that "all
you say of C. S. Peirce's remarkable capacities and acquisitions
is true, and I heartily wish that it seemed to me possible for the
University to make use of them," but that is where the matter
ended. Peirce did not get the job.

Meanwhile Peirce in 1891, after receiving his small legacy,
had resigned from the Coast and Geodetic Survey and retired
to Milford, Pennsylvania. He cannot have been in these years
too downcast, to judge from a description of him given by
John Jay Chapman, when by chance he sat down next to Peirce
at the Century Club one day in August, 1893:

"Went to the Century, where I happened to sit down next to
Charles Peirce, and stayed talking to him ever since, or rather
he talking. He is a most genial man—got down books and read
aloud. He began by saying Lincoln had the Rabelais quality.
It appears he worships Rabelais. He read passages from Carlyle
in a voice that made the building reverberate. He also read from
an Elizabethan Thomas Nash—a great genius whom he said
Carlyle got his style from, but he is wrong, Nash is better . . .
and Peirce read with oriflamme appreciation. He then talked
about—plasms—force, heat, light—Boston, Emerson, Margaret
Fuller, God, Mammon, America, Goethe, Homer, Silver, but
principally science and philosophy—a wonderful evening. It was
ask and have, and, but that he talked himself positively to sleep
with exertion, he would be talking yet, and I have many more
things I want to ask him, chiefly, Helmholtz. He is a physical
mathematician mechanician, that sort of a man of a failed life
so far as professional recognition goes, but of acknowledged

extraordinary ability, and is positively the most agreeable person in the city. He is a son of old Professor Peirce, is about 55 and is like Socrates in his willingness to discuss anything and his delight in posing things and expressing things. In fact I got to answering him in the style of Plato's dialogues. . . . He has a theory that the laws of mind and matter are the same and he doesn't believe in the conservation of energy. He explained this at length—and he frightened two or three gentlemen who came near while he was doing it so that they won't come to the Club for a month. They looked at him in wonder, crossed themselves, and went away."

When Gilman retired from Johns Hopkins in 1901 to become president of the Carnegie Institution of Washington, one of the early applications for a grant came from Peirce. He asked for funds to complete his treatise on logic. There were more than a score of supporting letters. The application was rejected. The matter was laid before Mr. Carnegie himself who is reported to have said: "That is just the sort of case I desired to help. If they will manage the thing right and help just such cases I will give not ten but twenty millions." Two years later, on April 9, 1895, Peirce tried to get Gilman to send him summer pupils, saying: "It has always been my desire to establish a summer school of philosophical studies here. . . . If the Johns Hopkins would aid us to make our philosophical academy, we might arrange to let the University have the place when we are done with it." Nothing came of this.

Peirce still had ten years to go. He corresponded with scholars, he kept working, neighbors reported that lights were on at all hours of the night, but there was no money in all this. When Peirce died in 1914, as Philip P. Wiener reports, "there was no money even for a decent burial. His widow sold all his manuscripts to Harvard University for five hundred dollars."

3. The Birth of Pragmatism

EINSTEIN FOUND A patent office a good place in which to do some basic thinking; Peirce working in the Harvard Observatory, on assignment from the Coast and Geodetic Survey, found this a good vantage point from which to launch some earlier American thinking. He thought, he read, and he discussed his ideas with others. Perhaps it was his father and Chauncey Wright who got him into this habit of discussing. Ten years after graduation we find him without a professorship but with a job of sorts and plenty of energy to organize a small but select discussion club of kindred souls who like himself were interested in the impact of science upon philosophy. This was not an undergraduate club. These were men in their thirties and forties, with minds of their own, who under the faltering leadership of Peirce crossed paths just long enough and frequently enough to enable Peirce to hatch a new philosophic movement.

"It was in the earliest seventies," says Peirce, "that a knot of us young men . . . used to meet, sometimes in my study, sometimes in that of William James. . . . Mr. Justice Holmes . . . will not, I believe, take it ill that we are proud to remember his membership, nor will Joseph Warner, Esq. Nicholas St. John Green was one of the most interested fellows, a skillful lawyer and a learned one, a disciple of Jeremy Bentham. His extraordinary power of disrobing warm and breathing truth of the draperies of long worn formulas, was what attracted attention to him everywhere. In particular, he often urged the importance of applying Bain's definition of belief, as 'that upon which a man is prepared to act.' From this definition, pragmatism is scarce more than a corollary; so that I am disposed to think of him as the grandfather of pragmatism. Chauncey Wright, something of a philosophical celebrity in those days, was never absent from our meetings. I was about to call him our corypheus; but he will better be described as our boxing-master whom we —I particularly—used to face to be severely pummeled. . . . John Fiske and, more rarely, Francis Ellingwood Abbot, were sometimes present. . . . Wright, James, and I were men of science. . . . The type of our thought was decidedly British. I, alone of our number, had come upon the threshing-floor of philosophy through the doorway of Kant, and even my ideas were acquiring the English accent."

Elsewhere Peirce says: "In the sixties I started a little club called the Metaphysical Club. It seldom if ever had more than half a dozen present. Wright was the strongest member and probably I was next. Nicholas St. John Green was a marvelously strong intelligence. Then there were Frank Abbot, William James, and others. It was there that the name and doctrine of pragmatism saw the light."

Peirce is somewhat vague about the exact years when these meetings took place. Feibleman sets the dates as 1872–1874. At any rate Peirce had by this time given a dozen years of study to his own system. The other men there had equally well-developed and pronounced views of their own. The lifework of the remarkable Chauncey Wright was almost over. He died in 1875. When the club faded out it was Peirce who undertook to write up the gist of some of the club discussions in the form of two articles, stillborn but later made famous by James. These articles were *The Fixation of Belief* and *How to Make Our Ideas Clear,* published in the November, 1877, and January, 1878, numbers of the *Popular Science Monthly,* then a somewhat different journal from what it is now. In any exposition of the views of Peirce these two articles take pride of place. Since Peirce went out of his way to tie them up with a "knot" of men with whom he debated these items, it will pay to take a brief look at each of these coshapers of pragmatism.

Peirce singles out Chauncey Wright, an ardent evolutionist, who had gone personally to see Darwin and had got from him a specific assignment. Darwin asked Wright, who had had psychological training, to investigate along evolutionary lines the origin of human self-consciousness. Darwin himself in 1871 had just brought out his *Descent of Man*. Wright, who at the time of the club meetings, was in his early forties, set to work with a will. In the *North American Review* of April, 1873, he published a remarkable article showing how by putting old capacities to new uses man might have arrived at self-consciousness. In speech the tongue and the lips are put to new uses. "Natural selection is not necessarily concerned in the *first* production of any form, structure, power, or habit, but only in perpetuating and improving those which have arisen from any cause whatever." It is not necessary to create a new soul, but only to perfect the mind as an instrument of survival. Wright comes to the strange conclusion that the self is not naturally selfish. He explained how love of self is social in character and leads to a love of mankind. Wright quotes Cicero: "Nature has inclined us to the love of mankind; and this is the foundation of laws."

It is easy to see that Peirce and Wright might have a great deal in common. Wright, like Peirce, stressed the gradual development of human from animal powers, thus obtaining the vista of a very long, slow growth still open at the end. Unlike Peirce, he was antimetaphysical, and believed in the complete ethical neutrality of science. The nature that science investigates is a completely amoral process. Also Wright was an unabashed nominalist, and on this point must have clashed sharply with Peirce.

Nicholas St. John Green, exactly the same age as Wright, died in 1876, one year after Wright. Wright and Green were close friends. So was John Fiske a crony of Green's. Philip P. Wiener tells us that "on Sunday mornings Green—who was not a churchgoer—often went with his son, Frederick, to visit the portly, pipe-smoking, beer drinking historian and cosmic evolutionist in his home on Berkeley Street." Green and Fiske must have had some stimulating talks together. Green, a successful lawyer who also did some teaching of law, had a reputation of not letting anyone do his thinking for him. He preferred criminal and personal injury cases, which he found of human interest. Doubtless he looked upon criminals as curious people with curious beliefs that they were willing to act upon. In his teaching of law Green had something to do with instituting the case method of study. Studying cases instead of treatises brought him into line with that pragmatic interpretation of jurisprudence to which Justice Holmes, also a member of the club, made even greater contributions.

Along with the study of cases Green advocated the historical approach. Perhaps he got this from Fiske. A lot of historical research is needed to understand law in the modern manner. Along with Peirce, Green opposed the idea of absolute standards and infallibility—how could it be otherwise when law is drawn from a tangled mass of court decisions accumulated in the course of time? There is no eternal law of nature, divorced from the struggles of man and written in the stars. Here he is echoing his master Jeremy Bentham, antimetaphysical advocate of utilitarianism, seeking "the greatest good for the greatest number." Green was given to pithy statements, such as: "The law of the status of women is the last vestige of slavery."

There were two other lawyers in the club, Joseph B. Warner and Justice Holmes. Joseph B. Warner, according to Philip P. Wiener, would not have figured at all in the history of American philosophic thought if Peirce had not mentioned him as a member of the Metaphysical Club. He got his A.B. from Harvard in 1869 and an A.M. in 1872. He was a student in Chauncey Wright's small course of university lectures in psychology in 1870, in which Wright used Bain as a text. Bain's book, *The Emotions and the Will* (3rd edition, 1873), contains the famous definition of belief as "that upon which a man is prepared to act," referred to above. Warner was interested in the higher education for women, and active in founding Simmons and Radcliffe colleges. He helped Holmes edit *Kent's Commentaries on American Law* in 1873. Warner was engaged by Royce to protect Royce's interests in the litigation with Abbot. Here he was on the wrong side of the fence, which fits in with his view of the law as having little to do with the fine points of ready-made ethics. According to Warner, the lawyer cannot always follow his own conscience. He is a hired defender who on different days finds himself on opposite sides. "The law, so far as it goes, is his conscience here. In invoking that he is

not immoral, he is non-moral—administering a system artificial
and positive, for which he is not responsible. . . . Justice does
not descend, in answer to our prayers, pure and undefiled from
heaven. It is struck out, with pain and sweat and conflict, in
the private disputes of men. Our system is not devised primarily
to discover truth, nor is a lawyer chiefly a searcher after truth."
Warner regarded court trials as a "visible struggle, old as the
world, of all the passions of anger, hate, greed, and avarice, less
wild than of old, but still full of their inherited spirit, and now
forced into an arena which, excepting war itself, is left as
the only battlefield for these irrepressible fighting instincts of the
race." The ruthlessness of some lawyers he attributed to "traits
which yet survive in the human animal." It is plain that the
impact of evolution was causing a great ferment among lawyers.

The third lawyer member, not very active in the club
perhaps but certainly a voice to be heard, was Oliver Wendell
Holmes, born 1841, later associate justice of the Supreme Court,
and therefore another of the thirty-year-olds who sometimes sat in
on this historic club. James himself was a year younger, and pretty
well a junior in the club. Holmes, outspoken, bluff and hearty,
was later inclined to pooh-pooh all of James's pragmatism as
wishful thinking. Chauncey Wright was his man. "Chauncey
Wright, a nearly forgotten philosopher of real merit, taught me
when young that I must not say *necessary* about the universe,
that we don't know whether anything is necessary or not. I believe that we can *bet* on the behavior of the universe in its
contact with us, and so describe myself as a *bet*-abilitarian."
Both Holmes and Green advocated a secular development of
law. For Holmes "the life of the law is not logic but experience."
Study the cases. He had what has been called a predictive
theory of law which studies "what the courts will do in fact."
Our Constitution is "an experiment as all life is an experiment.
The felt necessities of the time, the prevalent moral and political
theories, intuitions of public policy, avowed or unconscious,
even the prejudices which judges share with their fellowmen,
have had a good deal more to do than the syllogism in determining the rules by which men should be governed." Justice Holmes,
along with Chauncey Wright, had the evolutionary outlook in

his bones— ". . . the official theory is that each new decision follows syllogistically from existing precedents. But just as the clavicle in the cat only tells us of the existence of some earlier creature to which a collarbone was useful, precedents survive in the law long after the use they once served is at an end and the reason for them has been forgotten."

These were not just boys that Peirce was playing around with in his club. They were men who either had already developed or were about to develop strong views of their own. These ideas of theirs, as is true also of Peirce's ideas, all center around the new impact of science brought home by the epoch-making achievements of Darwin. John Fiske's entire work centers around evolution. Like Peirce, he had a turn for the cosmic aspect of things. Fiske started out with an exaggerated respect for Herbert Spencer and his own work reads like Herbert Spencer with a dose of theism added. Fiske's *Outlines of Cosmic Philosophy Based on the Doctrine of Evolution* was published in 1874. He was then thirty-two years old. Certainly as a member of the Metaphysical Club John Fiske must have been able to speak eloquently on his own point of view. He was a voluminous writer and talker, interested in history, philosophy, God and the destiny of man. One of the things he especially emphasized was "the lengthening of infancy which ages ago gradually converted our forefathers from brute creatures into human creatures. It is a babyhood that has made man what he is. . . . There is a period after birth when . . . character can be modified. . . . A door is opened through which the capacity for progress can enter."

When Francis Ellingwood Abbot took his Ph.D. at Harvard he was already forty-four years old. At the time of the Metaphysical Club he was nine or ten years younger, but as early as 1868 he had resigned from his Unitarian pulpit. His book *Scientific Theism* appeared in 1885. It proclaimed "the objectivity of relations, as opposed to the principle of the subjectivity of relations, which is the essence of the nominalistic doctrine of universals inculcated by modern philosophy." "Experience," said Abbot, "is the beginning and the end of the scientific method. . . . The scientific method . . . is a living organic process, the

true and only organon for the discovery of truth. . . . The
Scotch school held, not only that the things which we perceive
exist, but also that they exist as we perceive them; whereas the
philosophy of science will hold that the crudities of sense-percep-
tion . . . are to be corrected by scientific discovery. . . . Now
the root of modern idealism . . . is . . . the theory that nothing
can be known except 'phenomena,' and that all phenomena
depend for their existence on individual consciousness alone.
It is this theory of phenomenism, the life-principle of modern
philosophy, which most formidably opposes the theory of . . .
scientific realism or scientific ontology." These words by Abbot
could have been spoken, and certainly were reiterated and
stressed over and over again, by Peirce. No wonder that in
Abbot's troubles with Royce Peirce stood by Abbot. It is little
comfort to know that later Peirce received an apology from
Royce for the way he had treated Abbot.

Last, but no midget in the Metaphysical Club, was William
James, who with Wright and Peirce was a "laboratory" man.
The three laboratory men, the three lawyers, along with Fiske
the formidable evolutionist, banded together around a cloud
of ideas which Peirce condensed into the doctrine of pragmatism.
The impression left on James by Peirce was a lasting one, and
although Peirce wrote the first articles on pragmatism and put
them into print, it was James who twenty years later put both
Peirce and the articles back into circulation by a startlingly original version of pragmatism, the gist of which has already been
given, and the exact relation of which to the pragmatism of
Peirce has been much discussed. Meanwhile do not expect
from Peirce any wishy-washy amalgam of what these seven
men at the club must at one time or another, jointly or separately,
had been talking about. Nothing like that. These men were spar-
ring partners. What Peirce gives us in his articles is an exhibition
of his own thought—pure and unadulterated Peirce. In these
articles he takes or leaves what he likes, and in his own free and
easy manner lays down exactly what he himself thinks.

The titles of the two articles—there were others but the first
two are the most important—state very plainly what the articles
contain and what the discussions at the club were chiefly about:

The Fixation of Belief and *How to Make Our Ideas Clear*. Peirce is primarily interested in how people can make their ideas clear and how people do and can fix their beliefs, that is, clarify these beliefs and nail them down. There are good reasons for starting with the second of the articles, which deals with how to make your ideas clear. This problem was not original with Peirce. It was asked by Descartes, and again a little later by Leibnitz. Each had an answer, and now Peirce has a third answer. Peirce reviews the answers given by Descartes and Leibnitz, which supply what one might call the European approach, and then supplies an American approach and shows just how this differs from the European.

Descartes represents a clean break from medievalism. Like many truly great philosophers Descartes is easy to read. Anyone who has read him will never forget the intimate, almost biographical way in which he explains that in the education of his day everything seemed unclear to him until he came to mathematics. He never got over wondering at the beauty and clarity of mathematics, and he asked himself why the rest of our knowledge could not be equally clear. On this he pondered till he found what he considered a solution, following his famous doubting experiment. Doubt anything, doubt that the heavens exist, that the soul is immortal, doubt all you can, but you cannot doubt that you are thinking up new doubts. You are thinking, therefore you exist. *Cogito ergo sum!*

The impulse back of this doubting spree is a simple one: clear out all obscure rubbish until you are left with a single indubitable idea which is CLEAR. Then start from that. Descartes's "I think, therefore I am," was a first clear thought outside the sphere of mathematics. This was exactly what he was looking for. He was so glad to find this one new cornerstone of clear thinking that from it he quickly, all too quickly, built up again a whole edifice of what he deemed were equally clear thoughts, all in the highly controversial, nonmathematical field. Very early in this facile game of reconstruction Descartes, who after all was a firm and rather timid Catholic believer, established, on what he considered new lines, that God existed and that the whole world of matter and mind existed, much along the lines of what was then considered orthodox and could now be comfortably believed in. His *Discourse on Method* was published in 1637, and was in every respect in its day and age a remarkably forward-looking work. The approach was new, his analysis was a fresh one, and if his final results were not startling this was all the more reassuring to readers who shared his orthodox opinions. However, his quick return to firm ground caused some of the sharp thinkers who succeeded Descartes to look upon his method with suspicion.

It would be interesting to go down the line and say much more about Descartes and the thinkers who succeeded him, but beyond a brief mention of Leibnitz, who preferred to stress another way of making your ideas clear, right here the interest is in what Peirce had to say about the Cartesian method of making ideas clear. It will also be left to Peirce to expound the modification made by Leibnitz. Both Peirce and Whitehead began their views by attacking Descartes. Peirce attacked the Cartesian doubt, and Whitehead the Cartesian bifurcation of the world into mind and matter. With the fundamental point of divergence from Descartes in mind, the philosophies of Peirce and Whitehead stand out just as clear-limbed as the Cartesian structure.

The first thing Peirce condemned was artificial doubt. You cannot just doubt at will any more than you can surprise yourself at will. Some beliefs are so essential a part of our biological environment that from ingrained habit we find it impossible to doubt them. An honest search reveals not one but many indubitables. Not merely that the self exists, but that others exist, that animals exist, live, eat, run, and breathe as we do we cannot really bring ourselves to doubt. The acid test is that every moment of our lives we are willing to act on these beliefs. Santayana's doubt, although he really thought he carried it further than Descartes did, would by Peirce if he had mentioned it be condemned on the same grounds. Santayana, unlike Descartes, soon landed himself exactly where Peirce stood, namely, in the middle of things, in the common sense situation. On this Santayana and Peirce could not be in more complete agreement.

Peirce says we should begin not with universal doubt but

with the world of common sense, and then look around for the best way of refining this crude knowledge of common sense. Peirce did agree that "a few clear ideas are worth more than many confused ones," and that the "very first lesson that we have a right to demand that logic shall teach us is how to make our ideas clear." But Peirce has a sharper and a more critical view of what is involved in a "clear" idea. "When Descartes set about the reconstruction of philosophy, his first step was to (theoretically) permit skepticism and to discard the practice of the schoolmen of looking to authority as the ultimate source of truth. That done, he sought a more natural fountain of true principle, and thought he found it in the human mind. . . . Self-consciousness was to furnish us with our fundamental truths. . . . But since, evidently, not all ideas are true, he was led to note, as the first condition of infallibility, that they must be clear. The distinction between an idea *seeming* clear and really being so, never occurred to him. Trusting to introspection, as he did, even for a knowledge of external things, why should he question its testimony in respect to the contents of our own minds? . . . He was further led to say that clearness of ideas is not sufficient, but that they need also to be distinct, i.e. to have nothing unclear about them. What he probably meant by this (for he did not explain himself with precision) was, that they must sustain the test of dialectical examination; that they must not only seem clear at the outset, but that discussion must never be able to bring to light points of obscurity connected with them."

If you know a man well enough not to mistake him for another, that is one stage of being clear about that man. If you know an idea well enough not to mistake it for another, you may be said, in a sense, to have a clear idea. It would be better, thinks Peirce, to say that you were then familiar with that idea. Ordinary men are familiar with many ideas that in themselves are not clear at all. There are ideas so familiar that men hug them to their bosoms, they hang on to them for dear life, when all the time the ideas may be not only unclear but exceedingly obscure. So we need something more than familiarity. The quality these obscure ideas need to be supplemented by is distinctness. "A distinct idea is defined as one which contains nothing which is not clear."

The distinctions made by Descartes were according to Peirce, "somewhat developed by Leibnitz. This great and singular genius was as remarkable for what he failed to see as for what he saw. That a piece of mechanism could not do work perpetually without being fed power in some form, was a thing perfectly apparent to him; yet he did not understand that the machinery of the mind can only transform knowledge, but never originate it, unless it be fed with facts of observation. . . . Abstract definitions played a great part of his philosophy. It was quite natural, therefore, that on observing that the method of Descartes labored under the difficulty that we may seem to ourselves to have clear apprehensions of ideas which in truth are very hazy, no better remedy occurred to him than to require an abstract definition of every important term. Accordingly, in adopting the distinction of *clear* and *distinct* notions, he described the latter quality as the clear apprehension of everything contained in the definition; and the books have ever since copied his words. . . . That much admired 'ornament of logic'—the doctrine of clearness and distinctness—may be pretty enough, but it is high time to relegate to our cabinet of curiosities the antique *bijou*, and to wear about us something better adapted to modern uses."

Thus Peirce, so far as ways of making our ideas clear is concerned, condemns both Descartes and any improvements which Leibnitz is supposed to have made on Descartes. Peirce considers that (1) familiarity and (2) definitions are not good enough methods to make our ideas clear. We need to do something entirely different: we must connect ideas up with action. That is the new and modern point of view. In this way Peirce gives the modern supplement to Descartes and Leibnitz. "The whole function of thought is to produce habits of action." To develop the meaning of an idea "we have, therefore, simply to determine what habits it produces, for what a thing means is simply what habits it involves. . . . Thus we come down to what is tangible and practical, as the root of every real distinction of thought, no matter how subtle it may be; and there is no distinction of meaning so fine as to consist in anything but a possible difference of practice."

"It appears, then, that the rule for attaining the third grade of clearness beyond familiarity and definition is to: Consider what effects, which might conceivably have practical bearings, we conceive the object of our conception to have. Then, our conception of these effects is the whole of our conception of the object." This is Peirce's famous pragmatic maxim. Here is another version which he gave of this same maxim: "In order to ascertain the meaning of an intellectual conception one should consider what practical consequences might conceivably result by necessity from the truth of that conception; and the sum of these consequences will constitute the entire meaning of the conception."

"Let us illustrate this rule by some examples," says Peirce, "and, to begin with the simplest one possible, let us ask what we mean by calling a thing *hard*. Evidently that it will not be scratched by many other substances. The whole conception of this quality, as of every other, lies in its conceived effects. . . . Let us next seek a clear idea of Weight. This is another very easy case. To say that a body is heavy means simply that, in the absence of opposing force, it will fall. This . . . is evidently the whole conception of weight. It is a fair question whether some particular facts may not *account* for gravity; but what we mean by the force itself is completely involved in its effects." Next he takes up force and finds that force is what accounts for changes in motion. "Whether we ought to say that a force *is* an acceleration or that it *causes* an acceleration, is a mere question of propriety of language, which has no more to do with our real meaning than the difference between the French idiom *il fait froid* and its English equivalent *it is cold*. Yet it is surprising to see how this simple affair has muddled men's minds. In how many profound treatises is not force spoken of as a 'mysterious entity,' which seems to be only a way of confessing that the author despairs of ever getting a clear notion of what the word means!"

Thus looking to what actions are involved in ideas helps to make ideas clear. It also clears away a lot of rubbish. "Pragmatism is not," says Peirce, "a *Weltanschauung* but is a method of reflection having for its purpose to render ideas clear. . . . It ought in the first place to give us an expeditious riddance of ideas essentially unclear. In the second place, it ought to lend support, and help render distinct, ideas essentially clear, but more or less difficult of apprehension." Peirce also points out that it "shows that supposed problems are not real problems."

Doubt is not something conjured up for amusement by an arm-chair philosopher, and then disposed of once and for all by some legerdemain leading straight back to what we believed before. Doubt is something that assails ordinary men many times a day in connection with perfectly ordinary problems. Will John be home in time for dinner? is a real doubt of sorts, and one that requires certain decisions followed by appropriate action. There are also doubts, major ones, that science deals with in ways and by tests that are much more elaborate. But long before science came upon the scene men had ways of dispelling doubt, since life goes on and action must proceed. Peirce enumerates four. This brings us to Peirce's other paper: *The Fixation of Belief.*

Returning again to his starting point, Peirce gives his own analysis of doubt: "Doubt is an uneasy and dissatisfied state from which we struggle to free ourselves and pass into the stage of belief; while the latter is a calm and satisfactory state which we do not wish to avoid, or to change to a belief in anything else. On the contrary, we cling tenaciously, not merely to believing, but to believing just what we do believe. . . . Belief does not make us act at once, but it puts us into such a condition that we shall behave in a certain way, when the occasion arises. Doubt . . . stimulates us to inquiry until it [doubt] is destroyed. . . . The irritation of doubt causes a struggle to attain a state of belief. I shall term this struggle *Inquiry.*" Dewey takes over this term from Peirce. Inquiry is the method by which we try to get rid of doubt. It is the only sure way. Peirce makes a short survey of the way most people go about banishing doubts and nailing down their own beliefs. This leads to the four methods of belief fixation.

1. The Method of Tenacity

One way of retaining the beliefs you were born with, or any other favorite set, is to go on reiterating them. Keep on repeating these beliefs to yourself; become familiar with them; make them your own. In politics you pick out your party, then read every morning the paper that favors your party, attend rallies, and end up a good party man. You are ready to fight for your candidates at the drop of a hat. You are an active defender of your beliefs, and you keep these beliefs alive by reading, hearing, and talking about them each day. You are ready to support action based on those beliefs and do not inquire too closely into how these beliefs were acquired. They suit you and you are ready to back them up. You cling to them with tenacity. Very often beliefs are acquired from others who transmit them by this same method of reiteration. Start repeating to a child over and over again certain beliefs, and the child will, so to speak, grow into them.

Peirce says: "I admire the method of tenacity for its strength, simplicity, and directness. . . . But this method . . . will be unable to hold its ground in practice. The social impulse is against it. The man who adopts it will find that other men think differently from him, and it will be apt to occur to him, in some saner moment, that their opinions are quite as good as his own, and this will shake his confidence in his belief. . . . Unless we make ourselves hermits, we shall necessarily influence each other's opinions; so that the problem becomes how to fix belief, not in the individual merely, but in the community." This leads to the second method of fixing belief.

2. The Method of Authority

"Let the will of the State act, then, instead of that of the individual. Let an institution be created which shall have for its object to keep correct doctrines before the attention of the people, to reiterate them perpetually, and to teach them to the young; having at the same time power to prevent contrary doctrines from being taught, advocated, or expressed. Let all possible causes of a change of mind be removed from men's apprehensions. Let them be kept ignorant, lest they should learn of some reason to think otherwise than they do. Let their parents be enlisted, so that they may regard private and unusual opinions with hatred and horror. Then, let all men who reject the established belief be terrified into silence."

This was written in 1878, but it could stand as a prescription for a totalitarian state. Peirce has much more to say on this method of authority which has "immeasurable mental and moral superiority to the method of tenacity. Its success is proportionately greater; and, in fact, it has over and over again worked the most majestic results. The mere structure of stone which it has caused to be put together—in Siam, for example, in Egypt, and in Europe—have many of them a sublimity hardly more than rivaled by the greatest works in Nature." These organized faiths, whether religious or political, appeal to men of whom it is the highest impulse "to be intellectual slaves." "But," Peirce continues, "no institution can undertake to regulate opinions upon every subject. Only the most important ones can be attended to, and on the rest men's minds must be left to the action of natural causes. This imperfection will be no source of weakness so long as men are in such a state of culture that one opinion does not influence another —that is, so long as they cannot put two and two together. But in most priest-ridden states some individuals will be found who are raised above that condition. These men possess a wider sort of social feeling; they see that men in other countries and in other ages have held to very different doctrines." Doubts begin to spread. "The willful adherence to a belief, and the arbitrary forcing of it upon others, must, therefore, both be given up." Thus we are led to a third method of fixing belief.

3. The Method of Reason

This is based on principles agreeable to reason. Sometimes these are called "first" principles. Peirce also calls it the *a priori* method; some have called it the method of taste. This method lacks the arbitrariness of the second method; at least, it tries to make an appeal to reasonableness. Think up any fairly complete and consistent system of thought and to many it will appear to be true just because it is reasonable and uncontradictory. "Systems of this sort have not usually rested upon any observed facts, at least not in any great degree. They have been chiefly adopted because their fundamental propositions seemed 'agreeable to reason.' " Hence, as Peirce observes, agreeable to reason "does not mean that which agrees with experience, but that which we find ourselves inclined to believe."

"Plato, for example, finds it agreeable to reason that the distances of the celestial spheres from one another should be proportional to the different lengths of strings which produce harmonious chords. Many philosophers have been led to their main conclusions by considerations like this. . . . This method is far more intellectual and respectable from the point of view of reason than either of the others which we have noticed. Indeed, as long as no better method can be applied, it ought to be followed, since it is then the expression of instinct which must be the ultimate cause of belief in all cases. But its failure has been the most manifest. It makes of inquiry something similar to the development of taste; but taste, unfortunately, is always more or less a matter of fashion, and accordingly metaphysicians have never come to any fixed agreement. . . . And so from this . . . we are driven . . . " to a fourth and final method.

4. The Method of Science

We all need beliefs of some sort. You cannot act without them. Even animals have a set of beliefs. In fact, Peirce was all for starting out, as Santayana did, with this animal set of beliefs, but he soon saw that these beliefs lead us into logic. Man invents logic, and slowly perfects this invention, until in recent times it has become a method of dealing satisfactorily with new facts along the lines of science. Peirce shows how the scientific method expands the function of logic. To the well-known deduction and induction methods of logic Peirce adds a third procedure, the method of hypothesis, the only method of dealing with new facts. You frame an hypothesis which seems to cover the facts, and then you test it, to see whether it actually stands up or not. Do the facts bear it out? If not, discard the hypothesis. Publish your methods of testing so that others too can try it out. In this way men can gradually build up a widening array of tested hypotheses, for anyone to try out, so that he who runs may read. What these hypotheses do is to uncover more and more of the truth. And the truth shall make you free, not merely to speak out but also to join the world-wide body of fellow workers who more and more agree on more and more things. This growing consortium of open-minded experimenters is what Peirce keeps his eye on. They are the hope of the world.

For all his apparent sympathy with the three spurious methods of belief fixation—and Peirce has some good things to say about each one of them—the point should not be lost that Peirce unequivocally condemns them all in favor of the fourth and scientific method of belief fixation. On this he expends his full talents. The two articles in *Popular Science Monthly* were followed by a lifetime of effort in expounding the method of science.

4. The Unlimited Community

ONE AIM OF science is to improve the conditions under which we live. Electric lights, cars, better roads, and the thousand and one other things science brings may not be all that is needed for better living, but they help. The American philosophy of meliorism, or the belief that the world can be made a better place to live in, takes many forms, but from its start in Franklin it has not neglected practical items. Peirce, James, and Dewey all give science a central place in their system, but in the way that each of them handles this big subject these men correct and supplement each other. American philosophy thus gets to be not the work of any single man but a cooperative effort all the time undergoing improvements.

Both Peirce and James agreed that we live in a tough world of changing beliefs requiring new adjustments in human thinking. Both tied up thought with action. What this means is that both became more and more alive to the dynamic side of the universe stressed in evolution and in the new studies of motion that had been going on ever since the days of Newton. It is the change from a static to a dynamic world that preoccupied both of these men. Both hit upon the "objectivity of relations" as a dogma to put into the spotlight. This somewhat technical expression is merely another way of stressing movement, motion, and activity. In a static world you can study the sun and the earth as if they were standing still. In the modern world you can no longer do so. The relations between them, that is, their relative motions and positions with regard to each other, are just as objective, just as real, and just as important to study as the objects themselves. James gave this new interest in the relations of things to each other some of his best rhetoric; Peirce evolved a new logic of relations.

In daily life it is well known that everything around us lives and moves. But the eye of the philosopher, ever since Plato, has been on the faraway things that seem fixed. Now both James and Peirce bring philosophy nearer home by starting out with common sense. In all this there is the closest agreement between these two men, but now comes a divergence. In the 1898 California address in which James revived pragmatism he restates the Peirce maxim as follows: "The effective meaning of any philosophic proposition can always be brought down to some particular proposition, in our future practical experience, whether active or passive; the point lying rather in the fact that the experience must be particular, than in the fact that it must be active." Twice James uses the word "particular." James makes pragmatism of direct and personal concern to the particulor person. Peirce, on the other hand, always stressed the general. Peirce wrote James a letter asking: "What is utility, if it is confined to a single person? Truth is public." For Peirce "the opinion which is fated to be ultimately agreed to by all who investigate, is what we mean by truth."

For Peirce the quest for truth is a crusade for all mankind, leading theoretically to a community of true believers. This vision James, with his eye on his own troubles in coordinating his personal life, did not share. It might have been better all around if Peirce too had paid more attention to straightening out his personal difficulties by adjusting himself, as James did, to the practicalities of life, but, strange to say, he lost his living but saved his philosophy, while James made a brilliant success of his life but actually weakened his pragmatism by making it too personal.

In reading what F. C. S. Schiller, the brilliant English pragmatist, had to say in his *Studies in Humanism,* Peirce remarks: "Mr. Ferdinand C. S. Schiller informs us that he and James have made up their minds that the true is simply the satisfactory." This was altogether too much for Peirce to swallow, and it is not entirely clear that James himself went as far as Schiller did. Certainly Peirce never held anything resembling such a view. John Dewey too was distressed at the growing divergence between the two chief proponents of pragmatism and, while siding with Peirce, shoves the shoulder of a mediating brother between the two. It is all set forth in his lucid article printed at the tail end of *Chance, Love, and Logic.* Dewey makes out that for Peirce "pragmatism identifies meaning with formation of a habit, or way of having the greatest generality possible, or the widest range of application to particulars." This is the viewpoint of science, which tries to account for countless particulars through more and more general laws. Moreover, to Peirce "not only are generals real, but they are physically efficient."

Logic was for Peirce something based on the facts outside. It studied the way these facts are related, and the way these relations can be expressed in general laws. This is the only way of getting some agreement between the beliefs of mankind. The method of science with its quest for proved and established laws is quite different from any system of promoting individual beliefs through reiteration. In fact James at times comes perilously near to adopting the arbitrary method of tenacity. In questions not yet decided by evidence, why not believe what you want to believe? This, according to both Peirce and Dewey, is a most dangerous procedure. It is much better to admit that we do not know. In his *Will to Believe* James goes beyond science, and if you study just the two preliminary articles of Peirce which James drew upon, there is some excuse for confusion. It is easy to see how James might get some wrong ideas. Here are some of the things Peirce says:

"With the doubt, therefore, the struggle begins, and with the cessation of doubt it ends. Hence, the sole object of inquiry is the settlement of opinion. We may fancy that this is not enough for us, and that we seek, not merely an opinion, but a true opinion. Put this fancy to the test, and it proves groundless; for as soon as a firm belief is reached we are entirely satisfied, whether the belief be true or false. . . . The most that can be maintained is that we seek for a belief that we shall *think* to be true. But we think each one of our beliefs to be true, and, indeed, it is a mere tautology to say so. . . . If the settlement of opinion is the sole object of inquiry, and if belief is of the nature of a habit, why should we not attain the desired end, by taking as answer to a question any we may fancy, and constantly reiterating it to ourselves . . ." and Peirce launches into this as the first of four ways in which men actually do fix their beliefs. Certainly in his paper on *The Fixation of Belief* Peirce does show how easy it is for men by various methods to learn to believe a lot of things that are not true.

What seems to make matters worse is that even beliefs obtained by the fourth method are not absolutely true in the sense that they are not subject to correction. Newton's law of gravitation was subject to correction when three hundred years later men failed to establish that the ether exists. Much of our knowledge is the absolutely best that we can get, but none of it is forever uncorrectable. Peirce uses the word "incorrigible." The position is very similar to that obtained by physicists when they say that all motion is relative. This rules out absolute motion. It does not rule out motion. Similarly the absence of absolute finality does not rule out the kind of truth that fully warrants our belief.

It is easy to see how James defending relative truth against the absolutists of his day could get himself into difficulty. James, an excellent psychologist, was after all neither a mathematician nor a logician. He was easily maneuvered into saying that to all intents and purposes what you believe is true, and he had a hard time living down this superficial view of pragmatism, not held by either Peirce or Dewey. What was needed here was not a facile defense, not word-fencing at all, but an overhauling of the whole system of Aristotelian logic. Both Peirce and Dewey saw this, and both tried to provide just such a logic. But it was Peirce, and not James, who was especially equipped to break new ground in logic.

Peirce was appalled when, twenty years after his original articles had been written, he saw what James was making out of his pragmatism. "After waiting in vain, for a good many years, some particularly opportune conjecture of circumstances . . . the writer . . . feels that it is time to kiss his child good-by and relinquish it to a higher destiny . . . he begs to announce the birth of the word 'pragmaticism' which is ugly enough to be safe from kidnappers." In this semihumorous way Peirce shows his resentment at what others have done with his pragmatism. Specifically he mentions James, who used it to stand for his "radical empiricism," and Schiller, who used it for his "anthropomorphism."

So he redubs his pragmatism pragmaticism but the substance of it remains unchanged.

"The present writer having had the pragmatist theory under consideration for many years longer than most of its adherents, would naturally have given more attention to the proof of it." And to make his position more clear Peirce goes back to the notion that no one can doubt at will. You can suppose that a thing is not true. For example, after your father is dead, you can for the sake of argument suppose that he is still alive, but that is quite different from doubting that he is not dead. "Now that which you do not at all doubt, you must and do regard as infallible, absolute truth. . . . If your terms 'truth' and 'falsity' are taken in such senses as to be definable in terms of doubt and belief . . . well and good: in that case, you are only talking about doubt and belief. . . . Your problems would be greatly simplified, if, instead of saying that you want to know the 'Truth,' you were simply to say that you want to attain a state of belief unassailable by doubt. . . . Belief is not a momentary mode of consciousness; it is a habit of mind essentially enduring for some time . . . and like other habits, it is (until it meets with some surprise that begins its dissolution) perfectly self-satisfied."

What Peirce is here saying is that "truth" is a big word, and what it stands for depends upon the background you give it in your whole philosophy. For this reason Santayana found it necessary to work out an entire system with different realms of being, in which essences are eternally true but existences are not. For this reason Dewey preferred to avoid the word "truth" altogether and to speak instead of warrantable assertions. For this reason Peirce is here trying to pin his reader down to a limited universe of discourse in which truth is for the time being defined in terms of belief and doubt. But this is not the whole story.

Both men, James and Peirce—in fact all the men thus far considered—are committed to the realist position. This means that they believe in a world independent of human thought. So does science maintain this, as Peirce, following Abbot, points out. And when James maneuvered himself into a position where he seemed to give up this realist position he was getting into a fix whereby with Hegel, whom he loathed, he was led to say that man makes his own truth. No wonder Peirce shook his head over the rash enthusiasms of this espouser of his early, perfectly sound, but not yet fully developed views. It is not necessary to call Peirce's views pragmaticism and James's pragmatism; they are the same. Both are of the melioristic persuasion. For James to put the stress on the particular and Peirce on the general leads to a clarification. It is entirely possible that this induced Peirce to work all the harder on his logic with its emphasis on a new kind of universal.

James, Dewey, Santayana, Peirce all belong to the same family. It is somewhat as if in discussing transportation one were to take up in succession trains, trucks, airplanes, and vehicles in general. There are radical differences in emphasis and detail, but the family resemblance never falters. James is a powerful individualist, but not a lonely one. Peirce is a lonely man, but not an individualist in the sense that he was always fighting for his own advancement. Peirce and James were the most intimate of personal friends. They were college friends, club friends, and in later life Peirce half in playfulness made his middle initial stand for Santiago or St. James, the friend in need who had always helped him. No matter how much Peirce may have differed with James on certain minor points, it was after all Peirce's brain child that James was developing, and James gave a perfectly legitimate psychological interpretation of the Peircian point of view. James and Peirce both started from the same baseline of a world bursting with creativity. James wished to give himself and others every scope for self-deployment. He did a fine thing in stressing that in this broad land there is room for diversity. He gloried in the pluralistic aspect of his thought-world. Peirce, starting at the same place, looked at the creativity from a slightly different angle. He asked: To what end? His answer was to the end of channeling this diversity into lanes of achievement, which can be done by subsuming the diversities under simple laws which enable us to make predictions. We need control over nature as well as control over ourselves. Always Peirce was thinking of the way the human mind classifies, seeks out uniformities, and after finding a law, uses this law or equation to help mankind climb to higher levels of achievement. Always he thought in terms of mankind rather than in terms of the greatly varying individuals composing mankind.

It is easy to see how, if we had had our minds on how to avoid those world wars that came right after James and Peirce died, we might not get very far by stressing the fierce uniqueness of the individuals that James wanted to safeguard, and how Peirce's idea of all working together on one grand task of finding the truth might from this point of view be more helpful. Both ideas can, of course, very easily be run into the ground. To sacrifice individuality to uniformity is just as bad as giving up all idea of working together because each of us has to be true to himself. On the other hand, both ideas can work together beautifully. The world needs the creativity of its great minds. These great minds can in turn work together for humanity. To say that Peirce stressed the general and James the particular is to say no more than that each supplements the other.

Both James and Peirce come down hard on the mistake of stressing things to the exclusion of the relations between these things. On this point they insist with a sort of fierceness. James almost outdoes Peirce in saying that on this point we must supplement the "atomistic" British empiricists who end up with unconnected sensations pouring into the brain. The relations pour in too, says James. Betweenness, togetherness, upside-downness the world is full of—relations are jumbled together with objects. To all this Peirce could say Amen and more. Peirce invents a way of handling these relations. He made more of them than even James did. He carries this stress on relations farther than James did. One might say that James used the bonds between objects as a means of helping him to retain these precious individual sensations and to give them more reality by showing how in the world outside us these individual sensations are sustained by objective relations. Peirce, on the other hand, studies the resulting network of objects and relation in a genetic way and notes a trend: laws supervene on unrelated particulars, and one of the delights of the human mind is to trace just such laws, and possibly help them along.

Again both men outdo each other in insisting on the importance of habits. James veers off in the direction of showing what habits can do in a psychological way toward integrating the life of an individual. This is a perfectly legitimate way of developing the theme of the importance of habit. On the other hand, Peirce notes that habits operate everywhere in nature. James does not deny this. James too uses the illustration of a piece of paper that once folded retains its crease. But Peirce begins an almost metaphysical study of the entire universe to show how truly fundamental a thing habit-taking can become. In it he finds the possible origin of all law. The world gets habits, and so do we. Peirce is paving the way for an organic view of nature of the sort that Whitehead establishes. Peirce claims that the whole trend of evolution is in the direction of taking on more and more uniformities. Always, since hydrogen and oxygen found each other, the world is seeking and finding new combinations that work and that can lead to other combinations. The vision of a habit-taking universe is what fascinated Peirce, and he stressed this sweep toward generality as a triumph of reason.

5. The New Logic

IN HIS *Preface to Logic* (1944) Morris R. Cohen notes: "In the history of ideas the past century is one marked by an extraordinary development of logic. A discipline which had remained for more than 20 centuries in approximately the state to which the mind of Aristotle reduced it, suddenly entered upon a period of rapid growth and systematic development. While the essential elements of the Aristotelian logic have not been overthrown or shaken, the labors of Boole, Peirce, Shroeder, Frege, Russell, Whitehead, and a host of fellow workers have produced a calculus of classes and calculus of propositions in which the Aristotelian theory of the syllogism is seen to occupy only a tiny corner." The new thrust of logic is also discussed by Bertrand Russell:

"Throughout the Middle Ages, almost all the best intellects devoted themselves to formal logic, whereas in the nineteenth century only an infinitesimal proportion of the world's thought went into this subject. Nevertheless, in each decade since 1850 more has been done to advance this subject than in the whole period from Aristotle to Leibnitz. People have discovered how to make reasoning symbolic, as it is in Algebra, so that deductions are effected by mathematical rules. They have discovered many rules besides the syllogism, and a new branch of logic, called the Logic of Relativity (this subject is due in the main to Mr. C. S. Peirce), has been invented to deal with topics that wholly surpassed the powers of the old logic, though they form the chief contents of mathematics." In the vast and feverish new activity on logic Peirce gets credit for working out the Logic of Relations. Although Peirce is sometimes called the Father of Symbolic Logic, this is an exaggeration. Peirce did no more than play an important pioneer role in the development of

symbolic logic, but he was one of the very first to see the far-
reaching philosophic import of this new growth in logic, which,
by the way, is very closely connected with the new growth
in mathematics. To quote Russell on this particular point:

"Many of the topics which used to be placed among the
great mysteries—for example, the natures of infinity, of continuity, of space, time and motion—are now no longer in any
degree open to doubt or discussion. Those who wish to know
the nature of these things need only read the works of such
men as Peano or Georg Cantor; they will there find exact and
indubitable expositions of all these quondam mysteries."

The first point, then, to be made on the new logic is that its
affinity with mathematics is very close. Because of his training
in mathematics Peirce was able to see this clearly. Some, perhaps
quite rightly, say that the whole of mathematics has now become
a branch of logic. Peirce himself did not go that far, but he did
stress the point that logic desperately needed widening out
to include many other relations besides that of inclusion and
exclusion to which Aristotle in his syllogisms had kept it tied
down. Things are related in many ways and when so related
are said to be functions of each other. Functional relations of
the most varied kinds can be expressed in mathematics and in
logic.

It is impossible in any short space to go into technical details
on the intricacies of mathematical logic, but the general reader
can quickly grasp the new freedom and the expanded scope of
logic if he recalls how readily the scientist of today puts all his
new discoveries in the form of a mathematical equation. These
equations, like the Old Man of the Sea, can assume any form
demanded by the occasion. From the infinite forms supplied by
mathematics which has now become a kind of logic we can
select the ones that fit the observations. Then in turn the
form may suggest new observations. Thus Einstein may find
a new branch of mathematics worked out some time ago to be
exactly what he needs to fit the new facts as he sees them.

Take a child into a clothing store and there will be many fine
clothes in that store, but what you are looking for is something
that exactly fits and suits the child. Don't forget the child. Don't

forget nature. The big thing about logic is that it has to fit. Only the clothes that fit have any real worth. That is what Peirce means when he says that the new logic has to do with truth. One of the big contentions that Peirce makes over and over again is that logic deals with truth. In connection with the old logic it had been drilled into scholars that logic and truth had little to do with each other. Many a syllogism may be logically sound and quite untrue. With logic so slippery it was not easy to see how it could be useful; in fact, many used it to mislead. Peirce, however, always stresses that the whole purpose of the new logic to help us to discover the truth. Hypotheses are of no value unless tested and found to work. Furthermore, successful hypotheses can be most useful in pointing the way to new discoveries. In all this there is nothing very mysterious; it is just that men are beginning to grasp the full philosophic import of the scientific method.

The second great feature about the new logic is its close connection with symbols or signs. Peirce sometimes calls the new logic the science of signs. He goes into tremendous detail on signs and on the semantic aspects of logic. He coins dozens of bizarre new terms. Many pages of Peirce are almost pure mathematics. However, unlike the mathematician, Peirce also takes time out to explain the philosophical and even the metaphysical aspects of all this. Presently we shall see that, like Santayana, Peirce begins to speak of different realms of being, and this realm of symbolic representation is one of them.

A sign is a sign of something to somebody. We are the kind of animal that has invented this triadic kind of horseplay. Not content with things and our reactions to them, we invent signs and learn how to react to signs in the absence of the things themselves. Every time you hear a conversation or you yourself engage in one that game of sign manipulation is being practiced. Signs give us the realm of meanings. It will pay to go back a little further and see how a Scottish philosopher, Reid, came to clearness on the matter of signs. This is by no means unrelated to what Peirce is developing because he makes a special point of sometimes referring to his views as "critical commonsensism," and Reid was the father of the Scottish school of common-sense philosophy, Peirce taking over and refining what Reid had discovered. As Buchler remarked, Peirce starts his views with the best he finds in Locke, Reid, and Kant.

Thomas Reid (1710–1796), in 1764 published his *Inquiry into the Human Mind on the Principles of Common Sense*. There is a close connection between Reid and Locke. Locke, the man from whom early Americans learned so much, had a system of thought that stood up like a solid structure on three basic pillars: mind, matter, and ideas. According to Locke, we have the mind, we have ideas, and we have the world of matter which these ideas represent. Ideas represent things. "What things?" said Berkeley, who ends up by knocking out altogether this third pillar of matter. Some people at the time thought that this was a very profound view. Not so Samuel Johnson, who when asked by Boswell how he would refute the Berkeley doctrine reacted as follows: "Sir," said he, kicking a stone so hard that his foot rebounded, "I refute it thus!"

Next came Hume, a Scot and a skeptic, who knocked out another of the three pillars. The mind is really the self, but of the self too we have merely ideas. To Hume the mind was nothing but a string of ideas. If Berkeley was the right wing of the school founded by Locke, Hume represented the left wing. Berkeley denied matter; Hume denied mind. Ideas were left without support. Something similar had happened in the physical world when, as a result of research by Newton and others, objects were left without support. Loose planets and stars floated in the ether. These bodies, explained Newton, were held together only by the law of gravitation. Hume was ready with a similar law of the mind. This was the law of the association of ideas. Ideas clump together and form clusters and systems much as planets do. Thus we are left with the structure of mental life, the result of chance and the laws of association. Matter and mind were left, and to Hume the ideas were copies of sense impressions.

For the version of Locke which found wide acceptance, even in early America, recourse must be had not to Berkeley, nor to Hume, nor even to Locke himself, but to Thomas Reid, that other Scot, the fourth man in this quartet of worthies. From

Reid we get a new insight into what ideas really are. They are really something we can do without. In other words, Reid knocks out the third pillar, the ideas. We observe things direct. We do not see the idea of a house. We see the house direct. Hence the naïve common-sense aspect of the Reid view.

The way Reid examines the question is to write a whole book on the five senses through which sensations, ideas, or whatever they are, are supposed to enter the mind. He begins with the sense of smell and ends with sight. He hammers away at one finding: the sensations are not like the objects. A fragrant smell is not shaped like a rose, nor does it in any other way resemble a rose. The pain of a sword prick in no way resembles a sword. Over and over again he drives home his contention that there is no similarity between ideas and objects. This in spite of the fact that Locke, Berkeley, and Hume had all accepted the notion that ideas were copies of objects.

Ideas are not copies, faint or otherwise, of objects. Reid reserves to the last his analysis of sight because in sight we do have a retinal image and it does look as if here we have likeness between sensation and object. Reid goes deeply into the subject, giving physiological details, citing medical treatises of the day, and showing, among other things, that if the optic nerve is severed you have a retinal image but no sight. You can focus the image of an object on the sensitive skin of the human hand, but still there will be no sight. Whatever seeing is, it is something entirely different from the reception of facsimile images. Nine tenths of the book is taken up with the negative thesis that sensations, ideas, and words are not copies of objects.

The constructive part of the book is surprisingly sound and modern, though very short. Sensations, ideas, words are all signs. There is no more reason why a sign should be like the objects signified than why the word "apple" should taste like an apple. Reid's basic contention is that we live in a world of real objects and that it is the business of the mind to manipulate signs that in turn help us to manipulate objects.

Peirce takes it up from there. Peirce makes signs the starting point of a whole new view of human thought. Reid, like Columbus, had made an adventurous voyage, and after a long journey finally set foot in America, only to withdraw almost immediately, content to have made the great discovery that ideas are signs. Now Peirce starts exploring the new continent. Says Peirce: "The woof and warp of all thought and all research is symbols, and the life of thought and science is the life inherent in symbols; so that it is wrong to say that a good language is *important* to good thought, merely; for it is of the essence of it." All thoughts are signs. Logic is the science of laws. Logic is not just the name for certain vague and abstract laws of thought. Logic deals with facts. It is not correct to say that logic has nothing to do with truth. Logic has everything to do with truth. It is man's chief instrument, through science, for the finding of truth. Now it becomes apparent why Peirce is so interested in logic.

Instead of giving us just a copy or a duplicate of the external world, signs translate impacts of the world into something that we can retain and put to use. They give the world a meaning for us. The meaning of meaning is that it gives us the insights we need in order to put to use certain tractable portions of our environment. This is quite different from making a copy. Thus Peirce stresses the semantic import of logic. The only way we have of making the world understandable is to make it understandable for us. "We have no conception of the absolutely incognizable," says Peirce, and that is a sentence worth pondering. The only meaning a world can have is a meaning for us. It is human or nothing. It is wrong to say that our only hope is to try to make it human, for we can't do anything else but try to make it human, and we have been at it fairly successfully for years. With food all you can do is eat it; if it nourishes you it is food, otherwise it is not food. No one argues that food only SEEMS to nourish us. With the brain what we human beings do is to understand the world; and the very fact that thought, like food, sometimes satisfies us, sometimes fits and fits beautifully, has metaphysical import. There should be no foolishness about thought not fitting the world or not touching the world. It does not RESEMBLE the world, but it does give it MEANING—and that is all we need. Thereupon the way to further advancement and control is wide open. The logic of science is the key, and by this Peirce means the key to the structure of the world. Those who try to discard his metaphysics, or to separate his philosophy from his metaphysics, are on the wrong track. The metaphysics is an essential part of the philosophy.

A third big thing in Peirce's logic is that it is shot through with the idea of chance. His logic is (1) closely related to mathematics, (2) a science of signs, and (3) a theory of probability. The universe is neither fixed nor certain; there is a good chance that something can be done about it. All through American philosophy runs the theme that this is a world of opportunities. For Franklin it meant among other things that this is a world in which the common man can make a living and rise in politics. For Emerson it meant that this is a world in which compensation for rights and wrongs are meted out here below in this life. For James it meant free will. Life is a process in which human beings can play a creative part. Thinking is not just contemplation but an active participation in this creative process by which the human race enlarged its role in the universe. Dewey carried all this further by accepting wholeheartedly the evolutionary point of view by which through cultural inheritance man can cumulatively pass on what he has come to know and thus increase his power to change his environment. To this Santayana added a great deal of embellishment by showing in detail how a civilized person can, even in a materialistic universe, lead a life of reason. But no one until Peirce came full circle and went to the roots of the matter by maintaining that the universe itself is fabricated from chance operations. Peirce worked out the implications of the close kinship between freedom in the heart of man and spontaneity outside.

Peirce points out: "Aristotle often lays it down that some things are determined by causes while others happen by chance. Lucretius, following Democritus, supposes his primordial atoms to deviate from their rectilinear trajectories just fortuitously, and without any reason at all. To the ancients, there was nothing strange in such notions; they were matters of course; the strange thing would have been to have said that there was no chance. So we are under no inward necessity of believing in perfect causality if we do not find . . . facts to bear it out." Later Peirce says: "We are brought, then, to this: conformity to law exists only within a limited range of events and even there is not perfect, for an element of pure spontaneity or lawless originality mingles . . . with law everywhere. Moreover, conformity with law is a fact requiring to be explained; and since law in general cannot be explained by any law in particular, the explanation must consist in showing how law is developed out of pure chance, irregularity, and indeterminacy." Peirce never loses sight of Darwin's spontaneous variations. "The principle of sporting is the principle of irregularity, indeterminacy, chance. It corresponds with the irregular and manifold wandering of particles in the active state of protoplasm. It is the bringing in of something fresh and first."

After centuries of more and more emphasis on heredity, or compulsion from above, behind, and everywhere, there comes a change in the climate of opinion to a new insistence on freedom and spontaneity. American philosophy from Franklin on plays down heredity and plays up humanity's ability to govern its own future. To this movement Peirce gives new vitality by putting spontaneity into the invisible structure of things. In anchoring chance deeply inside the structural elements of the universe Peirce is anticipating some very recent trends. Professor F. S. C. Northrop, in his Introduction to Heisenberg's *Physics and Philosophy*, compares Einstein who "could not allow God to play dice" with Heisenberg who claims: "Experience on black-body radiation requires one to conclude that God plays dice." Stated less figuratively: "Perhaps the most novel and important thesis of this book is the author's contention that quantum mechanics has brought the concept of potentiality back into physical science . . . physicists found it impossible to account theoretically for the Compton effect and the results of experiments on black-body radiation unless they extended the concept of probability . . . to the ontological role." In plain words: physics reinstated probability in the very heart of being.

So has biology. Biology has done this by showing that the operations of chance are not so hard to understand as people thought they were. Chance used to be considered synonymous with confusion. It is not so at all, for the simple reason that chance never operates in a vacuum. Something always limits it, and then what you get are pathways, directions, and goals. When you throw dice the fact there are only from one to six spots on each side of a die makes possible certain general predictions. In the same way the fifty-two-card deck is a limited universe, and the smooth Janus-faced penny tossed up in the air even more so, and therefore even more simply predictable.

In evolution, too, there are certain limiting conditions the operation of which is called natural selection, defined by Julian Huxley as "the differential survival of variants in relation to the conditions of life." Agreeing with Professor R. A. Fisher, Huxley looks upon natural selection as "a mechanism for generating an extreme degree of (apparent) improbability." Huxley considers this improbability "of such a high order that it could never have been produced by chance alone without the aid of natural selection, any more than monkeys tapping on typewriters could ever produce a play of Shakespeare. Given the facts of life and the known extent of biological time, such apparently improbable results as the protective resemblance of a Kallima butterfly to a dead leaf, or the evolution of organs of stereoscopic color vision like our own eyes, become comprehensible and scientifically explicable."

The same point is made by Erwin Schrödinger from a different angle when he makes the living organism delay death by feeding on negative entropy, drawing upon the order of the environment. An organism has the astonishing gift of sucking orderliness from its environment, and thus escaping atomic chaos, by actually producing order from disorder. C. G. Darwin, says: "We start with a prejudice against probability and end up by using it almost exclusively. Rightly or wrongly, roughly or scientifically, we apply rules of probability every day." Peirce devotes many pages to the mathematics and the implications of probability. One of the simplest paragraphs he has on the subject is the following:

"The theory of probabilities is simply the science of logic quantitatively treated. There are two conceivable certainties with reference to any hypothesis, the certainty of its truth and the certainty of its falsity. The numbers *one* and *zero* are appropriated, in this calculus, to marking these extremes of knowledge; while fractions having values intermediate between them indicate, as we may vaguely say, the degrees in which the evidence leans toward one or the other. The general problem of probabilities is, from a given state of facts, to determine the numerical probability of a possible fact. This is the same as to inquire how much the given facts are worth, considered as evidence to prove the possible fact. Thus the problem of probabilities is simply the general problem of logic."

In his remarkably lucid Preface to the volume of excerpts from Peirce called *Chance, Love, and Logic* Morris R. Cohen explains that from his exact scientific work Peirce learned that nature was not so precise and regular as most people think. In his work on the pendulum he had to do some very fine measurements and he became quite an expert on the margin of error. Nature shows many minute departures from strict law. True constancy you get only in mass phenomena. Peirce developed quite an advanced view concerning the statistical nature of law. From all this he arrived at the idea that there are no absolute and invariable laws of nature. Regularity is a matter of gradual growth. Moreover, from Duns Scotus, who was very fond of the word "haecceitas" or "thisness," Peirce absorbed an appreciation of underived individuality. Such underivable diversities, spontaneities, and novelties are not illusory. They are the real thing. Peirce referred to this view as *tychism*, according to which "Chance is prior to law." Cohen says Peirce got his tychism from Chauncey Wright, who likewise was a believer in genuine novelty and used to speak of the "cosmic weather." Along with Wright, Peirce made the chance variations of Darwin's biology central to his whole system of thinking.

Dewey wrote a whole book on the quest for certainty, maintaining that in this quest men had been on the wrong track, but he never made it quite clear what it was that the modern world had in the place of certainty. The answer is probability. Peirce makes it very clear wherein the logic of today differs from the logic of yesterday. What happened to logic is that it changed from the indicative to the conditional mood. Instead of saying: Man is mortal, Socrates is a man, therefore Socrates is mortal, all these is's are mounted on if's. Modern logic is couched in the form of conditions. If so-and-so, then thus-and-thus. All arguments are thrown into the form of conditional statements. First we get a hypothetical, then a future side. The "iffy" nature of the new logic keeps us on the constant *qui vive* for facts. In logic we are manipulating hypotheses that need checking.

Absolute No and Yes are replaced by shades of probability. What are the chances? is the modern question. In days of old the world was predetermined. Men wanted it that way. They wanted a world of certainty. They wanted to be sure. They hated to take a chance. In the Master of the fate of the world lay our only hope. Some hope had to remain because man could not live without it. Essentially the situation is not different today; by putting their hope in science men, in a sense, make it their religion. But it is a more strenuous religion in the sense that much more depends on us. The new logic is the old dichotomous logic which always tried to make you answer Yes or No widened out into a query which instead of Yes or No makes you answer, "It depends." This includes the possibility that a part of what happens may depend on us. The road is left open for us to play a role. In the phraseology of Oliver Wendell Holmes, we all become betabilitarians.

A pendant to chance is fallibility. Buchler points out: "Peirce's conception of truth allows for the instability of theories, and even for scientific disagreement on a given theory. It characterizes scientific investigation as a communal process of settling belief. A hypothesis may be called true and yet be subject to refinement, for *beliefs are relative to evidence.* As our method of uncovering new evidence grows, our beliefs are corrected and restated." Buchler is also quite right in maintaining that Peirce's doctrine of fallibilism is "of deeply revolutionary import." If all knowledge is fallible, the world is open, and all inquiry proceeds on the assumption that it stays open.

Peirce himself stresses "that in order to learn you must desire to learn, and in so desiring not be satisfied with what you already incline to think." The quest for truth is a passionate quest. And it never ends because the world keeps changing and can be made to change. "For years," says Peirce, "in the course of this ripening process, I used for myself to collect my ideas under the designation *fallibilism;* and indeed the first step toward *finding out* is to acknowledge you do not satisfactorily know already; so that no blight can so surely arrest all intellectual growth as the blight of cocksureness; and ninety-nine out of every hundred good heads are reduced to impotence by that malady—of whose inroads they are most strangely unaware! Indeed, out of a contrite fallibilism, combined with a high faith in the reality of knowledge, and an intense desire to find things out, all my philosophy has always seemed to grow."

6. Modes of Being

IF PROBABILITY is built into the structure of the universe, some changes must be made in our notions of being. First there was motion that had to be built in, even into the heart of the atom. Then there was acceleration—in the broad sense that things affect each other, they cause changes, such as those by light falling on a photographic plate. Neither the plate nor the light is alive but there is here something that comes pretty near to sentience or sensitivity. And now there is probability. A certain amount of contingency is built in. There is creativity going on right now in the world.

Peirce saw red at the word nominalist. Why? The root of the matter is that Peirce, like Santayana, believed in more than one mode of being. The mark of the nominalist has always been that he recognized only one mode of being, only the individual particles are real. The rest was moonshine. What particularly riled Peirce was that modern scientists sometimes took the skeptical attitude that universals exist only in the mind.

Peirce, like James and Santayana, believed in the external reality of a thick world, not just the thin world of dancing atoms and empty space. There were two additional things, qualities and laws, that would not disappear even if the human race did. The qualities are in the things; the laws are habits which operate outside. These are not just things in our own head, or figments of the interaction between men and their environment. All American philosophers shared this fundamental view of Peirce's, but not all gave it the same amount of careful thought. James was vehement in his protests against those who discard the polychrome and multifarious world of sense. Secondary qualities and relations were as real as anything else. Santayana added tertiary qualities. Dewey went along with all this, and Peirce, like Santayana, built it into his metaphysics.

Santayana arrived at his realms of being through studying appearances. Peirce did the same. Both started from a species of phenomenology in which consideration was given to whatever appears to the mind whether this be in dreams, in imagination, in thought, or in observation. Then, said Peirce, almost immediately one discerns three large classes or types of appearances: "The first comprises the qualities of phenomena, such as red, bitter, tedious, hard, heart-rending, noble . . . beginners in philosophy may object that these are not qualities of things and are not in the world at all, but are mere sensations. Certainly, we only know such as the senses . . . reveal. . . . It is sufficient that wherever there is a phenomenon there is a quality. The qualities merge into one another. . . . Some of them, as the colors, and the musical sounds, form well-understood systems.

"The second category of elements in the phenomena comprises the actual facts . . . we feel facts resist our will. That is why facts are proverbially called brutal. Now mere qualities do not resist. It is the matter that resists. . . . All that I here insist upon is that quality is one element of phenomena, and fact, action, actuality is another." Thirdly, there is law. "Law is not in the world of quality and of fact yet it governs the world." At another place Peirce says: "The third category of elements of phenomena consists of what we call laws when we contemplate them from the outside only, but which when we see both sides of the shield are called thoughts. Thoughts are neither qualities nor facts. They are not qualities because they can be produced and grow, while a quality is eternal, independent of time and of any realization. Besides, thoughts may have reasons, and indeed, must have some reasons, good or bad. But to ask why a quality is as it is, why red is red and not green, would be lunacy."

To get a fresh start on this triple-decked ontology, Peirce called the three modes of being: firstness, secondness, and thirdness. These new names had no old associations to confuse us. He also spoke of the monad, the dyad, and the triad, pointing out that qualities were single, but that in facts there was always a polarity of something opposing or resisting something else, and that in thirdness came representation, a sign standing for an object to a person. This latter is a triadic relationship.

Peirce has many other things to say about these three Modes of Being or Categories. For one thing he claims there cannot be more than three, because anything more complicated can always be broken down into one of these three, but thirdness cannot be broken down into a dyad, nor the dyad into a monad. Three realms or categories is all there are. Santayana had four, but it is easy to fit Santayana's realms into the three here set forth. Essence and Matter correspond fairly well with Peirce's first and second categories, and Spirit has much in common with what Peirce calls Thought, Law, and Representation. Truth should be put with the essences or divided between essence and representation. There is no great conflict here. Both are elaborating different modes of being, the point being not just how the division is made, but that there is more than one type of being.

Firstness is the realm of spontaneity, freedom, and originality. According to Peirce, "the world is full of this element of ir-responsible, free originality. Why should the middle part of the spectrum look green rather than violet? Why was I born in the nineteenth century on earth rather than on Mars a thousand years ago? Why did I today sneeze just five hours, 43 minutes, and 21 seconds after a certain man in China whistled (supposing this did happen)? . . . The idea of First is predominant in the ideas of freshness, life, freedom."

Secondness "is the conception of being relative to, the con-ception of reaction with, something else." Peirce is fitting his realms together much more smoothly than Santayana did. Here we have a master logician at work; also a dyed-in-the-wool scientist who is not afraid to speak up to the mathematician and the physicist. Secondness "is the main lesson of life. In youth, the world is fresh and we seem free; but limitation, conflict, constraint, and secondness generally, make up the teaching of experience."

"The existence of things consists in their regular behavior. If an atom had no regular attractions and repulsions, if its mass were at one instant nothing, at another a ton, at another a negative quantity, if its motion instead of being continuous, consisted in a series of leaps from one place to another without passing through any intervening places, and if there were no definite relations between its different positions, velocities and directions of displacements, if it were at one time in one place and at another time in a dozen, such a disjointed plurality of phenomena would not make up any existing thing." A certain regularity is mixed in. "The flow of time, for example, is itself a regularity." This regularity hints at another realm, that of laws, or thirdness. The three realms are not separated by chasms or high walls. They fit admirably together into one universe, our world, as we know it. According to Peirce, "we need not, and must not, banish the idea of the first from the second; on the contrary, the second is precisely that which cannot be without the first. . . . Firstness is an essential element of Secondness," and Thirdness may be regarded as a "medium between Second and First. . . . Thirdness is nothing but the character of an object which embodies Betweenness or Mediation in its simplest and most rudimentary form."

Thirdness brings Firstness and Secondness into relation with each other. In our thought we handle qualities and objects as belonging together. Thirdness is a combining of elements into special combinations important from our point of view. "A combination is something which is what it is owing to the parts which it brings into mutual relationships." Many laws bring whole series of facts together so that we can thread our way among them and predict what facts are further, under certain conditions, going to happen. Laws outside, thoughts inside, and communication between man and man are all activities illustrating thirdness. This idea of thirdness leads Peirce to a clear-cut theory of why and how we can know so many more things than the other animals. It comes from using a sign-process. It comes from our ability to draw inferences. Thinking is the drawing of inferences as to what may happen. Guided by past experiences it makes us the best guessers in the world.

In a book of *Studies in the Philosophy of Charles Sanders Peirce*, edited by Wiener and Young, there is an article by

Professor William Reese of Drake University which neatly pulls together some of the scattered items on Realms of Being. Reese points out that there is one realm that all agree on, nominalists and realists alike, namely, existence, the one that Peirce calls secondness and Santayana calls matter. Common sense, too, cannot help but believe in this realm of solid fact. Now, Peirce extends the scope of reality in the direction of firstness and thirdness, or less abstractly, in the direction of qualities and thoughts.

Aristotle had two realms, the actual and the possible, but his idea of the possible remained very vague. Nevertheless, actuality and potentiality have been woven into human thinking for two thousand years. Potentiality is, in a sense, the world of tomorrow. Although we live in the world of today, we also give a good deal of thought to the world of tomorrow. We must take into account the possibilities of tomorrow. In a sense the world of today is going to bring forth the world of tomorrow. Tomorrow's world is not spandy new and totally unconnected with the world of today. In the same way all the yesterdays of the world are bound up into the world of today. The yesterdays have left their mark. In our own life we feel that our past is part of our present self. It has been incorporated. Now, this is exactly what Peirce is doing; he is tying up the future and the past with the present. Hence three realms. There are times when Peirce plainly makes the past a part of thirdness. "The past is the storehouse of all our knowledge," says Peirce. He argues that the facts of history can be recovered. They belong to knowledge. He does not think that the past is hopelessly beyond the reach of knowledge. "Who can guess what would be the result of continuing the pursuit of science for ten thousand years, with the activity of the last hundred? And if it were to go on for a million, or a billion, or any number of years you please, how is it possible to say that there is any question which might not be solved?" The past is there rooted in the present. We can see today what happened in the stars ages ago. The mysteries of time are only beginning to be tackled.

Past, present, and future tie up together, and those who too narrowly believe only in the present fail to enrich the present in the way that they should. This is the gist of what Santayana does with his realms of being, and it is also what Peirce does. Both Peirce and Santayana are working on the problem of showing us how these other realms fit into and enrich the realm of actuality. The logical maxim is: whatever is needed to explicate reality must be given a place within reality. Of course no one in real life ignores the world of everyday actuality, but the question is whether in accepting the world of actuality we do not by implication have to accept also two more worlds, roughly the world of tomorrow and that of yesterday. It is logically indefensible to deny them altogether and to say that they are nothing. They are part and parcel of the world of actuality and must be given a status within reality. They are needed to account for what is. The distinctive feature of Peirce's metaphysics is that he roots the future and the past not merely in our own heads but in the external world. Like Dewey, he makes thinking a process that has something to do with the shaping of the world itself.

7. A Guess at the Riddle

SOME COMMENTATORS on Peirce ignore his metaphysics. It is as if they said that we have here a man who was good at mathematics and science but also was given to some wild speculations that go far beyond these sciences, and the less said about these speculations the better. Everyone remembers Newton's work in physics but by common consent all ignore what he said about the Book of Revelation or biblical prophecies. The two sides in Peirce are not so far apart as that, but a fairer analogy might be to compare him with a man like Descartes, who begins with extreme doubts and then rather quickly recovers himself, or Kant, who writes a highly skeptical *Critique of Pure Reason* and then in his *Practical Reason* apparently reverses himself and ends up, like Descartes, as a true believer. In the same way it is sometimes said that Peirce starts life as a radical, is gradually and deeply disappointed with his lack of success, and ends up with some ultra-conservative views on theology and on general conformity. Science is a religion making eventually for an unlimited community of true believers, and, moreover, God is in his heaven and all is right with the world. In my opinion a close reading and study of what Peirce wrote and of what his best commentators make of him does not confirm this view. The commentators who accept the whole man and find in him a remarkable degree of simplicity, sincerity, and consistency throughout are on the right track.

Anyone who reads rather hastily the extensive passages which Peirce has written about God might jump to the conclusion that here certainly he has thrown all his logic to the winds and fallen back upon those feelings for which he has such a great and strange respect. I say "great and strange" because we are dealing with a logician. Does a logician, in matters of theology, fall back on the heart? There is no reason at all why he should not do just that if he will give us his reasons and explain the matter to us. Somehow we expect Peirce to be honest with the reader. Peirce is never a diplomat, he does not write to please anybody in particular, he is penning a long discursive diary with no double talk or *arrière pensée*. And his paragraphs on metaphysics and theology are no exception. It is not true that he is here doing exactly what he condemns James for doing, namely, saying what he wishes to believe rather than trying to get at the truth.

For one thing, Peirce is not at all unwilling to talk about these things. Most scientists keep their religious views in a separate compartment or, when consulted on the subject, immediately excuse themselves, saying that such matters are outside their sphere. To Peirce nothing metaphysical seems inapropos, and he goes right ahead asking himself questions. One cannot help liking his refusal to be reticent. He seems anxious to answer every question fully and frankly. So he asks himself: "Do you believe in the existence of a Supreme Being?" And then proceeds immediately to point out that "Hume, in his *Dialogues Concerning Natural Religion,* justly points out that the phrase 'Supreme Being' is not an equivalent of 'God,' since it neither implies infinity nor any of the other attributes of God, excepting only Being and Supremacy. This is important; and another distinction between the two designations is still more so. Namely, 'God' is a vernacular word and, like all such words, but more almost than any, is *vague.* . . . I will also take the liberty of substituting 'reality' for 'existence.'" Here Peirce inserts a little note to the effect that "reality" is a fairly new word. Albertus Magnus first imported it into philosophy, but it did not become at all common until Duns Scotus, in the latter part of the thirteenth century, began to use it freely. Then he continues: "I define the real as that which holds its characters on such a tenure that it makes not the slightest difference what any man or men may have *thought* them to be, . . . here using thought to include imagining, opining, and willing (as long as forcible *means* are not used); but the real thing's character will remain absolutely untouched."

Note that Peirce is not really losing his logical acumen. This definition, replete with repetitions, parentheses, enumerations, and italics might have been written by a lawyer. After all this Peirce is finally ready to commit himself: "So, then, the question being whether I believe in the reality of God, I answer, Yes." Meanwhile it should be remembered that Peirce has already made his readers aware of his division of the universe into three realms of being, and, in the above, he makes it very clear that the Deity is not to be placed in the realm of existence, or Secondness. It must then be either in Firstness or in Thirdness, both of which have reality.

Another thing to note is how strongly he stresses that most of our precious everyday words, including the word "God," are vague. Peirce as a logician has definite meanings for such words as "vague" and "general." He says, "I have worked out the logic of vagueness with something like completeness." The contrary of vague is definite; the contrary of general is individual. "Anything is *general* in so far as the principle of excluded middle does not apply to it and is *vague* in so far as the principle of contradiction does not apply to it." "A sign is . . . *vague,* in so far as . . . it reserves for some other possible sign or experience the function of completing the determination. 'This month,' says the almanac-oracle, 'a great event is to happen.' 'What event?' 'Oh, we shall see. The almanac doesn't tell us that.'" This is Peirce's illustration of something vague—it might be anything. Another illustration used by him is that the term "animal" is vague with respect to whether the animal is male or female. It might be either. To say that it is a female does not contradict its being an animal; nor does its being male. We just don't know; the term is vague in that respect. Most ordinary words are vague in the sense that they are not too definite. When you say, "Oh, he's a pretty good fellow," the rejoinder is likely to be "Just what do you mean by that?"

In saying that the term "God" is vague Peirce does not necessarily mean anything disparaging. He may even think that it is better to leave it that way. In the same way taking it out of the realm of existence of brute fact pushes it into the direction of ideality, which seems appropriate. In this connection Charles

Hartshorne, who has made a considerable study of the idea of God in a number of philosophers, points out that Peirce reverses the orthodox position. For orthodoxy God is pure actuality, whereas Peirce substitutes pure potentiality. In many ways it seems more right and logical to stress infinite possibility rather than absolute completeness. Making the divine something that is gradually being actualizied or incarnated puts Peirce in line with what some of the other American philosophers have been saying.

Peirce is not going to be trapped into saying anything that is too definite. Perhaps what we need here is not so much sharp ratiocination, and certainly not argumentation, as something more guided by feeling. We need here a kind of reverie for which Peirce coins the term "musement." About God Peirce muses: "I have often occasion to walk at night, for about a mile, over an entirely untraveled road, much of it between open fields without a house in sight. The circumstances are not favorable to severe study, but are so to calm meditation. If the sky is clear, I look at the stars in silence, thinking how each successive increase in the aperture of a telescope makes many more of them visible than all that had been visible before. The fact that the heavens do not show a sheet of light proves that there are vastly more dark bodies, say planets, than there are suns. They must be inhabited, and most likely millions of them with beings much more intelligent than we are. . . . What must be the social phenomena of such a world! How extraordinary are the minds even of the lower animals. . . . Let a man drink in such thoughts as come to him in contemplating the physico-psychical universe without any special purpose of his own. . . . He will ask himself whether or not there really is a God. If he allows instinct to speak, and searches his own heart, he will at length find that he cannot help believing it. . . . Do you believe this Supreme Being to have been the creator of the universe? Not so much to *have been* as to be now creating the universe. . . . I think that, vain as it is to attempt to bring to light any definite meaning from the idea, it is nevertheless true that *all reality* is due to the creative power of God. . . . I think we must regard Creative Activity as an inseparable attribute of God."

"The Christian religion, if it has anything distinctive . . . is distinguished from other religions by its precept about the Way of Life. . . . Now what is this way of life? . . . As far as it is contracted to a rule of ethics, it is: Love God, and love your neighbor . . . the belief in the law of love is the Christian faith. 'Oh,' but it may be said, 'that is not distinctive of Christianity! That very idea was anticipated by the early Egyptians, by the Stoics, by the Buddhists, and by Confucius.' So it was. . . . Christians may, indeed, claim that Christianity possesses that earmark of divine truth—namely, that it was anticipated from primitive ages. The higher a religion the more catholic. Man's highest developments are social; and religion, though it begins in a seminal individual inspiration, only comes to full flower in a great church coextensive with a civilization. This is true of every religion, but supereminently so of the religion of love. Its ideal is that the whole world shall be united in the bond of a common love of God accomplished by each man's loving his neighbor. Without a church, the religion of love can have but a rudimentary existence; and a narrow, little exclusive church is almost worse than none. A great catholic church is wanted."

The above is given as a sample of the deceptively simple way in which Peirce writes about religion. In discoursing on the religion of love, Peirce more than once refers to Henry James, Sr., the Swedenborgian, who defined ordinary love as love for what is in conformity to one's self, but who contrasted this with "creative love, all whose tenderness . . . must be reserved for what is intrinsically most bitterly hostile and negative to itself." God loves his enemies—those who hate him. Several times Peirce refers with approval to this particular insight of James the Elder which, as Peirce thought, shows evil and hatred as overcome by love. "Thus, the love that God is, is not a love of which hatred is the contrary; otherwise Satan would be a coordinate power; but it is a love which embraces hatred as an imperfect stage of it . . . yea, even needs hatred and hatefulness as its object. For self-love is no love; so if God's self is love, that which he loves must be defect of love, just as a luminary can light up only that which otherwise would be dark."

In short, the more closely and carefully one reads and rereads what Peirce has to say on religion the less definite and concrete it all seems. Although skimming through it might give one the impression of simple piety, there is nothing here corresponding to a specific creed; it is more on the order of what is found in Paul Tillich. There is no anthropomorphism. "But perhaps the wisest way is to say that we do not know how God's thought is performed and that it is simply vain to attempt it. We cannot so much as frame any notion of what the phrase 'the performance of God's mind' means. Not the faintest!"

"The hypothesis of God is a peculiar one, in that it supposes an infinitely incomprehensible object . . . continually tending to define itself more and more, and without limit. The hypothesis, being thus itself inevitably subject to the law of growth, appears in its vagueness to represent God as so." Elsewhere he says outright: "God probably has no consciousness." Or again: "Pure mind, as creative of thought, must, so far as it is manifested in time, appear as having a character related to the habit-taking capacity." The state of taking habits "must tend to *increase itself*. For a tendency to act in any way, combined with a tendency to take habits, must increase the tendency to act in that way." Here he identifies the divine principle with the habit-taking principle, but it bothers him that habit-taking alone is not enough, since "there are some habits that carried beyond a certain point eliminate their subjects from the universe. . . . Thus a tendency to lose mass will end in a total loss of mass. A tendency to lose energy will end in removing its subject from the universe." As to immortality: "*Some* kind of a future life there can be no doubt of. A man of character leaves an influence living after him. It is living: it is personal. In my opinion, it is quite proper to call that a future life." Most people would not think so. He ends up a paragraph on immortality by saying: "I really don't know anything about it." It is evident that he does not believe in personal immortality.

Hartshorne thinks that Peirce in his deity is giving a name to primordial potency. There is something outside of us in nature that from time immemorial men have been inclined to call God. The only question is what is it and how little or how well can we describe it. He also thinks that if Peirce had given as much thought to the development of this part of his philosophy as he did to other parts he would have stressed more the implied bridge between potency and actualization, and not left his God quite as remote as he did, accessible only to the vague direct perception of musement. Whitehead's ideas are remarkably similar to those of Peirce, and Whitehead has his epistemology better worked out than Peirce has. It is possible that Whitehead here also may supplement Peirce.

Alfred North Whitehead:
Inspired Metaphysician

1. The Belated Immigrant

THROUGHOUT HIS LIFE Alfred North Whitehead always had one eye on the alert for new worlds to conquer. After a distinguished career in mathematics in sheltered Cambridge University, England, this late-maturing scholar pulled up stakes to transfer to the turmoil of London University. "This experience of the problems of London, extending over fourteen years (1910–1924)," said Whitehead, "transformed my views. . . . The seething mass of artisans seeking intellectual enlightenment, of young people from every social grade craving adequate knowledge, the variety of problems thus introduced—all this was a new factor in civilization." At Cambridge he had worked with might and main at mastering and imparting to others the new ferments in mathematics, not moving on until he had prepared for print, with a bright pupil of his, Bertrand Russell, the three-volume *Principia Mathematica*, a monumental landmark in mathematical logic. That done, he looked ahead to the exciting task in London, where as professor at the Imperial College of Science and dean of the Faculty of Science, as well as chairman of the Academic Council, he broadened his interests to include the entire field of science, along with administrative problems.

This was still not enough. Out of the blue, six years after World War I, in which the Whiteheads lost a son, came the call to another continent and to a still wider field of conquest. As Lucien Price in his *Dialogues of Alfred North Whitehead* tells the story: "His invitation to Harvard came in 1924, a complete surprise. The letter was handed him by his wife on an afternoon which was dismal without and within. He read it as they sat by their fire, then handed it to her. She read it, and asked, 'What do you think of it?' To her astonishment he said, 'I would rather do that than anything in the world.'" So at the age of sixty-three he faced a new career at Harvard, and this time his work was to embrace nothing less than the entire field of philosophy. He came to America, he saw, and he conquered. At Harvard, like a newly inspired votary, he produced in rapid succession his final masterworks in philosophy. In *Science and the Modern World* (1925), *Process and Reality* (1929), and *Adventures of Ideas* (1933) he reached the same peak in metaphysics that the *Principia Mathematica* had reached in mathematics. This exposition based on mathematical and scientific principles was exactly what American philosophy needed. It was poetic justice, too, that this should happen at Cambridge, Massachusetts, by a man from Cambridge, England, who occupied the chair that might have been held by the luckless Peirce. Ten years after the death of Peirce, almost as a bright and brilliant reincarnation, comes Whitehead. Not only that, but the systems of thought of these two broad-statured mental figures, are in detail after detail unbelievably alike.

"The similarities between their philosophies," says James Feibleman, "are simply astounding. . . . We may safely assert that Peirce had not read Whitehead, since he died before the latter's important work in philosophy was published. The reverse is not so clear; but since there is no reference in Whitehead's books to Peirce, it is likely to be true; for Whitehead could not have read Peirce without being excited by him sufficiently either to quote him or to refer to him in some way. . . . Both were deeply affected by the reaction to Hume and Descartes, by the realistic English tradition since Reid, and by modern science. Both men were in full revolt against the nominalistic philosophy, and both inveighed against its effect on the modern world. They shared a common sympathy for the realistic outlook, and described their metaphysics as varieties of realism, yet were equally sure that, in Whitehead's expression, 'The really profound changes in human life all have their ultimate origin in knowledge pursued for its own sake.'" Nothing unites two people so much as a common enemy. Both Whitehead and Peirce repudiate point for point the nine items enumerated by Whitehead in his Preface to *Process and Reality:* (1) unwarranted distrust of speculative philosophy; (2) faith in ordinary language as always adequate to philosophy (mathematicians know better); (3) the faculty-psychology; (4) the subject-predicate form of expression; (5) the sensationalist doctrine of perception; (6) the doctrine of vacuous actuality; (7) the Kantian doctrine of the objective world as a construct from subjective experience; (8) overgreat faith in *ex absurdo* arguments; and (9) belief that a logical inconsistency always indicates antecedent error. There are further similarities. Feibleman accounts for all these striking resemblances by the identical influences which bore on both men and by the fact that both were devotees of mathematics and of logic.

More reasons for considering Whitehead a prime contributor to American philosophy will be given presently, but because Whitehead wrote his philosophy here, because he dovetails so closely into American philosophy, and above all because he, as a late but vigorous immigrant, so fully exemplifies the dauntless spirit of the New World, he must be counted among the sages of American philosophy. After retiring from his professorship at Harvard in 1936, he continued to make America his home until he died in 1947, at eighty-six, having been born in 1861. Lucien Price, a guest at many gatherings in the Whitehead home, took down the table talk during some vigorous final years, and tells what Whitehead was like: "He was now in his eighties. There was not the least evidence that his intellectual powers were waning. In fact, the current was being stepped up. During those final years at their apartment in the Hotel Ambassador, when our sessions might begin as early as seven-thirty in the evening and last until after midnight, he would finish fresher than he began. . . . The retention of his power he owed to moderation in all things. His abstemiousness was marked. He ate sparingly. Table wine was admissable. No smoking. He seemed never to have craved stimulants. The sight of this ruddy octogenarian, clear-eyed, clear-skinned, without a mark of the customary indulgences, was, as time went on, not the least of his impressiveness. Another and greater impression was the spectacle of his living, in a four-room apartment, a larger life, more free, more spacious of spirit and intellect than most others could have lived in affluence. . . . His calm, his magnanimity, the vastness of his concepts reduced the trivialities of daily living to their true dimensions. . . . One felt that here was a man who was not afraid . . . of the vast enigma of human destiny or the immensities of the universe. In those awesome spaces he was at home and at his ease. This is what it means to be a philosopher."

The Whiteheads had three children, two sons and a daughter. It was the younger son, Eric, an aviator, who was killed in World War I. As Price explains, "Only as one came to know them gradually year after year did one even remotely understand how Eric's loss was felt. Finally they could talk of him eagerly and with laughter, for Whitehead once said that the most vivid wordings of grief or attempts at consolation by those masters of speech, the English poets, to him 'only trivialized the actual emotions.'" Feelings in Whitehead's philosophy, as in Peirce's, are fundamental. In fact to Whitehead we are indebted for an understandable exposition of how feelings increase the basic store of human knowledge. Here he supplements Peirce.

John Dewey, too, goes out of his way to show how fundamentally alike he and Whitehead are in certain basic views. Experience has often been restricted, both by empiricists and by their opponents, thinks Dewey, to certain selected activities of the organism—chiefly the sense organs. This, according to Dewey, is one of the most extraordinary and uncalled-for errors of human belief. He notes that Whitehead, like himself, repudiates this restriction. Then he quotes Whitehead: "We must appeal to evidence relating to every variety of occasion. Nothing can be omitted, experience drunk and experience sober, experience sleeping and experience waking, experience drowsy and experience wide-awake, experience self-conscious and experience self-forgetful, experience intellectual and experience physical, experience religious and experience sceptical, experience anxious and experience care-free, experience anticipatory and experience retrospective, experience happy and experience grieving, experience dominated by emotion and experience under self-restraint, experience in the light and experience in the dark, experience normal and experience abnormal." All of this John Dewey, the philosopher of experience, most heartily approves. "Moreover," opines Dewey, "we philosophers are authorized to use traits of immediate experience as clews for interpreting non-human and non-animate nature." More particularly Dewey, like Whitehead, thought that physical science could help us to explain consciousness and do this "without engaging in the dogmatic mechanistic materialism that inevitably results when Newtonian physics is used to account for what is distinctive in human experience." Whitehead has the closest of affinities with both Dewey and Peirce.

If anything, Whitehead is still closer to Santayana and to James. Parts of Whitehead sound like deep reverberations from Santayana, and Santayana he had certainly read, going so far as to use certain of the technical terms coined by Santayana. And as to James, Whitehead takes a vital part of James's abortive metaphysics, the part which shows how one portion of experience can get to know another, and makes this into a cornerstone of the Whiteheadian metaphysics. In man the rest of the world is getting to know itself. It is too much to say that for this purpose man was born—that he should understand the rest of the world—but the fact remains that this is what is beginning to happen, and the clear-cut chronicler of this recent development is Whitehead. And man, as Whitehead develops this thesis, grasps the world not so much through intellect as through feeling. A philosophy so wide in its scope, ranging so far beyond the ordinary confines of intellect, is going to be, in its unfolding, more like a work of art than like a reasoned philosophy.

A number of men have specialized on Whitehead and written books about him, among them A. H. Johnson of the University of Western Ontario, to whom it seems that "The twentieth century has produced few men whose achievements in the fields of mathematics and philosophy can surpass those of Alfred North Whitehead. His is not a mere technical excellence. It is a competence which, on occasion, is adorned by an unexcelled brilliance of vivid expression. . . . Learning sits lightly on his firm shoulders; a sparkling, somewhat ironic, humor shines through his discourse. The prolonged humility of the truly wise dignifies his utterances. To persons in all walks of life his is a rare exemplification of cultured charm and humility."

Ivor Leclerc of the University of Glasgow, another expert who has written an excellent book on Whitehead, says: "We are

accordingly compelled to follow him in some of this detail, although . . . we shall not enter into the full complexity of Whitehead's analysis—an analysis which surpasses in the extent of its
detail and meticulous rigour anything which has so far been
achieved in the entire history of philosophy." Elsewhere, near
the beginning of his book, Leclerc claims that the difficulties of
Whitehead's metaphysics have "been greatly exaggerated by
incorrect and misleading approaches."

The approach here advocated, namely, that of taking Whitehead's thinking to be in many ways a continuation of the standard
American line of thought, may seem presumptuous, but it does
give us an easy and a ready entree into Whitehead's ideas. Whitehead was universally beloved in America. He acquired a host of
followers in this country, not merely in the academic world but
conspicuously among a very wide circle of laymen and readers
generally, interested, as he himself was, in the broader aspects
of culture. It is the humanity of the man and his profound up-to-
dateness that draws readers to him. In putting Whitehead in line
with other American sages, when he came here not as a refugee,
not as a stranger, but as a beloved professor, one might say,
who liked it so well here that he made America the place in which
to live out the rest of his life, there is no wish to appropriate
anyone who does not belong here, nor to acquire credit to which
this country has no right. On the contrary, so many Americans,
first and last, have come to this country from Europe that there
is no feeling at all that Whitehead does not belong.

For that matter, all American philosophy is overwhelmingly
British in tradition. From the start American thought has been an
overseas branch of British thinking, and it seems singularly fitting
that the man who puts the crown on what others have worked at
in this country should come to us straight from England. Whitehead is the one emissary who could make Americans feel that in
thought they had never been separated from England at all, or
rather that the mother country and all its domains are now again
one as never before. To achieve this reamalgamation is not the
least of Whitehead's great services, and he did it by managing to
become as American as his hosts. To think of completing any
sketch of basic American philosophy without including White-

head would be like building a house and leaving off the roof. If Whitehead was English rather than American, he does manage to get an American spirit into the body of his thought, and as long as Americans have any interest in their own philosophy they are going to have to study and to include this very wise man who came to Harvard to write those key books containing his maturest insights.

2. Enlarge Your Mind!

I⊤ ɪs ɴoᴛ at all unusual that in the course of human events a man has to enlarge his abode. There has been an increase in the family, perhaps it was only a new hobby that brought in new gear, maybe it is keeping up with the Joneses, but when one gets more things than the house will hold, the only thing to do is to enlarge it. The mind is no different. To accommodate a growing store of indispensable items or to keep up with new discoveries, every so often, the mind needs its boundaries expanded, the walls of prejudice knocked down, and new storage spaces built for new displays. I think Whitehead learned this lesson from mathematics.

In 1911 Whitehead wrote for the Home University Library a short and popular *Introduction to Mathematics*. It was reprinted as a paper-bound book in 1948. Today such popular introductions to the various sciences have become commonplace, but Whitehead's mathematical primer was in its day and age quite an eminent "potboiler." It was most authoritative and most readable, for one thing, because he sprinkled his text with stray asides, such as: "Lord Beaconsfield, in one of his novels, has defined a practical man as a man who practices the errors of his forefathers." It also contains a great deal of information on how the number system kept expanding. Numerals can be traced back to the seventh century. The Romans used letters. Can you imagine doing long division with Roman numerals? The Arabic numerals have been a wonderful shorthand. They relieve the brain of an enormous amount of work, and this is true of all good symbolism. The zero, or tenth digit, is of crucial importance. In the number 51, the position of the 5 makes it stand for a fifty, but 50 itself cannot be written without zero. This is its first function. Secondly, it gives us an important way of writing an equation, with the zero as the right-hand member. A third function occurs in the rule that 0 times x is zero. It broadens the mind just a little to know that something multiplied by zero is zero.

An important first extension of numbers, that is, of whole numbers, was fractions. These are very old, going back to 1700 B.C. A fraction is really a ratio. The Greeks found out about incommensurable ratios, not exact fractions of the original length, a strange idea when you come to think of it. In a right-angle triangle, with sides of unit length, the hypotenuse is not an exact fraction of the sides. There is no fraction which exactly represents the square root of 2. We can approximate it but never quite equal it. Room had to be made for these incommensurables. They belong with the fractions. The incommensurables, with the fractional and integral numbers, make up the class of real numbers. We should add the negative numbers. Positive and negative numbers can be interpreted as operations, like steps backward or forward. They first arose to denote an excess or defect from some standard weight.

Decimal fractions came in about 1700, another great advance. By the aid of such clever symbolisms as decimal fractions, and equations with zero as the right member, we can make transitions in reasoning almost mechanically by eye without even using the higher brain faculties; and merely putting down figures—what a relief from memory strain. "It is a profoundly erroneous truism repeated by all copybooks and by eminent people when they are making speeches, that we should cultivate the habit of thinking of what we are doing. The precise opposite is the case. Civilization advances by extending the number of important operations which we can perform without thinking about them. Operations of thought are like cavalry charges in battle—they are strictly limited in number, they require fresh horses, and must only be made at decisive moments."

The family of real numbers consists of rational and irrational numbers; the rational ones divide into integers and fractions; the integers into positive as well as negative integers and zero. This is only a good beginning. Next come the imaginary numbers. These come from such simple equations as x squared equals minus 2. We get a new foundling on our doorstep in the shape of the square root of a minus number. The square root of minus 1 has come to be looked upon as the head of all imaginary numbers and given the special designation "i." These imaginary numbers, to which Whitehead devotes Chapter 7 in his little book, when they arose in equations were, as Whitehead explains, "simply ruled aside as nonsense. However, it came to be gradually perceived during the eighteenth century, and even earlier, how very convenient it would be if an interpretation could be assigned to these nonsensical symbols." A good use was found for them. They could be diagrammed. They were presently admitted to the family of numbers as members in good standing. They are as numerous as the real numbers, and now they live side by side with them in the family of complex numbers. A complex number is a combination of a real and an imaginary number. Whitehead closes his chapter on imaginary numbers by saying: "One of the most fascinating characteristics of mathematics is the surprising way in which the ideas and results of different parts of the subject dovetail into each other. During the discussion of this and the previous chapter we have been guided merely by the most abstract of pure mathematical considerations; and yet at the end of them we have been led back to the most fundamental of all the laws of nature, laws which have to be in the mind of every engineer as he designs an engine and of every naval achitect as he calculates the stability of a ship. It is no paradox to say that in our most theoretical moods we may be nearest to our most practical applications."

The house of numbers is still not large enough. Room must be made for transfinite numbers. How they fought Georg Cantor when he first brought them in! The Hebrew letter aleph with a zero subscript, aleph-null—why should the legitimate family admit these queer constructs in which, by definition, the part is equal to the whole? Nevertheless, it and the number C, not the symbol standing for 100, but another member of the transfinite family, with more to follow, come trooping in. Mathematics is like the packaging industry, the more things there are to pack the stranger the containers. Sooner or later the most fanciful of containers is found to fit something that occurs in nature, as when Einstein put to good use a non-Euclidean geometry which he found fully constructed and ready to be used. Peirce, who was also a mathematician, at one place marvels at this curious way in which the human mind can make containers so many of which turn out to fit the facts.

The way arithmetic and geometry have been bursting at the seams, the way the whole subject of mathematics has in the past hundred years been experiencing a phenomenal growth, is bound to give a mathematician the idea that the mind must be kept open for new concepts. Such concepts may seem positively weird until it is found that they can be manipulated, possibly by the same rules already in use elsewhere, and that they help us to understand and to control formerly puzzling behavior, mayhap in the very innards of nature, such as when scientists after two years of unprecedented endeavor rigged up an atomic explosion. This is more frightening than reassuring, but so I am sure was fire when it was first clumsily manipulated and then brought under control. Enlarge the mind! Keep thinking! Keep trying! Success may come.

The spectacular advances in logic and in mathematics are bound to have reverberations in philosophy. Instead of calling a halt on new phenomena, we enlarge the confines of our understanding to admit new facts. Never let the mind stop growing. If our logic needs to branch out, let it sprout. Even if for two thousand years the logic of Aristotle was big enough, there is no reason why forever and ever we must stop at the logic of Aristotle. The men who expanded geometries have also been expanding logic. We have seen the deep interest that Peirce had in a functional logic covering all relations, and infinitely more Protean than the Aristotelian syllogism. Whitehead follows suit. One of his earliest technical books was a *Universal Algebra*, published in 1898. Here he examines forms of togetherness. Just what do we do when we add, subtract, multiply, and divide, that is, put things together and separate them again? This is going to be the technical foundation of a profound metaphysics, dealing with the genesis of order. In his small popular volume on mathematics, Whitehead makes the point that great truths ripen slowly. He quotes Shelley:

As thought by thought is piled, till some great truth
Is loosened, and the nations echo round.

One of the great inventions along mental lines was the calculus
of Newton's day, which gave mathematicians new power to understand the exact behavior of falling bodies (correcting Aristotle) and the motion of the planets. This turned out to be just
a beginning. Always human knowledge, no matter what advances
it makes, seems to be just beginning. There is always more beyond, and more understanding needed to grasp it. Gravitation
gives way to relativity, followed by quantum mechanics and an
uneasy ferment of waves and particles. The point here is that
Whitehead is familiar with the mathematics involved. We should
treat with respect his attempt to unite the logic of feeling with
the logic of intellect into a new type of intellection by which he
claims to be able to account, better than heretofore, for some of
the puzzles of creation both within and without the human
mind.

Sometimes a camera gives us the reverse of slow motion. Instead of seeing the swing of golf club, or the penetration of bullet
into a glass of water, slowed down to where we can observe
exactly what did happen, we see a plant that took years to grow
have its life condensed to a matter of twenty minutes or so.
Then we see the seed sprout, put forth leaves, a bud slowly
forming, and eventually bursting into full flower before our very
eyes. In that same way the knowledge that it took centuries to
put painfully together bit by bit is in the textbooks of today
given us in magic condensation so that a single man in the morning of life can span the ages and absorb almost in a flash the
wisdom of an entire geological epoch. For this there is needed an
expansible mind. Things that the mightiest brain simply could
not do a few centuries ago are now done and done easily by
ordinary youths. Of such stuff is the mind of man. And sometimes
it is possible to see a little of that new knowledge bursting in
upon us right before our eyes, as when both Dewey and Peirce
refuse to accept intuition, and then along comes Whitehead to
untangle the situation and show how it can and must be accepted.

James had flirted with the idea of two kinds of knowledge, but

Peirce would have none of it. Nor Dewey. No direct knowledge. Everything is inference, said these master logicians. Yet Whitehead is just as good a logician. We are reminded of those transfinite numbers that just seemed too absurd to accept, and yet, once in, how marvelously they help untangle the concept of infinity, and clear up opaque paradoxes that had withstood the intellectual pummelings of a few thousand years. Before the chemistry of today formerly impossible transmutations are child's play. Hume demolishes causation, and there that bright intellect is forced to stop. Now along comes Whitehead with a kind of intellection that once more ties cause and effect together, but in order to do it he has to throw out Peirce and Dewey's ruling against intuition. Few philosophers have studied intuition with any thoroughness. Bergson was an exception. But to Bergson intuition was something to replace, not to supplement, the intellect. For Bergson the intellect falsifies. Science schematizes and, as in dissection, destroys the pulse of life. Most theories of intuition have looked to intuition for salvation, a short cut to truth. This is not logic but mysticism. Mysticism is not Whitehead's way. No one as deeply versed in the triumphs of mathematics as Whitehead was could countenance the surrender to obscurity implied in mystic intuition. We need an advance out of and not a backward step into the fastnesses of former ignorance. How can feeling be more than a guess? How can a philosophy of feeling be worked in as an understandable part of a rational scheme? That is Whitehead's problem, and that is what a large part of his new expansion of philosophy is all about.

As stated, James had an inkling of two kinds of knowledge, one of which he called "acquaintance with" and the other "knowledge about," pointing also to the twin words of this kind in other languages. Peirce, although he ruled out all immediate knowledge other than inference, did admit that in secondness, in actual existence, there is the shock of resistance when one comes up against something real. There is a contact, a meeting, the awareness of an encounter where consciousness faces and in a sense recognizes at a glance the existence of something. Dewey with characteristic candor describes this as a sort of recognition or grasping of "discriminate objects recognizable in a context involving use." It is into this aspect of knowledge, involving a direct grasp, that Whitehead probes.

In a general way all American philosophers have agreed that thought should be tied in closely with action. Making thought part of a reflex arc between stimulus and action is giving it a new context and a wider role. This makes it impossible henceforth to sever thinking from the rest of our behavior; in other words, this reinterpretation of thought has philosophical repercussions. If Whitehead can show that feeling can be true knowledge, he is intertwining thought with behavior even more intimately than Peirce and Dewey did.

But none of this is going to be at all clear until we get some grasp of how Whitehead sees the actual structure of the universe. Just as one can get no insight into the accomplishments of modern chemistry unless some study is first made of molecules and atoms, so it must be understood first of all what Whitehead means by "actual entities." This is a term that Whitehead coins to indicate the building blocks of the universe, not just the physical universe but the whole works; and in making that distinction we are putting our finger on one of the difficulties in understanding Whitehead. He is from the start against bifurcation. His first books were on science rather than on philosophy, and they were all aimed at breaking down that wall which we all almost instinctively erect between mind and matter. The scientist especially has been thoroughly indoctrinated to feel that what he studies is atom configurations, without stopping to realize that he himself is just that—a similar configuration of atoms. Somehow man feels himself across the great divide—studying atoms but not of them.

This Whitehead tries to avoid. He feels that this bridge between us and the rest of the world must disappear if ever we are to understand what it means to "know" things. Hence when he makes the building blocks of the universe "actual entities," it is understood that we too are made up of these same "actual entities." Does this make Whitehead, like Santayana, an avowed "materialist"? Not quite, and not necessarily, because Whitehead is metaphysically less naïve than Santayana was and he has at his disposal greater resources in the way of scientific delvings. His view of matter is different. The universe is not dead matter at all. It is a process now going on, and the constitutive elements of that process are creative centers, technically known as actual entities, although they could just as well have been called something else. The universe consists of millions of creative centers of energy, not dead atoms nor just a crazy Brownian movement of dancing particles, as Santayana, without going into the matter, might lead one to think, but centers of more or less carefully interlocked and controlled energy, always covering more than a single instant. There are no single instants. There are small durations which Whitehead calls the "specious present." The specious present is not a line between past and future, but a "saddleback" covering a portion of the past and of the future. The continually perishing past gives up its burden to a host of future entities. This is what time means. Or rather, out of the perishing past, the entities that are gone, the future entity chooses what it is going to perpetuate.

This is a rough and a crude picture, but it is nearer to what is actually going on than the billiard-ball atoms of the crass materialism of a former day. There is more respect today for what is going on inside the world of the infinitely small. Nuclear physics has been expanding, and thinkers have more and more closely intertwined space and time. Temporality is of the essence of what is going on and choice is at the heart of things. We need a new metaphysics, and Whitehead tries very hard to give us just that in his *Process and Reality*. What we need is some glimpse of how, in a permissive way, the past might help us build the future and still not control it in the old deterministic manner. We need some adumbration of a nonmechanical view that is neither mystical nor vitalistic. Such a view will have to draw on the new mathematical logic and still not give up the old ideal of rationality. It can be done if we are willing to enlarge our minds.

3. The World Is Alive!

AMERICAN PHILOSOPHY began its career by accepting the vast mechanical world of Newton into which life seemed to have come as an afterthought. To take away some of the bleakness of this ruthless mechanism, Newton, who was a devout Christian, supplemented his conception of nature by a theism taken straight from the Christian Bible. Newton believed in revelation. In fact, from his studies of gravitation Newton plunged so deeply into studies of Bible prophecies in the Book of Daniel and in the Book of Revelation that for a while some of his friends began to think that his sanity was in the balance. Slowly he recovered, became more worldly-minded, began as master of the Mint to live in better style, was knighted, and toward the end of his life was dragged into a disgraceful dispute about whether he or Leibnitz had invented the calculus.

Newton's theism bothered the youthful Franklin, who saw the inconsistency of maintaining free will in a mechanical world set going by an all-powerful Deity, yet he had no good alternative. He retained the Newtonian view but softened it by stressing good works and presenting a pragmatic argument in favor of a lesser God who loved and rewarded human virtue. He also flatly rejected revelation. Emerson took up the matter where Franklin had left off. He discarded the theological heaven and hell as metaphysical supplements to a mechanical universe and tried instead to describe a universe in which an ever-present Deity played a constant role by, so to speak, running the mills that slowly grind out justice. Emerson was more poetical than logical, but his insight was true, and his semipantheistic world was not a sloppily sentimental one. Men had to save their own souls, and Emerson was sure they could.

Then came James with many new suggestions. The most startling innovation was an original psychology abolishing the soul substance, as Emerson had abolished a physical heaven and hell. He confirmed the Emersonian idea of the Deity as an interested coworker, but what was even more important, he tackled the problem of how, without a soul and without an all-powerful Deity, one physical part of the world could get to know another part of the physical world. He embarked on a naturalistic epistemology. Fundamentally this comes down to showing how the world can get to know itself. On this fascinating idea James could do no more than make a start. But that start was important. It was the first real attempt to bridge the body-mind gulf, the Cartesian dualism of mind and matter, basic to Western philosophy for three hundred years. Whitehead was fascinated by this aspect of James. He thought that James had made exactly the right start on this problem. For this reason he classed James among the truly original thinkers of this world. Said Whitehead:

"In Western literature there are four great thinkers. . . . These men are Plato, Aristotle, Leibnitz, and William James. Plato grasped the importance of the mathematical system. . . . Aristotle . . . inherited from Plato, imposing his own systematic structures. Leibnitz inherited two thousand years of thought. . . . His interest ranged from mathematics to divinity, and from divinity to political philosophy, and from political philosophy to physical science. These interests were backed by profound learning. There is a book to be written, and its title should be, 'The Mind of Leibnitz.' Finally there is William James, essentially a modern man. His mind was adequately based upon the learning of the past. But the essence of his greatness was his marvellous sensitivity to the ideas of the present. He knew the world in which he lived, by travel, by personal relations with its leading men, by the variety of his own studies. He systematized; but above all he assembled. His intellectual life was one protest against the dismissal of experience in the interest of system. He had discovered intuitively the great truth with which modern logic is now wrestling."

These words occur at the beginning of Whitehead's *Modes of*

Thought. After this initial tribute to William James, Whitehead devotes the better part of eight lectures to explaining in simple words how he expands the Jamesian view that in man the world is beginning to understand itself. James spoke of a neutral stuff, neither physical nor mental, but which could go either way. Here Whitehead continues. James's neutral stuff, neither matter nor spirit, comes out in Whitehead not as a single stuff but more, as in Leibnitz, in the form of innumerable bipolar entities, one pole material and the other mental, using these words as suggestions rather than as hard and fast delimitations. Thus we get the groundwork of a new pluralistic realism.

First of all, says Whitehead, note that our bodies are as much a part of external nature as a river, a mountain, or a cloud is a part of nature. Where does the body leave off? Not just that the food we reach for and eat gets to part of the body, but molecules pass in and out, functioning as parts of us and parts of sticks, stones, and vegetables. "The human body is that region of the world which is the primary field of human expression. . . . Wherever there is a region of nature which is itself the primary field of the expressions issuing from each of its parts, that region is alive." Here we get the beginning of a "field" theory of life. Thus far we have "actual entities" plus a "field" that comes alive. Even an atom is a center or a field of energy rather than a substance. Such fields range all the way from inorganic nature to highly organized living things. Whitehead's world is permeated with the notion of "organisms." What we have is not inert substance but organized formations actively functioning. Also note that things are alive long before they are conscious. Whitehead rightly notes that among living things consciousness is the exception rather than the rule. Some kind of sentience or "feeling" functions unconsciously. By no means all animals have fully equipped sense organs. Certainly microbes and plants, although they are living things, do not have the sense organs we do. All the attempts to reconstruct the universe from bits of information furnished by human sense organs, or the sense organs of other highly developed mammals, is bound to break down because it overlooks the manifestations and adjustments of living things involving those deeper feelings that precede or underlie or are the raw stuff from which those very sense organs can develop. We are beginning at the wrong end.

"The role of sense-experiences consists in the fact that they are manageable. . . . The pitfall of philosophy is exclusive concentration on these manageable relationships, to the neglect of the underlying necessities of nature. Thus thinkers repudiate our intimate vague experiences in favour of a mere play of distinct sensations, coupled with a fable about underlying reality. . . . During many generations there has been an attempt to explain our ultimate insights as merely interpretive of sense-impressions." Instead, says Whitehead, philosophy should be "the attempt to make manifest the fundamental evidence as to the nature of things." Philosophy he defines in several ways, but a favorite dictum of his is that philosophy is a "criticism of abstraction." By this he means that when you abstract you are going in the wrong direction. You are thinning things out. You are landing yourself in a net of abstractions, away from the concrete world. Concretize, add, and multiply—this is a curious insight for a mathematician to get but Whitehead has it unmistakably. "The aim of philosophy," he says, "is sheer disclosure." Do not exchange the workaday real world of living entities for a handful of abstractions. One of the truly remarkable things about Whitehead is that in spite of authoring the *Principia Mathematica*, three volumes full of equations, he does not think that the world and the fullness thereof can be put into an equation. If he hated equations, as James did, we might discount this belief of his as an antipathy, but Whitehead loved equations. He knew them and worked with them as magnificent tools of human thought, yet in his metaphysics they disappear. The scaffolding falls away, and the living, breathing world, a palpitating entity, lies disclosed. Nature expressed in equations is a tool, an abstraction, just the thing for an engineer, but philosophy is a critique of abstractions. It keeps on saying: Beware of abstractions. Whitehead has a famous phrase: "misplaced concreteness," and by this technical expression he means to hit the human foible of misplacing the concreteness of the world into those abstractions which man spins in his head. Thus we come to think that these ghostlike abstractions are more real than anything else. This is a mistake, the mistake of misplaced concreteness. Keep the concreteness where it belongs—in the living universe.

Follow the world of sense data, and what happens? We get small bits of matter perceived by the eye, ear, nose, palate or skin. The whole story is unfolded in the works of Descartes, Locke, Berkeley, and Hume. The solid world tumbles out of sight between the two stools of mind and matter. It is the mind that contributes the secondary qualities. These qualities are the first to go. Colors, smell, and taste are not in the object. Locke thought only the primary qualities remained outside in the objects. Berkeley soon corrected him on this. The primary qualities also fall out. The world out there becomes more and more schematic. It is truly a world of quality-less atoms pulled around by invisible laws.

Can it be that sense perceptions are more in the nature of practical guides? That sense perceptions do not provide data for their own interpretation was the great discovery made by Hume. That is why his *Treatise* remains a start for further thought. These objects so glibly accepted by literature and common sense move around supposedly in empty space. Air too occupies space. But what about outer space? How does light get through? What carries it? A very subtle form of matter, called ether, was assumed. Ether was the last stand of matter.

Newton found how bits of matter large and small attract each other, and with his laws of motion gave an explanation of celestial mechanics. Bits of matter, bodies, had stresses between them. That was the fundamental idea. But why these stresses? "In this determination he made a magnificent beginning by isolating the stresses indicated by his law of gravitation. But he left no hint, why in the nature of things there should be any stresses at all. . . . By introducing stresses . . . he greatly increased the systematic aspect of nature. But he left . . . mass and stress—in the position of detached facts devoid of any reason for their comprescence. He thus illustrated a great philosophic truth, that a dead nature aims at nothing. . . . Combining Newton and Hume we obtain a barren concept . . . that modern philosophy from Kant onwards has . . . sought to render intelligible. My own belief is that this situation . . . should not be accepted as the basis for philosophic speculation." Kant accepted both Newton and Hume and only got in deeper. In the end the whole notion of empty space has had to be eliminated from recent science. The spatial universe is a field of force, a field of incessant activity. The bits of matter, as self-identical supports for physical properties, also have been eliminated. Gone is the ether, which was nothing but a final form of dead matter. For a while ether remained with ordinary matter making knots and imposing stresses and strains throughout the whole of the jelly-like ether. In this way an immense unification was effected between light, heat, and electricity. The theory was profusely elaborated and then collapsed.

The collapse came when matter was identified as energy. That step was enough to cave in the whole struture. Matter vanished. The modern view expresses everything in terms of energy. "There is no possibility of a detached, self-contained local existence. The environment enters into the nature of each thing. In truth, the notion of the self-contained particle of matter . . . is an abstraction. Now an abstraction is nothing else than the omission of part of the truth. The abstraction is well-founded when the conclusions drawn from it are not vitiated by the omitted truth." But this abstraction was vicious. It did omit essentials. These are now being supplied. Still the old, deeply embedded view hangs on. Scientists in one field still work with the presuppositions, thirty years old, in another field. Geneticists find it hard to think of genes in any other way than hard isolated bits of matter not influenced by their surroundings. All of us cannot begin to think of bodies other than bodies simply located in space. Space to us may condition objects, but it does not necessitate them. We still think of space as empty. Instead, "there are no essentially self-contained activities within limited regions. . . . Nature is a theater for the inter-relations of activities." Passive space is out of date, and inappropriate. "The fashionable notion that the new physics has reduced all physical laws to the statement of geometrical relations is quite ridiculous. It has done the opposite. It has thus swept away space and matter, and has substituted the study of the internal relations with a complex state of activity."

As Justice Holmes said, the universe is not in us but we are in the belly of the universe. Aristotelian logic is inadequate. "The disease of philosophy is its itch to express itself in the forms, 'Some S is P,' or 'All S is P.'" It does not even do much good to ask how much of S is in P. Quantitative notions do not get us very far metaphysically. "Indeed quantity itself is nothing other than analogy of functions within analogous patterns. . . . The laws of nature are merely all-pervading patterns of behavior." Every science is an abstraction from the full concrete happenings of nature. Yet many leaders in natural science strive hard to keep them apart. The autonomy of the natural sciences has its origin in a concept of a world of nature now discarded. "Suppose we agree that Nature discloses to the scientific scrutiny merely activities and process. What does this mean? These activities fade into each other. They arise and then pass away. What is being enacted? What is being effected? It cannot be . . . 'merely a bloodless dance of categories.' Nature is full-blooded. Real facts are happening."

The older view, regarding nature at an instant, was a cross section. Cross sections, even under the microscope, are dead. "Nature at an instant is . . . equally real whether or not there be any nature at any other instant, or whether or no there be any other instant. Descartes, who with Galileo and Newton, accepted this conclusion . . . explained endurance as perpetual re-creation at each instant." The fatal contradiction in the Newtonian cosmology was the absence of time. It was merely bits of matter occupying this region at this durationless instant. "Velocity and momentum require the concept that the state of things at other times and other places enter into the essential character of the material occupancy of space at any selected instant." The differential calculus did not help because all Newton needed was the value of a function at a selected point. Newtonian physics required solely the limit of the function at that point. For the modern view "at an instant there is nothing. Each instant is only a way of grouping matters of fact." There are no separate instants—only creative advance, which takes the form not of an instant but of a saddleback straddling past and future, also called the specious present.

In nature, abstracted from the notion of life, we are left with an activity in which nothing is effected. This activity discloses no ground for its own coherence. All we have is a formula for succession. Of course it is always possible to be content with an ultimate irrationality. The popular positivistic philosophy adopts this attitude. But if a hundred thousand years ago our ancestors had been such positivists, we should have had no civilization. Insects visit flower—interesting fact, and nothing further to be said. "At present the scientific world is suffering from a bad attack of muddle-headed positivism. . . . We are told that there is the routine described in physical and chemical formulae, and that in the process of nature there is nothing else." The origin of this is the dualism in respect to mind and nature which since 1600 has continued to obsess us. "The effect of this sharp division between nature and life has poisoned all subsequent philosophy. For some, nature is mere appearance and mind the sole reality. For others, physical nature is the sole reality and mind is epiphenomenon." There is no fusion. "The doctrine that I am maintaining is that neither physical nature nor life can be understood unless we fuse them together as essential factors in the composition of 'really real' things whose inter-connection and individual characters constitute the universe."

Life is the self-enjoyment of a process of appropriation. What is appropriated is the antecedent functioning of the universe. We live off things as they were. Second, there is creative activity belonging to the essence of each occasion. This creative activity elicits unrealized potentialities. It brings about a creative advance. It is a process involving duration. The notion of an instant of time as important is nonsense. Third, life has aims, that is, it excludes alternative potentialities. Free will is inborn. We can choose novelty. We select enjoyment rather than death and pain.

In one sense the abstractions made by science have led to a good result: they allowed simple things to come first. The laws of nature were disclosed, but none of these give the slightest trace of necessity. "There is no necessity in any of these ways of behavior. They exist as average, regulative conditions because the majority of actualities are swaying each other to modes of interconnection exemplifying these laws. New modes of self-expression may be gaining ground. We cannot tell . . . after a sufficient span of existence our present laws will fade into unimportance. New interests will dominate . . . our spatio-physical epoch will pass into . . . the past, which conditions all things dimly and without evident effect on the decision of prominent relations." A genuine optimism is not ruled out.

Whitehead does say that the "massive laws, at present pre-vailing, are the general physical laws of inorganic nature." Apparently these disclose no aim, but in human life aim does play a great role. "Scientific reasoning is completely dominated by the presupposition that mental functionings are not properly part of nature." On the other hand, he concludes that "we should conceive mental operations as among the factors which make up the constitution of nature." Six types of occurrences are found in nature: human life, animal life, plants, single living cells, large-scale inorganic aggregates, and minute happenings such as those in the atom. These occur as an unbroken series with no sharp lines anywhere. "The different modes of natural existence shade off into each other. . . . The human individual is one fact, body and mind." We are healthy when the body is healthy. We enjoy vision when there is no eyestrain; we enjoy life when there are no disturbing aches. "The whole complexity of mental experience is either derived or modified by such functioning." The state of mind comes directly from the preceding state of our conscious experience. The body is mine, the antecedent experience is mine. The continuity of life does not depend on consciousness. We sleep or we are stunned. The same person recovers. Gaps in consciousness are not gaps in life. "The soul is nothing else than the succession of my occasions of experience, extending from birth to the present moment. Now, at this instant, I am the complete person embodying all these occasions. . . . We have to construe the world in terms of the bodily society, and the bodily society in terms of the general functioning of the world."

Each occasion presupposes the antecedent world as active in its own nature. This is the doctrine of causation, "the trans-ference of character from occasion to occasion. I shape the activities of the environment into a new creation, which is myself at this moment." "Life is the enjoyment of emotion,

derived from the past and aimed at the future. It is the enjoyment of emotion which was then, which is now, and which will
be then. This vector character is of the essence of such enter-
tainment." Thus each occasion is an activity "of concern, in the
Quaker sense of that term."

From any study, even a superficial one, of Whitehead one
cannot but arise with a new reverence, as with Schweitzer, of
life. Perhaps this reverence is not, in the case of Whitehead,
so much a feeling that life in all its forms should be saved as a
marveling at the ubiquity, ingenuity, and pervasive power of
that organizing principle that permeates both the world and
ourselves.

4. The Seamless Robe

WHITEHEAD USES THIS expression in connection with his views on education, but it fits equally well his entire philosophy. That too hangs together, not as a piece of patchwork but as a closely knit sleeve taking the form of a complete garment.

Every philosophy must first of all decide what it is that is "really" real. Aristotle spoke of just that, the really real, and for him it was being. To say that may be a good beginning, but it is not enough. Do we mean by this the thinnest kind of being, that somehow spreads over all things and is left when all else is taken away? Or should we, with Whitehead, try to start with the thick creative core of things, some kind of self-propagating building block that knows how to keep going and how to add to itself? Self-creativity is probably the deepest and most universal process in the world. Anyone can see that it involves organization of some sort. Centers of assimilating, self-organizing activity and the interactions and even competitions between them are what modern philosophers keep in view. Whitehead's philosophy, in particular, is a philosophy of organisms.

It should be stated immediately that "actual entities" combine easily into what Whitehead calls "societies." These are of the most varied sort. A stone is a society, so is an atom, so are all the animals, and so are we. A molecule, a plant cell, and a human civilization are all structured societies. Societies attain practically unlimited variety of structure and degree of complexity. Thus in saying that everything is composed of "actual entities" there is no undue simplification. It is like saying that nylon is coal tar. Living societies require food, a form of robbery pursued in their search for intensity. Living things seek not just preservation but intensity, which is a form of enjoyment. All societies seek "self-satisfaction," another technical term. Whitehead has been reproached for taking ordinary words and turning them into technical terms. The saving grace is that he is generally careful about defining them and fairly skillful at putting across to the reader exactly what he means. If in spite of all that we disregard his explanations, the resulting confusion is of our own making. This habit Whitehead has of using ordinary words may lead to what sound like startling statements, such as that the whole world is composed of persons. But a personality is defined as a unified control of millions of living centers. Come to think of it, you and I, as persons, are just that.

There is considerable difference in the degree of centralization of living societies. Worms and jellyfish, some of them, can be cut in two and survive. They are poorly centralized, but man is different. He cannot, like grass, have his head cut off and survive. Is such centralization in any way connected with the intensity of the living process? Whitehead does manage to have his philosophy keep on confronting you with new questions and new points of view, and that is perhaps a sign that his philosophy itself is on the growing edge of things. Somewhere Whitehead remarks that plants are truly democratic—no centralization; but along with progress in a certain direction we do get more central control. Without going, at this point, further into the higher reaches of terrestrially organized societies, it is best first to get some notion of what Whitehead means by prehension.

Prehensions lead into Whitehead's theory of perception. Every philosophy has a theory of perception. This is an essential part of the explanation of how knowledge comes about. We have a percept, roughly speaking, of the color red, that is, we perceive it, and we have a concept of the color red, that is, an idea of it, possibly containing a definition. Unless there is worked out some notion of what is meant by perception, and how perception can be differentiated from the more intellectual conception, there is no adequate theory of the origin of knowledge. Whitehead, to start with, coins the technical term "prehension." Cutting off the usual prefixes and leaving us with the naked Latin root gives us prehension, a fancy word for primitive grasping. Grasping and sucking are fundamental activities carried on by fetuses and babes as well as adults. Some monkeys have prehensile tails, and even plants "grasp" visible and invisible supports, such as air and water as well as light, which they build into their systems. All actual entities, even crystals, molecules, and atoms, can capture, hold, or dismiss, perhaps, only a charge of electricity. Enough has been said to show that prehension is a broad term. All actual entities continue their existence by acts of prehension taking place during the saddleback of duration, between past and future, when the past is, as it were, selectively "sucked" or "prehended" into the future. To call prehension a form of knowing is reminiscent of ancient biblical terminology when to "know" a woman meant to have carnal intercourse with her.

Feeling is deeply involved. In this, too, Whitehead is close to Peirce. According to Charles Hartshorne: "An important contribution involved in Peirce's view is his uniquely vivid sense of the spontaneous, creative, or chance-character of the life of feeling. . . . Another contribution is in the recognition of the basic rôle of sympathy in reality. Feelings react with other feelings, but in this reaction is involved some degree of participation in the qualities of these other feelings. A feeling feels the feelings to which it reacts." If Peirce got that far, it is not surprising that Whitehead is right up with him and ahead of him.

It is not easy to translate these basic transfers of feeling into the high-sounding terminology of cognition. In the subliminal processes of propagation we are nearer to the seed-growing kind of activity than to cerebration. Any really adequate theory of how the present gets to know and to embody, and even to improve, the past must include the nether as well as the upper reaches of epistemology. *Epistemé* is simply the Greek word for knowledge. In Greece, to this day, a university is still a panepistemion. Epistemology with Whitehead stretches deep down into biology and even into nuclear physics.

Of the three avenues that a human being has to knowledge, two are perceptual and one conceptual. The conceptual way of knowing is the best understood and most completely analyzed mode. For the two "perceptive modes" Whitehead has specific names: (1) presentational immediacy and (2) causal efficacy.

The first chapter in his little volume called *Symbolism* deals with the perceptive mode of presentational immediacy. Although this is a special name, what Whitehead means by it is what most of us mean by sense perception. Through the sense perception of sight or smell or any other of the senses there are immediately given us certain objects of sense. It is the second mode of perception, causal efficacy, that constitutes a new discovery.

Perception by means of causal efficacy is something even the lowest animals have. These animals may not yet have highly developed senses, but they do have the feel and the reaction of causal efficacy. Whitehead quite rightly maintains that "the dog never acts as though the immediate future were irrelevant to the present" and even "a flower turns to the light with much greater certainty than does a human being, and a stone conforms to the conditions set by its external environment with much greater certainty than does a flower." Among men "certain emotions, such as anger and terror, are apt to inhibit the apprehension of sense-data; but they wholly depend upon a vivid apprehension of the relevance of immediate past to the present, and of the present to the future . . .

"This latter type, the mode of causal efficacy, is the experience dominating the primitive living organisms, which have a sense for the fate from which they have emerged, and for the fate toward which they go—the organisms which advance and retreat but hardly differentiate any immediate display. It is a heavy, primitive experience." Presentational immediacy, on the other hand, is something sophisticated. It takes leisure and highly developed sense organs to stand still and have time to contemplate the passing show with all its detail of color and sound. This is a refined enjoyment of the details of an exterior world. To take these highly civilized sense data and to make of them primitive protocol fragments out of which to construct the world is to start at the wrong end. No wonder such attempts are sterile. Better, with Whitehead, descend to the grass roots. The bulk of life is unconscious. Many of our internal organs do their work by feel in the dark, and do it very well, as when bleeding is stopped and a small cut healed without any call on the higher centers of consciousness at all.

Hume had only "presentational immediacy." He left off half
the process. With Hume only the present moment remained.
Even memory went. There was no easy way of disclosing extended actual things. You might wonder, when you turned away
from a tree, whether the tree still existed. Way down, observes
Whitehead, this view has in it the naïve assumption of time as
pure succession. But "pure succession is an abstraction." It
leaves out "the conformation of state to state, the later to the
earlier," that is the very essence of time. "Thus the immediate
present has to conform to what the past is for it. . . . It expresses
the stubborn fact that whatever is settled and actual must in
due measure be conformed to by the self-creative activity. . . .
According to Hume there are no stubborn facts. Hume's doctrine
. . . is certainly not common sense." Kant admits that causal
efficacy is a factor in the world but he holds that it does not
belong to perception. "It belongs to our ways of thought about
the data." Here Kant goes off the track.

Whitehead makes our commerce with the world around us a
much more intimate and intricate process than do most philosophers. For him to know a thing is not too different from to feel,
taste, or even eat it. Knowing moves nearer to digestion and
breathing and ceases to be primarily a brain function. When we
get to know things they become part of us. In fact, the brain is
more likely to abstract. It takes in only a schematic view, which
may be very important but is not the whole story. Here we
have the thick versus the thin world again, and this time the
real world is not only "stereo" but rich. Whitehead wants to
keep in all the flavors of all the senses, plus the intense organic
feelings of our more primitive selves and the emotional insights
of the creative artist. The combined avenues of knowledge, all
lined with their own special antennae, link us together with a
squirming world not as insensitive or as dead as we thought
it was.

A pivotal idea in Whitehead is his theory of time, built
around the "specious present," the bridge, saddleback, or link
between past and future that is not just a dividing line but an
actual duration. The units of time are small "epochs," hence
Whitehead also refers to his temporalism as "epochalism." "Time

is a sheer succession of epochal durations. But the entities which succeed each other . . . are durations. . . . Temporalisation is not another continuous process. It is an atomic succession. Thus time is atomic (i.e. epochal), though what is temporalised is divisible."

In the chapter on relativity in *Science and the Modern World* Whitehead goes into this in detail, showing how his view differs from the classical scientific materialism which presupposes a definite present instant at which all matter is simultaneously real. Following the implications of relativity, there is no such thing as a unique present instant. "You can find a meaning for the notion of the simultaneous instant throughout nature, but it will be a different meaning for different notions of temporality."

Following relativistic notions, Whitehead uses the term "extension" for spatialization and temporalization taken together. How extension is itemized or divided "depends upon . . . the actual entities constituting the antecedent environment. In respect to time, this atomization takes the special form of the 'epochal theory of time.'" Taking a hint from this epochal theory of time and from some of the notions developed in Royce, Charles Hartshorne, who has a definite bias for the psychical, tries to commit Whitehead to the picturesque notion developed by Royce that different beings may have different specious presents. "Thus whereas a man experiences events lasting over something like a tenth of a second as a series of events, and cannot distinguish distinctly those lasting much less than a tenth of a second, there might be individuals who would experience a millennium as a single happening, and others for whom a millionth of a second would be a distinct experience." Hartshorne claims that "this principle is also stressed by Whitehead," and that it "is contrary to all reasonable analogies to think that even all animals have just the same span to their specious presents; much less, that the higher animals and microbes, or microbes and atoms, could do so." He makes these variations "in principle infinite in extent—for if there be a specious present of a tenth of a second, why not one of a millionth of a second, or of a million years, or a billion." This is reminiscent of the Psalmist: "For a thousand years in thy sight are but as yesterday." It also recalls what happens in dreams when days pass in minutes and vice versa, but Royce and Hartshorne tie this up with consciousness in a way that Whitehead never does. In life consciousness is the exception for Whitehead and nowhere does he sanction the idea that somehow even a planet might be conscious. James, following Fechner, did flirt with this idea, but in Whitehead, as in Peirce, temporality is extended downward into feeling. There is a great deal of sentience and sensitivity in the world far beneath the threshold of consciousness. Whitehead does not, however, definitely make consciousness a part of the nether spectrum. Together with the deeper feelings, which through sympathy seem to understand each other, it forms higher in the scale a part of the seamless robe of life.

5. Existence versus Essence

Modern American, like Western European, philosophy has a tendency nowadays to probe more and more deeply into the tissues away from the head. Exploration of the ethereal region of high abstractions emanating from the head continues also, but not without parallel attention to inside upwellings of anxiety or joy. A long line of philosophers and psychologists from Schopenhauer to Freud have been stressing the unconscious. All over the world it is coming to be recognized that surface cerebrations are not the whole story. In America the pragmatic attitude made thought a part of action. Tying up the brain with the rest of the nervous system was a first step to including also the deeper reaches of dreams and semireveries, the whole complex of what Watson calls "unverbalized" behavior. Whitehead is fully aware of all this. As in Europe intellectual existentialism comes to a head in Heidegger, so a parallel movement here climaxes in Whitehead. He goes so far as to give the organic upheavals of geology, the tensions within the atom, and the metaphysical interplay of mathematical assumptions a place in his philosophy.

It remains in this section to outline some further details of Whitehead's metaphysics. Thus far only the taproot has been examined. One main thing in Whitehead is his sustained attack on "bifurcation." "What I am essentially arguing against is the bifurcation of nature into two systems of reality. . . . One reality would be the entities such as electrons which are the study of speculative physics. This would be the reality which is there for knowledge; although on this theory it is never known. For what is known is the other sort of reality, which is the byplay of the mind. Thus there would be two natures, one

427

is the conjecture and the other is the dream." Instead Whitehead elaborates a single system from cerebration to atomic energy with no gaps or fences separating mind from matter. The whole fabric of knowledge gets to be one with the web of life itself.

Peirce and Santayana had various realms of being. How does Whitehead stand on this? Where are the essences of Santayana and the firstness of Peirce? For Whitehead too actual entities are not the only kind of entities there are. In addition to actual entities and to the combinations of these in "societies," there are what Whitehead calls "eternal objects." These are called eternal not because they outlast everything else but because these "eternal objects" recur in succeeding stages of the actual entities. They are the samenesses in a welter of change—very much like Peirce's qualities. Eternal objects supply a certain continuity in the actuality which "is incurably atomic." The actual entities are the individual pulsations of existence, the individual concrescences. No other entities are actual. In this there is close agreement with Santayana. Santayana also keeps on saying that essences do not exist. Whitehead is a little more specific in that he calls the eternal objects derivations of the actual entities. They are forms that ingress. They are literally ingredients. Another way of describing them is to say that they are potentialities. "An eternal object is always a potentiality for actual entities." They are potential not actual. The mistake of Plato was to make eternal objects actual. The potential is not actual, and thinking that it is, can turn life upside down by making human existence revolve around a realm of remote potentialities instead of around things, less ideal, but more actual here below.

As illustrations of "eternal objects" Whitehead cites: "whiteness, hardness, sweetness, thinking, motion, man, elephant, army, drunkenness, and others." These are taken from Locke. Any idea, particular or universal, is an eternal object. Whitehead's definition is: "Any entity whose conceptual recognition does not involve a necessary reference to any definite actual entities of the temporal world is called an 'eternal object.'" The orientation may be a bit difficult, but if we start as both Santayana and Peirce did from phenomenology, we shall find that ideas loom very large. We are so accustomed to thinking of the mind as an immaterial substance that exudes ideas that it is next to impossible to think of ideas in a non-subjective manner. Now suppose you are a phenomenologist. You are just examining what appears. You are not assuming that bifurcation into mind and matter that we have been taught since childhood. Now we might call ideas objects of a sort. Whitehead calls them eternal objects, which stresses the aspect that ideas are not like events. What happened on July 4, 1776, just can't recur. It can't happen again. There is an irreversible direction inherent in events that we do not find in these other objects which Locke called ideas and which Whitehead calls eternal objects.

Eternal objects ingress into events. They are infinite in number. They can be arranged in hierarchies and become very complex. Eternal objects are not solely associated with human minds. You can get possibilities in a test tube just as well as in a brain. There is choice everywhere and choosing is evaluating. The world is full of values. The things you choose you make your own. There is here an element of appropriation. Organisms lower in the scale than man also deal with values. Even a flower turns to the light, and to a cat a mouse means something. These creatures may not have ideas but they do have values. Whitehead lays down in his *Process and Reality* "That the fundamental types of entities are actual entities, and eternal objects; and that the other types of entities only express how all entities of the two fundamental types are in community with each other, in the actual world."

It is clear that Whitehead, like Peirce and Santayana, and possibly Aristotle, does have at least two realms of being, potentiality and actuality. With these two words the realms are merely characterized in a most general way; Whitehead himself goes into great detail. But what about that third realm for which Peirce makes out such a strong case, the realm of law? This third realm too comes to its rights in Whitehead, if what Whitehead says about religion is taken as covering very largely what Peirce said about the innate drift of the world toward more and more order. Whitehead's God is that force that in a gentle manner or, as Whitehead puts it, by offering

us the "lure" of potentialities makes for righteousness. Whitehead's notion of God needs a separate section, but right here
it can already be stippled out that it is not at all difficult to
interpret Whitehead in such a way that between him and Peirce
there is a substantial and fundamental agreement also on the
delineation of a third realm. For Peirce thirdness was law on
the outside and thought on the inside, characterized in both
aspects by a mediating of the other two realms. Whitehead says,
as noted above, that there are only two fundamental types of
entities and that the other types of entities only express how
these two fundamental types interact; but then he does, as will
be indicated more fully presently, make out a case for a special
drift in this interaction and something that helps bring this
about. It would not be difficult to interpret this as an emerging
third realm.

Between existence, essences, and any further guidance by a
lure, there is no doubt that Whitehead, in common with preceding philosophers, gives the priority to existence. It makes
existence none the less wonderful that out of it should come a
directional persuasion, or a lure. Aristotle, when he had done,
felt the need of positing a First Cause or Prime Mover, but
Whitehead posits a sort of lure and thus gives life a specific
drift.

6. What Is Civilization?

A MAN's ETHICS comes out in his Shangri-La. The kind of world he wants is the kind of world he gets, if he works at it. The kind of civilized world that Whitehead wants to see is a world that has in it adventure, art, truth, beauty, and peace. Putting adventure first does not mean that Whitehead is fond of hunting lions in Africa. By adventure he means something much more quiet and much more intense, as well as more truly wild —the unleashing of the free play of the imagination. Do not copy the past! Do not fall in love with and imitate the classics, not even the classics of the Greeks, who themselves copied nothing. Follow the forward reachings of the psyche whose finiteness is not an evil. Here Whitehead is speaking of the adventurous spirit, as does Santayana, who all too hastily concluded that the spirit could not rise above matter and yet resolutely pursued the things of the spirit. The adventurous man is not by inclination afraid of what is new. Instead of being a standpatter, negativing every innovation, he is eager to look into what is new, to see if there is anything there that might be put to use.

Whitehead speaks of the divine Eros, or urge, toward the finite realization of almost impossible things. Of course there are intrinsic incompatibilities that even God Almighty cannot surmount, but you never know what you can do until you try. There is one way of looking at evolution that makes the whole thing blood, sweat, and tears; but there is another view of it that sees the succeeding triumphs as the constant climb to higher levels—higher not in the sense of better but in the sense of having within them a greater range of possibilities, just as a keyboard of eighty-eight notes has a greater range than a toy piano with

431

eight or ten keys. Every prize civilization has in it certain types of perfection; and when men look at these accomplishments, their hearts are gladdened.

Without adventure civilization is in full decay. Creativity stops with satire—Lucian, Voltaire, Gibbon, to whom Whitehead adds Strachey in England and Sinclair Lewis in the United States. When the freshness is gone, it is time to turn to something new. Whitehead improves on Peirce by stressing that there are many different, and equally charming, types of order. The increase of order need not be limited to the advancement of a single type of regularity. On the contrary, it is contrast that counts. We need contrasts in our world, discriminations and reaches, the full-range keyboard, plus something else—a sort of forward march all along the line. Somehow Whitehead very definitely ties up contrasts with his definition of consciousness. After pointing out again how rare, comparatively speaking, is consciousness in the phenomenon of life, he defines consciousness as something that arises only when the ideal is opposed to the real. Only an animal that can frame hypotheses so as to see clearly possibilities other than the confronting facts is conscious in the human sense, where consciousness has risen to the heights of self-consciousness. Human consciousness is permeated with the feeling of contrast between what may be, what might have been, and what is. Sometimes what might have been is brought to pass, but often only partially so, and hence there is often attached to life a tinge of sadness, a cloud which may or may not have a silver lining—hope that what might have been will still come about through others (your own children?). No one quite fulfills his capabilities; hence yearning like "a thing with feathers" keeps nesting in the soul; hence, too, consciousness is often quite the reverse of contentment. There is a difference between happiness and contentment or, worse still, resignation.

Whitehead speaks of three metaphysical principles, all three of which he thinks are wrong. One is that there is a halt when perfection is reached. This amounts to a denial by Whitehead of static perfection. The slightest acquaintance with the dynamic thrust of Whitehead's thinking indicates that this he must do. Plato saw in mathematics a changeless perfection. Whitehead never. Whitehead agrees with Dewey and goes beyond him in rejecting mathematics and everything else when it poses as a finality. "Aristotle introduced the static fallacy by another concept which has infected all subsequent philosophy. He conceived of primary substances as the static foundations which received the impress of qualification. . . . The taint of Aristotelian logic has thrown the whole emphasis of metaphysical thought upon substantives and adjectives, to the neglect of prepositions and conjunctions. This Aristotelian doctrine is in this book summarily denied. The process is itself the actuality, and requires no antecedent static cabinet."

The second off-color metaphysical principle gives perfection only one single and selective line to follow. There are always other perfections which might have been but which are not. It denies the richness of perfection. It is the essence of adventure that the woods are full of game. Of course every inventor knows that not all ideas can be realized; there are certain lanes and grooves to follow; there are intrinsic incompatibilities even among goods; but every now and then among a thousand thorns there blooms a brilliant rose. And roses have seeds. And ten feet away from the roses may grow a tulip tree or something still more worth examining.

The third metaphysical principle that runs awry "concerns the doctrine of Harmony." To make harmony just a pattern of things already there is "tame, vague, deficient in outline and intention." Harmony is more exciting than that, and the reason we settle for such tameness again goes back ultimately to Aristotle with his rigidly separate primary substances. Essentially such a primary substance cannot develop. It cannot take up into itself any genuine novelty. It will be recalled that Whitehead has his "actual entities" feed on two things, former actual entities and eternal objects. But, according to Aristotle, "no individual primary substance can enter into the complex of objects observed in any occasion of experience. The qualifications of the soul are thus confined to universals. According to the metaphysical system that I suggest to you, this Aristotelian doctrine is a complete mistake." Whitehead continues: "The individual, real facts of the past lie at the base of our immediate experience in the present. They are the reality from which the occasion springs, the reality from which it derives its source of emotion, from which it inherits its purposes, to which it directs its passions. At the base of experience there is a welter of feeling, derived from individual realities or directed towards them." Thus in a world composed of societies of actual entities it is "the enduring individuals, with their wealth of emotional significance," which appear in the foreground.

It is remarkable how large a place Whitehead gives to art and beauty in his picture of a well-balanced civilization. Adventure, art, beauty, truth, and peace—art and beauty are both mentioned but goodness is not. Even in speaking of the divine, which is the embodiment of goodness, Whitehead finds it convenient "to dwell upon the tender elements in the world, which slowly and in quietness operate by love . . . but are a little oblivious as to morals." Beauty and truth and art, as life goes here below, are all of them often "a little oblivious as to morals." Morals change from place to place and from age to age, but art, excellence, and, in a rough way, the pursuit of truth run onward in recognizable form throughout the ages.

Art, in the sense of endless experimentation as to what elements can work together in slow or short rhythms within the framework of local conditions, seems to be the never-ending preoccupation of nature. "Beauty is the mutual adaptation of the several factors in an occasion of experience. . . . Adaptation implies an end. Thus Beauty is only defined when the aim of 'adaptation' has been analysed. This aim is twofold. It is in the first place, the absence of mutual inhibition. . . . When this aim is secured, there is the minor form of beauty, the absence of painful clash, the absence of vulgarity. In the second place, there is the major form of Beauty. . . . This . . . introduces new contrasts. . . . Thus the parts contribute to the massive feeling of the whole, and the whole contributes to the intensity of feeling of the parts."

In his further detailed explanation of beauty Whitehead goes deeply into the structure of nature's processes: conformation to essentials of the past, but always a groping toward new contrasts and a greater intensity of feeling. He is anxious to avoid any dead level of perfection. This is a process, not a tableau. There is a plea for irregularities or discords that can be resolved. To Whitehead "even perfection will not bear the tedium of indefinite repetition." Beauty cannot be divorced from spontaneity. It must jump into new orbits. And one beauty skips another beauty, since "finitude involves the exclusion of alternative possibility. . . . This is fortunate. For otherwise actuality would consist in a cycle of repetition, realizing only a finite group of possibilities. This was the narrow, stuffy doctrine of some ancient thinkers."

Harmony, if it is not just a tame acceptance of what is already there, Whitehead keenly welcomes, outdoing Santayana in his description of it as a driftlike push, "one of the strongest forces in human nature. It is at the base of family affection, and of the love of particular possessions. This trait is not a peculiarity of mankind alone. A dog smells in order to find out if the person in question is that *It* to which its affections cling . . . the original *It* commands a poignancy of feeling. . . . The worship of relics touches upon the pathology of such concerns. . . . Art at its highest exemplifies the metaphysical doctrine of the interweaving of absoluteness upon relativity . . .

"It appears . . . that Beauty is a wider, and more fundamental, notion than Truth. . . . Beauty is the internal conformation of the various items of experience with each other, for the production of maximum effectiveness. Beauty thus concerns the inter-relations of the various components of Reality. . . . The teleology of the Universe is directed to the production of Beauty. Thus any system of things which in any wide sense is beautiful is to that extent justified in its existence. It may however fail in another sense, by inhibiting more Beauty than it creates. Thus the system, though in a sense Beautiful, is on the whole evil in that environment. But Truth has a narrower meaning in two ways. First, Truth . . . merely concerns the relations of Appearance to Reality. . . . But in the second place the notion of 'conformation' in the case of Truth is narrower than in the case of Beauty. For the truth relation requires that the two relata have some factor in common." In truth there is "the bare fact of a certain limited relationship of identity. . . . In

other words, a truth-relation is not necessarily beautiful. It may
not even be neutral. It may be evil." Here Whitehead puts his
finger on a facet of truth that is often forgotten. One of the
noblest pursuits of man is the pursuit of truth, but why? Not
necessarily to leave truth as it is. We need to know the truth
lest we walk in error to our own destruction. The main things
blind organisms do not see is the truth. Thus they lose the clue
of adaptation, but in itself, as Whitehead remarks, "truth is
neither good nor bad."

Within the wrapped-up layers of Whitehead's views on truth
and Beauty lies that view of consciousness which indicates why
truth and beauty so greatly concern a being who is conscious.
"The factor in experience that renders Art possible is consciousness. . . . Consciousness is that quality which emerges into
the objective content as the result of the conjunction of a fact
and a supposition about a fact. . . . It is the quality inherent in
the contrast between Actuality and Ideality, that is, between
the products of the physical pole and the mental pole in experience. . . . Thus consciousness, spontaneity, and art are
closely interconnected. . . . Science and Art are the consciously
determined pursuit of Truth and Beauty. In them the finite
consciousness of mankind is appropriating as its own the infinite
fecundity of nature. In this movement of the human spirit types
of institutions and types of professions are evolved. Churches
and Rituals, Monasteries with their dedicated lives, Universities
with their search for knowledge, Medicine, Law, methods of
Trade—they all represent that aim at civilization, whereby the
conscious experience of mankind preserves for its use the sources
of Harmony."

Concerning goodness in and by itself Whitehead has little
to say. Like Santayana, he is inclined to give his ethics an
aesthetic basis. "Goodness is the third member of the trinity which
traditionally has been assigned as the complex aim of art—namely,
Truth, Beauty, and Goodness. With the point of view here
adopted, Goodness must be denied a place among the aims of
art. For Goodness is a qualification belonging to the constitution
of reality, which in any of its individual actualizations is better
or worse. Good and evil lie in depths and distances below and

beyond appearance. They solely concern inter-relations within the real world. The real world is good when it is beautiful."

Adventure, truth, beauty, art, and—peace. Peace need not kill off adventure. Apart from peace "the pursuit of Truth, Beauty, Adventure, Art can be ruthless, hard, cruel; and thus, as the history of the Italian Renaissance illustrates, lacking in some essential quality of civilization. The notions of 'tenderness' and of 'love' are too narrow, important though they be. We require the concept of some more general quality, from which 'tenderness' emerges as a specialization. We are in a way seeking for the notion of a Harmony of Harmonies. . . . I choose the name 'Peace' for that Harmony of Harmonies which calms destructive turbulence and completes civilization. . . .

"The peace that is here meant is not the negative conception of anaesthesia. It is a positive feeling which crowns the 'life and motion' of the soul. . . . Peace carries with it a surpassing of personality. . . . It is primarily a trust in the efficacy of Beauty. . . . The trust in the self-justification of Beauty introduces faith where reason fails to reveal the details." Because peace is not anesthesia it does not necessarily wipe out pain. "Peace is the understanding of tragedy, and at the same time its preservation. . . . Each tragedy is the disclosure of an ideal:—What might have been, and was not: What can be. The tragedy was not in vain. . . . The deepest definition of Youth is, Life as yet untouched by tragedy. . . .

"The vigour of civilized societies is preserved by the widespread sense that high aims are worth-while. Vigorous societies harbour a certain extravagance of objectives, so that men wander beyond the safe provision of personal gratifications. All strong interests easily become impersonal, the love of a job well done. There is a sense of harmony about such an accomplishment, the Peace brought by something worth-while. Such personal gratification arises from aims beyond personality. . . . Beyond the soul, there are other societies, and societies of societies . . . each in its measure, claim loyalties and loves."

Whitehead discusses fame, and he discusses supreme sacrifices, such as that of Regulus who, after warning the Romans, voluntarily returned to Carthage, with the certainty of torture and death. He discusses both the grandeur and the insufficiency of moral codes. There is no unique and single "type of perfection at which the Universe aims. All realization of the Good is finite, and necessarily excludes certain other types." He speaks of this as the "secret of the union of Zest with Peace. . . . In this way the world receives its persuasion towards such perfections as are possible for its diverse individual occasions."

Is there something outside, any general trend, or anything at all helping our ideals along? "The question . . . is whether there exists any factor in the Universe constituting a general drive towards the conformation of Appearance to Reality." The answer cannot come "as a result of argument." We have to fall back on direct "first-hand experience." At the same time: "It must be remembered that the present level of average waking human experience was at one time exceptional among the ancestors of mankind. We are justified therefore in appealing to those modes of experience, which in our direct judgment stand above the average level. The gradual emergence of such modes, and their effect on human history, have been the themes of this book." Whitehead is speaking of his *Adventures of Ideas*.

7. The Imprisoned God

THE QUESTION as to whether "there is any factor in the Universe constituting a general drive towards the conformation of Appearance and Reality," the appearance in this instance being man's own ideals, is not answered in *Adventures of Ideas*. Whitehead has written much, but very little of it deals directly with religion. There are a few pages in *Process and Reality* and a few more in *Science and the Modern World*, and there is also *Religion in the Making*. Put all these together and one gets a short but remarkably definite account. Like Peirce, Whitehead neither emphasizes nor sidesteps the subject of religion. Peirce's father was a convinced theist, and Whitehead's father was a clergyman, giving Whitehead a background, roughly speaking, of broad Church of England. Neither of the sons was a theologian, nor wanted to be, yet, like Dewey, James, and even Santayana, it is easy to consider both of these philosophers as essentially religious men. They do not reject religion; the question is, what do they mean by religion?

Whitehead's problem is at bottom the same one that faced Peirce. If as the result of your studies you fervently hold that the world is an open system, having in it real chance, spontaneity, and adventure, you cannot in the end turn around and make it all fixed again—either way—that is, you cannot confidently prophesy either doom or victory. The outcome is not fixed. No specific end is determined. Whitehead, with Peirce, rejects the implacability of law. Law is just the average way in which things now behave. Everything may change, even the laws themselves. There is nothing behind and outside of the universe to determine its course. Whitehead particularly stresses self-creativity. Peirce had the added difficulty that his theory of knowledge was not worked out as completely as that of Whitehead. There was no place in it for intuitions. In his discussion of what the divine portends he had to fall back on some very vague "musings." Whitehead has a sharper view of what perception may involve, and his insights into what in the phantasmagoria of things may be divine is much more definite, but also more difficult in its almost mathematical formulations.

The question is not whether there is in the world an element or a principle or an influence which men may call divine, but whether we can also call this God. Whitehead, like Peirce, has no qualms here. He plainly calls it God, and goes on to state in highly technical terms just what he means. Some good expositors have found Whitehead's idea of divinity so different from the usual ideas of the past that they think he should not have called it God, but just a "Principle of Concretion" or some such other abstract name. Whitehead, however, is never averse to using ordinary words and giving them new and sometimes highly technical meanings.

Something has already been said on what Whitehead thinks God is not. God is certainly not something so completely outside the universe and so different from it that we cannot even begin to conceive of what he is like. Such a God would be in no sense either a help or an explanation. We are making him the Great Unknowable. If we say that for some reason, we do not know why, he made the world we are only deepening the mystery. We are explaining unknowns by greater unknowns. If we say, in the nature of the case, we are finite, and he is infinite and as far above us as we are above the worm, we are again using terms as mystifications. We know pretty well just how we differ from the worm—the distance between us and the worm is by no means infinite. Such plays on the ununderstandability of a term like "infinite," or "absolute," or "ground of existence" are especially sure of rejection by Whitehead, who knows very well how mathematics has recently succeeded in defining terms formerly indefinite. He himself is a pioneer in the advanced type of mathematical thinking that has resulted in new extensions to logic. To cross swords with him you must at least understand and get beyond the

Principia Mathematica. Abstract conceptions which might evade or confuse the average man are not beyond men of the caliber and training of Whitehead. He cannot therefore be put off with abracadabra.

"It is childish," says Whitehead, "to enter upon thought with the simple-minded question, What is the world made of? The task of reason is to fathom the deeper depths of the many-sidedness of things. We must not expect simple answers to far-reaching questions. . . . The notion of God as the 'unmoved mover' is derived from Aristotle. . . . The notion of God as 'eminently real' is a favourite doctrine of Christian theology. The combination of the two into the doctrine of an aboriginal, eminently real, transcendent creator, at whose fiat the world came into being, and whose imposed will it obeys, is the fallacy which has infused tragedy into the histories of Christianity and Mahometanism."

Whitehead also speaks of the "brief Galilean vision of humility" that "flickered throughout the ages, uncertainly," and was replaced by the deep "idolatry, of the fashioning of God in the image of Egyptian, Persian, and Roman imperial rulers. . . . The Church gave unto God the attributes which belonged exclusively to Caesar. . . . In the formative period of theistic philosophy . . . three strains of thought emerge which . . . fashion God in the image of an imperial ruler . . . of a personification of moral energy . . . of an ultimate philosophical principle. Hume's *Dialogues* criticise unanswerably these modes of explaining the system of the world." Then Whitehead says he would like to add another speaker to "that masterpiece, Hume's *Dialogues Concerning Natural Religion.*" This speaker would explain in the first place that "God is not to be treated as an exception to all metaphysical principles, invoked to save their collapse. He is their chief exemplification. Viewed as primordial, he is the unlimited conceptual realization of the absolute wealth of potentiality. In this aspect, he is not *before* all creation, but *with* all creation. But, as primordial, so far is he from 'eminent reality,' that in his abstraction he is 'deficiently actual'—and this in two ways: His feelings are only conceptual and so lack the fulness of actuality. Secondly, conceptual feelings, apart from complex integration with physical feelings, are devoid of consciousness in their subjective forms."

Anyone who wants to go fully into the technical details concerning the primordial, consequent, and even the superject nature of divinity, and in just what sense this God is a Person, need only make a thorough study of what Whitehead has to say on this subject. His ideas on divinity in no sense negate or throw out the other parts of his broadly scientific philosophy on which our chief interest has been centered. Charles Hartshorne, who has made somewhat of a specialty of studying what various philosophers have to say on God, thinks that Whitehead's ideas of God offer the most technically adequate version of a conception of God which a score of philosophers and theologians of great distinction, and hundreds with humbler attainments, have been working out since the fifteenth century, and especially during the past one hundred years.

European existentialism divides into a theistic and an atheistic branch. The American movement in philosophy, paralleling existentialism, has not split up in this manner. Modern theologians are unwilling to reject reason altogether in favor of a heart which can believe a thing although it is absurd. They stick doggedly to a growth, a broadening, and an expansion of reason. Even Heidegger and Sartre, leaders of the left-hand branch of European existentialism, may be said to be working out an enlarged view of rationality, which, however, in their case has in it no return to theism. In America, with the possible exception of Santayana, the general trend has been to avoid the extreme conclusions, also with regard to theism. Whitehead time and again points out that science changes, philosophies change, and so do religions. The theology of the Bible starts with a "Thou shalt not" God thundering commands from Mount Sinai and ends with a tender shepherd who loves his flock. In our own country we have watched the trend from Calvinism and Puritanism through New England Unitarianism to a present-day almost secular theology more and more inclined, since the vigorous thinking goes into other fields, to take a back seat. Those who do not sidestep religion—and Whitehead is one who does not sidestep it—surprise us by the highly technical nature of their theological thinking. As in other chapters dealing with Whitehead there has been no attempt to go deeply into technical details, so there shall be none here. Instead, as in former chapters, there is merely an attempt to state clearly and in general terms what Whitehead's main ideas are.

This boils down to what is meant by a divine element in the universe. First of all it is IN the universe, not outside it. How could anything be outside all there is? Let us not start or finish philosophy with a childish contradiction in terms. The business of philosophy is to expand, not to deny rationality. This insistence on rationality that we get from our two final philosophers, Peirce and Whitehead, is neither a small nor a vague matter. Some have said that the enlargement of the top of the spinal cord into a brain is a disease. Intellectuality is a hazard. Back to the ways of the thoughtless blood! Creep in the grass like a snake, feel the dew on your naked body, crawl back closer to—no, INTO the earth again. Become a rock! Progress lies backward! Not so these men. They see room ahead. They hope for an enlargement of rationality—a new faith in reason.

Our recent thinkers end with three realms of being. The third realm, that of thought, rationality, and law, is still rather vague, but the other two, existence and essence, are each decade being etched with increasing clearness, and there is a new urgency in stressing the primacy of existence. The head is no longer letting us live in the clouds. Science is no longer abstract. The whole thrust of intellection is turning downward deep into our own component atoms. We can no longer slough off mortal coils and save our souls by going to heaven. Let the rest of creation perish while the thin thread of a disembodied soul joins the Great Spirit in what?—in a new creation? Why? This one to which we are so deeply committed is already well advanced. Is there no God in it at all? Perhaps that is what the vague theism of Peirce and Whitehead is all about. They retain a built-in God, who, quite rightly, is not going to do everything for us but who, in a sense that future thinkers may increasingly particularize, is of some sort of help. There is something in the universe answering the human thirst for righteousness and beauty. Franklin, Emerson, James, even Santayana, and certainly Peirce and

Whitehead think so. We need not believe them. We can write doom in the stars, but the Seven Sages refuse to do so.

Whitehead leaves us with something that is strangely like permissive legislation on the part of the universe. Go ahead, mankind, create your own God. In a sense, man has always been doing just that, making his gods in his own image. Our own must be in the best sense human. Whitehead begins to lay down some specifications that can be justified by what an advanced scientist already knows about the world, but the chief discovery is that there is permissive legislation. There is not just actuality. There is also possibility. And this possibility is such that more of the divine may gradually emerge. Men, or creatures like them, may keep coming and continue not only to multiply but also to subdue the earth.

On this planet we may, with warheads loaded with new bombs, blow the bulk of mankind to pieces. We may not. We do not have to. Even if we do there will certainly be lone survivors. And if we do not try to destroy the masses there is a good chance that men may turn more and more to fusion rather than to disruption. With spaceships in the offing, a first inkling of men from outer space is going to throw earthlings together as never before. With billions and billions of suns, why may some of them not be spawning planets with spirits like our own? With or against us—who knows? But in a twinkling what is left of mankind would unite. Men have looked to the skies, whence cometh our help, with upturned faces for so long that it would not be too great a surprise if some help really came. Such fancies are farfetched but not impossible. Our own transformations and evolutions into higher capacities may continue. The speech we learned to use as signals from one to another individual may serve with nonearthlings too. If so, all our training in other-worldliness, like Ben Hur's muscles developed while rowing as a slave in the galley, will not have been entirely wasted in that great day of the chariot race with other planets. Are these fanciful imaginings? On the contrary, they are a legitimate concomitant of straight, hard, fancy-free thinking.

That is the message of these final theistic musings of both Peirce and Whitehead. In the universe—and the universe exceeds our second-rate sun with its mediocre planets—there is imprisoned a God. It is possible that such a God can find utterance only through beings who work hard at increasing what they call their intelligence. It is really possible that, in the nature of things, there is no way for the divine impulse in us to develop except through the exercise of human choice and freedom. We are free either to kill off ourselves and any terrestrial divinity there may be inside of us at the same time or to go on living and see what happens. Whitehead means something like this with his lure of persuasion. The dumb world wants to become more intelligent. Ask the worm that became a man. Ask the race of men who may someday become nearer to the gods in the sense that they will have more to say of what becomes of the world than we do now. We are still pretty helpless, but the worm was more so.

American excelsiorism is more romantic than European existentialism. Whether because of the greater scope of the New Continent, its much shorter history, or just because in world wars up to now America has not suffered as much as other parts of the world, there is more genuine hope left in the foremost thinkers who laid the foundations of American philosophy. It has been our business to report that this is so.

Index